THIS IS ENVIRONMENTAL ETHICS

THIS IS PHILOSOPHY
Series editor: Steven D. Hales

Reading philosophy can be like trying to ride a bucking bronco—you hold on for dear life while "transcendental deduction" twists you to one side, "causa sui" throws you to the other, and a 300-word, 300-year-old sentence comes down on you like an iron-shod hoof the size of a dinner plate. *This Is Philosophy* is the riding academy that solves these problems. Each book in the series is written by an expert who knows how to gently guide students into the subject regardless of the reader's ability or previous level of knowledge. Their reader-friendly prose is designed to help students find their way into the fascinating, challenging ideas that compose philosophy without simply sticking the hapless novice on the back of the bronco, as so many texts do. All the books in the series provide ample pedagogical aids, including links to free online primary sources. When students are ready to take the next step in their philosophical education, *This Is Philosophy* is right there with them to help them along the way.

This Is Philosophy, Second Edition
Steven D. Hales

This Is Philosophy of Mind
Pete Mandik

This Is Ethics
Jussi Suikkanen

This Is Political Philosophy
Alex Tuckness and Clark Wolf

This Is Business Ethics
Tobey Scharding

This Is Metaphysics
Kris McDaniel

This Is Bioethics
Ruth F. Chadwick and Udo Schuklenk

This Is Philosophy of Religion
Neil Manson

This Is Epistemology
J. Adam Carter and Clayton Littlejohn

This Is Philosophy of Science
Franz-Peter Griesmaier and Jeffrey A. Lockwood

This Is Environmental Ethics
Wendy Lynne Lee

Forthcoming:

This Is Philosophy of Mind, Second Edition
Pete Mandik

This Is Modern Philosophy
Kurt Smith

THIS IS
ENVIRONMENTAL ETHICS

AN INTRODUCTION

WENDY LYNNE LEE

WILEY Blackwell

For general information on our other products and services or for technical support, please contact our Customer Care Department within the United States at (800) 762-2974, outside the United States at (317) 572-3993 or fax (317) 572-4002.

Wiley also publishes its books in a variety of electronic formats. Some content that appears in print may not be available in electronic formats. For more information about Wiley products, visit our web site at www.wiley.com.

A catalogue record for this book is available from the Library of Congress

Paperback ISBN: 9781119122708; ePub ISBN: 9781119122722; ePDF ISBN: 9781119122715

Cover design: Wiley

Set in 10/12pt Minion Pro by Integra Software Services Pvt. Ltd, Pondicherry, India.

SKY10035359_072222

CONTENTS

ACKNOWLEDGMENTS

It is customary to thank all of the people, friends, family, and colleagues, whose patience and forbearance make research and writing possible. There are plenty of these folks, and they know who they are. This book, however, requires a different introduction. It began as a meditation on the implications of the climate crisis for environmental ethics. Not because there aren't many other issues confronting an ecologically beleaguered planet and its citizens, but because climate change poses an existential crisis for human beings, for communities, and for every living thing with whom we share the earth and its atmosphere. Like so many of its predecessor crises—pollution, species extinction, resource exhaustion—the climate crisis is substantially anthropogenic. Human greed, excess, recklessness, and hubris are its causes. Unlike its predecessors, however, the climate crisis has the potential to render life no longer worth the struggle that is living.

Then, two things happened that altered the course of this book. First, and without warning, my daughter, Carley, died. Then the coronavirus pandemic descended and began to devour the world. The first still leaves me speechless. The second must be spoken and theorized. Covid-19 must be understood as the environmental crisis it is at the juncture of human chauvinism, ecological destruction, rapacious capitalism, and ever-increasing greenhouse gas emissions. The pandemic is not, as we might prefer to believe, simply a moment in time; it foreshadows an anguished future we could act to deter through will and foresight; though we haven't so far. Of course, it's not this simple. Some refuse to wear masks; others risk infection to help us breathe. Some deny the climate crisis; others are forced to flee its consequences. Both the pandemic and the climate crisis evolve in ways we can model, but not really predict. And most of us live somewhere between soldiering on, enculturated cognitive dissonance, outrage, and doing the best we can. The root-message of any ethic is: do better by the other who is you. Pandemic teaches us we cannot resurrect the dead. But while coronavirus will meet its match in a vaccine, for a while, the only armor we have against the climate crisis is thoughtful, deliberate, and collective action driven by the decision to care for others, listen to science, and make a reclamation of humility. The tipping points are right in front of us—climactic, viral, civilizational. We can do better. I would like to say: if only we had the right moral compass. The future will arrive. But it's late in the day.

For Carley Aurora Lee-Lampshire, my "Carlita Bonita,"
"Car-Bob" to her friends.
I love you to the moon and back.
8.28.88–1.18.20

ABOUT THE COMPANION WEBSITE

A Companion Website for *This is Environmental Ethics* can be accessed at https://thisisphilosoph.wordpress.com

There is a website for each title that hosts material such as an instructor pack with teaching resources and resources intended to aid student learning.

INTRODUCTION: ENVIRONMENTAL ETHICS IN THE ERA OF ECOLOGICAL CRISIS

One Planet, Many Worlds

What may be most striking about the incredibly dynamic terrain of contemporary environmental ethics is that while its many, sometimes competing, ideas, theories, and principles are grounded in philosophical thinking about moral issues, they're also driven by a deep-going sense of duty to speak to a world whose planetary conditions are changing in potentially ruinous ways that demand urgent, deliberate, informed, and collective action.[1] There are three basic truths to keep at the forefront: first, ecological conditions are existential conditions. Second, the crises we currently face, especially the climate crisis, mass human and nonhuman migration, war over access to clean water, and the potential for future pandemic, clarify the relationship of the ecological to the existential in ways pressing and paralyzing.[2] Third, like most other emergencies, environmental, economic, social, and geopolitical, the climate crisis impacts some in dramatically disproportionate ways. Global North and global South, human and nonhuman, rich and poor, women and men, brown, black, and white—no single metric of impact will be comprehensive save the obvious: exceeding the tipping points to measurable irreversible change signaled by Amazon rainforest die-back, Greenland Ice Sheet disintegration, Arctic permafrost melt, West African and Indian monsoon shift, extreme and more frequent weather events, and their ancillary impacts on human and nonhuman migration, food security, geopolitical violence, and species extinction.

Still, we tend to compartmentalize "environmental," segregating it from other domains of moral concern. Yet some of our most difficult moral questions erupt from our reflections in one domain that hemorrhages onto others: trash incinerators built in working-class neighborhoods, mining leases on

This is Environmental Ethics: An Introduction, First Edition. Wendy Lynne Lee.
© 2022 John Wiley & Sons, Inc. Published 2022 by John Wiley & Sons, Inc.
Companion Website: https://thisisphilosoph.wordpress.com

indigenous lands, food deserts, economically stressed communities washed away by tsunamis or burnt to the ground by firenadoes. We can't avoid these social, economic, and geopolitical intersections. The climate crisis is no more solely an environmental emergency than exploring for oil in the Arctic is solely the province of energy demand, or that the Covid-19 pandemic and its many evolving variants is merely a matter of public health.[3] Each threatens serious environmental consequences for every living thing that dwells on the planet's surface, under its soils, in its waters, over its lands, or within the bodies of every creature, living and dead. But as impact is unequal, it may be that our greatest moral crisis is not, at least in the first place, the failure to act, but the refusal to *know*. A realistic environmental ethic must then make a priority *epistemic responsibility*, that is, an understanding of the current state of the planet's environmental conditions and its atmospheric integrity is key to formulating personal moral compass, just social and economic policy, and ultimately global consensus about the future sustainability of the only home most of us will ever know: Earth.

Put another way: we may be tempted to think narrowly about climate change, reserving our concern to its environmental impacts, themselves enormous, of melting polar ice caps, shifting bread-baskets, habitat loss, extinctions, firenadoes, extended drought, bomb cyclones, vanishing shore lines, and the like. This seems like quite enough. But the fact is that climate change is a *crisis* because it poses at least as great a challenge to the ways in which we *think about* the planet's capacity to support life, its limited resources, vulnerable tenants, and its geopolitical stability as it poses to more immediate and tangible concerns like combatting firenadoes, bomb cyclones, or rapid viral spread. We tend, in other words, to be geared to the crisis right in front of us, but the climate crisis is also, and fundamentally, about the future. It disrupts many of the comforts and conveniences we take for granted in the privileged global "North," and it exacerbates much of the hardship that renders life in the developing world of the global "South" tenuous.[4] It raises critically important questions about who all counts as "we" with respect to access to critical resources like clean air, potable water, and food. Dividing those agents, institutions, and governments most culpable for the crisis from those most harmed, climate change makes it all the harder to ignore what we already know about social and economic inequality.[5] It alters the planet's capacity to recuperate from the abuse to which we subject it, enthralled as we remain by the myth of its endless treasure trove of resources and inexhaustible atmospheric toilet. It forces us to rethink whether it makes sense to conceive everything as a potential commodity. The climate crisis, in other words, disrupts not only the planet, but the *world*, or more precisely, the many and diverse *worlds* of human culture, religion, government, economy, politic—each interwoven with the ecologies upon which their tenants, human and nonhuman, wealthy and poor, entitled and disenfranchised depend.

In short, the climate crisis raises crucial, but difficult questions not only about what we value and why, but about *who* gets to decide value—and with what authority. Five observations seem certain:

- The climate crisis *will* impact all of us one way or another.
- Some human communities will bear its brunt in far greater ways than others.
- Environmental crisis tends to provoke new geopolitical antagonisms and worsen old ones. This includes war, as well as the ecological ruin and greenhouse emissions that come with war.
- Capitalism, a system of economic exchange rooted in the largely unchallenged assumption that all value can be converted to exchange or commodity value, plays a central role in environmental destruction, pollution, geopolitical violence, species extinction, and the climate crisis.
- An unprecedented number of nonhuman animal species will confront loss of habitat, starvation, and migration. But one of the most ethically troubling legacies of the *Anthropocene*, the age of human industrial domination, is extinction.

Climate change simply *is* the greatest challenge of our times. Yet, for too many it seems not to feel that way. Despite the fact that it's human-made, an *anthropogenic* crisis, despite the fact that we have decades of science apprising us of its implications, sustained attention to it tends to be eclipsed by emergencies experienced as more immediate, urgent, and visceral: food insecurity, gun violence, human migration, human trafficking, the opioid crisis, pollution, terrorism, viral outbreaks. In one way, it's not hard to see why: compared to the sheer terror evoked by the Covid-19 pandemic, the climate crisis feels like a problem that can safely be put off to the future.

We often hear the common refrain that we have always had fires, hurricanes, tsunamis; that climate "alarmists" are simply using weather as a rhetorical tool to argue for more restrictive "one-world" government whose aim is to control what we eat, how we live, where we travel. Or, as this line of thinking has begun to fade in the face of more frequent and more extreme weather events, we're invited to replace outright denial with the idea that, just as we put a man on the moon, brought back the Kihansi Spray Toad from the brink of extinction, and developed a highly effective vaccine for SARS-CoV-2 (Covid-19) at warp speed, we can "techno-wizard" our way out of the climate crisis. For too many, of course, climate change isn't a future crisis but a daily confrontation with drought, water shortage, food insecurity, and disease—a confrontation whose message is clear: to put off to the future what demands action in the now is *nihilistic*. That is, insofar as we know that today's emergencies are a harbinger of tomorrow's, and that tomorrow's can only be mitigated, if they can be, by what we do today, failure to act is effectively a concession to death for every living thing on the planet. Ecological nihilism is neither hyperbole nor reckless speculation. It's reality can be made gut-wrenching in the obliteration of towns like Greenville or Paradise California, charred beyond recognition by drought-fueled firenados. Its impacts are inescapable to any objective survey of the capitalist endeavor to monetize human and nonhuman life. Consider the slaughter of Sumatran Elephants for their tusks, toxic chemical dumping by industry to avoid more costly pollution statutes, or outsourcing human labor to the developing world's lower wages and lax safety and environmental regulations.

The Time Is Now

If this assessment of our current planetary state of affairs seems dark, it's because the necessity for a robust, courageous, inclusive, and deeply self-reflective ethic could not be more urgent. Consider a rough analogy: we know that left untreated cancer will metastasize and become calamitous for the patient. Treatment may not eradicate the disease, but early aggressive attention can mitigate against damage to tissues and organs. Imagine, however, that early on in a treatment regimen a patient tests positive for Covid-19, becomes sick, decides to suspend the cancer treatment, recovers from the virus, and then, feeling better, doesn't return to the chemotherapy. Will the patient live? No; and we rightly regard her behavior as self-defeating. Indeed, we'd urge her to return to chemotherapy, pointing out that her struggle with coronavirus may well have been made worse by the fact that she smokes and that the cancer had begun to metastasize to her lungs. We'd remind her that the root cause, if not of contracting the virus, but of its severity in her case is likely the smoking responsible for her cancer diagnosis. The patient is, of course, different from a planet that can't decide for itself to suspend "cancerous" emissions of greenhouse gases. That is the moral burden we bear to recognize that environmental conditions are existential conditions, that in having the planet "smoke" we are imperiling it and every living thing that lives within its "body." We know that human activities produce the "carcinogens" that generate "malignancy" for the planet's atmosphere. Like a smoker whose battle with Covid-19 is made worse by lung cancer, we know that a compromised climate will only add to every other environmental crisis. Yet, insofar as we ignore the intersection of the climate crisis and the planetary dilemmas made more volatile or even deadly by it, we're like a patient who, recovered from the virus, returns to the cigarettes; except the planet is the patient, and we're forcing her to smoke. Or, more precisely: life on planet Earth *is* the intimate relationship between the planet, its atmosphere, and the evolutionary history of its species.

To appoint ourselves to the status of unbeholden to these facts is the essence of *human chauvinism*: the presumptive view that planet Earth exists *for* us, that we are entitled to its resources and treasures, and that self-interest—including its commercial incarnations—are the irrefutably rightful domain of human domination. Human chauvinism is not human-centeredness; whereas the former seeks primarily its own advantage, the latter takes "centered" to be a call to moral and epistemic responsibility. Whereas human chauvinism is an outrage to virtually any ethic that would seek to impose conscience on human activity, human-centeredness can offer a point of departure for deep-going reflection on our ideas of rightness or wrongness. Put simply: whereas human chauvinism is characterized by arrogance, entitlement, and little concern for the future of others, human-centeredness can be re-imagined as a practice of epistemic responsibility, thoughtful humility, and a commitment to a baseline incarnation of the *precautionary principle*: first, do not harm. The difference between chauvinism and centeredness is the difference between the contemporary nihilism of the Anthropocene and whether what comes next turns out to be livable and for whom.

The Covid-19 pandemic illustrates this difference in a number of ways. There's one aspect of viral outbreak, for example, that makes it more hazardous than cancer: the virus is contagious, and it's in just this respect that it offers another window into the climate crisis. Part of what makes a virus, especially one capable of asymptomatic spread, so terrifying, is that it's not contained to a single individual. SARS-CoV-2 (Covid-19) spreads primarily in aerosolized droplets like coughing, sneezing, or singing from people who may or may not know they're infected, many of whom ignore *Center for Disease Control* (CDC) guidelines like mask-wearing that are designed to protect others from infection.[6] Feeling fine, the asymptomatic behave as if nothing has changed, spread the virus, infect, and potentially cause fatal illness in others who (or whose family) may never be able to identify the source of transmission. The virus-variants perfect this form of spread even among the vaccinated. Climate change denial spreads in similar fashion. We know the climate is warming; we see reports of extreme weather events, flooding, drought, disrupted animal migration patterns, extinctions. Yet we behave as if Earth and its atmosphere are not "infected" with this anthropogenic blight, going about our lives as if the planet really were an endless fount of clean water, hydrocarbons, and healthy soils, the atmosphere a boundless receptacle for greenhouse gases and other toxins. We set the example for everyone around us, especially our children. This is denial, and is its own kind of contagion.

Sometimes climate change denial is, however, more deliberate. Thinly veiled behind appeals to freedom or individual rights, denial of the climate crisis spreads as surely as do calls to antimasking rallies. The grandma who drives her gas-guzzler to Thanksgiving dinner, refusing to wear a mask or socially distance, manifests not only a faulty notion of freedom, but disregard for the future of her family's health and the planet's upon which it depends. The dad who shows up at a schoolboard meeting to decry "oppres-sive" vaccination requirements and circulate misinformation about the na-ture of mRNA vaccine technology jeopardizes not only his own children's health, but an entire community's. The point, however, of comparing the climate crisis to a pandemic is not simply that what's significant about a pandemic is reducible to the ways it can shed light on the impacts of climate change (or vice versa). It's that many of the behavioral dynamics at work in denial of the climate crisis have analogues in other domains. Understanding what drives denial, the tendency to minimize, the pretense that there is no crisis, the resort to conspiracy explanation and other forms of cognitive dis-sonance can help us to see similarities and differences, to weigh their moral relevance, and to make more consistent and rational judgments about our own actions and those of others. Appeal to a distorted notion of "freedom," for example, is not all that different for those who refuse to wear a mask during a pandemic than it is for those who refuse to consider driving more fuel-efficient vehicles. Both fail to acknowledge that "freedom" is not the freedom to cause harm to others, and both effectively ignore that aspect of freedom that entails responsibility.[7]

Although caution is always warranted, drawing analogies to other kinds of crises—cancer, pandemic disease—can serve to remind us that these same forms of cognitive dissonance have very real, often measurable, impacts on the way that, for example, zoonotic transmission, habitat encroachment and loss, extreme weather events, deforestation, the interaction of co-morbidities and viral outbreaks, human and nonhuman migration, and even geopolitical conflict become mutually fertilizing crises. It's a critical charge of the sciences to decipher these layers of connection in order to develop strategies to combat the climate crisis *and* the prospect of future pandemic, inequitable vaccine access *and* food insecurity, the extinction of polar megafauna *and* acceler-ated oil exploration in Arctic waters. We can no more afford to ignore these mutually fertilizing volatile relationships than we can assign California fire-nadoes merely to poor forest management, or the significantly higher rate of infection, hospitalization, and mortality among African Americans from coro-navirus merely to poor diet.[8] What we'll discover are the limits of our systems of moral judgment and the roles that forms of social domination and structural inequality play in our actions and evaluations. In many ways, it's the limits that tell the real story behind the crises that imperil our future and the futures of all the others with whom we share the planet. Both the climate crisis and the Covid-19 pandemic have the feel of a Mother Nature striking back at her way-ward, wasteful, selfish children. But an apology and a promise to do better will not suffice. We have much work to do. Still, that doesn't mean—doesn't have to mean—that we cannot do better. Seeing where we are is a point of departure. It's a "canary in the coal mine" call for an environmental ethic that takes it as vital to orient itself not only in ethics, but in the world as we find it. The time is now because where we find the planet and its many worlds is in trouble.

Environmental Ethics Is about the Present and the Future

We have a tall order. The environmental ethic we need must not merely be grounded in the recognition that we live in an era of crisis, but that the crises we face make talk of the *future* critically important. Whether and what human agents owe to the future is its own difficult question. But insofar as crises and our responses to them mirror human interests and priorities, the fact that we know that the intersection of climate change and viral outbreak can generate potentially apocalyptic consequences implies that there are still too many of us that don't take the future very seriously. For some, preventing and mitigating crisis is a life's work. The epidemiologists, virologists, and public health experts, as well as the heroic doctors, nurses, and healthcare workers, who save our lives from infection are of necessity thinking primarily about the crisis right in front of them.[9] But this doesn't mean that the future won't inform public health policy, therapeutic intervention, vaccine development, the management of viral variants, evolving diagnostic strategies, and comprehension of the prognosis for "long haul" patients in vital ways. Likewise, climate scientists, meteorologists, ecologists, zoologists, geneticists, chemists, and geologists, along with environmental activists, organizations, and policy-makers have been working to alert us to the effects of climate change across a range of patterns—weather, ecology, migration, crop losses, deforestation, and genetic alteration for decades.[10] Understandably, patterns may not evoke the same visceral urgency as do images of gasping patients waiting for ventilators. But as we know from the science, less directly evocative does not mean less urgent; instead, it suggests that an environmental ethic relevant to the twenty-first century must be able to show not only that "crisis" can mean as much applied to a slower moving catastrophe as it does to the sick patient who can't breathe, but that morality is as much about the future as it is the present. Measured in terms of sheer scale, the climate crisis may well suffocate far more.

Acclaimed climate scientist Michael Mann argues in *The Madhouse Effect* that our reluctance to confront the climate crisis is telling, that it exposes a deep-going hypocrisy at the heart of our capacity for moral decision-making.[11] On the one hand, we insist that morality is outward-looking; it's not merely about rationalizing self-interest, cost/benefit analyses, or risk avoidance. Morality is not merely prudence; rather it's about the *moral considerability* of others, the world beyond ourselves, the present and the future. On the other hand, Mann points out that our expressions of environmental commitment often fail to align with the actions necessary to realize the values they encompass. We can and should debate what moral considerability means and to whom/what it applies, though it's difficult to exaggerate the urgency of action right now.[12] Yet, without this key idea—that there exist features of things such as being a living thing or a necessary condition for living things, or having the capacity for sentience, or being endangered, or occupying an ecological role as predator or prey, or being beautiful—that make such things morally considerable and therefore something worth the effort to preserve to the future, it's hard to see what could act as an impetus to action. One difficulty is that what counts as morally considerable isn't a given in any ethic; it's rather a product or a consequence of the ethic we decide to adopt. If, for instance, sentience—awareness and the capacity to suffer—is a value of that ethic, nonhuman animals become morally considerable in very definite ways that might preclude eating them; if beauty, a concerted effort to preserve wilderness; if biotic diversity, policies and laws to protect endangered species from extinction. And, of course, there will be conflicts. What is more worth moral consideration, the individual sentient creature or the species? Does a forest still qualify as a beautiful wilderness if there's a road carved through it? Who's moral worth is greater in a dispute over grazing range, the rancher and her livelihood, or the endangered grey wolf? The aim of an environmental ethic is not necessarily to make these questions easy, but to make them *thinkable*.

The climate crisis bears on all of these questions, and the reason is because climate change is *anthropogenic*. It's *caused* by human activities, personal, industrial, geopolitical.[13] To be sure, some capitalist ventures and industries are more culpable than others for greenhouse gas emissions.[14] But insofar as consumption is the driver of industrial activities such as mining for fossil fuels, the mass manufacture of products, and industrial scale agriculture and animal agriculture, responsibility for addressing the climate crisis cannot be limited only to those who compete for our dollars.[15] Crises themselves affect consumption in environmentally relevant ways. Consider, for example, the increased demand for wood pulp in the form of toilet paper, carboard boxes, and packaging during a pandemic,[16] the negative impacts for biodiversity of rising disinfectant use,[17] or the drivers of climate refugeeism.[18] Or, consider the complex relationship between the Covid-19 pandemic, differing forms of consumption, and the emission of greenhouse gases. *National Institutes of Health* (NIH) researchers Tanjena Rume and S.M Didar-UL Islam report an unexpected positive environmental consequence owed to the lockdowns imposed in many countries: "due to movement restriction and a significant slowdown of social and economic activities, air quality has improved in many cities with a reduction in water pollution in different parts of the world." These indirect, but nonetheless welcome effects of the pandemic are, however, quickly overshadowed by the negative: "increased use of PPE (e.g., face mask, hand gloves etc.), their haphazard disposal, and generation of a huge amount of hospital waste has negative impacts on the environment."[19] Both are about the consumption of hydrocarbons; using less gas but consuming more disposable plastics—all during a lockdown. We might be tempted to think of PPE (personal protective equipment) as something other than consumption because its use is a matter of necessity, but the atmosphere neither knows nor cares whether the greenhouse gases emitted in its production and use are PPE, plastic water bottles, car exhaust, or children's toys. As Mann would likely observe, however vital to combatting Covid-19 is the manufacture, use, and disposal of PPE, our life-saving activities contribute to the conditions that will make the next pandemic more possible. Insofar as the manufacture, use, and disposal of PPE adds to the climate crisis, it increases the likelihood of ecological impacts like habitat loss that, in turn, increases the potential for interaction between virus-carrying nonhuman animals and human beings. In effect, we're robbing Peter to pay Paul. Or, more specifically: we're robbing the planet's future capacity to recover from a rapidly warming atmosphere in order to combat a present menace—owing a debt to the future we're insuring we'll be in no position to pay.

The cost of the mutually fortifying relationship between the climate crisis and the pandemic could in fact be devastating if we fail to act aggressively, decisively, and now. Rume and Islam make several suggestions to mitigate against the increase in greenhouse gas emissions including the use of public transportation, renewable energy, and improved wastewater treatment, but difficult questions remain about how to entice (or compel) corporations beholden to their mining leases, (or poised to make windfall profits manufacturing plastic face shields, disposable gowns, or ventilator tubing),[20] to engage in more environmentally friendly forms of production, transportation, and distribution. For capitalism, the primary objective is profits, not human welfare.[21] Given that objective, as well as the long history of environmental destruction perpetrated in the name of profit, it's no surprise that from the point of view of the creative entrepreneur, a pandemic is no different than discovering a new coal seam, inventing a new microchip, or finding new fodder for an advertising campaign. As Matthew Limb, writer for BMJ (*British Medical Journal*) reports, fear of infection is a commodity too valuable to waste:

> Firms trading in alcohol, tobacco, junk foods, gambling, infant milk formula, and fossil fuels are "leveraging" the coronavirus crisis to burnish their brands, build influence, and advance their strategic interests, often to the detriment of wider public health and sustainability goals, shows the research from the NCD Alliance and a multi-university and multi-agency consortium of researchers known as SPECTRUM, based at Edinburgh University, that focuses on the commercial determinants of health and health inequalities… The analysis found that companies have adopted four broad approaches: tai-

lored marketing campaigns and stunts tailored to the pandemic; corporate social responsibility and philanthropy programmes; pursuit of partnerships and collaborations, such as with governments, international agencies, and non-governmental organisations; and attempts to shape favourable policy environments.[22]

That many of the costs of the pandemic, including the ways it will be exploited, and the contribution these capitalist ventures will in turn make to the climate crisis, will be borne by those who can least afford them is also not surprising. Covid-19 outbreaks have ravaged Native American reservations already blighted by drought.[23] Ramped-up meat production by companies looking to cash-in on stay-at-home orders endangers already poorly paid workers, brutalizes "food" animals, and disgorges mammoth loads of greenhouse gases into the atmosphere.[24] Struggling front line and gig economy workers are more likely not only to be exposed to the virus, but to go home to food desert communities exploited by "alcohol, tobacco, junk food, gambling, infant milk formula, and fossil fuels" corporations seeking to build their social responsibility portfolios off the pandemic.[25] The issue here is not only that by putting the profits of greenhouse gas polluting industries ahead of human welfare and environmental integrity we've turned a blind eye to the future that will pay for it, but that having done so it seems like rank hypocrisy to then pretend that a McDonalds who offers free "Thank you" meals to healthcare workers during a pandemic signals compassion.[26] It doesn't; it is advertising for a company whose meat supply comes partly from illegal deforestation in the lungs of the world—Brazil's vanishing rain forests.[27]

The Climate Crisis Is the Greatest Moral Challenge Humanity Has Ever Faced

Even if human beings were the only species on the planet that mattered, it's hard to reconcile our evinced devotion to moral principle with our plainly self-interested and reckless behavior, especially with respect to the implications of the climate crisis for vulnerable human populations in virtue of race, sex, gender, economic wherewithal, and geography. And, of course, many would argue that human beings are not the only species that matter.[28] But in whatever way we see that important question, the upshot's clear: any ethic that seeks merely to expand on the moral values we currently espouse in hopes of making them fit the crises we now face is in danger of failing its most vital *moral* responsibility: to ask whether our systems of moral decision and judgment have served us well. What we'll discover is a mixed bag. True; Nazi fascism was defeated, at least for a time, in WWII. True; SARS-CoV-2 (Covid-19) can likely be controlled by an effective vaccine—if enough people take it. But, also true: white nationalist fascism is on the rise in many Western countries. Five hundred thousand Americans died by February, 2021 from Covid-19, 4.2 million worldwide by July. True: the climate crisis has already left wide swaths of the planet more scorched than every battlefield of every war in human history.

Some argue that the implications of climate change have been exaggerated, and that decision-making about how to mitigate its effects has become too saddled with emotion, even "delusional."[29] Images of polar bears searching for ice, Puerto Rican citizens bracing for the next hurricane season, or farmers confronted by drought like a scene from *Grapes of Wrath*, they argue, make for ill-advised points of departure for cool-headed policy. Becoming better stewards of the planet surely doesn't mean abandoning capitalism, just regulating against some if its more egregious excesses. We've already seen "sustainability" become part and parcel of many a marketing platform, from Amazon's fleet of electric delivery trucks to the creation of the Impossible Burger, each a piece of techno-wizardry that portends a brighter future.[30] Perhaps what we need is an *Operation Sustainability* that, can achieve for the climate what *Operation Warp Speed* achieved in the development of a vaccine to combat the Coronavirus Pandemic.[31] We've successfully addressed issues like the ozone crisis, DDT, or air pollution in the past. The climate crisis needn't be any different.

This all seems reasonable—rising to a great moral and civilizational challenge with great ideas and innovation. The problem is that climate change *is* different—*very* different. Like previous environmental crises, climate change is the product of human, all too human activities—but not just any. The carbon footprint of the villager who walks an ever-greater distance to secure potable water is far fainter than the suburb-dweller who drives a gas-guzzling SUV to the local Super Walmart for milk and eggs. The extractive industries that mine hydrocarbons, precious minerals, soil nutrients, human labor, and manufactured animal bodies, generate both mammoth profits and mammoth greenhouse gas emissions. They bear a great deal of the blame for our current environmental dilemma. But the role of consumers cannot be ignored either, especially as economies in countries with large and growing human populations such as China and India expand, creating their own burgeoning contribution to ecological deterioration.[32] Insofar as capitalist enterprise is rooted in the idea that economic growth is a limitless proposition, and thus in its false correlate that the planet is a bottomless reservoir of extractible resources, its atmosphere an inexhaustible vault for the release of greenhouse gases, our behavior is not adequately captured merely by the idea that it's *human-centered*. The Anthropocene is not merely the age of run-away self-interest but of a human chauvinism characterized by the revolutionary idea that all value is exchange value—that all things can be effectively exhausted by a cost and a price. According to this ethos of capital, the planet exists *for* human beings, at least some of us are *entitled* to exploit, despoil, and dispose of it, and what counts as progress is the accumulation of wealth.

The Sun around which worthwhile labor revolves in the capitalist world-view is economic growth fueled by the production and consumption of goods and services. But what endless production and consumption require are endless resources for raw materials, labor, and waste disposal. The capitalist ethos captures the idea that the only interests worth valuing are interests that can be quantified and monetized. Since only human beings can act as *agents* of capitalist exchange, all other things, living and nonliving, organic and inorganic, are assigned to the status of resource, instrument, commodity, or obstacle to growth. Yet even this sketch of the operational premises of capitalist exchange doesn't go far enough. What the histories of particular forms of commodification, for example, slavery, sex-trafficking, animal agriculture, or labor outsourcing illustrate is that, from the point of view of capitalist enterprise, human beings are as likely to be understood as commodities as are oil wells or wood lots. Many are in fact made especially vulnerable to industry's rapacious need for labor by institutions and practices that take full advantage of existing structural inequalities premised on race, sex, gender, indigenous status, and geography.[33] Like the Covid-19 pandemic, the climate crisis offers a window into these inequalities, exposing the many ways in which capitalism exploits the competition created by poverty to get some of its most onerous and dangerous work done at the lowest possible wage. The pandemic merely widens that window—exposing, for example, how low-wage meat-packing plant workers, many from indigenous or immigrant communities, become disposable "essential workers" during an outbreak; or how women are emblematic of "last hired, first fired" when corporate profits are threatened by a lockdown.

In one sense the climate crisis presents us with something brand new—a genie out of a bottle that no regulatory regime, political will, global governance, or social justice movement is prepared to contain; mitigate perhaps, but not halt. In another sense, the climate crisis simply clarifies the fact that the face of human chauvinism is predominantly white, male, Western(ized), wealthy, kleptocratic, and nihilistic in its breathtaking capacity for the denial of fact. Or better: what our arrival at the climate crisis shows us is that our behavior toward Earth is nihilistic. A finite planet cannot support a myth of endless resources, and therefore cannot support the prospect of endless opportunity to convert resource into exchange value, commodity into profit. To pretend that all of this "endless" is the case is kleptocratic: the theft of what is not ours on the falsehood that everything is property because the value of everything is reducible to exchange. Not everything is replaceable; for example, the atmosphere. While Al Gore's 2006 *An Inconvenient Truth* gave voice to this fact we're really just beginning to wrestle with what a future radically altered by the capitalist ethos might mean: more frequent and calamitous firenados, tsunamis, earthquakes, volcanoes, snow bomb-cyclones, more virulent disease outbreaks, more ancillary effects like mass migrations, starvation, and war over existential necessities like clean water.[34]

The kleptocratic nature of the capitalist ethos has thus another meaning: the translation of disaster, even as it threatens the conditions of a particular industry's own survival, into profit-opportunity. Fully consistent with this ethos is that Northern California firenados present an opportunity to profit on private fire services, that hurricanes in the Gulf of Mexico offer a bonanza for insurance companies, that a new market for "preppers," folks ready to "bug out" when civil unrest over access to basic necessities reaches a boiling point, are booming industries. *Disaster capitalism just is capitalism in the display of its kleptocratic character.* It's nihilism because, as *An Inconvenient Truth* showed us back in 2006, the planet cannot sustain this sort of brutality. The climate crisis is thus a dilemma of moral foresight that cannot be blamed solely on the chauvinism of human individuals. It's also not a crisis merely due to lack of relevant knowledge or technology.[35] The climate crisis is a creation of an economic ideology that is inconsistent with planetary facts, whose realization comes at immense cost to those who can least afford it even as it rewards handsomely those in a position to promote the myths on which it depends.[36]

Still, these observations aren't really news. As such, it remains a mystery why we have not acted more aggressively to mitigate at least some of the worst effects of glabal warming. much suffering could have been avoided.[37] Some theorize that the human psyche is not well-built to fully appreciate crises that stretch over long periods of time and extend far into the future. They argue that while we can see tsunamis and fires, we can't see climate change *per se*, so it feels like something we can put off. We acknowledge the crisis, as if that somehow counts as a mitigating action.[38] It doesn't, of course. This too bears comparison with the Covid-19 pandemic. Just as some keep driving their gas-guzzlers, eat out at steakhouses—or, comfortably quarantine and turn to ZOOM meetings, having steak dinners delivered by GIG economy workers, others enjoy no such entitled economic or social luxury. Driving for Uber to deliver for GrubHub to supplement a job as a frontline worker at a meatpacking plant contributes to greenhouse gas emissions, but few would hold the wage laborer to the same standard of culpability as the ExxonMobil CEO for the climate crisis. Still, the Earth is no more in a position to assign blame than it's a magically renewable bastion of resources and commodities. Earth is home to a complex, evolving, and diverse array of living and nonliving things, including us, including bacteria, including viruses. But the planet can no more reconstitute rapidly calving polar ice shelves than our very best scientists can bring the 4.2 million Covid-19 dead back to life. We can't bring back species driven to extinction during the Anthopocene. Species like the Golden Toad were driven to extinction by climate change–enhanced drought.[39] We can't fix the lives of Syrian refugees driven by dry water wells into the hands of Islamic State terrorist recruiters.[40] We can't undo the damage done to babies infected by the Zika virus whose mosquito-borne vector widens as the planet warms.[41] Once the planet's coral reefs are gone, they're gone.[42]

The difference, then, between an "ordinary" environmental crises and climate change isn't that "ordinary" may not mean "devastating." It often does mean exactly that. As Rachel Carson lays out in *Silent Spring*, the impacts of chemical pollutants on the shells of bird's eggs reverberates across entire ecosystems. The difference is that the climate crisis poses an existential threat for every living thing on the planet because it jeopardizes the very atmosphere upon which all life on Earth depends. Crises like pollution, habitat for endangered species, or coal mine acid run-off can be addressed through clean-up efforts, regulation, education, and conservation, but climate is not a thing we can simply "clean," and even if it was, its magnitude reaches beyond any mitigating effort not global in scale and international commitment.[43] In short, we can stop disgorging hydrocarbons into the atmosphere, but there's no reset button for the atmospheric conditions we've already created. We can try to rescue the countless species endangered by the crisis, but we can't fully predict what their loss will mean for other animal and plant species.[44] Indeed, we cannot predict with any precision the complex interaction between, for example, the preservation of nation-state borders, the migration patterns of climate refugees, exposure to viral outbreak, or the potential for border conflicts that can lead to war—all exacerbated by the climate crisis.

We Can Change

Put differently: we are not helpless, but the need for deliberate, well-informed moral action could not be more urgent. We must think much more seriously about how the planet is going to support a *world*, or better, the many *worlds* human beings have come to value. And we must think about these worlds as not merely sustainable, but in what a just and desirable world(s) might consist for those who come after us. Some, perhaps much, of what we have come to value we may not be able to sustain, and while ecological sustainability is necessary to the future, it's not sufficient to a future worth wanting. The post zombie apocalypse world is sustainable, but hardly desirable, and not every "world" is either just or morally defensible. But who decides these truly difficult issues, and on what criteria? Some decisions are more self-evident than others. For example, we can and should move decisively to write laws compelling industry to stop spewing CO_2 and methane into the atmosphere. Educating people about things over which we do have at least some control, for example, the impacts of what we eat, wear, to whom we are responsible on the planet's ecosystems should be a priority for every nation and culture. And there are some concrete examples that at least should be noncontroversial. Once we knew that plastic grocery bags suffocate seabirds, we saw a flurry of policy change aimed at persuading us to switch to reusable cloth containers.[45] When public transportation is made widely accessible, safe, clean, and reliable, people use it. The realization that methane is an even more potent greenhouse gas than CO_2 has moved many to demand alternatives to natural gas.[46] We know that mask-wearing goes a long way toward protecting others from viral infection.

We *can* change. But enduring positive change is often slow and unpredictable. For many, the climate crisis is at once too abstract to fuel a sense of crisis and too immense to calculate with any confidence what to do about it.[47] Climate science, moreover, is not reserved to a single discipline like climatology. An ideally informed public would then have some understanding of chemistry, physics, meteorology, geology, biology, zoology, genetics, ecology, botany, oncology, toxicology, neurology, among other sciences. Hence, it's not surprising that a scientifically undereducated public finds it easy to ignore the warning signs or deny the evidence of climate change altogether. Climate change, of course, is not the only issue where we can see that science is crucial to ethics. But it's hard to imagine a crisis where knowledge is more important—even if other crises like the Covid-19 pandemic seem more immediate. Ethics isn't merely about getting to the right policies or laws; it's about coming to a more acute picture of the conditions under which law and policy can claim a moral foundation. The climate crisis could not make this point more succinctly: it's not something we can just foist onto elected lawmakers and policy wonks. Laws aimed at regulating greenhouse gas emissions may help us *adapt* to climate change, but none are going to put the brakes on it, any more than the development of vaccines for viral outbreaks can prevent future pandemics unless we take them. Among the many jobs of an ethic is thus the provision of sound reasons to act. The questions we must ask are about big things like national and global policies, laws, and treaties—like the Paris Climate Accord[48]—but they're also about personal responsibility. What should *I* do? What difference can *I* make? It's on these latter questions that ethics is the toughest and the most critically important. We could, for example, stop driving cars, burning coal, and leave every remaining fossil fuel droplet in the ground. But unless we end industrial animal agriculture, we're unlikely even to slow the pace of greenhouse emissions in any meaningful way. Some decisions are, however, easier at least in the affluent West, than others: many of us *can* stop eating meat.[49] That's a choice possible for at least most healthy Americans, and if enough of us made that call, it could curb the impact of one industry whose contribution to the climate crisis is massive. Plus, going vegan comes with the morally reaffirming bonus that we're no longer party to at least one form of unnecessary suffering, animal agriculture. Difficult decision? Perhaps. But if this seems a more difficult *moral* decision than is wearing masks to protect others from viral infection, that may be a prime opportunity for self-reflection.

Personal choice thus forms one crucial axis of a realistic environmental ethic. But the careful examination and criticism of industry, its capitalist world-view, and its relentless drive for profit forms another. If animal agriculture treats the planet itself like a sewer for the industrial animal body waste pits, big oil and gas treat the earth's atmosphere as a limitless celestial landfill. [50] That factory farm waste pits are called "lagoons" makes them no less atmospherically hazardous than recent technology for drilling deep below the Earth's surface makes natural gas less perilous. [51] Besides the obvious environmental harms and hazards posed to human and nonhuman health, these are industries who externalize the costs of mitigating against pollution, restoring resources, and treating health consequences to taxpayers who foot the bill to clean up water-ways, reclaim habitat, and support hospital emergency rooms where possible. And it's rarely fully possible. After all, 100-year-old trees require 100 years to grow, dilution is rarely a good solution,[52] and extinction is forever. Add the climate crisis to this toxic brew and it's hardly surprising that these industries have begun to fuel something more than cars and planes, appetites and ex-panding waistlines, namely, righteous outrage and protest. As Naomi Klein says, "climate change changes everything."

One good example of growing public outrage is the response to the advent of hydraulic fracturing, "fracking," a method of natural gas extraction whose drill-bit to pipeline to offshore transport infrastructure does lasting damage to large swaths of land, creates the necessity for ozone-producing compressor stations, and requires a chilling number "deep-well injection" toxic waste dis-posal sites.[53] A fairly new technology, the aim is to break up shale deposits deep under the earth through a horizontal drilling process combined with the use of a chemical cocktail of "slickwater" explosives that generate small earthquakes, releasing the gas. The process requires millions of gallons of water for each "frack" to create pressure that, once exposed to the chemical cocktail, becomes "produced," water permanently made toxic via carcinogens like benzene. Such water can never be returned to use for consumption, and some of it also becomes radioactive in the drilling process.[54] While industry proponents argue that fracking is "environmentally friendly" in virtue of the fact that natural gas burns more completely than coal, methane, a byproduct of the hydraulic frac-turing process, is—on the long term—a more potent greenhouse gas than CO_2.

It's easy to see why, from many different points of view, fracking has become controversial. It opens a Pandora's box of issues ranging from violations of prop-erty rights,[55] the personhood of corporations,[56] the pollution of waterways, or injuries to well-pad workers.[57] These are all important issues, and each has its place at the intersection of environmental, economic, and social ethics. Yet, what connects them all is climate change for this simple reason: hydrocarbons not left in the ground will contribute warming to the atmosphere, and whether it's natural gas, oil, tar sands, or coal the more we extract, the more we'll consume; the more we consume, the greater the acceleration of greenhouse gases disgorged into the atmosphere; the greater that acceleration, the more devastating the implications, such as future pandemic. It might seem that issues revolving around property rights aren't really connected to climate change, but we need only look as far as the devaluation of property that's deforested, a water source that's contaminated, or soil depleted to see that rights to property only matter when the property is itself worth preserving.

Seven Basic Premises

Fortunately, developing an environmental ethic capable of helping us through the age of crisis doesn't mean we have to start over from scratch. What it requires is courage enough to adopt a critical attitude toward investigating how far our moral principles can take us and with what limitations. Can they be modified in ways that retain their character *as* moral principles, and yet be more responsive to the implications of the kinds of environmental dilemma we now face? We'll see that some principles, suitably re-tooled, fare better than others, but some will reveal themselves as more moral-sounding than moral-doing. Some are deployed, or even weaponized, as cover-stories designed to advance self-interest, often at irrecoverable cost to the planet's capacity to support life, and sometimes by the disaster capitalists. The right moral compass, however, can help us gain a more objective, critically well-informed understanding of the institutions—economic, social, educational, health-related, social, religious, and cultural—that are central to our lives and decisions. One of the most immediately valuable lessons that we can learn from the crises we face is that we can no longer afford to treat the planet's ecosystems and their inhabitants as mere background or fodder for human projects. What affects them affects us, and even on the most chauvinistic construal of why that matters, we can no more ignore it than we can pretend that California fires are not more ferocious and more frequent, or that we have had a hand in the viral outbreaks that kill our families and friends. Instead, our grounding presupposition is that nonhuman nature is a dynamic evolving actor whose body, incarnated as trees and rivers, vertebrates and invertebrates, living and nonliving things, interacts in countless ways with the bodies of human beings incarnated as individuals, families, and communities. Nonhuman nature affects and is affected by what human beings do; we're living things whose existential conditions are as dependent on nonhuman nature as are other living things. We do a good job of denying this fact by appeal to cultural tradition, technological know-how, or the capacity for inertia. But we age, deteriorate, and die as surely as do Walt Whitman's blades of grass.

This more critical approach to environmental ethics can be laid out along the rails of *seven basic premises*, each of which will govern our evaluation of the arguments we'll consider:

- First, *we're not alone on the planet*; we share it with a vast number of other people, nonhuman animal species, and biota upon whom we're existentially dependent, some of whom pose substantive danger to the future of human life.

- Second, *our actions can have consequences well beyond the immediate or near-term*. Although the complexity of the planet's ecosystems, atmosphere, species relationships, cultures, and histories can make prediction difficult, that doesn't relieve us the responsibility to consider the future—especially since it's the planet's future habitability that's endangered by the crises we have created.

- Third, *science must play a role as an essential partner at every level of decision-making*. This is true not only with respect to technological innovation, but for understanding biodiversity, our interdependent relationships with other peoples and species, the impact of human activities for human and nonhuman populations, and the capacities of human and nonhuman actors to adapt to a changing climate.

- Fourth, *other living things, human and nonhuman, aren't merely commodities*. Despite its increasingly apparent contribution to the conditions that produce famine, food insecurity, and disease, we continue to justify our consumption of animal bodies as key to "development" or "progress." We can no longer afford to exempt what we eat or wear from evaluating the environmental impact of its production. While many factors contribute to human hunger, the land required for animal agriculture, its production of greenhouse emissions, and the example that commodifying nonhuman animals sets for disvaluing some human populations only reinforces the human chauvinism responsible for the climate crisis.

- Fifth, we can't defend treating nonhuman animals and systems as commodities merely by appeal to the preservation of culture or tradition—however difficult a pill this is to swallow. This follows for at least two reasons;
  - Economic development disrupts and displaces culture, yet we endorse it as progress—risking hypocrisy concerning our efforts to justify, for example, eating nonhuman animal bodies.
  - Traditions aren't self-justifying. Just because a practice has a history does not by itself confer moral legitimacy on it. Many practices, for example, spousal battery, the abuse of animals as circus spectacles, or human slavery have "traditions" we now regard as indefensible.

To deny that climate change is anthropogenic (or deny it entirely) in the interest of preserving a particular tradition ignores the possibility the tradition is complicit—a defense both morally suspect and likely self-defeating.

- Sixth, *the planet's resources are limited*; contrary to what economist Herman Daly called "the myth of endless resources," the earth is not an inexhaustible storehouse of hydrocarbons, clean water, precious metals, or arable soil. The planet's atmosphere is not an infinite repository for industrial waste and greenhouse gases. While confronting the twin myths of endless resource and bottomless dumpsite is challenging—it *will* require a profound and sustained transformation of human behavior—no ethic stands a chance of saving us from our chauvinism without this operational premise. Until we take it as a given of decision-making that the shift to renewable forms of energy won't be enough without a sustained commitment to re-use, conservation, ecological restoration, and the strict regulation of pollutants, and that this commitment must act as the centerpiece of international agreements, national policy, community organization, and personal agency, we're unlikely to find ourselves able to confront the consequences of that failure.
- Lastly, although human chauvinism is the root cause of environmental crisis, this doesn't necessarily imply that a *rational human-centeredness* has no defensible place in an environmental ethic. Indeed, it does and it must if we're to articulate an ethic sufficiently persuasive to the only creatures on the planet equipped to make the kinds of dramatic changes necessary to sustain it into the future, namely, *us*. Whales aren't going to draft the next Paris Climate Accord. Chimpanzees aren't going to put a halt to diamond mining. One sparrow does not a Summer make. It's up to us, *all of us*, to reinvent a *human-centeredness* that takes what we now *know* about the planet and its denizens and translate that into an ethic that can see its way to a future worth the hard work to realize it. But this critical task cannot be left solely to those who currently benefit from the status quo. Hence one important part of articulating such as ethic must be to listen astutely and with humility to those who have borne the negative impacts of the myth of endless resources, those whose geographies, resources, labor, and bodies have fueled quite literally the voracious appetites of the Global North.

In short: we're not alone; actions have consequences; science is critical; nonhuman animals and ecosystems must be part of the moral equation; culture is important, but so is the planet's capacity to support life; planetary resources are limited; human-centeredness isn't necessarily chauvinistic, human interests do matter, and listening forms a crucial component of any ethic worth advancing. To some, these seven premises are obvious. To others, they seem radically out of step with what we've long taken for granted, namely, that we human beings are special and thereby exempt from the interdependencies and vulnerabilities that characterize other creatures. If the Covid-19 pandemic doesn't clarify for us that our sense of entitlement is misplaced, a planetary future driven by war over clean water will. It's not difficult philosophical concepts or complicated arguments that makes ethics "hard." it's that we have to change our ways—personally, collectively, economically, and politically.

Seven Key Objectives

One very old idea worth recuperating in our search for a point of departure takes us all the way back to the Ancient Greeks, namely to Socrates' claim that *the unexamined life is not worth living.* Much, of course, has changed. The world Socrates could take for granted as essentially eternal is an idea long shattered by the reality of a richer and more diverse, yet more fragile, planetary ecology. A life worth living in the age of environmental crisis will require the kind of courageous self-examination that can produce change in the way many of us live as well as the recognition of the enormous impact the climate crisis has already had. A life examined can mean changing the way "we" eat, what "we" wear, where "we" travel, how "we" get there, whether and how many children "we" have, where "we" live—*everything.* It can prod us to ask what we mean by "we." It will compel us to look more closely at what we mean by "worth," for whom, and under what conditions. If the point of adopting an ethic is to realize a life worth living, seeing what are our central questions is actually pretty straightforward, if hard to answer: what does "worth living" look like? Whose voices does it sound like? For whom? What should "worth living" be able to *do*?

The following seven criteria aim at helping us critically evaluate what's worth keeping as we examine some of the major theories in environmental ethics. Our goal will be to decide whether each of these can be met in light of the premises articulated above. Just as important, these are criteria that will help us decide what of those theories to let go, what has become antiquated, and what might undermine our quest for a life worth living in the age of the climate crisis. Here's what a contemporary environmental ethic must be able to *do* as part and parcel of such a life:

- First, it must *offer ways of thinking* about nonhuman nature, human and nonhuman animals, the future, and the planet that
  - Reach beyond the "mere" extension of moral principles intended for human use and application to other living things, ecological systems, and the planet as a whole.

- o Take as a governing premise species interdependence, their ecologies, and whatever endangers their survival, understanding these relations as central to "worth."
- Second, an environmentally oriented ethic must be able to *shine a bright, if not always flattering, light on the successes and failures of ethics* both as a branch of philosophy and as a human practice. Some would argue that our "moralities" have no more prevented us from spewing hydrocarbons into the atmosphere than they helped to prevent the rise of Nazi fascism, or are now offering us a way out of the Covid-19 pandemic. Others would hasten to point out that without moral principle to guide judgment we'd have no way to know what deserves praise or blame, no grounds for condemning bad decisions or policies and implementing good ones. Both are right, and neither *quite* right. But understanding how we arrived at this point, and how it might have been worse, or better, are key to understanding in what a sustainably desirable future consists.
- Third, a viable environmental ethic must help us *articulate strategies for imagining in what a desirable, ethically defensible, future consists* not merely for the few who are able to weather the environmental and geopolitical implications of our current dilemmas, but for the many, human and nonhuman. Such strategies are more important now than ever. Although there remain those who'd deny the climate crisis jeopardizes the capacity of the planet to support life, the science is as clear as are the facts of a warming planet for any number of other social, economic, and geopolitical issues.
- Fourth, an environmentally grounded ethic can help to *illumine a number of important issues human societies face* in a world whose interdependencies, relationships, conflicts, and crises intersect with specific ecologies and species, that is, *everywhere*. We cannot see this more clearly than through the lens of a rapidly spreading pandemic, the devastation left of whole communities by firenadoes and hurricanes, or the struggle for food and clean water. We can't simply add "environment" to moral judgment; issues like poverty, terrorism, human migration, food and water insecurity, demand serious consideration of precisely what roles are played by the causes of drought, disease, or food insecurity.
- Fifth, an environmental ethic must *help us see how the climate crisis forms a central component of moral judgment* for anyone committed to the idea that a life worth living for human beings includes access to basic goods like food and water security, access to medical care, education, national security. While we tend to overlook its significance, an environmental ethic must help us to rehabilitate other values, particularly the value of opportunities for aesthetic experience, for fun, and wonder. We can debate over what the aesthetic *in* experience might consist, but to ignore the value of the aesthetic is to ignore a critical aspect of what makes life desirable.

- Sixth, given the global nature of environmental crisis, a viable environmental ethic must be able to *remind us that ethics isn't merely a matter of what individuals do*; some of us are in position to recycle, go vegan, or ride bicycles instead of driving cars. Others struggle every day to secure adequate nutrition for themselves and their children in city food deserts; others still spend half their days foraging for firewood or carting clean water. Any environmental ethic that can live up to its commitment to a sustainable future must therefore also be allied with what governments, economies, cultures, militaries, and societies do. Environmental ethics, in other words, commits us, albeit in differing ways, from differing circumstances, to environmental, geopolitical, and social *justice*, and it's hard to imagine a more urgent time for clear-headed thinking about how individual moral decision-making intersects with the big picture of a warming planet.
- Seventh, a moral compass informed by a commitment to sustaining a habitable future *epitomizes what it means to do philosophy* in the broad sense that environmental ethics *is* future-directed *and* has its feet planted firmly in the soil of the perennial quest for a meaningful life. A desirable future is one for which meaning can be a tangible, possible project, an endeavor that can reach well-beyond mere survival. The climate crisis will compel us to think long and hard about that future, to think forward beyond the merely "sustainable." It will demand we think about the earth, quite literally, in terms of ecological conditions we can no longer afford to treat as inexhaustible. It will demand we think about ourselves as a species among others whose presence on the planet is as vulnerable to its changing climate as are the species endangered by often reckless human action.

Naomi Klein is right, climate change changes everything. But facts, even big ones, don't necessarily tell us what to do, much less how to imagine a life worth living endangered by the very practices and activities we take most for granted. Can an environmental ethic offer us an alternative vision of meaning that makes a livable future *desirable*? This is a very tall order. But it all starts, as we're reminded by the water protectors of Standing Rock, with the decision to enter that struggle: *Mni Wiconi*. Protect the water, because the water protects us all.

Summary and Questions

What distinguishes ethics as a field of philosophical inquiry from other disciplinary domains is that its work—the moral principles it explores—are always aimed at the judgments and actions of real people making decisions to resolve real dilemmas. This commitment to the actionable is especially evident in contemporary environmental ethics whose arguments are grounded in philosophical thinking about moral issues, but also driven by a sense of duty to speak to a world whose planetary conditions are changing in ways that demand urgent, deliberate, informed, and collective attention. Two key premises inform this branch of moral philosophy: first, ecological conditions are existential conditions. Second, the crises we currently face, especially climate change and the potential for recurring pandemic, remind us that decisions made in the present will impact the future. But impact is unequal. Indeed, any environmental ethic that does not at the same time pay close attention to the ways in which ecological crises like the climate crisis and the Covid-19 pandemic intersect with issues of social, racial, and economic justice will provide at best a distorted and incomplete picture of the moral life in the era of environmental crisis.

Like previous environmental crises, climate change is the product of human activities—but not just any. The carbon footprint of the villager who walks an ever-greater distance to secure potable water is far fainter than the suburb-dweller who drives a gas-guzzling SUV to the local Super Walmart for milk and eggs. It's also an easy thing to blame industries like the fossil fuel corporations, Big Box stores, and animal agriculture for the lion's share of the damage to the planet's atmosphere. But consumers, especially in the countries of the Global North, also bear responsibility, and as economies in countries like China and India expand, so too their consumer's contribution to pollution, waste, and greenhouse gas emissions. Insofar as capitalist enterprise is rooted in the idea that economic growth is a limitless proposition, it also presupposes the false correlate that the planet is a bottomless reservoir of extractible resources, its atmosphere an inexhaustible vault for the release of greenhouse gases. Under these conditions, human self-interest tends to be understood in the narrowly *chauvinistic* terms of a planet that exists *for* us, a worldview that, driven by the desire to preserve the myth of endless resources, is prone to precisely the willful ignorance and denial responsible for what is certainly the greatest environmental crisis of our time.

The antidote for ignorance and delusion, and therefore a critical component of a defensible environmental ethic, is science. Mitigating the effects of climate change will require global scientific consensus, international cooperation, and enduring personal commitment. While environmental ethics is not *about* climate change, it's hard to imagine any serious exploration of moral responsibility that doesn't take its causes and implications into account. This begins with listening to what the sciences tell us about the planet, its atmosphere, its oceans, and its species life. It means thinking long and hard about whether the moral principles that have guided human response to crises of the past are adequate to the present. Nonetheless, one very old idea remains wholly relevant to our present quest, the Ancient Greek philosopher Socrates' *the unexamined life is not worth living*. Socrates provides not only a point of departure but of return to a fundamental premise of all ethical inquiry, namely, that the value of life for any entity capable of asking that question lay in the capacity to examine and reflect in just what that life consists, who or what it affects, whether its legacy is one the future can remember because there will be successors to remember it.

1. Why is the climate crisis central to articulating an environmental ethic that makes sense for the twenty-first century? How is the prospect of future viral pandemic an environmental issue?
2. What role do inequalities of race, sex, gender, economic status, geography, and species play in our understanding of environmental dilemmas?
3. Why are the sciences vitally important to articulating an environmental ethic?
4. What's the difference between human chauvinism and human-centeredness? What is the myth of endless resources, and what role do capitalist economies play in any comprehensive evaluation of the causes of environmental crises?
5. Why is the concept of the future vital to developing an environmental ethic?
6. How is Socrates' idea that "the unexamined life is not worth living" relevant to environmental ethics?

Annotated Bibliography

Daly, Herman (1996). *Beyond Growth* (Boston: Beacon Press).
Provides a critical account of the myth of endless resources and its implication for climate change and other forms of environmental deterioration.
Jamieson, Dale (2014). *Reason in a Dark Time: Why the Struggle against Climate Change Failed and What It Means for Our Future* (Oxford: Oxford University Press.
Shows how our incapacity to think beyond immediate threats has thwarted our efforts to address climate change.
Klein, Naomi (2014). *This Changes Everything: Capitalism Vs. The Climate. Simon and Schuster,* New York.
Excellent and timely discussion of how we have ignored the warning signs concerning climate change, and how some of the planet's largest environmental organizations have let us down.
Lee, Wendy (2016). *Eco-Nihilism: The Philosophical Geopolitics of the Climate Change Apocalypse* (Lexington: Rowman and Littlefield).
Biting critique of the role that multinational capitalism and government inaction play in climate change and our failure to address it.

Mann, Michael (2016). *The Madhouse Effect: How Climate Change Denial is Threatening Our Planet, Destroying Our Politics, and Driving Us Crazy* (Columbia University Press).
Excellent and highly accessible discussion of the role of climate change denial in our failure to work toward solutions to mitigate this environmental crisis.
Plato (1997). *The Apology, 38a-5-6. Plato: Complete Works*, ed. John Cooper and D.S. Hutchinson (Hackett Publishing Company).
Dialogue of the trial of Socrates and his defense of the philosophically informed life.

Online Resources

1. "Environmental Ethics." *Stanford Encyclopedia of Philosophy*, https://plato.stanford.edu/entries/ethics-environmental.
2. "Fourth National Climate Assessment Update, July 2018," *GlobalChange.gov*, https://www.globalchange.gov/news/fourth-national-climate-assessment-update-july-2018.
3. "Coronavirus (Covid-19)," *United States Centers for Disease Control*, https://www.cdc.gov/coronavirus/2019-ncov/index.html.
4. "A 60 Second Guide to the Global North/South Divide," *Royal Geographical Society*, https://www.rgs.org/CMSPages/GetFile.aspx?nodeguid=9c1ce781-9117-4741-af0a-a6a8b75f32b4&lang=en-GB.
5. Hannah Brock, "Climate Change: Drivers of Insecurity on the Global South," *Oxford Research Group*, June 2012, https://www.files.ethz.ch/isn/146109/Climate%20Change%20and%20Insecurity%20in%20the%20Global%20South.pdf.
6. "Frequently Asked Questions: Spread," *United State Centers for Disease Control*, https://www.cdc.gov/coronavirus/2019-ncov/faq.html#Spread.
7. Emily Stewart, "Anti-Maskers Explain Themselves," *Vox*, August 7, 2020, https://www.vox.com/the-goods/2020/8/7/21357400/anti-mask-protest-rallies-donald-trump-covid-19.
8. Adam Vaughn, "How the Coronavirus has Impacted Climate Change—For Good and Bad," *New Scientist*, October 14, 2020. https://www.newscientist.com/article/mg24833040-900-how-the-coronavirus-has-impacted-climate-change-for-good-and-bad.
9. "Heroes of the Front Lines," *Time Magazine, Series*, 2020, https://time.com/collection/coronavirus-heroes.
10. *Climate Heroes*, https://climateheroes.org.
11. Mann Michael, *The Madhouse Effect: How Climate Change Denial is Threatening Our Planet, Destroying Our Politics, and Driving Us Crazy*, https://www.youtube.com/watch?v=rfjBM_BB-ic.

12. "The Grounds of Moral Status," *Stanford Encyclopedia of Philosophy*, https://plato.stanford.edu/entries/grounds-moral-status.

13. "Climate Change: How Do We Know?" *NASA: Global Climate Change*, https://climate.nasa.gov/evidence.

14. Matthew Taylor and John Watts, "Revealed: The 20 Firms Behind a Third of All Carbon Emissions," *The Guardian*, October 9, 2019. https://www.theguardian.com/environment/2019/oct/09/revealed-20-firms-third-carbon-emissions.

15. "A Brief History of Climate Change," *BBC News: Science and Environment*, September 20, 2013, https://www.bbc.com/news/science-environment-15874560.

16. Katie Mencke, "How Coronavirus Could Impact Pulp and Paper Demand," *Fisher International*, https://www.fisheri.com/blog/how-coronavirus-could-impact-pulp-paper-demand.

17. Ghulam Nabi, et. al., "Massive Use of Disinfectants Against Covid-19 Poses Risks to Urban Wildlife," *U.S. National Library of Medicine, National Institutes of Health*, July 9, 2020, https://www.ncbi.nlm.nih.gov/pmc/articles/PMC7346835.

18. Georgina Gustin and Mariana Henninger, "Central America's Choice: Pray for Rain or Migrate," *Inside Climate News and NBC News* (respectively), https://www.nbcnews.com/news/latino/central-america-drying-farmers-face-choice-pray-rain-or-leave-n1027346.

19. Tanjena Rume and S.M. Didar-UI-Islam, "Environmental Effects of Covid-19 Pandemic and Potential Strategies of Sustainability," *U.S. National Library of Medicine, National Institutes of Health*, September 6, 2020, https://www.ncbi.nlm.nih.gov/pmc/articles/PMC7498239.

20. "Plastic Industry Uses the Pandemic to Boost Production," *Green America*, 2020, https://www.greenamerica.org/are-single-use-plastics-increasing-during-covid-19.

21. Kristina Zucchi, "Main Characteristics of Capitalist Economies," *Investopedia*, May 7, 2019, https://www.investopedia.com/articles/investing/102914/main-characteristics-capitalist-economies.asp.

22. Matthew Limb, "Covid-19: Food and Drink Companies are Exploiting Pandemic to Further Their Brands, Analysis Finds," *The British Medical Journal*, September 11, 2020, https://www.bmj.com/content/370/bmj.m3548.

23. Jane Johnston, "Where Water is Scarce on Native American Reservations Covid-19 Spreads More Easily," *Circle of Blue: Where Water Speaks*, 2020, https://www.circleofblue.org/2020/world/where-water-is-scarce-on-native-american-reservations-covid-19-spreads-more-easily.

24. "Meatpacking Corporations Cash In On Pandemic While Family Farms and Consumers Foot the Bill," *High Plains Journal*, August 21, 2020, https://

www.hpj.com/opinion/meatpacking-corporations-cash-in-on-pandemic-while-family-farms-and-consumers-foot-the-bill/article_2ab81a2e-e319-11ea-9784-577a8ea2464d.html.

25. Elisa Braun, Laura Kayali, and Paola Tamma, "Coronavirus Pandemic Leaves Gig Economy Workers Exposed," *Politico*, March 19, 2020, https://www.politico.eu/article/coronavirus-pandemic-leaves-gig-economy-workers-exposed.

26. Drew Weisholtz, "McDonalds Giving Out Free Meals to healthcare Workers and First Responders," *Today*, April 21, 2020, https://www.today.com/food/mcdonald-s-giving-out-free-meals-health-care-workers-first-t179403.

27. Andrew Wasley, Alexandra heal, and André Campos, "Brazil: Investigations reveal that McDonalds, Burger King and Many Companies in the UK are Supplied with Meat from Illegal Deforestation Areas in the Amazon Rain Forest, Includes Company Comments," *Business and Human Rights Resource Center*, September 17, 2019, https://www.business-humanrights.org/en/latest-news/brazil-investigations-reveal-that-mcdonalds-burger-king-and-many-companies-in-the-uk-are-supplied-with-meet-from-illegal-deforestation-areas-in-the-amazon-forest-includes-companies-comments.

28. *Friends of Animals*, https://friendsofanimals.org/animal-rights.

29. Sterling Burnett, "Climate Change Alarmists are getting More Delusional in Their Predictions," *The Heartland Institute*, January 9, 2020, https://www.heartland.org/news-opinion/news/climate-change-alarmists-are-getting-more-delusional-in-their-predictions.

30. Alex Gray, "5 Tech Innovations That Could Save Us From Climate Change," *World Economic Forum: Global Agenda*, January 9, 2017, https://www.weforum.org/agenda/2017/01/tech-innovations-save-us-from-climate-change.

31. "Fact Sheet: Explaining Operation Warp Speed, 2020," *U.S. Health and Human Services*, https://www.hhs.gov/coronavirus/explaining-operation-warp-speed/index.html.

32. Andrew Freedman, "The Countries that Pushed Carbon Emissions to Record Levels," *Axios*, December 6, 2018. https://www.axios.com/china-india-us-pushed-carbon-emissions-to-record-levels-in-2018-1b1e171a-d46a-49b7-bc4a-7250942a1a7d.html.

33. S. Nazrul Islam and John Winkel. "Climate Change and Social Inequality," *United Nations Department of Economic and Social Affairs*, October 17, https://www.un.org/esa/desa/papers/2017/wp152_2017.pdf.

34. *An Inconvenient Truth*, https://www.imdb.com/title/tt0497116.

35. Martin Boucher, "Opinion: Climate Change is More Than a Tech Problem, so We Need More Than a Tech Sollution," *Ensia*, March 20, 2017, https://ensia.com/voices/climate-change-social-fix.

36. Naomi Klein, "How Power Profits from Disaster," *The Guardian*, July 6, 17, https://www.theguardian.com/us-news/2017/jul/06/naomi-klein-how-power-profits-from-disaster.

37. Beth Gardiner, "Coronavirus Holds Key Lessons on How to Fight Climate Change," *Yale Environment 360*, March 23, 2020, https://e360.yale.edu/features/coronavirus-holds-key-lessons-on-how-to-fight-climate-change.

38. Dale Jamieson, "The Misunderstood Risks of Climate Change," *Rock Ethics Institute, Youtube,* December 1, 2020, https://www.youtube.com/watch?v=SBfYRtcXL_g.

39. Andrew Curry, "Global Warming Didn't Kill the Golden Toad," *Science*, March 1, 10, https://www.sciencemag.org/news/2010/03/global-warming-didnt-kill-golden-toad.

40. Thomas L Friedman, "Without Water, Revolution," *New York Times*, May 18, 2013, https://www.nytimes.com/2013/05/19/opinion/sunday/friedman-without-water-revolution.html.

41. Greg Mercer, "The Link Between Zika and Climate Change," *The Atlantic*, February 24, 2016. https://www.theatlantic.com/health/archive/2016/02/zika-and-climate-change/470643/.

42. "How Does Climate Change Affect Coral Reefs?" *National Oceanic and Atmospheric Administration, National Ocean Service*, https://oceanservice.noaa.gov/facts/coralreef-climate.html.

43. "Is the United States About To Lose Its Best Conservation Program?" *The Revelator*, October 14, 2018, https://therevelator.org/lose-best-conservation-program/.

44. Chelsea Harvey, "Climate Change is Becoming a Threat to Biodiversity," *Scientific American*, March 28, 2018. https://www.scientificamerican.com/article/climate-change-is-becoming-a-top-threat-to-biodiversity.

45. "How Plastics Affect Birds," *International Bird Rescue*, https://www.bird-rescue.org/our-work/research-and-education/how-plastics-affect-birds.aspx.

46. Gayathri Vaidyanathan, "How Bad of a Greenhouse Gas is Methane?" *Scientific American*, December 22, 2015, https://www.scientificamerican.com/article/how-bad-of-a-greenhouse-gas-is-methane/.

47. Dale Jamieson, *Reason in a Dark Time.*

48. *United Nations: Climate Change, Paris Climate Agreement*, https://unfccc.int/process-and-meetings/the-paris-agreement/the-paris-agreement.

49. "Why Go Vegan?" *The Vegan Society*, https://www.vegansociety.com/go-vegan/why-go-vegan.

50. "Global Greenhouse Gas Emissions Data," *Environmental Protection Agency*, (EPA), https://www.epa.gov/ghgemissions/global-greenhouse-gas-emissions-data.

51. Robin Marks, "Cesspools of Shame: How Factory Farm Lagoons and Spray-fields Threaten Environmental Public Health," *National Resources Defense Council and the Clean Water Network*, July 2001, https://www.nrdc.org/sites/default/files/cesspools.pdf.

52. "Dilution," *Pollution Issues*, http://www.pollutionissues.com/Co-Ea/Dilution.html.

53. Mark Lallanilla, "Facts About Fracking," *LiveScience*, February 9, 2018, https://www.livescience.com/34464-what-is-fracking.html.

54. Jie Jenny Zou, "Fracking Produces Tons of Radioactive Waste: What Should We Do With It?" *Grist*, June 20, 2016, https://grist.org/business-technology/fracking-produces-tons-of-radioactive-waste-what-should-we-do-with-it.

55. Merrill Matthews, "Anti-Fracking Laws Vs. Property Rights," *Wall Street Journal*, July 31, 2014, https://www.wsj.com/articles/merrill-matthews-anti-fracking-laws-vs-property-rights-1406848564.

56. Mari Margil and Ben Price, "Pittsburgh Bans Fracking (And Corporate Personhood)," *Alternet*, November 16, 2010, https://www.alternet.org/story/148881/pittsburgh_bans_fracking_%28and_corporate_personhood%29.

57. Neela Banerjee, "Fracking Workers Exposed to Dangerous Amounts of Benzene," *Los Angeles Times*, September 11, 2014, https://www.latimes.com/science/sciencenow/la-sci-sn-fracking-benzene-worker-health-20140910-story.html.

1

MORAL PRINCIPLES AND THE LIFE WORTH LIVING

1.1 Philosophy and the Environment

1.1.1 Philosophy and the Life Worth Living

While many disciplines have a vested interest in the environment, its inhabitants and ecosystems, its biotic diversity, and its future stability, it falls to philosophy perhaps more than to any other to offer organizing concepts for a viable—actionable, livable, realistic—environmental *ethic*. Ethics isn't about what merely *is* the case, but what *should be*. As an organizing feature of our ways of life, moral decision-making always has one foot in the context or conditions of our present actions and another pointed toward the future. A life that lacks self-reflection concerning our place in the many contexts or roles we occupy, the impacts of our decisions on our relationships with others, human and nonhuman, present and future, is not as likely, as Socrates might have put it, to be a life worth living. Even from the point of view of simple self-interest, such a life is bound to reap more pain than pleasure, more sorrow than joy. The reason, of course, is that life on planet Earth includes more than human beings and human relationships. Our self-interested motives and the consequences that follow from our actions are rarely constrained to ourselves alone. Our lives include values that reach beyond the moral, for example, the aesthetic, the economic, the social, and the civic. As our recent confrontation with the Covid-19 pandemic surely reminds us, we cannot value our own health without valuing that of others, and as the climate crisis illustrates more clearly with each firenado, tsunami, or bomb cyclone, human actions have impact well beyond single communities, regions, and countries.

This is Environmental Ethics: An Introduction, First Edition. Wendy Lynne Lee.
© 2022 John Wiley & Sons, Inc. Published 2022 by John Wiley & Sons, Inc.
Companion Website: https://thisisphilosoph.wordpress.com

Every time we sit down to eat, buy a car, read a book, go on vacation—every ordinary thing we do—is woven throughout with the often invisible labors of other people, with institutions like governments, and systems of economic exchange that inform virtually every action, and with nonhuman nature, living and nonliving, plant life, and sentient animal. Our bodies bleed these intimate relationships; our cars run on them; our books are woven of fibers extracted from the wood of an industry that threatens several endangered species. Our aspirations are made realizable through the labor and resources of countless others, most of whom we'll never see or know anything about. Some are exploited in developing world cell-phone cities, banana plantations, diamond mines, sneaker factories, and sweat shops. Others become characters in dystopian novels and films that explore environmental apocalypse, the consequences of uncontrollable viral outbreak, species extinctions, or war over water scarcity. In these, the life worth living is displaced by stories of hardship and survival that often seem closer that we'd like to admit to the lives of people and their communities in the world as it is. They warn us of a world we do not want, but that the trajectory of our current environmental crises promise is coming. A robust practicable environmental ethic cannot save us from some of the crises we have already set into motion, but it can help us formulate plans of action that will blunt some of the impact and, if we act with well-informed deliberation and urgency, see our way to a more sustainable and more just future. In the spirit, then, of a modestly modified version of Socrates' claim, here are some important ideas that inform this work:

- *Moral considerability* raises the question whether a thing, living or nonliving, human or nonhuman, local or foreign, is worthy of consideration with respect to its welfare, and if so on what grounds. It's as often as not a difficult question to answer since while it might be easy to condemn ExxonMobil for harm to endangered Polar Bears, many other nonhuman animals, even if endangered, have not evoked similar empathy. And we needn't look much further than the history of coal-mining or the timber industry to see that ecosystems evoke even less consideration. One aim of moral considerability is to situate the examined life not only in the value of human beings, relationships, practices, and institutions across culture, geography, economic class, social status, and time, but to encourage recognition of the interdependencies that characterize the relationship of human beings to nonhuman nature, nonhuman animals,[1] and the planet's atmosphere. A life worth living derives value not only from the goods that accrue to self-interest, but from those made possible by a stable environment rich in biodiversity, connections with human and nonhuman others, and a deep-going appreciation of the idea that considerability is closely connected to justice—environmental, economic, and social.[2]

- *Science* forms a key component of a life worth living even, or especially, when it dislodges us from the bad habit of denial by its evaluation of the effects of human action for the planet and its atmosphere. It charts a course to a future habitable or otherwise, and thus lays before us the decisions we can still make. It illustrates for us is plain numbers, for example, CO_2 parts per million,[3] rising incidents of viral infection, the last living Javan Rhinoceros,[4] golden tree frogs, Sumatran elephants, or polar bears, the consequences of our recklessness and what, at our peril, we continue to ignore. Science reminds us of our finitude whether we're counting in ventilators or drought-scorched hectares, in bullet forensics or hurricane categories.
- *"Worth"* (or value) is an important idea whether we think it an intrinsic quality or not.[5] The concept of moral considerability needn't require commitment to the contentious claim that living things have value inherent or intrinsic to being that (kind of) thing, or that "worth" is a function of an intrinsic property of a creature or thing. Even if assigning "worth" is an activity (as opposed to a discovery), it doesn't commit us to assigning it solely with the aim of advancing human interests. Moreover, while worth is related to moral considerability, it's not identical to it. Something can, for instance, have aesthetic value without necessarily being *morally* considerable. One might race into a burning building to retrieve a painting because of its beauty, originality, or the fame of the painter. But surely, upon seeing a kitten sitting terrified in front of the painting, most people would get the kitten out first, even if the painting was lost. Most would find condemnable someone who reached for the painting, regardless its aesthetic value, over the kitten. Similarly, the political worth of a charismatic candidate is not the same thing as her moral considerability as a human being; she might be a fantastic speaker, but if we found out that she had threatened to murder her opponent, surely her political capital would be squandered.
- *Human-centeredness* need not imply human chauvinism, and while we may need reminding at times, "centeredness" needn't mean narrow self-interest, but rather epistemic responsibility. This idea can help us avoid the contentious issue of trying to decipher what has intrinsic worth by shifting the duty to assign value onto human decision-making, serious reflection concerning the morally considerable, and the duty to consider the possible consequences of our actions, individually and collectively. If we're the deciders, in other words, among our responsibilities is to recognize that the human chauvinism of our current trajectory has produced a poor quality of life for many, great suffering for some, loss of biodiversity, and that the ecological damage it has created is ultimately nihilistic. But it's also precisely *because* we're the deciders that this trajectory can be altered. We can't escape decisions, and decisions signal value; but we *can* individually, collectively, and internationally make better calls. This re-imagined human-centeredness leaves to the side intrinsic worth for the still rocky, but more promising

road paved by a commitment to the future informed by science. To be clear: science does not (and cannot) dictate moral action, government policy, or best practice. Indeed, far too often science is put to nefarious objectives. But, equipped with the right moral compass, what science can do is provide the foundation for a well-informed consideration of *fact*. Facts about a warming atmosphere, facts about the effects of toxic waste, coal ash, or ozone for human and nonhuman health, facts about the sentience of nonhuman animal species, facts about what supports or weakens ecosystem integrity—and countless others crucial to the very way we conceive a future for lives worth living. Adopting human-centeredness as an important aspect of the life worth living does not necessarily solve our moral problems, but it can serve as a reliable axis around which we can examine issues through a lens more objective, less chauvinistic; more oriented toward the imperiled future, less mired in the nihilism of the unsustainable.

Equipped to go forward with these important moral ideas, three difficult questions become apparent: (1) can any of our available, well-established, moral principles be *extended or expanded* in a way that not only demonstrates the moral relevance of what we're in a position to know, but provides direction toward making defensible judgments about what we should do in light of that knowledge? (2) Given that some version of *moral extensionism* offers the best route for developing an environmental ethic, what qualities, characteristics, or capacities, should we prioritize in nonhuman animal species and/or ecosystems such that our judgments of moral relevance lead to actions, policies, and programs whose impacts are environmentally sustainable, or better: tend to the desirable future? (3) Who and/or what should be the intended beneficiaries of moral extensionism, and why?

Moral extensionism is, of course, not really a new idea and several philosophers, including Peter Singer and Christopher Stone, among others, sought early on in the growing 1970s environmental movement to answer these questions, and thereby provide a robust defense of their intended beneficiaries. Still, fifty years have passed since their landmark arguments, and science has opened many doors to a deeper understanding of the similarities and differences that characterize our relationship to nonhuman animals, the ecological value of biodiversity, or the impacts of extractivist industries such as oil and gas drilling. These open doors raise anew the question how we ought to conceive the morally considerable, whether our twentieth-century theories are adequate in light of newly discovered facts, and whether an appreciation of the facts should prompt us to rethink and revise. This brings us to another modification of Socrates' "the unexamined life is not worth living":

- *Existential security is synonymous with a sustainable environment.*[6] Whatever endangers the planetary environment imperils the human condition.

Given a future impacted by environmental crisis, any environmental ethic consistent with a life worth living must include at least this straightforward incarnation of the *precautionary principle*: wherever an action, practice, policy, law, or (de)regulation implies a well-supported likelihood of causing harm to the planet's atmosphere and ecologies, thus to its capacity to support life, or its critical resources, water, air, soil, and biodiversity, the burden to demonstrate that harm will *not* occur as a consequence of that action, etc. falls directly on the actor(s) or agencies responsible for it.[7] If the responsible party is not able to show that harm, short or long term, will not be the result of that action, etc., caution councils that it not be undertaken. Policies, laws, practices, and regulations currently in force, but demonstrably culpable for harm (or failing to prevent harm contrary to their stipulated purpose), to ecosystems, their human or nonhuman members, are legitimate targets for review and potential repeal as inconsistent with at least minimum conditions of life worth living, namely, a sustainably protected atmosphere, clean water, breathable air, arable soil.

Taking the precautionary principle seriously could mean significant changes in the way many of us live. The aim of an ethic after all isn't necessarily to make us comfortable with what we already do; it's to make us think about what we *should* do.

Few understood the potential consequences of our current trajectory more clearly than writer and zoologist Rachel Carson when in 1962's *Silent Spring* she observes that

[t]he most alarming of all man's assaults upon the environment is the contamination of air, earth, water, rivers and sea with dangerous and even lethal materials. This pollution is for the most part irrecoverable; the chain of evil it initiates not only in the world that must support life but in living tissues is for the most part irreversible... The rapidity of change and the speed with which new situations are created follow the impetuous and heedless pace of man rather than the deliberate pace of nature. (6–7)

Yet even Carson might have been left speechless by the "chain of evil" that has given rise to the climate crisis and its likely cascade of irreversible implications. While this "assault upon the environment" ultimately affects the existential conditions for every living thing, it's important to see, as a number of ecofeminist, environmental justice, and indigenous theorists will show us, that climate change doesn't affect all human beings, all nonhuman animal species, or all ecologies equally. Developing world communities of the Global South, economically depressed communities in the Global North, and the increasingly beleaguered ecologies upon which they depend bear a disproportionate share of resource exploitation, pollution, and exhaustion. Thus, the challenge Carson poses to the "impetuous and heedless pace of man" is not merely a challenge to radically rethink what we mean by "moral considerability," but also to come to a clearer understanding of how structural inequalities of sex, gender, race, geography, indigenous status, and species inform social, political, economic, *and* environmental injustice.

1.1.2   The Precautionary Principle

Integrating the precautionary principle into the ordinary operations of our moral reasoning offers a clear point of departure toward a livable environmental ethic. But "clear" doesn't necessarily mean expedient. It means (at least): if X causes harm to human or nonhuman others, and it's not necessary to my life or health, I should (at least) reconsider it, possibly decide against it, or opt for a less harmful alternative even if it's not convenient. If the magnitude of harm is potentially great, perhaps I ought to forego it altogether. In my life as a public person or *citizen*, the precautionary principle might require even more: if I'm in a reasonable position to know this governmental policy, regulation, or law is likely to cause (or be causing) harm to human or nonhuman others, I (may) have a responsibility to make others aware of this fact and, depending on the magnitude of harm and an appraisal of the potential risk to myself or my family, I might have a moral duty to take public action (at least) in the form of alerting my elected representatives, participating in public actions, or joining with others in nonviolent civil disobedience.

The precautionary principle is thus somewhat like the Hippocratic Oath taken by physicians: *first*, do no harm.[8] What can make its application challenging is that we're used to thinking that human beings are special or privileged, that we're exempt from the laws of nature that govern other species, that we're entitled to use the planet's resources, including other living things, however we see fit. We like to think we know better, but we'd probably not be confronted with the climate crisis or the sheer magnitude of fatality from the Covid-19 pandemic had we acted both individually and collectively on the precautionary principle sooner. As Carson details in the foreboding elegance of *Silent Spring*, we didn't. Now we're left with the question whether this version of "*first*, do no harm," or for that matter any moral principle, will be enough to inspire us in sufficient numbers to undertake the hard work of re-imagining a world whose citizens take environmental stability so seriously that the possibility of other basic goods like justice (economic, social, geopolitical), or the exercise of rights, or the experience of things like beauty, joyousness, and laughter, seem unthinkable without it.

A truly frightening volume of evidence, however, suggests we're running in the other direction—away from any notion of a moral responsibility to the future. As environmental hero Bill McKibbon puts it: there's no vaccine for the climate crisis.[9] We go to considerable effort, contrary to fact, to convince ourselves that we're exempt from the existential constraints that govern the lives of other species of evolved animal whose members are born, eat, eliminate waste, reproduce, suffer, and eventually die. This is more than just hubris; it's delusion accompanied by denial.[10] We offer a thousand excuses to smoke, but we know our lungs aren't immune to cancer or emphysema. We eat the desiccated bodies of cows, pigs, chickens, and dogs, but we know we share more in common with other species of creature than not, especially the capacity for pain. We refuse to mask or socially distance, preferring to risk our own lives and those of our elders in order to pretend we're immune from the virus that killed our neighbor. We know that death comes for us just as surely as it comes for snails and Labradors, kings and commoners. Yet we behave as if our own lives were as inexhaustible a resource as the planet's—even though we know both of these are false. Human history is witness to the struggle to conquer death, a subset of that more grandiose venture to show-up the universe.[11] "Heedless," as Carson puts it, but—counterintuitively—more heedless now *because* we know more now.

Consider, for example, the vitriol displayed by some climate change deniers,[12] or the spleen vented at anti-masking "freedom" rallies.[13] It seems we can measure denial by the momentum it takes to avoid confrontation with fact. A legitimate worry, of course, is whether an idea as unpretentious as the precautionary principle can even be heard over all this noise. Given the crises we're facing, it's not crazy to wonder how bad things might have to get—how hot, how dry, how deluged, how burnt down, how polluted, how diseased, how terrorized, how diaspora—before we take seriously the fact that inaction is nihilism, and nihilism is resignation. But giving up also seems out of character for a species of scrappy pugilists like us. After all, human history is also witness to monsters like smallpox, cancer, AIDS, fascists, and autocrats—each different kinds of threats, but all united by the moral imperative that they must be defeated; some have, some will be, but the climate crisis? Some, like the emergence of fascists and autocrats, seem always to be with us, yet so too is the reaffirmation of democratic principles and institutions. Coronavirus variants like Delta are monsters partly the product of our own making, but so too is *Operation Warp Speed's* vaccine development.[14] The climate crisis is bigger than all of these and more. But what that means is that what might seem simply a point of departure for environmental ethics is actually a rubicon. We can either continue to race blindly toward apocalyptic world wars over water, oil, and food driven by escalating environmental crises, or we can change. "First, do no harm" points squarely in one direction.

1.2   Human Chauvinism versus Responsible Human-Centeredness

1.2.1   Human-Centeredness: Taking Responsibility

It's at this crossroad, where our capacity for principled action meets its equal in hubris, that we can begin to understand the difference between human-centeredness and the human chauvinism that endangers the planet's ecologies and species life. Centeredness is ubiquitous to human nature, and thus must be accounted for in any realistic ethic. It recognizes human beings as a species of animal limited or "centered" with respect to an evolved array of cognitive, epistemic, psychological, perceptual, and somatic capacities. For example, human beings have two eyes at the front of our heads and color vision, but none at the back, and limited visual range; we have ears that can hear just so far, noses that can smell just so much, legs that can only run so fast, and brains that, while we sport an impressive cognitive cortex, are prone to a litany of ailments ranging from Tourette's Syndrome to schizophrenia, Alzheimer's to autism.[15] We cannot help but be human-centered: we experience the world as members of *homo Sapiens*. But this fact doesn't imply an invitation to narrow self-interest. Just because we cannot experience the world as anything other than human beings doesn't mean that being human is the only worldview worth having, or even that it offers any special insight to the way things are.

The ways in which we act on our centeredness can be re-visioned consistent with an environmental ethic grounded in *taking responsibility* for the capacities *and* limits that define our species membership and our place in the planetary ecosystem. Such an ethic recognizes that human engineers, not Chimpanzees, can build nuclear power plants *and* weapons of mass destruction, and it acknowledges the possibility that our own intellect could be dwarfed by others yet undiscovered (or who've not discovered us). We know that the difference between human engineers and our close primate relatives, or for that matter, parrots, ferrets, and iguanas, is a matter of *degree* of cognitive capacity, not kind of animal.[16] Chimpanzees and human beings are both big-brained mammals. We're both social creatures capable of learning and culture; we both recognize and care for our offspring. We both experience psychological as well as physical pain. *But because only one can create a nuclear weapon, only one can take responsibility for the magnitude of destruction that is that weapon.* The theory of evolution has, of course, its own deniers, but like their climate crisis analogues it's not hard to discover that at the root of denial is human chauvinism, not settled science.[17]

While it's hard to imagine any defensible strategy for confronting environmental crisis not grounded in the relevant science, we must also keep firmly in mind that the same science that informs us of parts per million, vanishing shorelines, and tipping points, is also conscripted by governments and multi-national corporations to develop technologies that disgorge natural gas from shale deposits, weaponize nuclear fission, and create the Frankenseeds of GMO fame.[18] There are many difficult questions here, but one thing is clear: we can no longer afford to ignore the potentially negative environmental consequences of our technological development. We are the *only* animals culpable for the climate crisis in virtue of what we do with what we know. It's in precisely this sense that the ethical cannot be divorced from the epistemic. To claim intellectual superiority over nonhuman animals, and yet deny we're the cause of climate change is as transparent a form of hypocrisy as is applause for the SARS-CoV-2 vaccine while refusing to wear masks. Being this planet's smartest animals is not license to evade responsibility for what we do with brains we insist are so big.[19]

In short, a human-centered environmental ethic that seeks to avoid the pitfalls of human chauvinism must embrace humility, avoid hypocrisy, and value truth. Climate change denial is only one example of where these basic moral proscriptions have so far failed. Some still deny that cigarettes cause cancer, that the flesh on our dinner plates is the result of immense suffering, or that our sneakers are the product of child labor and wage-slavery. For a human-centered ethic, however, the denial of fact is a debauchery of reason, and where reason is treated merely as a tool for achieving human objectives, ethics can gain no traction.[20] Perhaps this explains where we are, but it cannot help us chart a course to a sustainable, or even habitable, future.

1.2.2   The Desirable Future

The appeal to knowledge in the service of environmentally defensible ends is at the same time an appeal to the value of a future that incorporates nonhuman nature as essential to the life worth living. But, as our current crises make clear, we cannot, as it were, "fake it until we make it" simply by driving more gas-efficient cars or sending donations to environmental organizations like the Sierra Club.[21] Indeed, insofar as many of these Big Greens avoid treating animal agriculture to the same blistering critique they aim at the fossil fuel industry, we must assume that for them demanding meaningful review of human chauvinism is a bridge too far. Driving an electric car still allows us to drive; giving up "meat" feels like we're being deprived of *food*. The latter doesn't secure a donor base; the former does.[22]

But the point is not simply to beat up on the Big Greens for their hypocrisy; it's that facts about the culprits of greenhouse gas emissions alone won't motivate us to change. We have to want to. We don't need philosophy to tell us about racism, heterosexism, classism, or speciesism. We are well aware; we *experience* it. Science can show us the difference between the extinguishable fires of past environmental dilemmas and the frying pan climate of the future. But even good science can't get us to put down our cigarette, lay off potato chips, or go vegan. Our only realistic hope, then, for escaping climate catastrophe is the decision to value the interdependencies, *the ecologies of our existential conditions*, and that is a *philosophical* as well as moral decision no matter our educations or experience. It's the philosophical project of deciding what counts as value and thus *what has value* that can help us see our way through to a future that, while it may be difficult to achieve, still can offer a life worth that struggle. In short, facts can't tell us everything we need to know about what to do but, suitably appreciated via the right system of value, they provide substance to epistemic responsibility, and epistemic responsibility provides the scaffolding for a moral responsibility informed by both the precautionary principle and a commitment to a future not merely livable, but desirable.

A life worth living thus takes its point of departure in appreciating the difference between the environmental crises of the past and the climate crisis of the present; it recognizes that decision-making must be undertaken *in light of* that difference, not *heedless* of it. A morally defensible ethic demands a transformation of disposition or attitude; it supposes a world wherein our only choices are about *how* we'll adapt, not whether we have to. It remains human-centered with respect to accountability, rejecting the chauvinism that feeds every form of injustice, social, economic, and environmental. It aims not to see through climate change in order to preserve the status quo, but takes climate change into account in order to gain a clearer view of in what our relationships to human and nonhuman others consist, what morally defensible motives look like given this world, and what a desirable future given this circumstance includes.

Articulating an ethic for a life worth living, even amidst crisis, is still possible. Indeed, incorporating the climate crisis into the operational premises of such an ethic is, comparatively, the easy part. What comes next is the harder work of hammering out moral principles, criteria for judgment and action, and, perhaps most challenging of all, what it means to be a good person, citizen, and member of a community made fundamentally global by the fact that the climate crisis knows no geographical or political boundaries.[23] Can we modify principles we already know to make them adaptable to the moral issues we're likely to confront? If Naomi Klein is right when she argues that climate change changes *everything*, issues we don't think of as "environmental" such as civil war, terrorism, disease, or human trafficking must be included in our environmental ethic precisely because they're impacted by the consequences of shifting weather patterns as well as the advantage taken by the beneficiaries of hierarchically structured social institutions of those already at risk. Consider an example: food. A warming planet increases the potential not only for drought, flood, crop-destroying insects, and blight, but also the necessity of insecticides, pesticides, and chemical fertilizers that, while preventing crop loss, are attended by a number of other hazards for soil, water, human and nonhuman health.[24] Few would contest the claim that food is the stuff of any ethic; little is more basic, more existential. But what counts as "food," how and where it should be cultivated, who should have access to it, and who's entitled to profit from its production, are all issues affected by a warming planet in significant and often unpredictable ways.

The prospect, moreover, that food crop production could be jeopardized by environmental conditions rapidly spinning out of control is doubtless a driver of climate change denial.[25] Hunger also fuels the vulnerability exploited by terrorist organizations looking for recruits,[26] or governments in need of an acceptable public narrative for restricting immigration.[27] The upshot is that any ethic we adopt *must* be able to address not only abstract philosophical questions about why we should value the environment; it must also be able to tackle the morally contentious intersection of issues that, while they may not be original to climate change, are clearly accelerated by it. Social, political, and economic justice are not only dependent on environmental stability, but are rather an expression of the value we invest in the future, the value we invest in a specifically *ecological* understanding of the planet as *home*. If the history of ethics has shown us anything it's that while appeals to concepts like moral consistency can move us to shame in our hypocrisy, shame rarely spurs us to action, much less to the kind of transformative decision-making that a life worth living in the age of climate change will demand.

1.3   An Aerial View of Moral Extensionism

1.3.1   Is Moral Extensionism a Good Idea?

Now that we have some grounding premises and a rough framework on the table, we can turn our attention to our first set of four questions:

- What moral principles characterize modern discourse in ethics?
- Can any or all of these be extended, expanded, or modified to address morally weighty *environmental issues*? Will we still recognize them as applications of their originals?
- Can any or all of these be extended, expanded, or modified to address issues concerning *nonhuman animals*? What qualities or capacities must a species of nonhuman animal possess to qualify for moral consideration?
- Can any or all of these be extended, expanded, or modified to address the often complex intersection of environmental, economic, social,

geographical, and political injustice that impacts vulnerable human populations? Where, in other words, do analyses of structural inequality fit into a practicable environmental ethic?

Three points about context and concepts: first, most moral decision-making is not the result of careful assessment of fact followed by application of principle. It might be a better world if this were true, and the aim of any discourse in ethics is, of course, to make that true. But, we typically don't write out our quandaries and options. We don't always discuss them attentively with others, or review decision variables before we act. We want to do the right thing, but we're ethically disorganized and tilted to self-interest. We tend toward "act now, justify later." As Rachel Carson shows, the trouble with this approach is that the impacts of environmental damage can be irrecoverable. Second, whether it's possible to extend some moral principles beyond human agents and communities to the environment and/or to nonhuman animals is as contentious as determining what qualities, characteristics, or capacities justify the inclusion of an animal, species, or ecosystem within the domain of moral considerability. Although it's commonplace in environmental ethics to treat the moral status of nonhuman animals as a separate domain for theory, we're going to eschew at least a rigid version of that distinction here on the grounds that it's demonstrably arbitrary, and as such distorts how we might understand important questions about the extension of moral principle:

- To what exactly does an extension of a particular moral principle apply? Does it make sense to extend some principles to a moral consideration of the status of nonhuman animals, but not ecological systems, or vice versa?
- What are the criteria for extending a particular principle? What difference does this make to articulating an actionable environmental ethic?
- Are these criteria defensible in light of what science tells us about what is included in or excluded from the extension?
- What difference, if any, do urgent environmental crises make to our appraisal of a given principle and its criteria for inclusion (or exclusion)?

These questions are important not because they're especially difficult, but because what the answers show is the extent to which the distinction between nonhuman animals and the ecologies they inhabit is itself more conventional than substantive, more an explanatory tool than a description of reality. There *are* distinctions to be drawn between living and nonliving, sentient and nonsentient, organic and inorganic. But the bodies of animals, from insects to lizards, to human beings, to mega fauna, are themselves ecologies—systems whose complex interactions, symbioses, and interdependencies are not necessarily neatly captured by the artifice of "animal" or "environment." Animal bodies, including human bodies, don't end at the boundary of skin, tentacle, scale, wings eyelash, or fang. Plant bodies may extend beyond their petals, leaves, stems, and stamens. The predator/prey relationship makes the bodies of some food for others. It makes waste, decay, and decomposition food for countless species of living organism.[28] Even questions about whether viruses behave sufficiently like bacteria to count as living are important here in that "living" belongs as much to chemistry as to biology, ecology, zoology, or even to philosophy, and is itself contentious.[29]

It's thus a mistake to treat "environment" versus "animal" as if the distinction "carves nature at its joints." Like the nature/nurture distinction, or metaphors like "king of the jungle," it helps us understand (however imperfectly) what things are and do, but that doesn't mean it offers reliable grounds for settling moral considerability. The more the sciences show us about the intimacy and complexity of relationships that compose eco-systems, the more evident that animal bodies are reflections of their ecologies, and that ecologies are made manifest as/in the bodies of animals. The upshot's important: whether a moral principle crafted for application to human beings and communities can be extended beyond its original intent will depend, at least in part, on the qualities, capacities, or characteristics that count for it as morally considerable. But what does so count is itself subject to review and revision as we learn more about nonhuman animal species, their ecologies, and their relationships to other living and nonliving things. Moral considerability is thus an epistemic charge as well as an ethical one, the precautionary principle its grounding point of departure.

1.3.2   The Problem of Sentience

Consider the possible extension of a principle that appeals to sentience, *the capacity for consciousness*, as a necessary condition of moral considerability.[30] It must assume (as a condition of application) that we can differentiate sentient entities from nonsentient ones neatly enough to determine to what our candidate principle applies: puppies but not petunias, black bears but not bacteria. When we look more closely, however, what we discover is that the sentience criterion not only relies implicitly on the animal/environment distinction, but on the assumption that the environment is essentially just material background or resource for sentient entities. It assumes, in other words, that we can know what counts as a sentient *living* thing as opposed to non-sentient living things, that we can identify non-sentient *nonliving* things, and that there's something about sentience, say the capacity for pain, that recommends it as a criterion for moral considerability, delegating all else to background, or necessary condition, but only so long as "necessary" remains the case. This is problematic in at least two ways:

- First, insofar as the bodies of animals are composed out of living and nonliving materials made available in their environments and through the bodies of other animals, it's not necessarily self-evident where a body ends and an environment begins. Skins are permeable surfaces; tissues, including muscle, organ, bone, and brain, are composed of the ingested processed bodies of other things. Bodies, their organs, bones, and tissues, *are* ecologies; they're ecologies that consume and produce bodies, living and nonliving. Sentient/nonsentient, living/nonliving must thus be understood as useful artifacts of explanation, but neither more nor less supported by nature than the animal/environment distinction.

- Second, consider the possibility of androids, *nonliving sentient entities.* The prospect that such feats of engineering might someday come to pass shows, among other things, that it is possible to divorce the capacity for consciousness from the capacity for pain, and that recognizing pain as a condition for moral considerability makes sense only if we're willing to deny it, for example, to women in labor who've opted for pain-relieving epidurals, or to people who suffer neurological conditions that depress their pain response.[31] It will do no good, moreover, to insist that the future existence of androids is unlikely. Their mere possibility demonstrates how fickle, and ultimately chauvinistic, are our definitions of what counts as morally considerable: we create sophisticated robots that mimic an extensive array of human abilities, but insist that should some future generation of these robots achieve consciousness, they're still not "like us," at least not enough to warrant consideration of their status as autonomous, self-regarding beings. In other words, we deny moral status to creatures who are sentient, insisting that they're unlike human beings in some other relevant way, yet we also deny moral status to androids who are sentient precisely *because* we have engineered them to be as humanlike as possible—yet deny them moral status anyways. This, of course, is simply arbitrary, and as such reflects the significance with which we invest sentience, so long as it's ours.

Sentience also raises serious issues not only of moral considerability, but of epistemic responsibility. The scientific consensus concerning what kinds of brains can support sentience is by no means settled. Dogs and cats are sentient creatures, but the jury remains out concerning jellyfish and Venus flytraps. Lobsters, goldfish, and honeybees did not use to rate very high on the sentience scale, but that thinking has evolved as we've come to understand more about cognitive activity across the broad spectrum of animal life.[32] To be clear, we're not entertaining the thesis put forward by, among others, the Bioneers that Poppies and Irises feel pain or deliberately lean into the sunshine.[33] But insofar as "sentience" is neither a fixed trait whose typical examples are settled science, nor a capacity that can be divorced from the ecological and evolutionary conditions that give rise to it, its significance as a register of moral worth must remain open to review.

1.3.3   What Counts as a Living Thing?

Consider a very different criteria of value, namely, *the capacity for being alive.* While a stone can be damaged, we typically don't think of it as a thing that can be harmed because it's not a living thing. A stone can be destroyed—but not killed. The kinds of entities included in the living thing criterion of value are, of course, many more than on the sentience criterion since being alive is at best a necessary but not sufficient condition for being sentient. The precautionary principle also has wider application for the living thing criterion since determining whether a thing is alive, generally, is less difficult to determine than whether it's sentient. We don't doubt, for example, that the slow-moving snail is alive even if we're not sure about its sentience, but we might mistakenly infer that a hologram was sentient, and thus alive, simply because it behaves in ways we identify as human. On one hand, then, "living" is a less contentious concept than "sentience" in that "living" offers a more obvious and measurable set of indicators such as respiration, heartbeat, nervous system response, cell replication, photosynthesis, growth, self-locomotion, consumption of nutrients, elimination of waste, or behaviorally evidenced brain activity. Nonliving does not, of course, necessarily mean "dead," but both mean nonsentient. On the other hand, once we consider indicators other than those we apply to organic entities, particular forms of electrical activity in a robotic brain, for example, determining what counts as "living" becomes more difficult. Explored in TV shows like *Star Trek: New Generation*, the android Data doesn't perform any activities from the list above, yet insofar as he considers himself to be a living thing, we'd be hard-pressed to deny it.

We also don't have to resort to science fiction to raise this more difficult question about what qualities define a living thing. Consider viruses. They behave in many ways like bacteria, yet such simple replicators may not quite rise to the bar of "living." Like bacteria, they pose a deadly health hazard to human and nonhuman beings. We actively seek to kill HIV, Ebola, and Covid-19 just as we take antibiotics for bacterial infection. Yet we don't regard this killing as murder, and we might justify that difference by arguing that murder requires the thing killed be sentient. But this too is problematic since fetuses up to at least 26 weeks' gestation are not yet capable of sentience, yet some regard abortion as murder.[34] We seek to destroy bacteria and viruses because they pose a hazard to human and nonhuman health, yet some argue that a pregnant woman has a duty to carry a fetus to term even if there is great potential for harm to her health or life. What's contentious, however, is less whether any of these are living things, but rather whether being a living thing confers a right to life, or if it does for some things but not others, what counts as the morally relevant difference. *When* something counts as living is also as difficult a question as *what*. Consider once more developing embryos. Few doubt that a clump of dividing cells is a living thing, but whether that fact alone gives it a *right* to life is hotly contested, at least for human embryos, precisely because so many of the other qualities we typically identify with living are not yet present. While some argue that merely being an instance of Homo sapiens confers the right to life from conception, others wrangle over when along the developmental trajectory, if at any time before birth, such a right emerges. And, of course, if it's merely "living" that confers moral considerability, even a right to life, the same criterion of value applies just as well to species of nonhuman animal as it does to human beings—raising difficult questions about the many ways in which we discount "living" when our interests are served by killing.

Another potential difficulty with "living" as a criterion of value occurs when we try to provide a convincing justification for the *exclusion* of *nonliving* things from moral considerability. Clean water, breathable air, arable soil—these are just some of the most obvious examples of nonliving things that, because they form necessary conditions for life on the planet, cannot be excluded from our judgments of value—at least if we want to avoid existential peril. Moreover, all living things die at some point, and decompose into biochemical translations of H_2O, oxygen, microbes, etc., and both philosophers and physicians have debated the point at which a living thing dies.[35] Our temptation might be to argue the difference is that water, air, and soil compose the environment whereas living things subsist *in* it; one *is* the environment, the other *inhabits* it. This seems reasonable, though it does raise the problem once again of treating the environment merely as the backdrop against which the actions of morally considerable agents play out, and a host of problems that accompany this artifact of human interest:

- First, even if we consign the environment to narrowly defined existential value as background, we're still left to clarify what *is* the environment from what's *in* it. If only the latter counts as morally considerable in virtue of including potentially living things, we have to decipher not only what qualifies as a necessary condition, but what of that environmental background can be excluded from consideration in virtue of not being existentially critical. Stones do not themselves form a necessary existential condition for any living thing, nor are stones alive. Yet mountains composed, among other things, of stones might form an ecosystem that, taken as a whole, provides the existential conditions for countless species of living thing. Similarly, dead animals can be, but aren't necessarily, food for living things. If not consumed, they become part of the biota that forms the soil for the cultivation and growth of living things later. Time doubtless plays some role in this calculation of value, but that role seems entirely dependent on many other factors—some calculable, some not. In short, it may seem sensible to assume that there exists a natural and morally relevant distinction between "the environment" and "living things in the environment." But insofar as direct questions like "how should we determine the value of stones?" quickly become intractable, we are inevitably compelled to review whether this distinction does, in fact, make sense. It may turn out that, while language invites simple distinctions, the existential conditions of actual living things and their ecosystems requires a much more nuanced appreciation of the limits of our concepts and the self-interest with which we invest them.

- Second, consider things *in* the environment: we certainly distinguish entities like rocks, puddles, and embankments from moss, tadpoles, and daffodils. We hold the former to be nonliving, the latter living. But insofar as we can stipulate many points of intersection, say, tadpoles swimming in puddles, daffodils growing out of grassy embankments, moss clinging to stones, it once again becomes apparent that merely stating that a tadpole is not a puddle is not all that informative; even less so in the case of the moss and the stone since some properties of the moss itself certainly derive from the stone just as the yellow of the daffodil may derive in part from chemical properties in the soil under the grass, or be affected by the angle of the embankment's tilt toward the Sun. In any case, the more we come to know about the biochemical properties of these living things as well as their evolutionary histories, the less obvious that the living/nonliving distinction offers much by way of explanatory value.

- Third, consider the extinction of a species of living thing. The relationship of species to environment is an intimate one informed by a range of evolutionary pressures and changing environmental conditions. Whole species can face extinction in as little as a single generation if conditions for its reproduction are not met. Yet, among these conditions are included many things, living and nonliving, each of which is itself *in* the environment—as opposed to being the whole of the environment itself. Indeed, if we conceive the environment as the collection or evolving sum of each of these factors, "the environment" begins to seem like a vacuous placeholder. Things like natural caves, ice sheets, abandoned shells, or decomposing bodies all offer homes to specific species of animal without which, as we've seen with climate change and polar bears, they can quickly become imperiled. If, in other words, we regard "species" as itself morally considerable apart from other qualifiers—living or nonliving, the capacity for sentience, what counts as an existential condition—this too seems to count against the usefulness of distinguishing "the environment" from "in the environment." Put differently: what natural selection teaches us is that species, including Homo sapiens, are embodied incarnations of environmental and evolutionary processes over time, very long stretches of time. The idea that a species can be abstracted and examined from its evolutionary history inevitably distorts the account of what it is; for "what it is" is an ecologically informed moment of time engaged in the struggle for survival, that is, the struggle to reproduce *that* moment.

For the purpose of articulating a realistic environmental ethic, however, what we need is something a bit more prosaic. We might think about the environment/in the environment distinction this way: living bodies *are* the environments for all kinds of things like bacteria, parasites, viruses; *and* living bodies occupy particular ecologies as agents and subjugates of various complex relationships—predatory, symbiotic, competitive, parasitic, cooperative, etc. We can recognize that distinctions like living versus nonliving are conventional, useful if limited fictions, without being committed to the view that the environment is mere background against which evolutionary history plays out. We can, in other words, consider the environment an enfranchised agent whose long, sometimes violent, often unpredictable trajectory makes our own survival a matter of making useful distinctions, drafting practical fictions, organizing a story of the "world," that bolsters our chances. That hubris gets in our way is not the only obstacle to an ethic that would otherwise keep "environment" at the forefront *as a useful fiction*, but hubris does tend to overshadow the humility we need to cultivate to have a chance of surviving our current endangered circumstance. Yet insofar as that hubris seems to be routinely translated into other fictions—the myth of endless resources, that all value is exchange value, and that qualities like sentience or even life pose no impediment to commodification—humility seems as far as the climate crisis seems ever closer.

For most, it's easy to grant that in the quest to identify what counts as the morally considerable it's important to cultivate qualities like humility, forthrightness, objectivity, and compassion. The reason is that ethics is about something more than prudence, more than avoiding the reckless or the crassly selfish, more than merely appearing to be good. But just as denial, cognitive dissonance, and willful ignorance are common traits of the human chauvinism that has led to so much environmental blight, so too false humility; that is, the pretense to concern dressed in the defense of policies or institutions behind which is the advance of motives selfish, profiteering, and sometimes even cruel. In defense of zoos, for example, some argue that captivity for the sake of preserving an endangered species from extinction effectively evinces a form of moral considerability because, like a Noah's Ark, it values the species if not the individual animals. But the principle winners are human zoo-goers, not zoo animals. Zoo captives are neither likely to know they're endangered nor experience captivity as good, no matter how humane the prison.[36] Conservation and restoration of habitat rarely enters that conversation, as the relevant lands have already been sequestered to human use. Indeed, one of the rarely acknowledged assumptions of the zoo argument is that we don't have any particular responsibility to preserve a species' original habitat in order to mitigate against the pressures that lead to extinction. But, of course, we might do just that.

Or consider the argument for eating animal bodies so long as they're raised as "free range," and not on factory farms.[37] This seems a reasonable compromise that, once again, appears to include cows, chickens, pigs, bison, dogs, etc., as morally considerable, until we realize that the people who observe us eating them probably don't know that what we're eating might have led a more or less natural life. Our fellow diners are reinforced as carnivores, animal agriculture continues unabated, and while "free range" may be conscience-saving, it rarely means a better life for factory farm animals. This seems, once again, like a violation of the precautionary principle: if our moral principles don't demand we set a good example, what are they for? In sum, taking moral extensionism as a serious candidate not only for an ethic, but for a life worth living presents some daunting challenges. How we define the range of application of a principle depends at least partly on how we define key terms like "living," "sentient," and "value." The traits of character suitable to making an environmental ethic capable of tackling urgent issue like the climate crisis possible stand in stark contrast with a deeply enculturated capitalism that would have us assume value is a function of marketability. There are also some very immediate, very urgent issues: if we aren't willing to extend moral consideration to unmistakably sentient creatures like chickens and cows, how much more difficult will it be to conceive the atmosphere as a worthy candidate? If being a sentient entity poses no impediment to commodification, does anything? For some, the difficulty of these questions leads to apathy or despair; realizing the nihilism inherent to the capitalist myth of endless resources can certainly lead to a kind of moral paralysis. Moral extensionism asks us to make some determination about what to include in our calculus of moral value. But perhaps it's the precautionary principle we should adopt as our North Star. That is, perhaps the right questions are less about inclusion and more about *exclusion*, less about coming up with qualifications for belonging to the moral community, and more about determining grounds for why a thing (or species, or ecosystem) should be left out. As we'll see, this approach won't make our task of articulating an environmental ethic easier, but it will solicit the qualities—humility, forthrightness, objectivity, and compassion—that make it an *ethic*.

1.3.4   Summary and Questions

Like the philosophical tradition generally, it's not surprising that study of the moral life has been reserved mostly to how we conceive the good for human beings, our relationships and institutions, our practices, customs, laws, and the expectations we associate with civilization. Environmental ethics, however, poses a serious challenge to how we understand our human-centeredness— our *anthropocentrism*. Insofar as we now know that human activity can have adverse, even devastating, consequences for nonhuman animals and ecosystems, rethinking what counts as a life worth living has become a priority for both personal and collective moral decision-making. While some concepts such as *moral considerability* take on renewed meaning and urgency, others like inherent worth seem more suspect, or at least less obviously useful, in the light of scientific discoveries that undercut some of our most basic assumptions about what constitutes an animal, consciousness, cognitive wherewithal, or even what counts as a living thing.

While a sustainable future may not be out of reach, we now know that sustainable doesn't necessarily mean desirable, and that even the lowest common denominator conditions for a desirable future demand expanding the range of moral consideration beyond narrow human interest. Part of what makes this achieving these goals difficult is that we haven't done a very good job of treating our fellow human beings equally, justly, or with compassion—let alone nonhuman animals or nonhuman nature. It seems that any effort to extend traditional moral principle, *moral extensionism*, requires some careful rethinking about how human chauvinism intersects with racism, sexism, and other forms of structural inequality. When we consider the potential impacts of the environmental crises we face, especially the climate crisis, it becomes clear that environmental justice cannot be divorced from social and economic justice.

Difficult questions arise as to whether any of the moral principles with which we're familiar can provide adequate grounds for their extension to nonhuman nature and/or nonhuman animals. If we're the narrowly self-interested chauvinists of our checkered history, this doesn't seem promising. But if our understanding of human-centeredness, anthropocentrism, can be reconceived to include *taking responsibility* for what we know about the consequences of our actions for nonhuman nature and nonhuman animals, we might be able to formulate versions of moral extensionism better-suited an environmental ethic that can meet the challenges posed by the climate crisis. We cannot undo the harm we've done to the planet, its atmosphere, and its inhabitants, but we needn't continue the destructive course we've thus far charted. Beginning, then, by embracing the *precautionary principle*—err on the side of caution, compassion, and care—our goal is to undertake a careful investigation of our moral principles to see whether some version of *moral extensionism* can be made to work toward a future desirable not only to the most fortunate, but to the least.

1. What is the basic idea behind moral extensionism, and why is it important to developing a sound and actionable environmental ethic?
2. What is the precautionary principle? How does it ground the basic conditions for an environmental ethic?
3. Distinguishing human chauvinism from human-centeredness, we've anchored the latter to taking responsibility not only for what we *do*, but for what we're in a position to *know*—epistemic responsibility. Why is this important to an environmental ethic?
4. What do we mean when we refer to the intersection of environmental stability and social or economic justice? Give an example where/when environmental destruction intersects with racism and/or sexism.
5. How are questions about sentience or the difference between living and nonliving things relevant to moral extensionism?

Annotated Bibliography

Bernstein, Mark H. (1998). *On Moral Considerability* (Oxford: Oxford University Press).

After developing a view of being a moral patient—an entity to whom we may owe moral consideration even if they do not owe it in return—Bernstein argues that we have "unjustly disenfranchised some individuals from our moral domain," and that recognizing this will "pave the conceptual groundwork for a detailed examination of the sorts of revisions that morality requires of us."

Birch, Thomas "Moral Considerability and Universal Consideration." *Environmental Ethics* 15 (4), (January 1993), pp. 313–32.

Referring to moral considerability as "practical respect," Birch argues that we replace "moral considerability" with "universal consideration" in light both of the latter's less compromised history in the "Western project of planetary domination," and its capacity to give greater attention to the "ethical obligations that arise from relating" with nonhuman others.

Carson, Rachel (1962 [1994]). *Silent Spring* (New York: Houghton Mifflin Company).

Cusimano, Cory. "*Defending Epistemic Responsibility.*" *Arche* 5 (2), (2012–2013), https://www.bu.edu/arche/5/cusimano.pdf

Cusimano defends against the claim that we cannot be held epistemically responsible because we do not exercise control over our beliefs.

Engel, Milan. "Ethical Extensionism." *Encyclopedia of Environmental Ethics and Philosophy* 1, (2008). https://www.niu.edu/engel/_pdf/Ethical ExtensionismPenultimate.pdf.

Engels offers a fine overview of several varieties of moral extensionism, including utilitarian, deontological, anthropocentric, and non-anthropocentric versions.

Fox, Warwick, ed. (2000). *Ethics and the Built Environment* (New York: Routledge).

In this edited work, Fox assembles a set of essays focused not on the "natural" environment, but the "built" which consider how we conceive the distinction between the "natural" and the "human-made" especially in light of our negative impacts on nonhuman nature.

Hale, Benjamin. "Moral Considerability: Deontological, Not Metaphysical." *Science Policy*. https://sciencepolicy.colorado.edu/admin/publication_files/2011.38.pdf

Hale's argues that "moral considerability should be understood narrowly and centrally as an agent-relative deontological question…in order to determine what obligations rational agents have to nonhuman others."

Harnad, Stevan. "Animal Sentience: The Other- Minds Problem." *Animal Sentience*, (2018), p. 100. https://animalstudiesrepository.org/cgi/viewcontent.cgi?article=1065&context=animsent.

Hiller, Rudy. *"The Epistemic Condition for Moral Responsibility."* Stanford *Encyclopedia of Philosophy*, (2018). https://plato.stanford.edu/entries/moral-responsibility-epistemic

Hiller surveys the conditions generally considered necessary for epistemic responsibility, namely, the freedom to act and the cognitive wherewithal to be held accountable.

Holly-Luczaj, Magdalena. "Artifacts and the Problem of Ethical Extensionism—Selected Issues." *Studia Humana* 6 (3), (November 2017). https://content.sciendo.com/view/journals/sh/6/3/article-p34.xml.

Holly-Luczaj argues for the extension of moral considerability to a specific subset of nonhuman, nonliving artifacts—usable things—as "beings which status can be improved or deteriorated through human activity.

Kim, Claire Jean. "Moral Extensionism or Racist Exploitation? The Use of Holocaust and Slavery Analogies in the Animal Liberation Movement." *New Political Science* 33 (3), (2011).

Kim argues that recent People for the Ethical Treatment of Animals (PETA) exhibits comparing animal rights abuses to the Holocaust or to slavery raises very difficult questions "about the intersection of race and species as hierarchical categories ordering social life…"

Klein, Naomi. "*Big Green Groups are More Damaging than Climate Deniers,*" The Guardian, September 10, 2013, https://www.theguardian.com/environment/2013/sep/10/naomi-klein-green-groups-climate-deniers.
In this interview, Klein argues that "there is a very deep denialism in the environmental movement among the Big Green groups," and that it is more damaging that right-wing climate change denial because the Big Greens continue to embrace market solutions, thereby steering us "in the direction of very poor results."

Lal, Sanjay. "Moral Extensionism and Nonviolence: An Essential Relation?" *The Peace of Nature and the Nature of Peace* 282, (2015), pp. 71–80.
Lal argues that placing an emphasis on similarities between human beings and nonhuman animals is an "essential aspect of maintaining a genuinely nonviolent…attitude toward nature."

Lee, Wendy (2016). *Eco-Nihilism: The Philosophical Geopolitics of the Climate Change Apocalypse* (Lexington: Rowman and Littlefield), pp. 78–80.
Lee argues that the concept of inherent worth (or intrinsic value) can neither adequately anchor moral considerability nor remain immune to being hi-jacked, even weaponized, to defend the superior moral status of the beneficiaries of an unequal and unjust social order.

Levin, Yuval. "*The Moral Challenge of Modern Science.*" *The New Atlantis*, Fall 2006, https://www.thenewatlantis.com/publications/the-moral-challenge-of-modern-science
Levin argues that while we generally understand science to be a morally neutral project, "modern science is about much more than a source of technology," and that what this entails is that we must "judge modern science not only by its material products, but also, and more so, by its intentions and its influence on the way humanity has come to think."

Light, Andrew. "Finding a Future for Environmental Ethics." *Ethics Forum* 7 (3), (2012), pp. 71–80.
In this essay, Light offers an explanation as to why environmental ethics has not yet "captured the attention" of moral philosophers, and what might be done about it.

Owen, James. "Virus infecting Virus Fuels Definition of Life Debate." *National Geographic*, August 22, 2008, https://www.nationalgeographic.com/science/2008/08/news-virus-infecting-definition-life.
What's the difference between a living thing and a "bag of genes"? This is the question Owen pursues in light of findings that suggest that viruses can infect other viruses—and make them sick.

Pierrehumbert, R.T. *"Climate Change: A Catastrophe in Slow Motion."* Harvard Law Review. https://www.cfa.harvard.edu/~wsoon/myownPapers-d/Pierrehumbert06-LawReviewCatastrophe.pdf

Pierrehumbert argues that "climate change is a catastrophe equal to nearly any other in our planet's history," and that "[h]umans have become a major geological force with the power to commit future millennia to practically irreversible changes in global conditions." Nonetheless, because climate change is about long-term atmospheric conditions—and not simply weather patterns—we find it difficult to take it seriously enough to take the necessary action.

Schwartzman, Peter. *"Climate Change and Water Woes Drove ISIS in Iraq."* National Geographic, September 14, 2017. https://news.nationalgeographic.com/2017/11/climate-change-drought-drove-isis-terrorist-recruiting-iraq

Schwartzman offers an example of the relationship between climate change-enhanced drought and vulnerability to being recruited by terrorist organizations like ISIS, in this case, in beleaguered Iraq.

Science Learning Hub. *"Characteristics of Living Things."* https://www.sciencelearn.org.nz/resources/14-characteristics-of-living-things

Offers a highly accessible set of basic characteristics of living organisms, including the capacity for respiration, locomotion, the ability to detect environmental change, and the capacity for growth.

Taylor, Paul W. (1986). *The Ethics of Respect for Nature: A Theory of Environmental Ethics* (N.J. Princeton: Princeton University Press). http://rintintin.colorado.edu/~vancecd/phil3140/Taylor.pdf.

Taylor defines inherent worth in terms of the notion that "Every organism, species population, and community of life has a good of its own which moral agents can intentionally further or damage by their actions." To have a good of one's own is to be able to be "benefitted or harmed."

UNESCO. *"The Precautionary Principle."* The United Nations Educational, Scientific, and Cultural Organization. http://unesdoc.unesco.org/images/0013/001395/139578e.pdf

"Born of environmental considerations, the precautionary principle has since matured into an ethical principle with a far broader scope and the potential value... as a policy guide..."

Warren, Mary Anne (2000). *Moral Status: Obligations to Persons and Other Living Things* (Oxford: Oxford University Press).

Addressing the central question, "What does it take to be an entity worthy of moral consideration?" Warren argues that there is no single quality or property that can identify such worth, but that we can articulate principled criteria to aid us in this determination.

Weston, Anthony (2009). *The Incompleat Eco-Philosopher: Essays from the Edges of Environmental Ethics* (Albany, NY: SUNY University Press.

Weston raises important questions about a number of concepts central to contemporary environmental ethics, including "inherent worth," and advocates a significantly revised version of naturalism.

World Food Programme. *"Climate Impacts on Food Security."* https://www.wfp.org/climate-change/climate-impacts

Profiles the intimate relationship between growing planet-wide food insecurity and climate change, particularly with respect to drought, extreme weather events, and access to available food stores.

Wuerthner, George, et al. (2014). *Keeping the Wild: Against the Domestication of Earth* (Foundations for Deep Ecology), p. 3.

Wuerthner and his colleagues explore whether we should embrace the Anthropocene—human domestication of the planet—or reinvest in tradition commitments to ecosystem conservation.

Zimmerman, Michael J. *"Intrinsic Vs. Extrinsic Value."* Stanford Encyclopedia of Philosophy, 2002. https://plato.stanford.edu/entries/value-intrinsic-extrinsic

Zimmerman offers a concise overview of what in the philosophical tradition has defined intrinsic value compared to extrinsic or instrumental value. He raises the question whether there really is any such thing, and whether it has the moral significance that has been attributed to it.

Online Resources

1. "The Moral Status of Animals," *Stanford Encyclopedia of Philosophy*, August 23, 2017, https://plato.stanford.edu/entries/moral-animal.

2. "Economic and Economic Justice," *Stanford Encyclopedia of Philosophy*, May 28, 2004, https://plato.stanford.edu/entries/economic-justice.

3. Rebecca Lindsey, "Climate Change: Atmospheric Carbon Dioxide," *NOAA: Climate Change*, https://www.climate.gov/news-features/understanding-climate/climate-change-atmospheric-carbon-dioxide.

4. Anna Funk, "Which Animals Are Going Extinct? The 32 Closest Ones Are Often Overlooked," *Discover Magazine*, November 16, 2020, https://www.discovermagazine.com/planet-earth/what-animals-are-going-extinct-its-not-an-easy-question.

5. Ronald Sandler, "Intrinsic Value, Ecology, and Conservation," *The Knowledge Project*, 3 (10), (2012), p. 4. https://www.nature.com/scitable/knowledge/library/intrinsic-value-ecology-and-conservation-25815400.

6. "What is Sustainability?" *UCLA Sustainability*, https://www.sustain.ucla.edu/about-us/what-is-sustainability.

7. "The Precautionary Principle," *The Silent Spring Institute*, https://silentspring.org/precautionary-principle.

8. "The Hippocratic Oath," *National Institute of Health: Greek Medicine*, https://www.nlm.nih.gov/hmd/greek/greek_oath.html.

9. Bill McKibbon, "Coronavirus and Climate Change," *YouTube*, May 14, 2020, https://www.youtube.com/watch?v=fdzxxndqDV0.

10. Amanda Erikson, "The U.S. has more Climate Skeptics than Anywhere on Earth. Blame the GOP," *The Washington Post*, November 17, 17, https://www.washingtonpost.com/../the-u-s-has-more-climate-skeptics-than-anywhere-el.

11. Ernest Becker, *The Denial of Death* (The Free Press, Macmillan and Company, 1973). https://humanposthuman.files.wordpress.com/2014/01/ernest_becker_the_denial_of_deathbookfi-org.pdf.

12. Rebecca Leber, "The Role Harassment Plays in Climate Change Denial," *Mother Jones*, https://www.motherjones.com/environment/2018/11/the-role-harassment-plays-in-climate-change-denial.

13. Luke Mogelson, "The Militias Against masks," *The New Yorker*, August 17, 2020, https://www.newyorker.com/magazine/2020/08/24/the-militias-against-masks.

14. "Fact Sheet: Explaining Operation Warp Speed," *U.S. Health and Human Services*, https://www.hhs.gov/coronavirus/explaining-operation-warp-speed/index.html.

15. Armand Schwab, "The Human Animal," *The New York Times*, September 13, 1970. https://www.nytimes.com/1970/09/13/archives/the-human-animal.html.

16. Alexandra Michel, "Humans are Animals Too: A Whirlwind Tour of Cognitive Biology," *The Association for Psychological Science*, May/June 2017, https://www.psychologicalscience.org/observer/humans-are-animals-too-a-whirlwind-tour-of-cognitive-biology.

17. Anna Muir, "10 Ways Chimps and Humans are the Same," *Jane Goodall Institute of Canada*, https://janegoodall.ca/our-stories/10-ways.

18. "Science and History of GMOs and Other Food Modification Processes," *U.S. Food and Drug Administration*, https://www.fda.gov/food/agricultural-biotechnology/science-and-history-gmos-and-other-food-modification-processes.

19. Shane Gunster, et al., "Why Don't You Act Like You Believe It? Competing Visions of Climate Hypocrisy," *Frontiers in Communication*, November 6, 2018, https://www.frontiersin.org/articles/10.3389/fcomm.2018.00049/full.

20. N. Kolodny, "Instrumental Rationality," *The Stanford Encyclopedia of Philosophy*, November 2, 2018. https://plato.stanford.edu/entries/rationality-instrumental.

21. *Sierra Club Foundation.* https://www.sierraclubfoundation.org.

22. Christopher Shields, "In the Shadows of Dominion: Anthropocentrism and the Continuance of the Culture of Oppression," *Electronic Theses and Dissertations*, Paper 2474, *East Tennessee State University*, 2015, https://dc.etsu.edu/cgi/viewcontent.cgi?article=3819&context=etd.

23. Nina Popovich, et al., "76 Environmental Rules on Their Way Out Under Trump," *The New York Times*, July 6, 2018, https://www.nytimes.com/interactive/2017/10/05/climate/trump-environment-rules-reversed.html.

24. Bashar Khiatah, "The Health Impacts of Chemical Fertilizers," *Amos Institute*, https://amosinstitute.com/blog/the-health-impacts-of-chemical-fertilizers.

25. Jean Daniel Collomb, "The Ideology of Climate Change Denial in the United States," *European Journal of American Studies*, Spring 2014. https://journals.openedition.org/ejas/10305.

26. Ben Doherty, "Climate Change Will Fuel Terrorism Recruitment, Report for German Foreign Office Says." *The Guardian*, April 19, 2017, https://www.theguardian.com/environment/2017/apr/20/climate-change-will-fuel-terrorism-recruitment-adelphi-report-says.

27. Elodie Hut, et al., "Covid-19, Climate Change, and Migration: Constructing Crises, Reinforcing Borders," *United Nations Environmental Migration Portal*, https://environmentalmigration.iom.int/blogs/covid-19-climate-change-and-migration-constructing-crises-reinforcing-borders.

28. "Predator-Prey Relationships," *New England Complex Studies Institute*, https://necsi.edu/predator-prey-relationships.

29. Luis P. Villarreal, "Are Viruses Alive?" *Scientific American*, August 8, 2008, https://www.scientificamerican.com/article/are-viruses-alive-2004.

30. Anton J. M. Dijker, "Consciousness: A Neural Capacity for Objectivity, Especially Pronounced in Humans," *Frontiers in Psychology*, March 17, 2014, https://www.frontiersin.org/articles/10.3389/fpsyg.2014.00223/full.

31. Keza MacDonald, "Being Human: How Realistic do we Want Robots to Be?" *The Guardian*, June 26, 2018, https://www.theguardian.com/technology/2018/jun/27/being-human-realistic-robots-google-assistant-androids.

32. Lars Chittka, and Catherine Wilson, "Expanding Consciousness," *American Scientist*, Nov-Dec, 2019, https://www.americanscientist.org/article/expanding-consciousness.

33. Kenny Ausubel, "Plants are Sentient Beings," *The Bioneers*, February 9, 2017. https://www.youtube.com/watch?v=couHXnRdIc4.

34. Sarah Zhang, "Why Science Can't Say When a Baby's Life Begins," *Wired*, October 2, 2015, https://www.wired.com/2015/10/science-cant-say-babys-life-begins.

35. Jeff Mason, "Death and Its Concept," *PhilosophersMag*, January 31, 2015. https://www.philosophersmag.com/opinion/17-death-and-its-concept.

36. Kelly Kaspar, "Zoos Should Leave the Ark Metaphor Behind," *Nature Research: Ecology and Evolution*, September 24, 2018, https://natureecoevocommunity.nature.com/posts/39133-zoos-should-embrace-the-un-sustainable-development-goals-to-achieve-their-wildlife-conservation-missions.

37. James McWilliams, "Why Free-Ranged Meat Isn't Much Better than Factory-Farmed," *The Atlantic*, December 7, 2010. https://www.theatlantic.com/health/archive/2010/12/why-free-range-meat-isnt-much-better-than-factory-farmed/67569.

2

TWO EXAMPLES OF MORAL EXTENSIONISM: PETER SINGER, TOM REGAN, AND THEIR CRITICS

2.1 The Capacity to Suffer: The Utilitarian Extensionism of Peter Singer

2.1.1 What Is Moral Extensionism?

A bit like hybrid apples, the philosopher's version of *moral extensionism* comes in many varieties, a feature both a great strength and an Achilles' heel.[1] Broadly, it's the view that while our traditional concepts of rights, moral standing, and moral considerability were intended for human beings, it may be possible to *extend* some or all of these concepts to at least some others typically assumed to be outside the moral community, or what some call the social contract. The extension of a moral principle depends, of course, on how we understand *to what* it would apply, and for what reasons. That project in turn demands that we sharpen key concepts such as "environment," "living," "sentient," "rights-bearing," "community," "contract," and "value," clearly enough to justify *to what* a specific principle would apply, to what it would not, and why. As we've seen already, this turns out to be more difficult than it seems at first glance. Indeed, moral extentionism is challenging for anyone who takes seriously human-centeredness as foundational to the examined moral life. Any moral agent who seeks to realize value beyond narrow self-interest, who takes "centeredness" as a call to responsibility as opposed to privilege, must offer justifying criteria, and must be willing to wrestle with the potential implications of an expanded "moral community."

This is Environmental Ethics: An Introduction, First Edition. Wendy Lynne Lee.
© 2022 John Wiley & Sons, Inc. Published 2022 by John Wiley & Sons, Inc.
Companion Website: https://thisisphilosoph.wordpress.com

Contrary to embracing a responsible human-centeredness, human chauvinism faces no such moral quandaries. For it, the extension of moral status to nonhuman others is neither desirable nor necessary. In fact, it's a counterproductive distraction from the pursuit of self-interest, especially the quest of economic interests that require the transformation of things, living and nonliving, sentient and nonsentient, into marketable commodities (more on this later). The expansion of notions like "rights" to nonhuman animals or to ecosystems poses a threat to a social and economic order that privileges the few—mostly white, male, Global Northern, and affluent—in ways reminiscent of the struggles of women, non-white minorities, and indigenous peoples.[2] Indeed, extending moral status to nonhuman animals poses an even greater threat to the social and economic hierarchy by demanding we consider what science now shows concerning, for example, nonhuman animal sentience, the value of biodiversity, the loss to ecosystemic integrity caused by extinction, and the effects of human excess on the planet's capacity to support life. Even where human chauvinism has, through centuries of struggle, come to terms with the evils of slavery, heteropatriarchy, racism, anti-Semitism, and the like, articulating criteria for the inclusion of nonhuman animals and ecosystems remains largely off its moral compass. Perhaps more disconcerting, given copious opportunity offered by the sciences to review prejudice and alleviate ignorance, is that the capacity for denial remains deeply rooted in human chauvinism's DNA: the prospect of sentience, the impacts of greenhouse gas emissions, the eternity of plastics, food insecurity, the shrinking availability of clean water, the loss of habitat, the potential for transmission of zoonotic disease, extinction. A compelling environmental ethic must be able to offer some insight into why denial (including its many cousins—the capacity to downplay, diminish, ignore, evade, obscure, distort) continues to be a powerful psychic, social, and economic driver of our failure to confront environmental crises, and how the right ethic might be able to overcome it.

An all too devastating example of human chauvinism and its consequences is offered to us, sadly, by the infection rate of the Covid-19 pandemic in slaughterhouses and meat-packing plants in the United States. As Megan Moltini reports, "nearly 5000 plant workers in 19 states" tested positive for the virus by late April, 2020, creating near-panic in the plants, forcing shutdowns, generating worry right along with an escalation in cases of sickness and death in surrounding communities and region.[3] The causes are not hard to identify: close working quarters involving a high potential for worker accident under soiled factory floor conditions. That people, especially healthcare, transportation, and food delivery workers, are terrified of the Covid-19 virus makes perfect sense; as of this writing there is no reliable treatment and no vaccine. But even if there were an effective vaccine, the prospect of variants remains a potent reminder of Covid-19's potential lethality. While the sheer terror of a story about the cost to human health and life sheds light on questions about whose lives matter, and thus on the social and economic inequalities exposed by the pandemic, it's the "human interest" story about farmers being forced to "euthanize," for example, their pigs that trains the brightest light on human chauvinism.

A "food" animal slaughtered *before* its body is dismembered and eventually eaten is "euthanized"; after, it's merely "processed." The use of euphemism in *both* cases functions, as Carol Adams argues, to conceal—to convert into an *absent referent*—the sentient entity killed and transformed into "food."[4] To be sure, some bemoaned the "euthanizing," just as using that term intimates, but few ask the question that philosopher Cora Diamond proposes, namely, should dismembered nonhuman animal bodies count as food? Very few ask whether the existence of slaughter houses and meat-packing plants is itself morally defensible beyond the effects of the working conditions on their human workers. But this *absence* exposes the hypocrisy at the heart of human chauvinism, at least in its global North incarnation. For even as President Trump moved swiftly to designate the food animal industry as "essential," thus requiring it to remain in operation during the pandemic, the condemnation of Chinese "wet" markets (wild animal street-level slaughter houses) grew louder. In other words, even as a cacophony of voices grew condemning the potential for zoonotic transmission from nonhuman animal species to human beings of a virus proving to be stunningly deadly,[5] the presupposition that the vehicle of transmission had to be some other species (or the species of "the other") remained uninterrogated. It's not sufficient, however, to conclude from this simply that human chauvinism has no single cultural or social expression, or even to recognize that it's nearly always to be found in association with other forms of structural inequality—sexism, racism, and classism—though these are both true. We must go further: in the face of significant dangers to health and life, the "others" of human chauvinism are not only more vulnerable to sickness and death, but are made so by the very social and economic structures that generate the conditions of sickness and death. Zoonotic transmission may be a viral event, but it is equally a socio-economic one presaged by habitat encroachment, resource pollution and exhaustion, human population growth, habits of consumption, and arguably, moral shortsightedness. In any case, what is true of zoonotic transmission is just as true, and for at least some of the same reasons, for the climate crisis.

Long before hockey-stick models showing an alarming uptick in greenhouse gas emissions or images of lonely looking polar bears, philosophers had already begun to re-think the question whether nonhuman entities and/or ecosystems count as worthy of moral consideration.[6] Wisely enough, they looked to moral principles readily available for inspiration and guidance, reasoning that insofar as they'd been adapted to address any number of human dilemmas beyond the scope of their original intention, they could surely be adapted to tackle issues relevant to the environment and/or to nonhuman animals. Perhaps principles that had been effectively utilized to end slavery could be put to work in the moral evaluation of zoos; important insights about equality that have (however gradually) been expanded to women, sexual minorities, and disabled persons surely have utility in assessing the moral status of nonhuman animals and perhaps even the environment itself. Perhaps notions like "respect for life" can be translated into laws protecting biodiversity. Perhaps consistency requires that the same moral condemnation we heap on Chinese wet markets be applied to American slaughterhouses and meat-packing plants. And perhaps there's no reason to reinvent the moral wheel; we simply need to identify whatever capacities or qualities that could extend a favored principle to new kinds of cases, and then see how well it fits.

2.1.2   Peter Singer's *Animal Liberation* and the Principle of Equality

Few embody this basic impulse behind moral extensionism more influentially than Peter Singer whose ground-breaking 1975 *Animal Liberation* offers a case for the extension of the *principle of utility* to sentient nonhuman animals in virtue of a capacity they share in common with human beings, namely, *the capacity to suffer*. If we have a moral duty, argues Singer, to maximize happiness and minimize suffering for at least those human beings relevantly affected by our actions, so too we have a duty—at a bare minimum—to take into consideration as an aspect of our moral decision-making the suffering of sentient nonhuman animals. Singer calls this the *principle of equality*:

> If a being suffers, there can be no moral justification for refusing to take that suffering into consideration. No matter what the nature of a being, the principle of equality requires that its suffering be counted equally with the like suffering—insofar as rough comparisons can be made—of any other being. If a being is not capable of suffering, or of experiencing enjoyment or happiness, there is nothing to be taken into account. So, the limit of sentience... is the only defensible boundary of concern for the interests of others. To mark this boundary by some other characteristic like intelligence or rationality would be to mark it in an arbitrary manner. Why not choose some other characteristic like skin color? (Singer, *Animal Liberation*, pp. 8–9)

Sometimes referred to as the *Greatest Happiness* principle or *consequentialism*, Singer extends the principle of utility to all those sentient entities capable of having an interest in avoiding suffering.[7] Such an interest requires neither intellect nor reason, but only the capacity to experience pain and pleasure. "The capacity for suffering and enjoyment," argues Singer, is a *prerequisite for having interests at all*, a condition that must be satisfied before we can speak of interests in a meaningful way," (*Animal Liberation*, p. 7). We can no more prevent suffering that occurs as a part of, for example, predation than we can keep the sun from rising, but this isn't Singer's point. He's not looking to disrupt the relationships that characterize the natural world; he's looking to disrupt the unnecessary suffering imposed on nonhuman animals through human action. We treat as morally considerable other human beings by refusing to participate in racism or sexism. We don't discard intellectually disabled human beings, Alzheimer's sufferers, or the permanently comatose. We wrangle over the moral status of human embryos.[8] So too, argues Singer, we must treat similarly sentient nonhuman animals by refusing to participate in *speciesism*:

> Racists violate the principle of equality by giving greater weight to the interests of members of their own race when there is a clash between their interests and the interests of those of another race. Sexists violate the principle of equality by favoring the interests of their own sex. Similarly, speciesists allow the interests of their own species to override the greater interests of members of other species. The pattern is identical in each case. (*Animal Liberation*, p. 9)

Unless, in other words, we can demonstrate that the brains of nonhuman animals are composed in such a way that, while we can feel pain, they cannot, we've no justification other than self-interest for refusing to extend moral consideration to them, that is, to consider the consequences of our actions with regard to their capacity for suffering. In short, for Singer, self-interest cannot support discrimination on grounds so arbitrary as species. From this point of view the factory farm is comparable to the gas chambers;[9] the zoo to the prison.[10] Skipping a stone across a lake causes it no harm; tossing a bag of kittens into a river to drown causes incalculable suffering and death. As Singer puts it: "A mouse… does have an interest in not being kicked along the road, because it will suffer if it is" (*Animal Liberation*, p. 8). We neither risk nor sacrifice anything of equal significance by refusing to eat animal bodies, visit zoos, or sanction animal cruelty.[11] Moreover, although human history offers an imperfect image of moral progress to be sure, it is a story of recognizing the wrongs of institutions like slavery and patriarchy. Singer would thus extend that recognition to the factory farm, the zoo, and to the use of nonhuman animals in all forms of experimentation (product testing, pharmaceutical, and medical). What we gain is moral consistency with respect to what, according to Singer, is the most important interest of any sentient entity, namely, the minimizing of unnecessary pain and the maximizing of the possibility of pleasure.

Let's take a step back for a moment, however, to consider the principle at the heart of Singer's moral extentionism. At its most basic, the principle of utility invests the morality of an action in its prospective consequences. What makes an action morally permissible, in other words, are the consequences that follow from it, that is, whether it maximizes happiness and/or minimizes suffering for those relevantly affected. Very generally, the "act" utilitarian determines

permissibility on the basis of each action, calculating the potential consequences for those affected from a range of possibilities given that action. The
"rule" utilitarian (probably the more realistic approach) settles on a set of morally defensible rules for calculating the quotient of happiness over suffering
over a range of possible scenarios and then seeks to consistently apply those
rules as the need to make decisions arise.[12] Most human agents are *utilitarians* at least in the sense that it's rare for us to pay no attention to the possible
consequences of our actions. We mostly do care; we mostly do think about
consequences; we mostly do aim to maximize happiness or at least minimize
suffering at least for our human fellows.

Moreover, we condemn those who appear to take neither notice nor care
for the effects their actions have on others. The woman who drives drunk and
plows into a family of five isn't excused having forgot how many cocktails she
consumed. The man who leaves his children in a hot car while he goes into a
bar for a beer isn't excused for not having been aware of the heat index. We
call such actions reckless, especially since the likely consequences were predictable, and the very speed and certainty of our judgment hints at a kind of
innate consequentialist inclination. Being a consistent utilitarian, however, can
be more demanding:

- How can I be reasonably sure I have made the right prediction about
  whether a particular action maximizes happiness and/or minimizes
  suffering? How do I know (if I adopt rule utilitarianism) what rule
  applies to what circumstance?
- To whom/what does my utilitarian calculation of "relevantly affected"
  apply? How do I know how expansive this circle should be? Who do
  I prioritize, and why?
- Are there varieties of happiness or pleasure that should never be maximized? Are there varieties of suffering that are acceptable on the way to
  some other good end?
- When do the ends, however good, noble, or just, justify the means when
  the means are morally suspect or even repugnant, or where they involve
  violence or violate some other value?

These are just some of the questions that confront the utilitarian—even before
we get to its extension to nonhuman animals.[13] Imagine, for example, a fifteen
year-old high school student who discovers she's pregnant. She has three choices:
abortion, have baby/keep baby, or have baby/give up baby for adoption. Who
is she morally obligated to consider in making this decision? For whom are the
consequences likely to be the most significant? Her parents? Siblings? Grandpar-
ents? The baby's father? Who comes first? Why? If the young woman's parents
are deeply religious and opposed to abortion, should she lie and have it to keep

from dropping out of high school? Do these ends justify those means? Should the father have veto-power over a decision he rejects? Is fifteen years old enough to make such weighty decisions? The point, of course, is that if decisions involving members of the human community can be morally fraught, those involving non-human beings or ecological systems are likely to be all the more so.

2.1.3   Weighing Interests and Predicting Consequences

It's easy to see how the application of a moral principle that places a high premium on predicting future outcomes, weighing the welfare of whatever "many" are relevant to its calculation against the potential losses or even suffering of the few, can invoke complex cost-to-benefit analyses. Moreover, trying to ascertain short-term consequences is one thing, but trying to perform an equally convincing assessment for the long-term can be nearly impossible. If the fifteen-year-old drops out of high school, will she become a social safety net statistic? If she gives up the baby for adoption, will she regret it later? Can she safely assume that pregnancy won't have negative heath impacts down the road? If it's challenging to be a consistent utilitarian with respect to other people, it stands to reason that it could only be more so in the case of sentient nonhuman animals. Hypocrisy is easy; it's moral consistency that's hard. We condemn the man who beats his dog but let pass unremarked the woman who orders the bacon-burger. We applaud the *Society for the Prevention of Cruelty to Animals*, but take our kids to the circus.[14] We solar panel our house, but fail to consider whose labor goes into the manufacture of the panels and at what cost to their well-being.[15] Here too the prediction of long-term over short-term consequences can make weighing relative interests difficult. Imagine advocating the protection of a population of goats against aerial extermination for the sake of saving a species of plant from extinction; then imagine a population of mice starving to death once the plants upon which they depend are gone. Or imagine, as some critics of the vocal young climate activist Greta Thunberg point out, calling out the fossil fuel industry for committing theft against the future of a sustainable planet only to have inadvertently encouraged other young adults to commit suicide in despair.[16]

Although Singer's argument, particularly his comparison of racism and sexism to speciesism, has had a good deal of influence with respect to the moral consideration of sentient nonhuman animals, it also raises several thorny questions. For example, because the aim of his argument is the prevention of unnecessary suffering, its primary focus individuals, it raises difficult questions concerning conflicts between the interests of individuals and the preservation of eco-systemic stability. Deer are sentient creatures, but the ecologies upon they depend can become irrecoverably degraded when their populations grow too large. A whole species of endangered plant life could be driven to extinction in the interest of refusing to cull the goat herd that feeds on it. Thus, we have to ask: should we be comfortable with preventing suffering if the cost is ecosystem (and often biodiversity) loss? Who/what should take priority in a conflict between individual suffering and resource depletion? What means are justified in the effort to combat ecosystem destruction if they're likely to produce suffering or even death? What about when it's the presence of human beings—dwellings, roads, dams, mining operations, farms—that pose the greatest threat to an ecosystem? Are there ever circumstances where the suffering of human individuals should count for less than the preservation of a seriously endangered ecology or species?

Insofar as this last question reintroduces the interests of human beings into the utilitarian calculus, it raises a second conflict: given the hunger and disease associated with poor nutrition in some human populations, and given that key proteins are made more accessible via the less expensive manufacturing processes of factory farms, isn't more happiness maximized, more suffering minimized overall through the maintenance of animal agriculture— even though it produces suffering on a scale far larger than the populations of human consumers it serves? Singer's response is that we'd be far better off to end industrialized animal agriculture, and then distribute the grains consumed by factory farm animals to human populations. No doubt, such an approach could reduce human starvation. But Singer misses another important consideration: while oppressive, the labor practices institutionalized in animal agriculture act both as a source of income for the poor and working classes. Hence, while the factory farm is a source of suffering for human and nonhuman beings, it is also itself an avenue to food security for the family that has no option other than to focus on the short-term goal of feeding hungry children.

While shutting down the factory farms and redistributing the grains may go some ways on the short term to alleviate hunger, it's hard to imagine an argument convincing enough to persuade the worker to go on strike while she has a family in immediate need of food. That she's paid a wage which guarantees her continuing dependency on the only job to which she has reliable access certainly serves the purposes of the meat processing business that employs her—even at the high cost of her health and her future prospects. In short, it's hard to see how arguments like Singer's, however morally compelling, are likely to produce real action toward long-term change; the stakes for those likely to make the biggest sacrifices to secure that change are just too high. In short, confronted with the sheer immediacy of food insecurity, Singer's revolutionary expansion of moral value seems aspirational, but hardly realistic. He may be right to draw comparisons between the racist, the sexist, and the speciesist. But insofar as Singer doesn't account for the fact that these "isms" are institutionalized as critical resources for an economic system that advantages a small class of beneficiaries through the exploitation of those traditionally excluded from power, his moral extensionism remains inadequate to address either the short- or long-term consequences of ending a global industry like animal agriculture. After all, if the short-term consequences are starvation or at least chronic food insecurity, it's hard to see how we get to the long-term environmental benefits. And it's hard to imagine the many other industries necessary to animal agri- culture—grain production, mining operations, large machinery manufacture, trucking—much moved by arguments whose focus is minimizing the suffering of individuals, even if their "what's for dinner?" advertising can make it look that way. Singer might respond, of course, that confrontation with economic reality might leave nearly any moral principle withering on the vine. Be that as it may, the need to speak to the racism, sexism, and speciesism that supply labor, bodies, and laboring bodies to capitalism is not diminished by the limits to date of our moral reasoning.

What Singer's moral extensionism can offer are useful avenues of comparison for organizing campaigns to combat hunger by showing how it's at least partly the product of an industrialized meat production that requires massive volumes of grain, or by showing, for example, how water bottled for human consumption has become popular in part due to the fear that tap water is polluted by herbicides, fertilizers, and insecticides sprayed on crops to grow the grain that will be consumed by the cattle, pigs, and chickens that end up on the dinner plates of those who can afford to buy meat. Hence, even the story of bottled water illustrates the ubiquity of social and economic inequality as well as its environmental consequences. A moral lens that expands the scope of whose suffering matters can help us see how a product as innocent-seeming as bottled water is intimately connected to larger issues such as the volume of plastics consumed by ocean-dwelling creatures, or even the distance develop- ing-world villagers have to travel to secure water for cooking, drinking, and washing. Serious issues of water security are not, moreover, problems only for the developing world. We needn't go further than Flint, Michigan to see that polluted drinking water is as entrenched an issue of class and race as is access to adequate nutrition, exposure to asthma-producing air-borne toxins, or the prospect of becoming a climate crisis refugee.[17] And it can only be measured as darkly ironic that the short-term response to the Flint crisis was to truck in a city's worth of bottled water.

Flint reminds us that while we might be tempted to think that the winners of resource exploitation live in the global North, and that the cost of the global North's consumption is borne mainly by the global South, this is largely false. What's also true is that the cost of being poor in the developed world can be just as high, especially for children. One response Singer recommends is to adopt a veg- etarian or vegan lifestyle, to effectively opt out of at least one aspect of this cycle of exploitation and suffering. But moving to a plant-based diet can be prohibitively expensive even for global Northerners, particularly in countries like the United States where the divide between the wealthy and the poor is ever-widening. Pollution, clean water scarcity, food insecurity, disease, and a changing climate know no borders, geographic or geopolitical, even when their impacts predictably affect those already made vulnerable by the structural inequalities of sex, gender, race, geography, indigenous status, or species. Mexican fishery collapse, Syrian drought, Ebola outbreak in West Congo, bee colony collapse disorder—all are drivers in the migration of human and nonhuman populations; all forebode consequences difficult to predict with any precision, resistant to the interests of companies and countries.[18]

2.1.4   Moral Extensionism and the Climate Crisis

Climate change could not offer us a better example of the kinds of dilemma the utilitarian faces: while we know the short-term consequences of flooded islands like Kiribati are bad for its citizens, how do we predict the long-term effects of this displacement?[19] While we know years of drought played a role in driving thousands of Syrians into the cities where, unable to find work, they became vulnerable recruits for terrorism, what will be the long-term effects of this Diaspora? What if Syrian water wells remain dry? What if Syrian land remains barren?[20] Singer reminds us that the value of a moral principle is *consistency* in its application, its impartial consideration of interests. But can we afford to be impartial when the damaging effects of environmental deterioration are borne so much more greatly by some than others? Or when corporate excess, government policy, or military venture predictably benefit a very few at the immense expense of the very many, human and nonhuman? While we might run into the burning building to save a human baby first, if we can return to save the dog at no significant risk to ourselves, Singer's moral extensionism requires we do so. But does the value of being consistent extend into the future such that—even if we could, for example, slaughter and consume nonhuman animals without their suffering—we're still obligated to refrain on the grounds that their production contributes to greenhouse gas emissions? Who is the "we" to whom this obligation applies? Does access to adequate nutrition make a difference to how we answer this question? According to Singer, whatever else distinguishes a child from a dog, they share the capacity to suffer equally; they obligate us more or less equally; they represent, especially the child, the possibility of the future. Clearly these questions are thus not merely about moral consistency, but how "we" should want to *live*.[21]

Whatever we decide about babies, dogs, and burning houses, we grasp the moral weight of a decision like this *because* it's urgent, *because* it's right in front of us, and because whether good or bad, its resolution is knowable. The climate crisis, however, presents us with a very different matter of scale, an urgency to be sure—but spread out over a horizon less obvious than a house burning down. On the one hand, the idea that the planet's "house" is burning down isn't far-fetched; even a small child can be made to understand how global warming will melt icebergs, raise ocean water levels, and erode shore lines. On the other, it's genuinely difficult to see the urgency of acting to mitigate climate change. It's not right in front of us, so it's easy to punt to the future. It's long-term, globally dispersed, and abstract; it raises tough questions about what "having interests," "relevantly affected," or "moral extension" mean in particular cases distinguished by geography, class status, species identity, or extant levels of environmental damage.[22] It demands we think long-term, that we work toward mitigation with limited knowledge always evolving in confrontation with new data.

Many of the most obvious negative impacts of the climate crisis expose the fault lines of structural inequality. They reveal factors relevant to other crises, for example, vulnerability to disease or the inability to escape the impacts of extreme weather events. However, in other words, we might want to see the climate crisis as a problem for the future, for an increasing number of human and nonhuman populations, it has become a terrifying fact of the present. There's also plenty of room for hypocrisy. One could be a consistent moral extensionist by becoming a vegan, driving a hybrid car, limiting the number of children, recycling, and by living in a tiny house—but still work as a defense contractor for one of the most polluting, greenhouse gas emitting, businesses in the world—the US Department of Defense. The difficulty with Singer's argument is that while it's certainly not a stretch to see the relevance of his discussion of suffering to future catastrophe, it is hard to see what action—as individuals and as societies—we ought to take. Because the foci of Singer's moral extensionism is the individual subject of suffering, it potentially pits the rights of individuals against the stability of ecosystems. For the same reasons, it also raises important questions at the intersection of race, sex, class, and species: what/who must we be prepared to sacrifice for the sake of mitigating against damage to the planet's atmosphere? Who decides?[23]

2.1.5   How Do I Know a Thing Can Suffer?

Another difficult issue for the utilitarian, even for short-term decision-making, is that while the moral duty to prevent unnecessary suffering is intuitively compelling, what counts as evidence of suffering isn't always as obvious as Singer's "rough comparability" might imply. Nonhuman animals evince suffering in their behavior, but can no more tell us what is the case than human newborns. The precautionary principle is likely our most reliable moral ally here, but few on the side of preventing unnecessary suffering are likely to hold it goes far enough at least in cases of nonhuman animals that we experience as very different from anything comparable to ourselves. The questions are daunting: some researchers in the marine sciences, for example, hold that invertebrates such as lobsters are unlikely candidates for suffering because their nervous systems are not able to support the requisite sentience.[24] Response to pain, they argue, isn't necessarily *experience* of pain. Yet new research suggests that lobsters, hermit crabs, and squid, among others exhibit behavior more sophisticated than autonomic response—deliberate avoidance of painful stimuli, and some invertebrate behavior, namely, that of octopi raise even tougher questions about sentience.[25] Singer recognizes that this is a problem even in the human case when he observes that:

> In theory, we *could* always be mistaken when we assume that other human beings feel pain. It is conceivable that one of our close friends is really a cleverly constructed robot, controlled by a brilliant scientist so as to give all the signs of feeling pain, but is really no more sensitive than any other machine. We can never know, with absolute certainty, that this is not the case. (*Animal Liberation*, p. 10).

Fair enough. But whether Singer's response to the possibility that we could be mistaken is sufficient—that is another question. He appeals to behavior, arguing that

> ... while this might present a puzzle for philosophers, none of us has the slightest real doubt that our close friends feel pain just as we do. This is an inference, but a perfectly reasonable one, based on observations of their behavior in situations in which we would feel pain, and on the fact that we have every reason to assume that our friends are beings like us, with nervous systems like ours that can be assumed to function as ours do and to produce similar feelings in similar circumstances. (*Animal Liberation*, pp. 10–11)

Who and what might feel pain, in other words, isn't just a "puzzle" for philosophers. And this is true despite the fact that human beings have a very checkered history with respect to the kinds of inferences Singer insists are "perfectly reasonable." On the one hand, if we readily drew the inference to the suffering of other human beings, perhaps we'd be less prone to the bigotries of our history. On the other, Singer has had tremendous influence, especially with respect to what we regard as food.[26]

There's something more going on here, something that either fuels our denial of the obvious, or something less evident than Singer recognizes. Perhaps we're not as capable of empathy as his appeal to comparability implies;

perhaps we are, but we're also creatures capable of rationalizing interests more chauvinistic than empathetic. Perhaps predicting consequences is too difficult to provide a foundation for moral considerability, especially as we're more and more confronted by events that draw our attention away from the plight of individuals—extreme weather events, global pandemics, and a significant increase in our understanding of what sorts of creatures can likely experience suffering. Perhaps determining what ends justify what means is more likely to encourage us to excuse suffering, especially given the conflicts created between self-interest and the sketchy future of planetary environmental stability. These are difficult issues, and they lead some philosophers to reject, or at least significantly modify, Singer's utilitarianism. One such is ecofeminist philosopher Cora Diamond. In "Eating Meat and Eating People" Diamond makes the provocative claim that "all such discussions" of the advantages of vegetarianism premised on the claim that nonhuman animals have a right not to be made to suffer unnecessarily are "beside the point." Indeed, the real issue, she insists, is that we do not eat other human beings regardless the status of how they died, (p. 2):

> All such discussions are beside the point. For they ask why we do not kill people… for food…. This is a totally wrong way of beginning the discussion, because it ignores certain quite central facts… *We do not eat our dead*, even when they have died in automobile accidents or been struck by lightning, and their flesh might be first class…. We also do not eat our amputated limbs…." (p. 2, italics in original)

These facts, as Diamond puts it, cannot be adequately captured by arguments about the moral significance of suffering because they *preempt* them. We'd find it repulsive to eat our own dead (or amputated human limbs) even had such persons not been subject to suffering, but we do not give arguments for this revulsion; rather, it's simply part of what it *means* to be a human person—that it is not a thing to eat. Hence, Singer's argument that questions about what it is morally acceptable to eat can be satisfactorily answered by reference to a right not to suffer fall flat at least to the extent that they ignore the "central fact" that arguments do not determine what counts as food. As Diamond makes the point:

> Now the fact that we do not eat our dead is not a consequence—not a direct one in any event—of our unwillingness to kill people for food or other purposes. It is not a direct consequence of our unwillingness to cause distress to people. Of course, it *would* cause distress to people to think that they might be eaten when they were dead, but it causes distress because of what it is to eat a dead person. (p. 2, italics in original)

For Diamond, in other words, there is something about the way we conceive a human being—something in the way we *refer* to human beings—that cannot be reduced to what we may or may not share in common with nonhuman animals, namely, the capacity for suffering. Hence, the attempt to draw a comparison between human and nonhuman animal suffering is bound to fall flat. "If he [Singer] admitted that what underlies our attitude to dining on ourselves is the view that *a person is not something to eat*," writes Diamond, "he could not focus on the cow's right not to be killed or maltreated, as if that were at the heart of it," (p. 3, italics in original). To be clear, this is not to say that there may not be other compelling arguments for vegetarianism. "I write this as a vegetarian," says Diamond, "but one distressed by the obtuseness of the normal arguments" (p. 3).

Several avenues of response to Diamond suggest themselves, but let's examine just one: does Diamond offer an argument or something more like an anthropological description of how human beings think about other human beings? If so, is her claim that she doesn't "think it an accident that the arguments of vegetarians have a nagging moralistic tone" more an expression of human chauvinism than an argument—*for or against* vegetarianism? In other words, while Diamond may be right that "it is normally the case that vegetarians do not touch the issue of our attitude toward the dead," it could also be true that this attitude discloses something more than a "central fact" about our disposition to other people at the intersection of death, human being, and what counts as food. Such attitudes may in fact betray the kind of human chauvinism arguments like Singer's are intended to interrogate—whether or not the vocabulary of "rights" offers the best tools. Diamond's no doubt right that the idea of raising people for "meat" would be met with moral condemnation. She may well be right too that this condemnation does not derive, at least in the first place, from a consideration of suffering. But this doesn't relieve us of the responsibility to consider the moral relevance of suffering.

Drawing the distinction, as does Diamond, between the reasons we don't eat people and reasons for going vegetarian might provide us with just the opportunity we need to reflect more deeply on what we do count as food and why, *and* what suffering we do count as morally relevant and why. If Diamond is right, the reasons that count against cannibalism and the reasons for becoming a vegetarian *are* very different; indeed, they may well belong to different conceptual categories. But this does not obviate the fact that nonhuman animals can suffer, and that Jeremy Bentham's insistence that "[t]he question is not can they reason, but can they suffer?" remains morally significant for any human being other than the committed chauvinist. The target of Diamond's distress, however, is not only Singer's extension of the principle of utility, but arguments that make rights even more central to their defense of nonhuman animals and extend well beyond questions about what counts as food.

These bring us to Kantian philosopher Tom Regan who appeals not to sentience or the capacity to suffer, *per se*, but to a narrower criterion, namely, self-consciousness, to what he refers to as *being-the-subject-of-a-life*. For Regan, inclusion in the moral community depends on the ability to *recognize oneself* as an entity capable of being the subject of one's own life. This doesn't necessarily require the ability to experience pain, and so it's not as tightly tethered to the utilitarian directive to maximize happiness and avoid suffering. It's thus not as closely aligned with Diamond's observation that the fact that we don't eat our dead has little to do with suffering; we *do* perpetrate suffering on other human beings *and* we don't eat our dead. But, as we'll see, it does raise important questions about whether "rights talk" is misplaced or, as Diamond puts it, "obtuse." Perhaps, for example, it is true that the only creatures (so far as we know) that can conceive the rule "this is not a thing to eat" and experience revulsion at the prospect of violating that rule are human beings. But this certainly doesn't preclude other species of animal—primates, cetaceans, some bird species, at least—from candidacy in "being-the-subject-of-one's-own-life" (or even some intellectually immature and/or disabled human beings). So, if an appeal to certain sorts of rights, like the right not to be eaten, the right not to be molested or tortured, etc., is not the right venue for recognizing what distinguishes such subjects from nonsubjects like turnips, what is? Unless we're prepared to concede to the human chauvinist that all but human beings are potentially "things to be eaten" (or otherwise consigned to mere use value), how do we assign value to nonhuman beings that are (at least potentially) the subject-of-their-own-lives? Regardless the "nagging moralistic tone," if not rights, what?

2.2   "Subject-of-a-life": The Kantian Extensionism of Tom Regan

2.2.1   *The Case for Animal Rights* and Immanuel Kant's Categorical Imperative

In 1983's *The Case for Animal Rights*, Tom Regan argues for an expansion of Immanuel Kant's Categorical Imperative to nonhuman animals who are capable of being "*subjects of their own lives*."[27] Typically, the Categorical Imperative divides into two formulations, both deriving their principle force from the foundational demand for moral consistency. According to the *universal law* (the Golden Rule) formulation, we have a moral duty to treat other *subjects* as we wish to be treated in virtue of the worth inherent to their capacity to act on their own interests and imagine a sense of their own futures. The self-awareness of some individuals, regardless species, invests them *as individuals* with the *right* to be treated with the respect and dignity accorded to persons; they are *subjects of their own lives*. Regan thus expands "subject" to include creatures that, although they may not share the same quotient of intellect, are nonetheless capable of something more than sentience. As Regan makes out the argument:

> To be the subject-of-a-life...involves more than merely being alive and more than merely being conscious. To be the subject-of-a life is to be an individual whose life is characterized by [having] beliefs and desires, perception, memory, and a sense of the future, including their own future; an emotional life together with feelings of pleasure and pain; preference-and welfare-interests; the ability to initiate action in pursuit of their desires and goals; a psychophysical identity over time; and an individual welfare in the sense that their experiential life fares well or ill for them, logically independently of their utility for others and logically independently of their being the object of anyone else's interests Those who satisfy the subject-of-a-life criterion themselves have a distinctive kind of value—inherent value—and are not to be treated as mere receptacles. (*The Case for Animal Rights*, p. 243)

For Regan, moral considerability accrues not to the ability to suffer, but to the capacity for events in the world to *matter* to an *individual*, including but not only the capacity for pain. Worth inheres in such a subject in virtue of its "logical independence" from the use that might otherwise be made of it by others.[28] If lobsters are capable of suffering but not of being subjects of their own lives, and octopi can suffer *and* are aware of themselves as such, octopi can be said to have worth inherent to their ability to *be* such subjects. octopi thus belong to the moral community, but not lobsters. It would consequently be wrong, on Regan's view, to treat octopi as food, but the same does not apply to lobsters even though the latter may be able to experience pain. Similarly, a brain condition known as *anencephaly*, defined by the *National Institutes of Health* (NIH) as "[a] baby born with anencephaly is usually blind, deaf, unaware of its surroundings and unable to feel pain" may belong to a species capable of very high cognitive function, but as an individual qualifies less as a-subject-of-a-life than a normal octopus.[29] A "mere receptacle" has value at most only with respect to its utility; lobsters are edible and anencephalic newborns may have value as organ donors.[30] A subject-of-a-life, however, has value independent of utility; it's the center of its own intentions, preferences, and can form a specific identity.

The distinction between subject-of-a-life and "mere receptacle" is thus critical according to Regan for determining to what or whom our moral obligations apply. The distinction can potentially affect everything from what we eat to what we wear, to organ donation, to what animals, if any, can be defensibly utilized in medical and/or product experimentation, to the morality of zoos or to owning pets. From the running of the bulls to rodeos, to circuses, to Burger King, what counts as a subject is a radically different kind of thing, argues Regan, that what counts as an instrument, a tool, a consumable, or a disposable.[31] The distinction is also central to determining what does and doesn't have inherent worth; presumably what does cannot be used without its express permission, and what doesn't have no such say. Some species are more obvious candidates for moral considerability on the subject-of-a-life criteria, some less. Because we're more likely to identify with higher primates such as Chimpanzees and Lowland Gorillas, we tend to rank them more highly; yet we tend to be inconsistent.[32] We're less likely, for example, to treat cetaceans—whales, dolphins, and porpoises—with the same respect even though they're likely at least as intelligent, communicative, and socially oriented as primates.[33] We're also more likely to treat our pet snakes, animals who may or may not qualify on Regan's criteria, as subjects-of-a-life, but ignore the lives of pigs, despite the fact that porcine are smarter and act on a wider range of emotion.[34] Like Singer's extension of the principle of utility, Regan's subject-of-a-life is agnostic about species *per se*, making its focus the individual. The obvious advantage of such a focus, of course, is that it lends itself to the compassion and empathy made possible by the experience of particular creatures in real time. The disadvantage is that by this same token the subject-of-a-life criteria is too often applied arbitrarily, prioritizing the imputed interests of nonhuman animals who happen to be close to us (like our pets) and ignoring those whose dismembered bodies appear in tidy plastic-wrap in the refrigerated meat section of the grocery store.

2.2.2   A Subject-of-a-life

Although Regan, following Kant, takes the capacity for being a subject-of-a-life to include inherent worth, we can make out Regan's argument for moral considerability without this concept. We can, for example, simply reserve moral considerability to those entities that have the requisite set of traits, leaving the door open to the discovery of additional species. We may, in other words, designate as rights-bearing whatever qualities that accrue to "logical independence," that is, that distinguish a subject-of-a-life from an entity whose value is fully exhausted in its use. The difficulties with this approach, however, are not resolved by substituting questions about what counts as inherent for an ostensibly simpler calculus of qualities relevant to being the subject-of-a-life. In the first place, it might turn out to be a be a Sisyphean task to specify precisely enough, across a wide range of species, in light of evolving scientific discovery in what qualities "subject-of-a-life" consists, how we should measure it, and by what means we might recognize it. But, second, even if we could accomplish this task, we have no good reason to think that human beings don't share many of these qualities with some—perhaps many—other species of creature.

This point is made succinctly by Lori Gruen in her essay, "The Moral Status of Animals." "Is there something distinctive about humanity," she asks, "that justifies the idea that human beings have moral status while non-humans do not?" No, argues Gruen, and among the qualities she rejects first is species membership:

> Species membership itself cannot support the view that members of one species, namely ours, deserve moral consideration that is not owed to members of other species. Of course, one might respond that it is not membership in a biological category that matters morally, it is our humanity that grounds the moral claims we make. Humans are morally considerable because of the distinctively human capacities we possess, capacities that only we humans have. (Gruen, "The Moral Status of Animals," *Stanford Encyclopedia of Philosophy*).

Even as we dismiss species membership as acceptable criteria for determining moral considerability, and turn instead to capacities, what we discover, argues Gruen, is that there are few (if any) capacities that we don't share in common with many other species of creature. In other words, once we shift from the plainly human chauvinist to a determination of qualities that constitute, if not inherent worth, at least the right to be recognized as a subject-of-a-life, we are confronted with an unnavigable dilemma: either we specify such qualities so narrowly that only a handful of species count, or we acknowledge that the task of teasing out what really does have the requisite qualities and what doesn't is far more Sisyphean than we had originally speculated. But, as Gruen makes clear, the attempt to satisfy the first inevitably leads to the second:

> But which capacities mark out all and only humans as the kinds of beings that can be wronged? A number of candidate capacities have been proposed—developing family ties, solving social problems, expressing emotions, starting wars, having sex for pleasure, using language, or thinking abstractly, are just a few. As it turns out, none of these activities is uncontroversially unique to humans. (Gruen, "The Moral Status of Animals")

In other words, even if we abandon the concept of inherent worth, adopting instead some notion of qualities or capacities to determine what counts as the subject-of-a-life, we run into the insuperably difficult problem of how to specify these in a way that's not simply arbitrary—or arbitrary in virtue of being human chauvinist. As Diamond might put it, "human being" remains the arbiter of value whether we acknowledge it or not. Just as "human bodies are things we do not eat" is not the product of an *argument* about what counts as edible, so too "developing family ties, solving social problems, expressing emotions, starting wars, having sex for pleasure, using language, or thinking abstractly" is not the product of an *argument* about what count as capacities that define a subject-of-a-life. Were they, we might imagine asking questions about other capacities, say, tail-chasing, perch-bouncing, or fence-jumping—but we don't. Gruen offers a cornucopia of examples of shared capacities, ranging from orangutans to wolves to elephants to chickens to horses, demonstrating that even on a narrow human-centered set of specified capacities, there is no non-arbitrary way of excluding so great a number of nonhuman animal species that the point of making the effort is lost.

Still, as Regan might well respond, the value of identifying what species of creatures count as subjects-of-their-own-lives is that it provides an avenue for demanding that at least some nonhuman animals not be exploited and abused. Consider, for example, a nonhuman animal that many count as emblematic of subject-of-a-life, chimpanzees. Among other things, chimps share significant genetic, anatomical, and brain function similarities with human beings; they have faces which express intelligence, curiosity, and the capacity for suffering. But chimpanzees also have a long history as experimental lab animals in, among other things, HIV/AIDS research, in programs whose beneficiaries are human beings and only human beings. Chimps are not, of course, consenting experimental subjects, even if they are subjects-of-their-own-lives. How then should we apply Regan's view of moral considerability to this story? In 2013 the National Institutes of Health (NIH) decided to retire all but fifty of some nearly 400 "surplus" chimps to sanctuaries:

> No longer needed for AIDS or space research and expensive to maintain, these chimps are now referred to as "surplus" animals. Some sit alone in small steel cages indoors, with no opportunities for exercise, play or companionship. Others are housed in pairs. Some have access to outdoor cages, while the luckiest ones live in small groups with access to large outdoor enclosures equipped with toys, rope swings, and other climbing structures... In addition to the chimpanzees currently housed in U.S. laboratories, another estimated 300 chimps are kept in zoos and exhibits. Of those in laboratories, the federal government owns or supports 900-1,000; the rest are owned by private research institutions that use them to study infectious diseases such as polio, malaria, hepatitis B, and HIV/AIDS. They have also been used in maternal bonding studies and to study the effects of space travel. In total, there are approximately 2,000 chimpanzees in the United States...In 2013, the National Institutes of Health (NIH) announced a plan to retire all but 50 of its research chimpanzees to sanctuaries or other similar facilities, and in 2015, they announced that those remaining 50 would also be retired to

sanctuaries. The NIH has also stopped breeding chimps for research and currently places strict standards on funding new research involving chimpanzees. Even though the NIH made the announcement and has made strides in reducing funding for research, in 2015, only 7 chimpanzees were relocated, and as of January 2016, 382 of the 561 NIH-owned chimps still remained in laboratories. ("Chimps and Research," NIH)

From the point of view of the subject-of-a-life criterion, the concept of the "surplus animal" is morally repugnant, and it's just this kind of commodification and exploitation that Regan seeks explicitly to counter, regardless the commodity value of chimpanzees as lab animals or even the medical value to finding a cure (or a vaccine) for HIV. The tough issue, as the NIH account exemplifies, is that its decision-makers were no closer to being able to clearly distinguish "mere receptacle" from "subject-of-a-life" in 2016 than they were in 2013.

On one hand, the NIH description of the "luckiest," Chimps who live in groups and have toys, clearly recognizes the subject-status of these animals; "[i]t is hard to ignore," they write, "the connection we sense… There, in those brown eyes, [is] curiosity, an invitation to reach out, to play, to be together, and to communicate. There is something almost human about the interaction." On the other, the passage refers to "no longer needed," suggesting that were chimps still useful and inexpensive to medical research, we'd be perfectly just in ignoring the brown eyes, curiosity, and "something almost human" interaction we might encounter in individual animals. Some might, of course, describe the face of the anencephalic newborn in similar terms, even though such infants don't enjoy anything remotely like the sentience of a chimpanzee. Others might, on these same morphologic (what looks like us) grounds, ignore the prospect that octopi can experience pain. Fierce debate characterizes the discourse over harvesting rare organs from anencephalic infants. Yet, little public uproar has attended the NIH's poor record for the sanctuary placement of lab chimps. Octopi sentience probably does not rise to the status of subject-of-a-life, yet few doubt the octopus' capacity for pain.

What cases like the NIH treatment of lab-chimps illustrate is how muddled is the reasoning even of the purported experts about what counts as a subject-of-a-life, on what criteria, determined by what means, and how respect owed to such subjects should be effectuated. If belonging to *Homo sapiens* is neither necessary nor sufficient to determine what counts as a subject-of-a-life, what privileges the anencephalic infant, the brain dead, or the permanently comatose? What makes it acceptable to commodify chimpanzees as disposable lab animals? To be clear, the moral we draw from these difficult questions is not distrust for scientific experts, but rather that while science can be an invaluable source of knowledge, that doesn't mean it's also a source for clear direction about what we *ought to do* with that knowledge; "is" is not "ought."

Regan's agnosticism with respect to species membership seems, like Gruen's, right insofar as this is plainly not requisite to being a subject-of-a-life. But our task is also not as easy as simply deciding to extend moral considerability to instances of *apparent* subjects-of-a-life merely because we recognize some creatures as such. Inference from behavior, a familiar-looking face, the capacity for language—none of these are sufficient on their own to determine whether an entity is the subject-of-its-own-life. Just as determining that human bodies are not something to eat has not been decided by arguments about what to eat, so too—we might at least wonder—has determining that the use of chimps as lab animals regardless the cost to the chimp has not been decided by the subject-of-a-life of the chimp, but rather by the necessity of finding a cure for a devastating *human* disease—AIDS. Twenty-first century sex robots have many of at least the behavioral qualities Gruen cites, yet, they're not subjects-of-their-own-lives. Bats seems like radically alien creatures, but are not only fellow mammals, but may indeed be the subjects-of-their-own-specific-experi-ence. From the point of view of animal agriculture, pigs are bacon machines—despite the fact that what the evidence shows is that they're intelligent social creatures capable of physical *and* emotional harm.

One way to frame a difficulty with the subject-of-a-life criterion, then, is this: given the goal is to articulate a well-reasoned livable ethic—a life worth living not liable to paralysis with indecision at every turn, it's simply not clear whether Regan's criterion advances that project. We can readily imagine Peter Singer raising some hard questions about whether the subject-of-a-life crite-rion is vulnerable to the objection that it invites us to identify such subjects according to a narrow view of human subjectivity—leaving out species of creature that seem more alien to us like bats and octopi. Indeed, human his-tory is rife with examples of human beings denying the moral status of other human beings in order to justify racism, sexism, anti-Semitism as well as their correlates: slavery, genocide, sex-trafficking. Singer might even go further: why should it count against a creature that, simply because it cannot recognize its interests *as* its interests, we have no duty to recognize interests it does have? An octopus may well not be able to formulate the idea that it has an interest in not experiencing pain, or even that it is *this* entity that has such interests. But it doesn't necessarily follow from this lack of recognition (in either respect) that an octopus has no interest in not suffering or that its suffering would somehow be less due to the fact that it does not know who—itself—is experiencing it.

Just as the capacity for suffering may have greater moral weight than Regan assigns to it, so too the lack of any capacity to feel pain or to become a subject-of-a-life may have no significant moral relevance in some cases. Consider the anencephalic infant: its parents may take it home, dress, feed, and bathe it until the baby dies after a few weeks. They'll administer to it as such because this is *their* baby. They may have been apprised of the facts, but it doesn't matter to them, and we don't begrudge them this. The point is *not* that we need a better understanding of *in* what a subject-of-a-life consists, or that without this understanding we're in a poor position to judge the rightness of the parents' decisions. The point is that what matters in this case simply isn't whether the baby is such a subject. *What matters is the parents' relationship to the infant* or, as Diamond might put it, that "their baby" has a profound meaning *to them* that requires no argument to defend it. Or, perhaps even more persuasive, what matters is that the parents are *suffering*, and that to alleviate *that* suffering may require administering to the infant as an aspect of their grieving. We don't begrudge them this precisely because the subject-status of their infant is not what's at issue. For Singer, their *pain* is what's at issue. For Diamond, it's "*their baby*"; for Gruen, it's that suffering is neither *unique* to human beings nor the only capacity we share in common with other species of creature. Even if we could, as in this case, make a clear determination whether something is a subject of its own life, it's not at all obvious that this fact determines what is owed to it, *or what may be owed to others* in virtue of it.

This too is possible: we may not *owe* to others anything other than a duty to avoid harm and a duty to noninterference. We could opt for a very spare *libertarian* construal of rights—the right not to be harmed intentionally or via preventable negligence, and the right to pursue our own objectives without impediment. But even on this view of rights, many of the questions Regan (and, implicitly, Gruen) raises persist: what criteria inform what counts as a person to which these rights apply? Could, for example, we make sense of an ecosystemic "person" insofar as its many species of organism are endangered by human encroachment? Or does this stretch "harm" too far? Can nonsentient entities like bacteria have a right to "pursue" their infectious goals without interference? Is this any odder a proposition than that an anencephalic baby has a right to avoid abandonment or euthanasia? Diamond would surely be right here to suggest that these are simply not the sorts of considerations animating the parents' decision to bring the baby home. Still, this decision seems different from, say, determining whether to put down an ailing Golden Retriever, or to stop eating pork. While each of these may have some connection to suffering, it's also possible than none do. While its certainly possible to articulate each of these in the vocabulary of rights, even the libertarian's, it seems strained, and it's not clear that it achieves any important moral objective. Moreover, for the most part we really aren't libertarians. We do offer sympathy, compassion, or approval, but these too are not arguments, and may cleave more closely to why we don't consume our own dead.

Context does matter. If the language of "owing" seems misplaced in any or all of these scenarios, it may be because our response to the parents of the anencephalic baby isn't *about* the baby (or the parents), the dog or its human companion, the vegetarian or the factory farm pig. Our disposition to each of these, and hence our actual behavior, may simply be *given* as part of the expected repertoire of a particular moral community. Yet, as Singer and Regan would likely point out, an unexamined faith in cultural norms and traditions is as vulnerable to hypocrisy as the unexamined life is not worth living; it most certainly lends itself to the human chauvinism that any environmental ethic is intended to thwart. Is it hypocrisy to treat the anencephalic baby as if it were the subject of a life when it isn't, yet treat the factory farm pig as a mere commodity when its capacity for sentience wholly eclipses the infant's? We would be no more likely to euthanize the baby than we would be to eat its body after it dies. Yet, this seems beside the point in important ways with respect to the potential moral considerability of the factory farm pig. One of these is that the concept of "owing" applies not only to what is owed to moral agents—the parents, the dog owner, the vegetarian—but to what we may owe to others who act as witness, counsel, confessor, or agent in some other capacity. Consider again the Covid-19 outbreaks in US meat-packing plants. As Rebecca Rainey and Liz Crampton report for *Politico*,

> President Trump can force meat-packing plants to stay open during the pandemic, but his own administration hasn't required employers to provide safety equipment to prevent the virus' spread… Twenty meat-packing and processing workers have dies from the coronavirus. At least 6500 have tested positive for Covid-19, showing symptoms, missed work, or been hospitalized… ("Workers Turn to Courts and States…," 4.28.20)

While, as the *Politico* piece makes clear, workers from many industries have suffered sickness and death over the course of the pandemic, workers in slaughter houses and meat-packing plants provide an especially stark picture of an industry that recognizes "food animals" as sentient creatures only insofar as the term "euthanasia" is applied to describe killing them *prior* to what would have been their slaughter and consequent "processing" as meat. The hypocrisy of this word choice, particularly as it is situated in the context of portraying industrial meat "farmers" as victims of the corona virus, is plain: factory farm animals are not both sentient creatures such that killing them amounts to euthanasia, and nonsentient such that slaughtering them incurs no terror or suffering.

Yet the hypocrisy that pervades our cultural attitudes doesn't end at the factory farm door. What this Covid-19 example illustrates is that, despite the value attributed to "human being" such that people are not, for instance, a thing to eat, as workers, people are apparently a thing to exploit, use-up, and discard once they're sickened or killed by the pandemic. It's not surprising, of course, that such workers are disproportionately poor and/or female and/or black and Latinx. It's not even surprising that factory farm owners are portrayed as the "real" victims of the virus; they're "compelled" to "euthanize" their animal stock when it's no longer profitable to maintain them. Just as casting the slaughter of pigs before they reach their final destination as euthanasia, but the slaughter itself as merely "processing," so too casting the meat-packing workers as "essential" such that they can be denied access to unemployment benefits if they refuse to choose their jobs over their lives. In both cases, the potential for harm is preempted by appeal to an ostensibly higher value, in this case a "food" supply chain cast as "necessary."

Here is the moral dilemma: on the one hand, the vocabulary of an "appeal to higher value" presupposes sufficient capacity for self-reflection that we at least recognize the potential for harm to be preempted; yet, as Diamond might point out, this recognition seems unlikely insofar as few other than philosophers and animal rights theorists appear to be worried about anything other than whether the cost of meat will rise, or whether meat itself will become scarce. Just as people are not a thing to eat, pigs—or rather "pork"—is. On the other hand, that meat producers utilize the terms like "euthanasia" indicates that they're capable of self-reflection sufficient to recognize the moral relevance of sentience. You kill a flower, but euthanize a dog. It's not just the philosophers and the animal rights theorists who get that distinction. The first case makes it easy to paper over the fact that factory farms are in no way necessary to the food supply chain (indeed, given their mammoth land, water, and hydrocarbon use, the reverse is true). The second makes it more difficult; hence, the industrial premium of assigning the status of "victim" not to the millions of cows, chickens, and pigs destined for terror, suffering, and death, and not to the workers, thousands of whom have already experienced the terror and suffering of the corona virus, some to the point of death, but to the corporate heads "forced" to choose either "euthanizing" their animals or terminating the employment of workers who deem their own health and lives of greater value than their low wage, infection-vulnerable jobs.

It's hard to imagine an example that offers a more compelling aerial view of issues relevant to an environmental ethic than the Covid-19 pandemic and its devastating consequences for workers and nonhuman animals in an industry whose environmental footprint is already enormous. As reported by Kyle Bagenstose, et al., in *USA Today*:

> The meat-packing industry has already been notorious for poor working conditions even before the coronavirus pandemic. Meat and poultry workers have among the highest illness rates of all manufacturing employees and are less likely to report injuries and illness than any other type of worker... And the plants have been called out numerous times for refusing to let their employees use the bathroom, even to wash their hands... ("Coronavirus at Meatpacking Plants Worse Than First Thought...").

Add to this the contribution of growing, slaughtering, and processing of millions of "food" animals, transport to market sites, and the distribution of waste to lagoons, rivers, and fields—and what we discover is that the primary and largest product of concentrated animal feeding operations are greenhouse gas emissions, and thus the climactic change implicated in environmental conditions made ripe for future zoonotic transmission of virus strains.[35]

2.2.3   Whose Subject-of-a-life Matters?

Let's leave the aerial view aside for a bit so we can look more closely at some other important features of Regan's argument for animals' rights. A common criticism of Regan is that subject-of-a-life suffers from inconsistent practical application because it offers inadequate guidance with respect to prioritizing whose rights count for more in a conflict. Such conflicts, moreover, are bound to arise; in fact, they're inescapable. What if chimpanzees stood alone among primates other than human beings as valuable to HIV research? It's easy to condemn maternal bonding research as cruel and unnecessary. In fact, we don't need the subject-of-a-life criterion for this; Singer will do. But is HIV a different issue in virtue of its lethality? Even if we acknowledge the chimp's personhood, can we justify seeing it as less than ours on any other but human chauvinist grounds? Can "subject-of-a-life" be something we can quantify?[36] If the lab animals were gibbons or Colobus monkeys, not primates, would we see their use in medical research differently? What about dogs, cats, pigs, and mice? How about androids—self-aware robots? If we invent them to be enslaved, and they revolt, does their origin have any bearing on their moral status?[37] The problem, in other words, is that it's one thing to recognize that some, perhaps many, non-human animals enjoy the capacity to be subjects-of-their-own lives, and that these have a right to be treated with respect in line with their personhood. But it's another thing to develop criteria for determining what exactly we can and cannot do with respect to such animals and under what conditions, *even if we recognize that value.*

Perhaps, as many might agree, chimps should not be used as research animals; should they also no longer be bred in captivity for zoos, even if the primate enclosures are state-of-the-art humane?[38] Factory farms should be closed; but does that mean that the slaughter of cows who have led natural free range lives is also immoral?[39] It's difficult for Singer to defend the claim that depriving a sentient creature of its life, so long as the killing is painless and the life has been a natural one, constitutes suffering. But it's equally difficult for Regan to defend the claim that *if* the conditions of imprisonment are consistent with what a chimp's life might have been like in the wild (or better), *if the chimp is in no position to tell the difference,* that using it as a lab animal for experiments painless and unremembered violates its being the subject-of-a-life. Our repugnance is not necessarily theirs, and it's arguably human chauvinism, not moral concern, to simply assume that our sensibilities about what it's *like* to be the subjects-of-our-own-lives is mirrored in their experience, even if they're primates like us, and potentially much less so if they're, say, octopi. It will do neither Singer nor Regan much good, moreover, to insist that a human being would resist being painlessly killed or that a human being wouldn't find even the most resort-like prison unjust. This kind of anthropomorphizing, treating nonhuman animals not as subjects, but as *human* subjects, is liable to misconstrue what might be in the animal's best interest, violate its rights, and could even lead to real harm.

No doubt aware of what we might call the problem of prioritizing value, Regan conscripts a useful distinction common to bioethics intended to help clarify to what-all subject-of-a-life may apply, even for those cases where agency is less obvious or lacking: the distinction between *moral agents* and *moral patients*.[40] Both can be said to have an interest in their own welfare; an agent can pursue that welfare on her/his own, a moral patient is dependent to some greater or lesser extent on others to insure their interests are satisfied. A typical human adult can make a judgment about whether it's safe to cross a street; a small child can't. But it's in both their interests to cross safely. The grown-up qualifies as a subject-of-a-life and a moral agent; the child a subject and a moral patient. But let's take a less obvious case: what about people who, suffering serious brain damage, have succumbed to a deep variety of coma called a *persistent vegetative state*? They can no longer reasonably be considered *moral agents* because they're no longer able to formulate independent intentions. But do they qualify as moral *patients*? The comatose individual is capable neither of acting on her own behalf nor experiencing care given by others in any fashion that matters *for* or *to* her.[41] She's not, for example, like a small child who, lacking a developed capacity for reason, can still voice desires, feelings, etc.; she's not even like the octopus who, though a very different kind of creature, nonetheless evinces evidence of intention independent of mere sentience or external forces. And she's not quite like the anencephalic newborn because she *was* a subject-of-a-life, and the newborn wasn't. As Regan makes this point:

> For example, young children and the mentally enfeebled of all ages lack the requisite knowledge and sometimes even the requisite physical abilities to satisfy even their own basic needs and correlative desires. If we do not act on their behalf, they will fare ill. But even in the case of these individuals, their having a welfare, being the experiencing subject of a life that fares well or ill for them, logically independently of their utility for us or of our taking an interest in them—this fact about them is not causally dependent on what we do to or for them…. And the same is true both of those moral patients (e.g., animals in the

wild) who can take care of themselves without the need of human intervention and of those humans who are moral agents. (*The Case for Animal Rights*, p. 244)

The child and the "enfeebled" can fare well or poorly; the coma-stricken patient cannot, at least not in any obvious sense that a subject-of-a-life requires. And this matters: while the distinction between moral agency and moral patience seems straightforward enough, what species, much less which individuals, meet this minimum criterion of being a subject-of-a-life—to be able to be benefitted, to have an interest in faring well—is a tougher determination to make than Regan accounts for in *The Case for Animal Rights*.

The difficulty isn't that we can't draw a distinction between, say, a mushroom and a beagle; mushrooms aren't sentient, beagles are. The trouble is that sentience admits of many *degrees* of awareness such that at what point the threshold for qualifying as a moral patient is met, either for a species or within a species, may be extremely difficult both to define and to detect.[42] Indeed, this distinction seems to demand the kind of expert that most of us, however well-intended, aren't. Determining whether/when a human fetus becomes a subject-of-its-own-life, or when a comatose patient may no longer qualify, or what species of invertebrate reach the threshold of moral patient are not issues that can be settled by anything other than science, and science, of course, is subject to the revision of its hypotheses; whales are not fish, the universe is not geocentric. A credible moral extensionism that seeks to establish self-consciousness as the beachhead for what counts as a subject-of-a-life needs to be able to show the morally relevant difference between lobsters and octopi, fetuses and babies, black flies and honeybees—if it can. But that moral extensionism either needs its practitioners to be experts, or it needs to be supplemented with the precautionary principle. But if we adopt the latter, erring on the side of caution, we'll apply Regan's criteria to particular cases of apparent sentience regardless whether their status as subjects-of-a-life is fully evident (say, honey bees), whether we know it, or are likely to know it in the future. We'd treat other living and/or sentient things with respect regardless species unless they posed a threat to our own welfare. But once we've arrived at this juncture, the subject-of-a-life criterion has, if not fallen by the wayside, at least been diluted sufficiently to be largely as unnecessary to moral judgment and action.

While Regan can certainly allow for what he calls the "respect principle" to remain open to scientific review, he also insists that it's a matter of "strict justice" that we act to make sure moral patients (and not just moral agents) receive the respect they're due: "[t]o deny that moral patients have inherent value, or to affirm that they have less inherent value than moral agents ... is arbitrary" (*The Case for Animal Rights*, p. 264). Setting aside inherent value in favor simply of the application of the respect principle to moral patients, we might conclude that this was fair enough; but although Regan lays out in detail the qualities he takes to indicate the presence of a subject-of-a-life, his criteria remains silent on the question, for example, whether *potential* subjects-of-a-life are included, or past-subjects like the comatose. What about the *recently deceased*? Can they qualify as honorary subjects? Does this have an expiration date? Do human eggs or sperm qualify in virtue of their potential to come together and gestate a baby? Does that apply to frogs as well as people?[43] When Regan argues that "[t]he validity of the claim to respectful treatment, and thus the case for recognition of a right to such treatment, cannot be any stronger or weaker in the case of moral patients than it is in the case of moral agents," he affirms the rights of a class of self-aware entities often made vulnerable to harm in the form of abandonment or exploitation. But this affirmation doesn't tell us *when* in the course from potentiality to actuality something constitutes a subject-of-a-life—or when it ceases to do so. And it's not obvious that the sciences are in a position to make that moral distinction either. Science may be able to tell us when a developing fetus is likely to experience the first bits of consciousness, but because it's unlikely to be continuous it remains a matter of judgment whether that first bit is sufficient to count as a subject-of-a-life. Science can't tell us, then, whether it's immoral to eat eggs, have an abortion, disconnect a feeding tube.

2.2.4   Subjecthood, Intellectual Wherewithal—and Zombies

Another issue for Regan is that although defining "subject-of-a-life" in terms of self-awareness seems reasonable, what counts is not only a matter for philosophical and psychological debate; it's also increasingly an issue for the sciences, especially neurophysiology and neuropsychology. Is some level of *intellectual wherewithal* even at the level of moral patient, necessary to consti-tute "subject"? How do we measure that? Is it sufficient to be able to recognize oneself as *a* something *in a mirror*? Or must one be able to recognize oneself as *this* something? How do we measure either of these? Could a self-aware android count as a subject-of-a-life? If I'm conscious of myself as something other than what I actually am—say I think I'm a Martian—am I still a subject of *my* subject-of-a-life? What role does my brain play in this drama? What about zombies?[44] They're typically depicted as unconscious—yet they behave as if someone's home, sort of. These are all issues tethered to the practical appli-cability and empirical relevance of the subject-of-a-life criteria. They matter to an environmental ethics because adopting Regan's moral extentionism would entail radical change in many human practices, both personal and profit-ori-ented. The adoption of Regan's animals' rights argument would have profound effects on the use of nonhuman animals in product research, and perhaps more importantly in light of the Covid-19 pandemic, medical research. The necessity of radical change would follow even if Regan's criteria for moral considerability is more exclusive than Singer's. Can I take my kids to zoos (or circuses) if I understand zoo animals as captives objectified for human entertainment? Should I be willing to be a volunteer in a Covid-19 vaccine trial knowing that the research subjects that came before me were monkeys? Should I give up eating "food animals"? Should I join ALF, the *Animal Liberation Front*, to protest, perhaps even sabotage animal agricultural operations?[45] Should I volunteer for the *Sea Shepherd* to combat whaling?[46] Should I ever go to a Sea World?[47] In one sense, Regan's subject-of-a-life achieves what Singer's appeal to suffering can't quite reach: criteria for the respectful treatment of nonhuman others even if we're unable to establish whether they can experience suffering. But there's another sense in which Regan is arguably throwing out the baby with the bathwater: if we can't always be certain a given species of animal has the capacity for suffering, how much harder will it be to determine what has the capacity for self-consciousness? If it's a tricky business for at least some cases to differentiate reaction to stimuli from experience of pain how much more so is it to tell the difference between a merely sentient creature and a subject-of-life?

And this really matters because whatever has value independent of utility can't simply be converted to resource, commodity, or entertainment. This isn't, however, an argument for adopting the concept of inherent worth. Indeed, the fact that we can adopt it, apply it selectively, and discard it at will probably tell us more about the potentially inflated value we attach to "human being" than it does about whether we're committed to the extension of moral consideration to others. "Subject-of-a-life," after all, privileges qualities paradigmatic of human agency. Hence, it's not surprising that Regan extends moral considerability to mammals, but not further to nonhuman animals that have the capacity to suffer, but for whom things cannot be said necessarily to matter. The subject-of-a-life criterion for moral considerability is, in other words, in danger of begging an important question: given that it takes qualities associated with being human to be paradigmatic of qualities that have moral value, can it epitomize a genuine extension of moral considerability, or does it merely make a few exceptions to human chauvinism? At the end of the day, does Regan's moral extensionism really value nonhuman animals *as* creatures worthy of moral consideration on their own, or as human analogues worthy of moral consideration because they're (a bit) like us?

2.2.5 A Feminist Critique of the Subject-of-a-life Criterion for Moral Considerability

Few capture Regan's privileging of the capacity for self-reflective reason implicit in the subject-of-a-life criterion better than Josephine Donovan in her essay "Animal Rights and Feminist Theory," where she argues that:

Regan's criterion in fact privileges those with complex awareness over those without.... I do not quarrel with the idea that adult mammals have a highly developed intelligence that may be appropriated to human reason; rather I question the validity of the rationality criterion... From a cultural feminist point of view the position developed by utilitarian animal rights theorists is more tenable in this regard because it dispenses with the higher intelligence criterion insisting instead on the capacity to feel—or the capacity to suffer—as the criterion by which to determine those who are to be treated as ends [and not merely means or tools]. (p. 355)

In its elevation of "complex awareness," really a synonym for "reason," over sentience and feeling, the subject-of-a-life criterion risks reproducing the very inequalities that Regan explicitly rejects, namely, the structural inequalities that buttress racism, sexism, and speciesism:

In the articulation of [John] Locke and the framers of the U.S. Declaration of Independence and the Constitution not all humans were in fact considered sufficiently rational to be considered "persons" entitled to rights: only while male property owners were deemed adequately endowed to be included in the category of personhood... Here as elsewhere in Western political theory women and animals are cast together." (pp. 353–4)

Insofar as the capacity for self-reflective reason is identified with being a white, male property owner, "persons" who, in virtue of their superior capacities, have a "natural right" to dominate those dependent on "mere" sentience or feeling, it's hardly surprising that Regan's own reading of "personhood," subject-of-a-life, reinforces a hierarchy of value that denies to women, non-white men, and nonhuman animals the status of moral agent. Although he rejects the divide Kant cleaves between human beings and nonhuman animals, he effectively reproduces it in his own privileging of reason as foundational to personhood. Thus, while Regan ostensibly modifies the Categorical Imperative in two substantive ways:

- Extending "the category of those having absolute worth or inherent value to include non-rational but still intelligent nonhuman creatures," (p. 354).
- Defining "non-rational but still intelligent" to mean "complex awareness" or "complex consciousness," (pp. 354–5).

He nonetheless undermines his argument for "absolute worth" by positioning "complex awareness" as a stand-in for reason via the disclaimer "*but still intelligent.*" Indeed, as Donovan points out, even if we could address the structural inequalities endemic to racism and sexism, "complex awareness" still excludes whole classifications of human and nonhuman being, some of whom can suffer and some who cannot, including "severely retarded humans, humans in irreversible comas, fetuses, even human infants" (p. 355). Regan's is thus not so much a rejection of Kant, but rather an attempt to extend of the range of the Categorical Imperative. Yet it's not obvious that, given the *way* the capacity for reason is built into "subject-of-a-life," that the moral considerability Regan claims for nonhuman animals can be extended beyond some qualifying human beings, some higher primates, and some cetaceans.

Given the conceptual inconsistencies in Regan's argument, argues Donovan, it's not surprising that some feminists favor Singer's more inclusive utilitarian approach in virtue of its appeal to the capacity for sentience associated with maximizing happiness and minimizing suffering. The attraction to arguments like Singer's, she argues, is not inspired merely by the rejection of reason as necessary to moral considerability; it's also motivated by the feminist project to recuperate, as Donovan puts it, *feeling*, as a vital element of moral judgment:

> Utilitarian animal rights theory has the virtue of allowing some flexibility in decision-making, as opposed to Regan's absolutist stance that no animal's suffering is justifiable under any circumstances… Singer insists, for example, that an awareness of consequences can and should influence the evaluation of an individual's fate in any given situation. This leads him to admit that "there could conceivably be circumstances in which an experiment on an animal stands to reduce suffering so much that it would be permissible to carry it out even if it involved harm to the animal…[I]f some experimental procedure would hurt a human and a pig to the same extent, and there were no other relevant consequences,…it would be wrong to say that we should use the pig…." (p. 357)

Part of what's important here is that the appeal to feeling, the capacity for suffering and pleasure, is a critical driver in the pursuit of particular consequences where the concept of equality does the important work. If the suffering of a pig in the performance of medical experiment can predictably reduce the likelihood of suffering for many human beings—*where the balance of happiness over suffering can be quantified*—it may be permissible to use the pig even at the cost of harming it. That the possible harm is explicitly included in the utilitarian moral calculus is a matter of treating *all* those potentially affected by an action as relative *equals*. As we discussed earlier, however, the utilitarian approach raises some difficult questions of its own about what ends justify what means, when the means predictably cause harm. Donovan gives voice to this worry when she observes that the necessity to quantify suffering is a "mathematization" of morally significant beings that:

[w]hile it recognizes sensibility or feeling as the basis for treatment as a moral entity, the utilitarian position remains locked in a rationalist, calculative mode of moral reasoning that distances the moral entities from the decision-making subject... Just as... Regan inherently privileges rationality, Singer's utilitarianism relapses into a mode of manipulative mastery. (p. 358)

At the end of the day, there may not be as much daylight between Regan and Singer as seems at first glance, at least according to Donovan. On her view, the problem for both the rights and the utilitarian approach is essentially the same: privileging a concept of reason that tends to exclude or devalue feelings or relationships rooted in compassion or care, and devalue these, however unwittingly, in the interest of reinforcing forms of structural inequality whereby some human beings—male, white, Western(ized)—are preemptively identified with reason and therefore entitled to make decisions about the significance of suffering or what counts as the subject-of-a-life. While the role that reason plays in Regan's subject-of-a-life operates at the "micro" level, determining who or what qualifies as a person, in Singer it operates at the "macro" level, privileging quantitative or calculative evaluations of suffering over the individual.

Donovan's critique has important implications for how we characterize human chauvinism: it privileges not merely human beings, but a specific subset, namely, some men in virtue of their racial, economic, and geopolitical status. It's not surprising that traditional approaches to ethics, including its varieties of moral extensionism, tend to reinforce the presuppositions that empower this subset. But we also cannot escape the fact that the environmental crises we now face—crises that have the potential to produce a mammoth and inequitably distributed quotient of suffering—have been sponsored by no means exclusively, but nonetheless substantially, by white, property-commanding, Global North men.

2.2.6   Summary and Questions

Moral extensionism is the view that although the ethical concepts with which we're most familiar were originally intended to help us sort out *human* moral dilemmas, it may be possible to *extend* some or all of these to at least some others. Whether these "others" are individual nonhuman animals, entire species, biotic communities, or even the planet in its capacity to support life, they've largely been relegated to the outside of the moral community; or, as some put is, they're not party to the social contract. To extend a moral principle beyond its original scope, however, is not merely a matter of making the moral considerability tent bigger. We have to draft criteria for determining to whom or what the extension of a moral principle would apply. We need a clearer bead on concepts like "human being," "nonhuman animal," "environment," "sentient," "nonsentient," "living," "nonliving," "rights-bearing," "community," "contract," and "value," among others—and that's a pretty tall order.

We can also expect that the proponents of human chauvinism will raise objections. After all, expanding notions like "rights" to nonhuman animals and ecosystems poses the same threat to the social and economic status quo as did the inclusion of non-white, nonmale, and non-Western(ized), people in days gone by. For some, the extension of moral status to nonhuman animals poses an even greater threat to the social order in that, because it relies on science to tell us about sentience, consciousness, the capacity for pain and the like, many of our assumptions concerning the difference between "us" and "them" are challenged—if not squarely defeated. It poses a serious threat to the view that the planet, its resources, and nonhuman inhabitants, exist for the sake of human use: it's far more difficult to treat a thing as a commodity once were confronted with the prospect of its moral considerability—the possibility that our moral ideals may be arbitrary in their presumptive exclusion of nonhuman beings.

We turn our attention first to utilitarian philosopher, Peter Singer, who argues that insofar as we have a moral duty to maximize happiness and minimize suffering—the principle of utility's central premise—for at least some human beings, so too we have a duty to take into consideration the suffering of sentient nonhuman others. Singer calls this the *principle of equality*: "[i]f a being suffers, there can be no moral justification for refusing to take that suffering into consideration." He then extends the principle of equality to sentient entities capable of having an interest in avoiding suffering, arguing that having such an interest requires not reason, but only the capacity to experience pain and pleasure. Just as the principle of equality provides the moral justification for condemning racism and sexism, so too, argues Singer, it shows us why speciesism—elevating one's own species over others—is wrong at least with respect to species capable of suffering.

Singer's argument for moral extensionism is convincing and has many adherents, but it is not without some of the same problems that hound its anchor moral principle—utility. These problems range from the dicey business of predicting consequences, especially long-term consequences, to determining to what precisely the principle of equality applies. Climate change offers us a particularly apt example: the range of its impacts are planetary. No region, time zone, species, landmass, body of water, sample of air quality, human population, or business will be spared. Yet, exactly the nature, onset, frequency, or harm of its impacts is incredibly difficult to model. We know that climate change left unabated will produce a very different planet at the dawn of the twenty-second century, but exactly how and with what temporal trajectory—that's a hard question.

We next turn to Tom Regan whose aim it is to extend Immanuel Kant's Categorical Imperative to a subset of living things, namely, entities who qualify as a "subject of a life." We have a moral duty, argues Regan, to treat such subjects as we wish to be treated in insofar as their capacity to act on their interests is analogous to our own. They may not share the same *quotient* of intellect, but they're more than merely sentient, and as such constitute persons. On Regan's view moral considerability isn't about the ability to suffer *per se*, but the capacity for events in the world to *matter* to an *individual*, including but not exclusive to pain. Such subjects have inherent worth in virtue of the fact that their interests are "logically independent" from their utility to others.

Regan's view, however, is also not without its problems. Even though there's some fact of the matter for individual cases about whether they qualify as subjects, few of us have the scientific *expertise* to make judgments that fall outside the obvious; we know chairs aren't subjects-of-a-life, but what about octopi? This leaves judgment open to the self-interested, the taken-for-granted, and the arbitrary—a far cry from the morally considerable. Another problem is that even if we could reliably determine what counted as a subject-of-a-life, prioritizing whose rights count for more isn't solved by Regan's criterion. Sentience admits of many degrees of awareness such that it's difficult to define, much less detect, at what point the threshold for qualifying as a subject is met. Lastly, is there some level of *intellectual wherewithal* necessary to being a subject? Is the capacity to recognize oneself as *a* something in a mirror enough? Or must it be *this* something? Could nonliving, but sentient, entities like androids count? If I think I'm a Martian am I still a subject of *my* life? What about zombies? Insofar as the subject-of-a-life criterion takes qualities associated with being human to be paradigmatic of qualities that have moral value, does it actually extend moral considerability, or does it just make a few exceptions to human chauvinism?

1. What is moral extensionism? What's one advantage? One disadvantage?
2. What is Peter Singer's utilitarian version of moral extensionism? What are at least two reasons to embrace Singer's argument? What are at least two of its problems?
3. How does the concept of sentience play an important role in the extension of moral considerability to nonhuman animals and nonhuman nature?
4. What, for Tom Regan, is a subject-of-a-life? How does inherent worth/value play a key role in his version of moral extensionism?
5. What is the criticism, leveled primarily at Regan, that Cora Diamond raises with respect to moral extensionism?

6. What are at least two problems that arise in the application of subject-of-a-life to moral decision making?

7. What criticism is raised against Regan and Singer by ecofeminist philosopher Josephine Donovan with respect to definitions of reason that reinforce the social and cultural entitlements of some—mostly white and Western(ized) men?

Annotated Bibliography

Adams, Carol (2015). *Neither Man nor Beast: Feminism and the Defense of Animals* (Brooklyn, NY: Lantern Books).
Essentially a manifesto, Adams traces the complex and multiple relationships between the ways in which nonhuman animals and women have been conceived as commodities by a patriarchal and human-centered Western culture.
Bagenstose, Ken, Sky Chadde, and Matt Wynn. "Coronavirus at Meatpacking Plants Worse than First Thought, USA Today Investigation Finds." *USA Today*, April 22, 2020, https://www.usatoday.com/in-depth/news/investigations/2020/04/22/meat-packing-plants-covid-may-force-choice-worker-health-food/2995232001.
Bagenstose, Chadde, and Wynn report on the extent to which the American meat-packing industry exposes workers to working conditions made especially hazardous due to the Covid-19 pandemic.
Blackfish. http://www.blackfishmovie.com.
Documentary traces the treatment of whales and other marine life at Seaworld amusement parks.
Diamond, Cora. "Eating Meat and Eating People." in Martha Nussbaum and Cass Sunstein (ed.), *Animal Rights: Current Debates and New Directions* (Oxford University Press, 2004), ch. 4.
Diamond offers a trenchant critique of Peter Singer's and Tom Regan's approach to animal rights, arguing that the kinds of considerations that effectively preempt any discussion of rights have more to do with uninterrogated cultural practices about what counts as a thing to eat.
Donovan, Josephine. "Animal Rights and Feminist Theory." *Signs* 15 (2), (Winter 1990), pp. 350–75.
Donovan argues that neither Tom Regan's rights-based theory for nonhuman animals rights nor Peter Singer's utilitarian approach to moral considerability are adequate, and both unwittingly reinforce racist and patriarchal norms. She argues for a cultural feminist approach that takes the feeling of connection to nonhuman life as its guiding moral premise.

Francione, Gary L. "Animal Rights Theory and Utilitarianism: Relative Normative Guidance," *Animal Legal and Historical Center*, 1997, https://www.animallaw.info/article/animal-rights-theory-and-utilitarianism-relative-normative-guidance.

Francione offers a good general introduction to Peter Singer's utilitarian view of animal rights.

Gould, James and Carol Grant Gould (1974). *Animal Architects: Building and the Evolution of Intelligence* (New York: Basic Books).

James Gould and Carol Grant Gould offer a compelling evolutionary account of intellectual wherewithal in the context of the capacity to build structures like nests.

Goodall, Jane. "Chimpanzees and Change." *Johns Hopkins CAAT Newsletter* 14 (1), (1996). http://caat.jhsph.edu/publications/Newsletter/Volume%20 14/Number%201/editorial.html.

Goodall argues against the claim that Chimpanzees are useful in AIDS research.

Gruen, Lori. "The Moral Status of Animals," *Stanford Encyclopedia of Philosophy*, Originally published July 1, 2003, revised August 23, 17. https:// plato.stanford.edu/entries/moral-animal.

Gruen argues that the sorts of qualities we have typically taken to justify human exceptionalism are not unique to human beings, and thus raise thorny questions about the way we treat nonhuman animals given that exceptionalism is false.

Jamieson, Dale (2014). *Reason in a Dark Time: Why the Struggle against Climate Change Failed and What It Means for Our Future* (Oxford: Oxford University Press.

Shows how our incapacity to think beyond immediate threats has thwarted our efforts to address climate change.

Maughan, Chris. *The Moral Status of Animals. IAS early Career Fellow*, https:// warwick.ac.uk/fac/cross_fac/iatl/study/ugmodules/humananimalstudies/ lectures/2/the_moral_status_of_animals_-_slides_2016.pdf.

Maughan offers a very compelling illustrated lecture that succinctly captures at least some of the issues at the intersection of animal rights and environmental ethics.

National Institutes of Health (NIH), "*Chimps and Research*," https://www. mspca.org/animal_protection/chimps-and-research.

This essay examines the language commonly used in the way researchers characterize their use of nonhuman primates in medical research, in this case for AIDS.

Rainey, Rebecca and Liz Crampton. "Workers Turn to Courts and States for Safety Protection as Trump Declines to Act," *Politico*, April 28, 2020.

https://www.politico.com/news/2020/04/28/workers-court-states-safety-protection-trump-217372.

Rainey and Crampton report on the failure of the Trump administration to invoke safety protections in American meat-packing plants during the 2020 Covid-19 outbreak.

Regan, Tom (1983). *The Case for Animal Rights* (Berkeley: University of California Press).

Regan extends Immanuel Kant's moral principle, the Categorical Imperative, to what he calls a subject-of-a-life—nonhuman animals capable of making themselves subjects of their own lives and actions.

Regan, Tom (2003). *Animal Rights, Human Wrongs: An Introduction to Moral Philosophy* (New York: Rowman and Littlefield).

Regan situates his argument for animal rights in the broader context of moral philosophy and human history.

Regan, Tom (2006). *Defending Animal Rights* (Urbana, Ill: University of Illinois Press).

Regan continues his argument in the defense of animal rights, addressing criticism and providing a discussion of specific issues.

Singer, Peter (2001). *Animal Liberation* (New York: Ecco Press).

This is Singer's groundbreaking work in the extension of the principle of utility to nonhuman animals, especially with respect to the right not to be made to suffer unnecessarily.

Singer, Peter. "*All Animals Are Equal*." https://spot.colorado.edu/~heathwoo/phil1200,Spr07/singer.pdf.

Here, Singer expands on his argument for nonhuman animal rights by comparing the animal rights movement to the movements to end discrimination against persons of color and women.

Singer, Peter. "Factory Farming: A Moral Issue," *The Minnesota Daily*, 2006. https://www.utilitarian.net/singer/by/20060322.htm.

Focusing specifically on Concentrated Animal Feeding Operations—CAFOs—Singer argues that the conditions of the lives of "food animals" is morally inconsistent with our commitment to avoid unnecessary suffering.

Singer, Peter (2005). *In Defense of Animals: The Second Wave*. New York: Wiley-Blackwell.

Singer reflects on his argument for moral extensionism, expands on its central premises, and addresses criticism.

Singer, Peter and Jim Mason (2006). *The Ethics of What We Eat: Why Our Food Choices Matter* (Emmaus, PA: Rodale).

Singer and Mason offer a moral and an environmental argument for veganism.

Online Resources

1. "Extending Moral Standing, Environmental Ethics," *Internet Encyclopedia of Philosophy*, https://www.iep.utm.edu/envi-eth/#H1.
2. Peter Singer, "All Animals Are Equal," https://spot.colorado.edu/~heath woo/phil1200,Spr07/singer.pdf.
3. Megan Molteni, "Why Meat-Packing Plants Have Become Covid-19 Hot Spots," *Wired*, May 7, 2020, https://www.wired.com/story/why-meatpacking-plants-have-become-covid-19-hot-spots.
4. Carol Adams, "Sexual Politics of Meat and the Absent Referent," *Earthling Liberation Kollective: Community Empowerment and Species-Inclusive Social Justice*, https://humanrightsareanimalrights.com/2015/01/02/carol-j-adams-politics-and-the-absent-referent-in-2014.
5. S. Mas-Coma, M.A. Valero, and M.D. Bargues, "Effects of Climate Change on Animal and Zoonotic Helminthiases," *Review of Scientific Technology*, 2008, Issue 27.2, pp. 443–52, https://pdfs.semanticscholar.org/ae11/3c126 ff26054d8411f0f2ad45c3206f7dc45.pdf.
6. Judy Weiss, "Michael Mann's Hockey Stick Gives Readers a Handle on the Science of Climate Change," *Citizen's Climate Lobby*, https://citizensclimatelobby.org/michael-manns-hockey-stick-gives-readers-a-handle-on-the-science-of-climate-change.
7. Ronald White, "The Principle of Utility," https://faculty.msj.edu/whiter/utility.htm.
8. Mark T. Brown, "The Moral Status of the Human Embryo," *The Journal of Medicine and Philosophy*, https://academic.oup.com/jmp/article-abstract/4 3/2/132/4931241?redirectedFrom=fulltext.
9. Peter Singer, "Factory Farming: A Moral Issue," *The Minnesota Daily*, 2006, https://www.utilitarian.net/singer/by/20060322.htm.
10. Peter Singer, "There's No Good Reason to Keep Apes in Prisons," *Wired*, May 26, 2015, https://www.wired.com/2015/05/peter-singer-no-good-reason-keep-apes-prison.
11. "Why Go Vegan?" *The Vegan Society*, https://www.vegansociety.com/go-vegan/why-go-vegan.
12. "Act and Rule Utilitarianism," *Internet Encyclopedia of Philosophy*, https://www.iep.utm.edu/util-a-r.
13. "Calculating Consequences: The Utilitarian Approach to Ethics," *The Markkula Center for Applied Ethics*, Santa Clara University, https://www.scu.edu/ethics/ethics-resources/ethical-decision-making/calculating-consequences-the-utilitarian-approach.

14. "Circuses," *People for the Ethical Treatment of Animals* (PETA), https://www.peta.org/issues/animals-in-entertainment/circuses.

15. Bibek Bhandari and Nicole Lim, "The Dark Side of China's Solar Boom," *Sixth Tone*, July 17, 2018, https://www.sixthtone.com/news/1002631/the-dark-side-of-chinas-solar-boom-.

16. Robinson Meyer, "Why Greta Makes Adults Uncomfortable," *The Atlantic*, September 23, 2019. https://www.theatlantic.com/science/archive/2019/09/why-greta-wins/598612.

17. "Water Crisis: Systemic Racism Through the Lens of Flint." *Report of the Michigan Civil Rights Commission*, February 17, 2017, https://www.michigan.gov/documents/mdcr/VFlintCrisisRep-F-Edited3-13-17_554317_7.pdf.

18. S. Nazrul Islam and John Winkel, "Climate Change and Social Inequality," *United Nations, Department of Economic and Social Affairs*, Working Paper No. 152, 10.17.

19. Mike Bowers, "Waiting for the Tide to Turn: Kiribati's Fight for Survival," *The Guardian*, October 22, 2017, https://www.theguardian.com/world/2017/oct/23/waiting-for-the-tide-to-turn-kiribatis-fight-for-survival.

20. Mark Fischetti, "Climate Change Hastened Syria's Civil War," *Scientific American*, March 2, 2015. https://www.scientificamerican.com/article/climate-change-hastened-the-syrian-war.

21. Peter Singer, "200 Pigs Versus One Baby," *Ave Maria Radio*, June 26, 2015, https://www.youtube.com/watch?v=PpkSbcPBHow.

22. "Curbing Climate Change: Why It's So Hard to Act in Time," *The Conversation*, August 17, 2017, https://theconversation.com/curbing-climate-change-why-its-so-hard-to-act-in-time-80117.

23. A. E. Cahill, et. al., "How Does Climate Change Cause Extinction?" *Proceedings of the Royal Society*, September 24, 2012, http://rspb.royalsocietypublishing.org/content/royprsb/280/1750/20121890.full.pdf.

24. Tamar Stelling, "Do Lobsters and Other Invertebrates Feel Pain?" *Washington Post*, March 10, 2014. https://www.washingtonpost.com/.lobsters./f026ea9e-9e59-11e3-b8d8-94577ff66b.

25. Katherine Harmon Courage, "Do Octopuses Feel Pain?" *Scientific American, Blog*, August 30, 2013, https://blogs.scientificamerican.com/octopus-chronicles/do-octopuses-feel-pain.

26. Bell Hooks, "Beyonce's Lemonade is Capitalist Money-Making at its Best," *The Guardian*, May 11, 2016. https://www.theguardian.com/music/2016/may/11/capitalism-of-beyonce-lemonade-album.

27. R. Johnson's, "Kant's Moral Philosophy," *Stanford Encyclopedia of Philosophy*, July 7, 2016, https://plato.stanford.edu/entries/kant-moral.

28. Lilly Marlene Russow, "Regan on Inherent Value," *Between the Species*, March, 1987. https://digitalcommons.calpoly.edu/cgi/viewcontent.cgi?referer= https://www.google.com/&httpsredir=1&article=1679&context=bts.
29. "Anencephaly," *Genetics Home Reference: National Institutes of Health*, https://ghr.nlm.nih.gov/condition/anencephaly.
30. Joyce L. Peabody, et al. "Experience with Anencephalic Infants as Prospective Organ Donors," *New England Journal of Medicine*, August 10, 1989, https://www.nejm.org/doi/full/10.1056/NEJM198908103210602.
31. Dylan Matthews, "It's Time to Put Down the Hemmingway and Accept that the Running of the Bulls is Horrifying," *VOX*, June 29, 2018, https://www.vox.com/2016/7/5/12072534/running-of-the-bulls-bullfighting-pamplona-san-fermin.
32. Anne Wooten, "What are the Smartest Primates?" *Discover*, January 10, 2006, http://discovermagazine.com/2006/nov/primate-iq-hierarchy.
33. George Johnson, "The Battle for the Great Apes: Inside the Fight for Nonhuman Rights," *Pacific Standard*, November 21, 2016, https://psmag.com/news/the-battle-for-the-great-apes-inside-the-fight-for-non-human-rights.
34. Andy Wright, "Pigheaded: How Smart Are Swine?" *Modern Farmer*, March 10, 2014, https://modernfarmer.com/2014/03/pigheaded-smart-swine.
35. S. Mas-Coma, M.A. Valero, and M.D. Bargues. "Effects of Climate Change on Animal and Zoonotic Helminthiases," *Review of Scientific Technology*, 2008, Issue 27.2, pp. 443–52. https://pdfs.semanticscholar.org/ae11/3c126 ff26054d8411f0f2ad45c3206f7dc45.pdf.
36. Jane Goodall, "Chimpanzees and Change," *Johns Hopkins CAAT Newsletter*, January 14, 1996, http://caat.jhsph.edu/publications/Newsletter/Volume% 2014/Number%201/editorial.html.
37. *I-Robot*, film, director Alex Proyas, 2004, https://www.youtube.com/watch?v=XtG-vK88K0Q.Viagas, Jennifer. "Captivity Affects Zoo Chimps' Mental Health," *Science, NBC News*, 7.5.11. http://www.nbcnews.com/id/43641745/ns/technology_and_science-science/t/captivity-affects-zoo-chimps-mental-health/#.XAMWBi2ZMvE.
38. James McWilliams, "Why Free-Ranged Meat Isn't Much Better Than Factory-Farmed," *The Atlantic*, December 7, 10. https://www.theatlantic.com/health/archive/2010/12/why-free-range-meat-isnt-much-better-than-factory-farmed/67569.
39. Morton Winston, "Moral Patients," *An Ethics of Global Responsibility*, http://ethicsofglobalresponsibility.blogspot.com/2008/02/moral-patients.html.
40. "Schiavo Autopsy Shows Irreversible Brain Damage," *US News*, June 15, 2005, http://www.nbcnews.com/id/8225637/ns/us_news/t/schiavo-autop syshows-irreversiblebrain-damage/#.XAMaUi2ZMvE.

41. Joshua Hehe, "The Different Degrees of Awareness," *Medium*, January 13, 2017, https://medium.com/@joshuashawnmichaelhehe/the-different-degrees-of-awareness-69cc39b1e0f6.
42. C. Allen, "Animal Consciousness," *Stanford Encyclopedia of Philosophy*, October 24, 2016, https://plato.stanford.edu/entries/consciousness-animal/.
43. Mike Mariani, "The Tragic Forgotten History of Zombies," *The Atlantic*, October 28, 15, https://www.theatlantic.com/entertainment/archive/2015/10/how-america-erased-the-tragic-history-of-the-zombie/412264.
44. *Animal Liberation Front* (ALF), http://www.animalliberationfront.com.
45. *Sea Shepherd*, https://seashepherd.org.
46. *Blackfish*, http://www.blackfishmovie.com.

TWO MORE EXAMPLES OF MORAL EXTENSIONISM: CHRISTOPHER STONE, HOLMES ROLSTON III, AND THEIR CRITICS

3.1 The Rights of Trees: The "Moral Standing" Extensionism of Christopher Stone

3.1.1 Moral Extensionism, the Concept of "Wilderness," and Human Chauvinism

It might seem at this point that we've strayed a bit from our original mission of drafting an *environmental* ethic. We've been focused on the question to what all can we extend moral principles like utility or the categorical imperative, and this compels us to consider capacities like consciousness, sentience, and intellectual wherewithal in order to gain a firm foothold on just how far moral extensionism can go. It might seem that we've not said much about the environment, at least directly, at all. But we're right on course. We've simply made it a point not to prejudice the question *to what* the possible extension of a moral principle might rightly apply. We've sought to avoid *exclusions* that would seem arbitrary—that would *be* arbitrary. Adopting a kind of agnosticism about what that range of inclusion might be will help us avoid treating the environment as mere background for human projects. We've already enlivened our discussion of the planet's ecosystems by introducing an array of human and nonhuman beings, as well as a range of capacities, interactions, and limitations. By refusing to adopt a rigid distinction between ecosystems and the countless species, cultures, and societies that inhabit their

This is Environmental Ethics: An Introduction, First Edition. Wendy Lynne Lee.
© 2022 John Wiley & Sons, Inc. Published 2022 by John Wiley & Sons, Inc.
Companion Website: https://thisisphilosoph.wordpress.com

deserts, plains, and mountains, their oceans, prairies, tundra, reefs, rivers, rainforests, and ice-flows we're reminded that "the environment" is a dynamic physical, social, and historical *event* as well as a *place* composed of many facets of chemical, biological, and evolutionary, but also predatory, symbiotic, parasitic, and social relationships.

By making one of our early foci the individual, we're reminded that the capacity for suffering occupies a particularly important role in any ethic, but especially any variety of moral extensionism for which sentience takes center stage. Because the life worth living grounds itself in respect for facts and science, whatever environmental ethic we adopt isn't likely to have room for the idea that "the environment" is a thing *out there*, a thing with which we can engage when it suits us and set aside when it doesn't. It doesn't—or at least it shouldn't—take a firenado, or images of climate crisis refugees, or a pandemic to teach us that organic and inorganic, sentient and nonsentient, living and nonliving, are themselves ecosystems in and among ecosystems. Yet, given the derelict ways we often treat them, it seems we can't be reminded too often that our bodies are ecosystems just like those of trees and cows and birds, and that our communities are ecosystems however we refer to them as "city" or "town," "village" or "metropolis."[1]

The history of those communities, however, is also the history of our expansion over the planet's land masses, waterways, oceans, and airspace. The way we've sought to characterize and justify various cultural and economic ventures offers insight into to the value of articulating an environmental ethic and into the ways human-centeredness has advanced, but also distorted and even thwarted the life worth living. In "The Trouble with Wilderness," for example, William Cronon argues that "the time has come to rethink" the concept of "wilderness," the environment "out there" illustrated in images of the "unknown" and the "refuge," the "alien" and the "paradise." Cronon argues that exploring the history of "wilderness" reveals that

> [f]ar from being the one place on earth that stands apart from humanity, it is quite profoundly a human creation—indeed, the creation of very particular human cultures at very particular moments in human history. It is not a pristine sanctuary where the last remnant of an untouched, endangered, but still transcendent nature can for at least a little while be encountered without the contaminating taint of civilization. Instead, it is a product of that civilization, and could hardly be contaminated by the very stuff of which it is made. (p. 7)

Cronon traces the history of the modern notion of "wilderness" as quite different from incarnations 250 years earlier as "'deserted,' 'savage,' 'desolate,' or 'barren,' (p. 8) or even earlier Biblical associations that refer to "places on the margins of civilization where it is all too easy to lose oneself in moral confusion and despair" (p. 8). He then remarks on the striking transformation of "wilderness" in the late nineteenth and early twentieth-century America that gave rise to the conservation movement with its competing narratives of, for some, a frontier, for others, a romantic or sublime escape, and for others still, adventure (pp. 9–10).

As Cronon shows, however, *for whom* "wilderness" provides the frontier of the rugged individualist (pp. 13–14), the romantic solitude of the poet (pp. 11–12), the sublime to the spiritual seeker (pp. 9–11), or adventurous quest to the explorer (pp. 15–17)—that "who" itself affords an opportunity to gain a clearer perspective on the ways in which human interests govern the meaning of such concepts. As Cronon shows, such interests turn out to be as much about how we *desire* to see ourselves as they are about the environment, and more often than we might want to acknowledge, what we desire most is to be seen as conquerors of "mother nature," commandeers of property, or developers of "endless" resources. For Cronon, the darker truth about "Wilderness" is that it signals a cover story for invidious displays of wealth; it appeals to an ethic of environmental conservation as a justification for acquisition and commodification:

> Thus, the decades following the Civil War saw more and more of the nation's wealthiest citizens seeking out wilderness for themselves. The elite passion for wild lands took many forms: enormous estates in the Adirondacks… cattle ranches for would-be rough riders on the Great Plains, guided big-game hunting trips in the Rockies, and luxurious resort hotels wherever railroads pushed their way into sublime landscapes… One went to the wilderness not as a producer, but as a consumer. (p. 16)

Part of Cronon's point is that such lands had to be convincingly portrayed as "wild" in order to become objects worthy of conquering as "property," exhibited as "wild" to be advertised as highly valuable objects of acquisition and domestication, a paradox that threads its way throughout twentieth-century images of "wilderness." "Wild" is essentially a billboard that serves to cultivate commodity value, having little to do with the untamed, and much to do with a kind of theater intended as marketing. Mountains become estates, the Great Plains become ranchland; railroads render the sublime into dusty hardtack towns and vanquished peoples. The American Bison is driven nearly to extinction, its market value rising as its numbers plummet.[2] The environmental cost of "wilderness" is mirrored, argues Cronon, in the social hierarchies that make its domestication possible. Had "wild lands" been widely accessible to regular soldiers returning from the Civil War, the social order that gave birth to "wilderness" would have been threatened with disruption; insofar, that is, as "wilderness" is deeply anchored in the racist politics of slavery, the anti-feminist politics of denying women the franchise, and the myth of endless resources, it is a reflection of social and economic drivers moving Westwards as well as the need to justify the immense human, nonhuman animal, and ecological cost of that conquest to those decimated by it. The picture Cronon presents us is a dark one. Once we strip away the mythology of the pristine and the untouched, however, an even darker reality of the human chauvinism implicit in "wilderness" begins to emerge. As Cronon explains:

> The movement to set aside national parks and wilderness areas followed hard on the heels of the final Indian wars, in which the prior human inhabitants of these areas were rounded up and moved onto reservations. The myth of the wilderness as "virgin," uninhabited land had always been especially cruel when seen from the perspective of the Indians who had once called that land home. Now they were forced to move elsewhere, with the result that tourists could safely enjoy the illusion that they were seeing their nation in its pristine, original state, in the new morning of God's creation. (p. 15)

Perhaps the most important lesson in the history of "wilderness" is not only that it's an invention of human chauvinism, but that human chauvinism has been realized in ways that reveal a relationship with nonhuman nature deeply imbued with the prejudices and motives that inform social hierarchies in human communities, as well as the capitalist aspirations driving Westward expansion. "Wilderness" can show us something about the ways in which culture is always, at least partly, about controlling nonhuman nature, making it over according to some human interests; but it also mirrors the often horrific cost to those who present an obstacle to the maintenance of that control. "The trouble with wilderness, argues Cronon, is that it quietly expresses and reproduces the very values its devotees seek to reject," namely, consumption, domination, and waste (p. 16). This is the central paradox: "wilderness embodies a dualistic vision in which the human is entirely outside of the natural," (p. 17). We'd not seek to return to something from which we were not alienated in the first place; yet "wilderness" wouldn't be the magnate it is but for the sense that we are somehow outside of it.

Insofar, however, as the values that the devotees of "wilderness" reject, or perhaps closer to the truth, *pretend* to reject—materialism, artificiality, waste— are tethered to a history of expulsion, brutality, flagrant racism, and genocide, it's not especially hard to predict that the consequences of that history will be an enduring legacy of suffering. Few examples could better illustrate that suffering and its intimate relationship to the land than the devastating effects of the Covid-19 pandemic on the Navajo Nation. Although the Navajo Reservation is the largest in the United States, encompassing more than 17 million acres across Utah, Arizona, and,[3] it's also among the poorest and most economically disadvantaged, including a sky-high rate of unemployment, an absence of electricity, running water, or indoor plumbing in at least a third of households, and chronic overcrowding in substandard homes that are often no larger than two rooms.[4] There are twelve regional healthcare clinics,[5] but like many (especially rural) hospitals across the United States, the *Indian Health Service* (IHS) found itself ill-equipped to confront a virus with few treatment options and no vaccine.

Among those to call attention to the rising number of Covid-19 cases and the gross inadequacy of the federal government response to the pandemic in Indian Country was the Chair of the *Natural Resources Committee* of the United States Congress, Raul M. Grijalva, in a letter to the US Department of Health and Human Services (HHS), where, among other issues, he queries how federal relief funds are going to be allocated, the long wait times for virus-testing, whether there's a plan for handling cases in multigenerational homes, and how scare resources like Intensive Care Unit (ICU) beds and personal protective equipment (PPE) are going to reach these rural communities.[6] The practical nature of his questions notwithstanding, the context of Grijalva's inquiry is clear to anyone who, like Cronon, understands the history of dispossession: the inferno of Covid-19 that spread through the Navajo Nation is the direct result of a deadly combination of highly polluted environmental conditions, long-standing paucity of educational and economic opportunity, the resultant chronically high levels of diabetes, alcoholism, and drug abuse, and lack of access to basic preventative healthcare on the reservation. As Kalen Goodluck reports for *Wired*,

> The novel coronavirus has ravaged much of the world, yet its impact has been particularly acute on the Navajo Nation, where it is pushing the tribes health system to its limits. Decades of negligence and billions of dollars of unmet need from the federal government have left tribal nations without basic infrastructure like running water and sewage systems along with sparse Internet access and an underfunded Indian Health Service.[7]

The wilderness imagined by the mostly white and wealthy is not what the indigenous peoples of the Americas have been left to scrape out a living, and it is manifestly not the uranium rich mining opportunity of which companies like United Nuclear Corporation took advantage—violating through pollution, working condition, and exposure to radioactive materials the basic human rights of the Navajo, the Hopi, and countless other Native American tribal peoples who worked at or lived near the mines. It is darkly ironic to be sure that the lands to which indigenous peoples have been discarded turned out to be highly profitable opportunities for mining the heavy metals used in the conduct of foreign wars by the American government's *Manhattan Project* and by the *United States Atomic Energy Commission*. But it's also a textbook demonstration of how the structural inequalities of racism and the intimate companion of "wilderness," namely, property, gave rise to a human chauvinism ill-suited to the containment of a super-spreader virus like Covid-19.

"One went into the wilderness not as a producer but as a consumer," writes Cronon, a claim that provides the vital link between the environmental, the economic, and the social that fuels the paradox of values espoused in the embrace of "wilderness" and, especially in the case of a pandemic, hastens its collision with the reality behind it. But what's also true, as Cronon argues, is that there would be no concept of "wilderness" as a *refuge* or *escape* were it not the case that this reality instantiated precisely the environmental destruction responsible for the hazards only the wealthy are equipped to escape. And, of course, "escape" is as much a myth as is "wilderness" since neither Covid-19 nor the climate crisis to which uranium mining contributes are reserved to the borders of nation states, geography, social or economic class, to race, gender, or sex.[8] Certainly, the wealthy mining company CEO can afford better healthcare, can live in safer more antiseptic environs, and can evade having to witness the consequences of his/her company's operations, but even he/she is constrained by the planet and its toxified atmosphere.

Yet, while we can perhaps disabuse mining company CEOs of their paradoxical fantasy, what can "wilderness" even mean to the disenfranchised Navajo mother who risks viral exposure going to work at a meat-processing plant in Gallup, New Mexico, in order to feed her family,[9] bringing home the virus with the paycheck, unintentionally infecting and killing her own parents who live with her and her children? Can "wilderness" be anything other than a grim reminder of environmental injustice to someone whose two-room dilapidated house lacks running water and the basic capacity for thorough sanitation? To someone reminded by her own parent's diagnosis of kidney damage that the water may be radioactive? Someone effectively forced to choose between money to buy food and healthcare for herself and her family? The Navajo mother certainly knows the uranium mining industry's toxic legacy of radioactive pollution, that it taints the drinking water and the soil of her community, jeopardizing the health of its members, human and nonhuman alike. The reminders are everywhere—in the warning notices outside barbwire fencing of abandoned mine sites, in the news reports of disease, and in the bodies of those afflicted. Her life personifies the intersection between environmental justice, economic justice, and human rights.

Yet for the Navajo mother there is no easy escape, no way to make substantive change out of her rights—and that is part of the cruelty. As Erin Klauk documents for *Integrating Research and Education*:

Despite efforts made in cleaning up uranium sites, significant problems stemming from the legacy of uranium development still exist today on the Navajo Nation. Hundreds of abandoned mines have not been cleaned up and present environmental and health risks in many Navajo communities. In addition to this, Navajo communities now have to face proposed new uranium solution mining that threatens the only source of drinking water for 10,000 to 15,000 people living in the Eastern Navajo Agency in northwestern New Mexico ... In terms of both short and long term environmental impact, uranium mining is by far the most problematic of any mining activity because radioactivity of the ore presents an intangible that cannot be chemically mitigated.[10]

No one calls this pristine wilderness, even if some—including those coerced by economic necessity to work in uranium solution mining—still call this land home; indeed, this land *is* home, and remains if not "wilderness" nonetheless sacred ground to the Navajo and the Hopi.[11] What word, however, captures the home, the long and sacred history, of land despoiled by, for example, by what Klauk details in the 1979 Church Rock disaster where a burst dam discharges "eleven-hundred tons of radioactive mill wastes and ninety million gallons of contaminated liquid pouring downstream towards Arizona"? It's surely not "wilderness," and it's unclear whether any extension or expansion of moral principles intended to navigate and resolve human conflict can be adequately outfitted to challenge the human chauvinism responsible for this disaster.

Catastrophes like Church Rock do, however, illustrate one of Cronon's central insights: land painted as "wilderness" by those socially and economically empowered to commandeer it was never wilderness to those who, for millennia, called it home. Now despoiled by uranium mining, that same land, though it remains sacred, cannot be home—at least if "home" means safety—even to those who try to scrape out a subsistence on it; it has been commodified, extracted, and abandoned in the quest for precisely that power to determine its, and its inhabitants' fates who have themselves been commodified as mine workers and abandoned as "Indians." If there are rights violated in this grim story, it's difficult to ferret out where they begin and end. This is not because there is no harm; it's because the harm is great, but also diffuse. The harm afflicts not only the indigenous peoples whose lives and lands are compromised, but the water contaminated, the animals poisoned, the trees uprooted, and the land scarred and left for desolate. The radioactivity left by the uranium mining, the climate altered by the greenhouse gas emissions of a packing plant waste lagoon, the invisible asymptomatic spread of a virus—all are harm. But even if we, like Singer and Regan, are ready to extend the notion of rights to the factory farm animals "processed" at the meat-packing plant in virtue of the sentience they share in common with the Navajo mother, can we make sense of such an extension to the trees? To the waterways? To the land? There are, of course, the rights of the Navajo mother to work under safe conditions, to have access to safe drinking water and health care, and to food security. But if it seems contrived to talk about her rights outside of the environmental, economic, cultural, and social circumstances that brought her to care for her elderly parents, to work at a meat-packing plant, to be dependent on bottled water, or to Covid-19, perhaps it does so because her rights are somehow connected to the rights of those things upon which she depends—the water, the trees, the land. Is Cronon's diagnosis of the history of "wilderness" grim only because what we glean from it is a chronicle of egregious human rights abuses? Certainly not for Cronon. If the story of "wilderness" is grim, it's because it illustrates the intimacy of the relationship between environmental, economic, and social justice. But its key player is wilderness. That is, its key players are the water, the trees, and the land. Can we extend the notion of rights to them? Or, perhaps better: can the rights of the Navajo mother be divorced from those of the water, the trees, or the land in any way that doesn't grossly distort the stories of all three?

3.1.2   Do Trees Have Rights? The Portability of Moral Standing

Whereas Singer's appeal to the principle of utility concentrates on the capacity to suffer regardless other differences between or within a species, Regan's narrower "subject-of-a-life" introduces us to the possibility of extending moral considerability to specifically sentient nonhuman individuals for whom things can matter, for whom "life" means a life recognized as such. Regan's criteria for membership in the moral community shifts the focus from what we can know about the capacity for suffering at the level of species to the status of particular subjects whose unique experience defines them as *this* subject. Rights-oriented theorist Christopher Stone retains Regan's focus on the individual, but makes his focus neither the capacity for sentience nor status as a living or nonliving thing. Neither, he argues, constitute necessary conditions for counting as morally considerable. Parting ways with both the appeal to suffering and to self-consciousness, Stone argues for a *moral standing* modeled after the legal status accorded to *nonsentient, nonliving* conventional entities like corporations, governments, or religious institutions. If human-made artifacts like businesses can count as persons protected by the law, so too nonsentient *living* things like trees. Both can be said to have an interest in avoiding harm; hence it stands to reason, argues Stone, that moral *standing* derives from the moral *considerability* of interests, and that interests can be represented as *litigable*, that is, they can be represented in a court of law where what governs a determination of whose interests take priority in a given case is presumed, at a minimum, to be the equality of the parties. If the interests of a business such as Exxon-Mobil can be represented in a court of law, why not a river? If a corporation can constitute a legal person, why not an old growth forest or a coral reef? If a government can be sued, why can't the plaintiff be a mountain? In short, if an artifact of human design can have moral standing, how much more so a *natural object?*

Stone makes his argument utilizing an historically oriented strategy that bears a family resemblance to Singer's, but Stone not only goes appreciably further to advance the interests of nonsentient living and nonliving things, he also *rejects* consciousness or even metabolic status as necessary conditions for moral standing. What history shows, argues Stone, is that although the extension of rights to "property," namely, enslaved populations, women, and children, may have once been "unthinkable," human societies have in fact made substantive, if bumpy, moral progress. Moreover, nonliving entities such as art works or ancient artifacts have long enjoyed the defense of their interests in being preserved against counterfeiters or looters. The Civil War ended slavery; women can vote; the law forbids child labor; corporations can sue; world historical sites are recognized rights-bearers. *The unthinkable of the past can become the unexceptional of the present*, and courts are more and more the venue of choice for resolving conflicts among rights-bearers.

Like Singer, Stone frames the struggles of women, ethnic, religious, and other minorities not only in terms of the political or civic aspirations of groups or classes, but in terms of the critical value of *being a thing that has interests* (whether or not these can be known or articulated by that thing). Moral standing is not a privilege that can be withdrawn due to a change in conditions, but a locus of *rights* intrinsic to what is *in the best interest* of a thing. Not having the capacity to stake a claim to those interests, moreover, does not, on Stone's view, weigh against having them. It's thus not only trees *per se* that have moral standing, it's *this* sequoia, *this* tributary, *this* migrating flock of Mallards, *this* geological configuration whose standing is predicated on having (at least) the same claim to be left unmolested (at a minimum) as those whose claims endanger them. Courts of law exist not to create rights, but to adjudicate conflicts among them. It's in this sense that moral standing is *portable*: it goes *with* the tree, the flock, the tributary, and it cannot be negated, cancelled, or denied solely because human interests competing for priority are presumed to have greater moral weight. Moral standing, in other words, confers certain effectively inalienable rights— such as to be represented as a fully vested party in a court of law.

Recognizing that nonhuman, even nonsentient, entities have moral standing with respect to their central interests does not, however, necessarily make resolving conflicts easy with respect to whose interests should take priority. Courts can provide an operational framework and a venue for litigating disputes, but they can't guarantee outcomes fully satisfactory to both sides. Still, among the great strengths of Stone's argument is that even interests not recognized by a particular entity themselves can be represented in a rule-governed credible *place*, a court of law, by a committed proxy who understands the relevant issues, risks, and potential outcomes especially for vulnerable litigants. Representation that can see beyond short-sighted human chauvinism and resist the preclusion of moral standing, especially where nonsentient entities are concerned, is key: the convenience to commuters of a planned free-way bypass doesn't diminish the trees' claim to moral consideration, but a court challenge could produce a compromise solution. That people like to eat bacon doesn't negate pigs' interest in avoiding slaughter, and the courts at least offer a venue where we can advocate for our porcine fellows. That a corporation wants to build a theme park at Yellowstone doesn't void the national monument's right to the preservation of its unique ecologies and species—yet, beyond pro-test, letter-writing campaigns, and demanding our representatives reject it, we can also sue on behalf of the monument. The difficult issue for an environmen-tal ethic like Stone's, however, is that while many cases may offer the prospect of compromise, not all do—especially where a very significant threat is posed to human health or other vital interest.

There are really two related, but distinct, issues here. First, while the courts can provide a space for litigating disputes among rights-bearers, the presuppo-sition that human interests ought to take priority and the consequent tendency to represent those interests *as* vital tilts decision-making in the direction of human-centeredness if not human chauvinism. Even where good-intentions prevail, determining what counts as a "vital interest" may be difficult and should not necessarily default to cases where "vital" is narrowly defined as "existential." Second, some human interests may be truly vital, if not existential, in other ways such as preserving health or a capacity such as sight or mobility. Whose interests take priority in cases that have traditionally involved the use of nonhuman animals in medical treatment or pharmaceutical research into, say, Macular Degeneration? Cancer? Alzheimer's Disease? We might agree that research into male pattern balding doesn't qualify as vital, but what about research into lifestyle disease—Type II Diabetes? Morbid Obesity? COPD? What about cases where the human interest may be truly life-saving, yet the research required to address it is likely to generate harm, suffering, or loss of life for its nonhuman animal test subjects? Do human beings always "win" in such cases? Who decides?

Stone may well be able to tackle this difficult kind of case, but before we examine his argument more closely, let's see how tricky it might be. Consider the use of monkeys, specifically monkeys bred for experimental use, in the urgent effort to develop a vaccine for Covid-19. It's clear that monkeys, espe-cially Rhesus Macaques, are the animal of choice for use in Coronavirus trials. The *National Institute of Health* (NIH) reports as a ray of hope, for example, that "a single dose of ChAdOX1 nCov-19, an investigational vaccine against SARS-CoV-2, has protected six rhesus macaques from pneumonia caused by the virus."[12] NIH goes on to detail the how and the who of the experimen-tal vaccine development, its use of chimpanzees in previous studies, and what might be expected as the research program moves forward. But what makes this example different from the conflicts concerning the moral status of the sequoia, the pigs, or Yellowstone is not that medical research necessarily occupies some special category of moral evaluation, at least not without a supporting argument, and it's not that the Rhesus Macaque is a close relative of human beings—though that fact has certainly generated plenty of protest over the use of monkeys and primates in medical research regardless how devastating the disease or condition.[13] What makes this example different is the sheer urgency, even panic, presented by a virus, Covid-19, that can be transmitted asymptomatically, has a relatively low but not wholly predictable rate of fatality, and that even with the development of effective vaccines, the prospect of variant strains of the virus more virulent than the original remains a serious issue.

The difference, in other words, isn't *in* the object of moral consideration; moral standing, argues Stone, is as *portable* as are the interests of an entity to exist and prosper unmolested. The difference is in *us*; it's in our daily witness of a rising human death toll, the prospect that a disease so monstrously infectious leaves its victims to die alone in hospital rooms on ventilators, if they make it that far. It's in the fact that Covid-19 poses a mortal threat that can spread undetected. The difference is in the fear created by a *novel* coronavirus. But what is the *moral* relevance of urgency? Fear? We do, after all, confront terrifying threats to human existence where many—not only animal rights activists—reject the use of nonhuman animal test subjects as cruel regardless the potential value of the research. We need look no further, for example, than the use of live baboons in car crash studies,[14] or studies of the effects of nerve gas.[15] Few doubt that car crashes and exposure to nerve gas are terrifying, and that at least car crashes are a realistic hazard. Knowing what happens to the human body in such cases certainly qualifies as critical, yet the prospect of using human test subjects abhorrent. Still, while car crashes will doubtless take many more lives than Covid-19, we don't see the urgency of knowing what happens when a human cranium plows through a windshield as justifying the use of Baboons to find out, not at least without an argument.

There are many reasons why we see car crash and nerve gas experiments with nonhuman subjects differently than we see the use of monkeys to develop a Covid-19 vaccine; reasons that offer a window into the role of human chauvinism in our experience of urgency or terror. Because, for example, driving a car is a voluntary activity, we feel as if we exercise at least some control over the potential hazards, a sense of control lacking in the asymptomatic transmission of Covid-19. Even knowing the likelihood of dying in a car crash is greater isn't likely to alleviate our anxiety about the virus. We could, of course, be exposed to nerve gas unknowingly, but because the likelihood of this is very low for most, the sense of urgency it generates waxes and wanes with reports of its use in war zones—even though we know dying from nerve gas is horrific. Covid-19, on the other hand, feels stealth: it sneaks up on us; it's everywhere;

it causes a suffering and untimely death. It feels distinctly unfair. Given these characteristics, surely, goes that defense, we don't even need to ask whether it's morally permissible to use nonhuman animals in research that might lead to treatment or, better yet, a vaccine. Judging by the evidence charting the rapid transition from laboratory to animal trial, it seems that this defense has been highly effective. Little hand-wringing over the potential for suffering attends the use of nonhuman animals—even monkeys, and the number of university and private industry labs jumping into the race to develop a vaccine using mice, monkeys, and other nonhuman animals grows daily.[16]

The question for Stone is essentially this: can arguments that appeal to a concept of moral standing specifically tailored to litigation in courts of law address dilemmas like the use of nonhuman animals, especially highly sentient animals, in researched deemed vital, on whatever grounds, to human interests? How far, in other words, can we expect moral standing to reach given *that* venue? This seems hard to judge given the sense of urgency that attends these kinds of cases combined with the uninterrogated assumption that at least some human dilemmas outweigh the rights of nonhuman entities, even where those rights are acknowledged; perhaps even where they're represented in a court of law. It's understandable that the anxiety generated by cases of vital human interest makes it *feel* like the demand for a resolution is justified, even at the cost of suffering for its nonhuman experimental test subjects. But like the spouse who shoots and kills the neighbor he/she finds in bed with his/her partner, understandable does not necessarily mean morally defensible; a conviction for manslaughter is probably still in the cards. Consider once more the Covid-19 pandemic: perhaps it feels inappropriate to even raise the question whether it's morally permissible to use nonhuman animals in medical research in *that* case. Maybe it just is what we have to do. But, as Singer would hasten to point out, the urgency of the research does not diminish the suffering of its nonhuman subjects; it doesn't (Regan) alleviate their anxiety and, argues Stone, the legal standing of a plaintiff in a court of law is not altered by the emotion that attends any particular case, but rather by a sober assessment of the costs and benefits relevant to the parties at conflict. Is it ethical to use nonhuman animals in medical research? Does a pandemic that threatens human life (though not the species Homo sapiens) count as a defensible exception even if we otherwise object?

The animal rights organization *People for the Ethical Treatment of Animals* (PETA) explicitly rejects this claim, demanding, for example, that the treatment of monkeys at the *Washington National Primate Research Center* where Covid-19 research is being conducted show that none have been exposed to the virus and that testing be suspended. In a public statement, PETA argues that, given the desperation for treatment and vaccine, the pandemic presents a "perfect storm" for animal abuse, and thus demand the animals be relocated to sanctuaries.[17] We need only shift the context slightly, moreover, to see that PETA has a point. As David Grimm reports for AAAS Science

Faced with her lab's imminent closure, Sunny Shin had already begun to fear she would have to euthanize large numbers of the mice she works on. Then, last Tuesday, the email came from her school's vice provost of research. "In response to the public health crisis caused by Covid-19," it read, "mouse/ rodent users should cull their colonies as much as possible." Shin, a microbial immunologist... had to deliver the bad news to her lab manager: euthanize 200 mice—more than three-quarters of their research animals—as quickly as possible... "It was heartbreaking," says Shin, "scientifically and emotion- ally." As thousands of the rodents began to be euthanized—they are typically killed with carbon dioxide and their necks are broken just to make sure... PETA first called attention to the effort, blasting them as a "killing spree."... But the heads of major lab animal facilities say the efforts are needs to ensure both the safety of their staff and the welfare of the remaining animals in their care.[18]

PETA defends the claim that such massive scale "euthanasia" amounts to a killing spree in that "[e]xperimenters are again choosing the path of convenience and simply killing animals that should have never been bought, bred, or experimented on in the first place." Yet, it's easy to imagine a scenario where many of these animals starve to death during the pandemic lockdown. We might also think about it this way: depending on just how we assess argu- ments like Singer's, Regan's or Stones for the moral standing, even the rights, of nonhuman sentient or nonsentient entities, we might find it comparatively easy to pull back the curtain on the fact that "euthanizing" factory farm pigs is as much an appeal to euphemism as is "processing" them, and with the same objective: it makes us feel better about what we eat. Should we see the "eutha- nizing" of mice in the same way? Does a circumstance of not being able to care for them make the carbon dioxide and neck-breaking easier to swallow? Does it matter that they're mice—and not monkeys, pigs, or dogs? Is our own terror at the prospect of not having a vaccine for a deadly virus *morally* relevant? If we are not ready to accord sufficient moral standing to monkeys such that a crisis would not necessarily justify our stripping it away, how close are we to recog- nizing the rights of trees? It would seem, not very.

3.1.3   Moral Standing versus Consequences/Rights versus Goals: What Matters More?

Stone is forthright about the fact that the struggle for the recognition of moral standing for nonhuman, and especially nonsentient, entities is far from over, and there are important issues that go beyond what counts as a vital interest. One is this: as the moral community expands and becomes more inclusive, those who have traditionally benefitted from the subjugation of others, that is, mostly white, male, and Western(ized) human beings, have gradually been forced to relinquish some of the unearned social, economic, and political privilege taken for granted as a birthright. Privilege, however, rarely gives up without a fight, especially with respect to economic interests. Hence, it's unsurprising that animal agriculture, commodity food production, "Big Box" retailers, and the hydrocarbon industries, interests that remain overwhelmingly dominated by this small class, assert their "rights" *as corporate persons* to the same representation Stone would see extended to natural objects like trees, rivers, and mountains. The issue is that while progress toward greater presence in courts of law has certainly been made, the kind of representation to which privilege has access remains better equipped to advance its interests than that available to those assigned the status of commodity, resource, or labor. Exxon has lawyers and lobbyists on permanent staff; the Arctic doesn't.

Consider, for example, the complex story of the northern spotted owl. As Eric Loomis reports for the *Washington Post*, in 2019 the Trump administration dealt a body blow to the Endangered Species Act by "allowing policymakers to consider economic impacts of protecting these plants and animals."[19] While large corporations such as Weyerhauser or Georgia-Pacific "stand to benefit the most from the eased regulations," President Trump specifically "touted the positive effects" for timber industry workers. Indeed, many applauded the move toward greater deregulation as job-saving for a struggling industry. But, Loomis argues, what a closer look reveals is quite a different story: the reinforcement of the economic inequality that endangers both the loggers, the northern spotted owl, and the ecologies of the Pacific Northwest. Loomis explains that as early as 1938, the *International Woodworkers of America* (IWA) recognized that a rapacious timber industry spelled doom not only for forest ecologies and their dependent species, but for the future livelihoods of logging workers, their families, and their communities. "The union spent the next decade demanding sustainable forestry that would lead to stable communities and healthy forests—as well as jobs," consistent pressure that ultimately produced the Wilderness Act of 1964.

Fast-forward to the "deindustrialization, automation, [and] outsourcing" of the 1970s, however, and it becomes quickly apparent that despite significant gains, the structural inequalities that empower the giant wood fiber corporations remain largely unaltered: logging workers are pitted against environmentalists working to preserve the last stands of Old Growth forest in the Pacific Northwest as they struggle to save their own jobs from automation and outsourcing. Environmental organizations like the Sierra Club advocate for what becomes the *Redwood Employee Protection Program* that "helped nearly 2000 workers get through hard times before the Reagan administration killed the program in 1981." By 1987, IWA sides with the corporations against environmentalists cast as hippies and tree-huggers. Yet, in a profoundly dark twist to this dark story, the timber industry scapegoats the northern spotted owl as an excuse to eliminate jobs, a "cynical but effective way," writes Loomis, "for the timber industry to deflect its own culpability for the conditions in which these communities found themselves." The fate of the northern spotted owl has hung in the balance ever since, but the species' potential extinction cannot be attributed solely to Trump administration deregulation. As Loomis and Cronon show, it's the history of what counts as a morally considerable thing combined with a social order that values and privileges some over others that informs the complex, often fraught, relationship between powerful industries, specific ecologies, the economic wherewithal of communities, their workers, and the species endangered by industrial activity. The timber industry may not have *carte blanche* to log however and wherever it sees fit, but its influence over politicians, the pressure to deregulate, and the economic stress of depressed Northwest communities gives it clout that private citizens, environmental organizations and worker's unions just can't leverage. That too is part of the history of the northern spotted owl.

As Cronin shows, it's because history is so often buried along with its casualties that reclamations of "person" beyond what we take to be its most current examples feel out of place. It's not surprising that Stone's argument for the extension of rights beyond what serves corporate interest seems disruptive.[20] That corporate persons nearly always win against their opponents, human or otherwise, fuels a bitter "life" cycle: Big Timber, Big Ag, Big CAFO, King Coal, Big Oil and Gas—these are the corporate ventures culpable for some of the most enduring harms to human health, human communities, and the ecologies upon which they depend. Even with the benefit of proxy representatives such as the Sierra Club, few among the casualties of the "Bigs" have more than a limited capacity to confront the economic and social order that subjugates and discards them. If anything has forced the multinationals to take more reflective stock of their own future profitability, it's the growing recognition that the resources upon which they depend are not, in fact, endless—that they can no longer *afford* to ignore the effects of their own rapacious histories. Faced with disease, firenadoes, hurricanes, floods, and food insecurity, the public, whose workers produce the wood pulp, soy, animal proteins, and hydrocarbons corporate giants depend on, have become harder to convince there's no relationship between production and disaster. Put differently: denial is a powerful driver of human behavior to be sure, but faced with its very real and costly consequences, even the "Bigs" have been compelled to look inwards at their business models' capacity to survive the next pandemic, the next climate-associated environmental disaster, the next loss of public confidence.

Yet, instead of confronting the root causes of the harm—that lethal marriage of human chauvinism and capitalism's dependence on a bottomless vault of resources and an inexhaustible atmosphere for the expulsion of waste—we turn instead to treating the symptoms. Like a physician who treats cancer by prescribing an aspirin regimen, we turn, for example, to building bigger dams and levies instead of reducing the greenhouse gas emissions that contribute to the production of ever more damaging floods. Instead of asking hard questions about how we might slow the rate of human population growth, we side with Blake Hurst against the "agri-intellectuals" who argues it's delusional to think we can feed the planet without the chemical fertilizers, insecticides, and herbicides that are the trademark of Big-Ag.[21] Instead of trying to prevent the next zoonotic transmission of a dangerous virus by restraining human encroachment into nonhuman animal habitat, or by discouraging bush meat markets, or even just by encouraging vegetarianism, we turn to medical research for therapeutics and vaccines. This is not to say, of course, that we should abandon dam-building or meat-eating or the pursuit of medical research in favor of a revolt against capitalism. But it is to highlight the vantage point from which we can see that it's the same toxic marriage of human chauvinism and the capitalist conversion of all value into commodity value that acts as the driver in all three. It's the profit-incentivized chauvinism that invites us to ignore the erasure of Native Americans in the fabrication of "wilderness," or to forget that loggers were once the vanguard of ecological conservation, or to never question whether medical research will be able to save us from virulent viral outbreak. It's no wonder that, at least during a crisis, the use of nonhuman subjects to develop treatments, cures, and vaccines rarely sees objection.[22] But it's not the crisis that makes their use obviously acceptable any more than we should regard it as obvious that the right thing to do is just keep building bigger and bigger damns or spreading more and more chemical fertilizer on exhausted soil.

3.1.4   Moral Standing and the Concept of the Future

Just as the histories of "personhood" are crucial to understanding how human activity is at the root of so much environmental destruction, species loss, and human suffering, so too concrete planning at the local, regional, national, and global level committed to the future is what's needed to incentivize the work necessary to realize it in ways desirable from the point of view of those least likely to have a say. Albeit in differing ways, what Stone and Cronon show is that whatever we might mean by "desirable," its decision-makers must include not only the entitled, but those whose moral standing is ignored and undermined. It's in this important sense that our concept of "rights" is (and must be) informed by a clear comprehension of the fact that coming to terms with past injustice means working to restore the communities, habitats, and ecologies that can exemplify the moral standing of their members. What recognizing the moral standing of trees needs to be effective is a vision of a world for which rights are *actionable*, yet one in which trees no longer require proxy representatives to defend them. We can imagine, after all, a just world where, due to scarcity of essential resources, respected entities are treated justly but where very little is desirable. We defend the interests of polar bears against Exxon-Mobil's arctic drilling permits because we think a future without polar bears is a future missing something fundamentally good. We defend the rights of rivers to be protected from acid mine run-off because we envision a future of a river that can support aquatic life, where we can fish or swim in sparkling clean water. We resist the logging of old growth forest in the US Northwest however much this pits us against timber corporations not only because we value endangered species like the northern spotted owl, but because we value ancient forests against encroaching human populations.[23] What made the environmentally devastating Deep Water Horizon disaster in the Gulf of Mexico disastrous wasn't only the loss of eleven human lives, but that it choked to death countless bottleneck dolphins, suffocated aquatic plant life, and dealt a crushing blow to an economically depressed region of the American South still reeling from Hurricane Katrina.[24] It projected a future where perhaps there would be compensation, perhaps even an effort at ecological restoration, but where—because the disaster was probably preventable, because it appears that profits were prioritized over the lives of people, dolphins, and the gulf ecology—what of the good was preserved was at least not obvious.

With respect to the values necessary to realizing a desirable future, the climate crisis could not be more relevant. What could be more *about* the future than atmospheric stability? On the one hand, facts are stubborn things. We either act to dramatically limit the emission of greenhouse gases into the atmosphere or the sustainability of the planet's ecologies and remaining species, including Homo sapiens, will be at risk. Our successors might find themselves, as David Wallace Wells puts it, confronted by an "uninhabitable earth."[7] We either begin to take seriously the important roles played by species impacted by the climate crisis including the large, the small, and the seemingly insignificant, Sumatran elephants, northern spotted owls, bottleneck dolphins, lichen, honeybees, or lemur leaf frogs,[25] or while the future might be sustainable, it might not seem worth fighting for. We either grapple more honestly with questions about who is this "we" who must take the lead to mitigate against the implications of climate change, or even a merely survivable future is likely to reproduce the same structural inequalities and forms of injustice that brought (or bought) us the crisis. On the other hand, as Brian Barry argues, recognizing that we have a responsibility to the future doesn't necessarily tell us what to do about it, much less for whom the fight is most urgent in the present (Barry, 93). And we can make things worse. Perhaps it sounds miserably dystopian, but we could imagine a future completely bereft of real trees, elephants, owls, dolphins, lichen, honeybees, or frogs, but plentiful in opportunities for virtual experience with holographic analogues under climate controlled domes, so-long established that few remember their "originals." It's this future, however, that fortifies Stone's most important presupposition: *moral standing is not time-dependent.* If trees have rights to exist unmolested, our duty to preserve the conditions whereby they can continue to exist unmolested is also not time-dependent. A towering Hemlock is not a holographic Hemlock. A Sumatran elephant swinging it head to swat flies is not a simulated elephant. Whatever replacements we can envision are at least morally irrelevant because the rights of natural objects and species to exist preempts whatever "we" think is adequate to "our" experience. And this "we" is, of course, itself highly contentious since both the production and access to virtual trees and elephants and may be profit-centered domains of the social order's beneficiaries.

The really difficult issue then is whether there will be any "we" willing to do the hard work of representing the rights of trees in a future beleaguered by the crises of the *present*—climate, viral pandemic, food insecurity, geopolitical violence, lack of clean water, human overpopulation—that tend to entrench human chauvinism, not disarm it. In our response to climate change, for example, our actions rarely follow our words of acknowledgment. However we decry Covid-19 as tragic, the move to normalize a daily death count of 2000 and an infection rate of at least 20,000 begins within weeks of the outbreak. We bemoan the problems of the so-called developing world all the while we ignore the food deserts in cities just a few hours away. Out of disgust with our capacity for denial, avoidance, and willful ignorance, one environmental activist suggests that the best response for those who say they "[c]are about the planet?" is to "[k]ill yourself."[26] We're not likely to take that advice, but it does capture the urgency with which we're confronted, as well as the conflicts we seem ill-prepared to navigate.[27] The countless head of cattle awaiting slaughter at a factory farm pose a direct threat to the climate.[28] How should we think about their moral standing as animals produced for the sole purpose of consumption? What about the moral status of the factory farm? Its operations may well jeopardize the health and lives of workers exposed unwillingly to Covid-19 on the slaughter line. But whose standing takes priority, and with what justification? The cow's? Worker's? The corporation's? One thing seems clear: however mercenary on the part of the corporation, prioritizing the rights of workers not to be infected over the rights of cattle not to be slaughtered is far more likely to get the plant closed down—but the corporation applauded—than protesting for the rights of the animals, even if the cows end up being "euthanized." Yet, imagine a very different case where a population of feral pigs destroy plants essential to carbon-absorbing forests. In this case the forest, given its claim to "being there first," is likely to win, and sharpshooters will likely be hired to cull the pig population.[29] We could also imagine a lumber company whose

CEO denies the moral status of an old growth forest by referring to trees as "wood fiber," claims that without permission to "harvest" it will likely have to outsource its operations, defends its rights to timbering as essential to the company's "survival,"[30] and is thereby absolved of any wrong-doing against "being there first."

Each of these cases is driven by a primarily human interest even if its beneficiaries include the environment. Whether corporate reputation, the disvalue we assign to feral or invasive species, a bottom line, the value we assign to age, or the perennial argument for jobs, the futures that derive from these decisions reflect not only *what* we value, but *for whom*. Consider a natural gas company seeking a permit for a hydraulic fracturing operation on top of a mountain laced with high value trout streams. If the community downstream sues to stop the operation arguing that "fracking" will diminish fishing and other recreational opportunities, they will likely win more stringent regulation than if they went to the defense of the mountain, the fish, much less the aquatic plant life. If they sued on the grounds that the mountain and its trout streams have moral standing *per se*, they'd be unlikely to see their suit gain much traction since the default position gives priority to human interests.[31] The strength of the corporation's position might actually be reduced, in other words, by *not* pitting it against the moral standing of the mountain, and instead looking to the strategy that makes for the best *future* outcomes.[32]

Put in plain terms: considerations of moral standing are not in every case likely to be comfortable bedfellow with the consideration of consequences—and this tension is a difficult one to navigate for any ethic. Questions about what we owe to the future, if anything, are made difficult by many things. The capacity to make predictions, what we might be willing to sacrifice in order to conserve something of greater value, whose interests should be prioritized, what is the place of nonhuman species and their ecologies in this calculation—all are challenging, and all the more so given the environmental deterioration we already face and the complex implications of the climate crisis for human and nonhuman life. To many the idea of setting aside a commitment to defend the moral standing of particular natural objects *as* those objects, even where the likelihood is that taking up that defense will mean a loss, feels like a kind of betrayal. They argue that we'd be sacrificing the very values we hope to preserve into a sustainable future, and without which that future offers little by way of a desirable world. Moreover, because a thing can have an interest and yet not be aware of it, as well as a right to see that interest met even if not equipped itself to meet it, it falls on us to represent and defend it. Who else is in any position to rise to that occasion? If we punt to the future hoping a different course of action will produce better consequences, it seems we've betrayed the very idea that moral standing is not time-dependent.

This is, of course, just another way to frame the standard dilemma for the utilitarian—when do the ends, however good, justify means that require sacrifice or harm? When do the interests of something to avoid harm outweigh the consequences that might result from the defense of its associated rights? My quite sentient elderly Maltese-Bichon, Mr. Luv-Lyte, may not have the intellectual wherewithal to conceive an interest in getting his rabies vaccine, but he clearly "has" such an interest in the sense that it's *in* his interest not to contract rabies. It's my responsibility as his guardian to see that he receives that protection, and perhaps even to set an example of important values like compassion or concern for the suffering and lives of others. Not only, after all, are these values relevant to any vision of the future, but all the more so for a future world altered by the climate crisis. In Mr. Luv-Lyte's case, it's pretty hard to imagine any "better future consequences" other than not contracting rabies to justify the vaccine. But what about the mountain case where, rather than defend its high-value trout streams, fracking opponents appeal to the recreational opportunities for vacationers precisely because this might achieve greater protections for the mountain? Do the ends justify the use of means that detract from the moral standing of the mountain itself, in effect reaffirming the same values held by the natural gas corporation, namely, that the mountain, its streams, and wild life, are commodities? What about the slaughterhouse case where going to defense of the cattle's interest in not being "processed" instead of workers exposed to Covid-19 may actually waste valuable time and cause more harm to the workers while the plant remains open? Whether near or far term, nearly all questions of what ends justify what means will be made more difficult by the extension of moral standing to nonhuman and nonsentient entities because having a right to exist unmolested preempts the temporal dimension of utility. Stone's right: considerations of moral standing are essential to any civil society. The issue is thus not merely how we predict possible consequences, but rather—even where we mostly can make such prediction—how do we decide in what kinds of cases interests ought to be prioritized, regardless the consequences, and in what kinds of cases consequences ought to have sway, even where rights are violated. It is, after all, one thing to grant that nonhuman, even nonsentient entities have a right to the representation of their interests just as do other nonsentient entities like corporations. We can even go so far as to repudiate our human chauvinism and work diligently to defend fairly and robustly the rights of things like trees and mountains. But it is still another and more difficult task to articulate criteria to determine in cases of highly consequential conflict whose rights take priority, why they should, given the possibility of harmful consequences—or, where the consequences are prioritized, how we reconcile that judgment with the violation of rights we recognize as significant.

3.1.5   The Interests and Rights of the Voiceless

Consider one more kind of case, one where an entity (or a species) is not in a position to defend its own interests, and where its loss, in one way or another, is irrecoverable. A stately, nonsentient, California old-growth sequoia can no more conceive its value or its interest in being saved from the construction of a highway than can my dog, Mr. Luv-Lyte, imagine rabies, but it's nonetheless in the sequoia's interest not to meet with a chainsaw. According to arguments like Stone's, it's the state's duty as the sequoia's guardian to protect it. It may even be the private citizen's duty to agitate to insure the state takes that duty seriously.[33] But whereas we might count the loss of the sequoia as irrecoverable in virtue of its age, beauty, and enormity, we might not regard the loss of a Maltese-Bichon in the same way. Mr. Luv-Lyte is irreplaceable to *me*, but not to Maltese-Bichons. Still, if saving the sequoia but risking rabies for Mr. Luv-Lyte seems somehow arbitrary, perhaps it's because it's not necessarily obvious *to what* moral standing attaches. What bestows moral standing on a thing? Particularly when, according to Stone, it's not sentience or even necessarily being a living thing? Is it some quality or set of qualities? Membership in an unusual species? Rareness? Beauty? Age? Size? Novelty? The trouble, of course, is that we can think of lots of things that might fit one or more of these characteristics, but that don't obviously qualify an entity as a candidate for moral standing. Covid-19, for example, is commonly called a novel corona virus, but few think novelty has much bearing on whether or not we'd eradicate it if we could. Progeria—a disease that afflicts only one in eight million children with the physical appearance of rapid-onset aging and hardening of the arteries, is rare. The red-lipped batfish is a strange-looking creature to be sure, but neither endangered nor something other than a fish. Yet, the lowest common denominator quality, mere existence, applies to every grain of sand, a position virtually none would adopt.

Another way to put this problem is that while the workhorse of rights-based arguments, "having an interest," offers direction once it's decided whose interests matter, it cannot determine whose those are. The near-uniqueness that may belong to an ancient sequoia doesn't by itself make its loss irrecoverable. People who have unique tattoos acquired early in life are not, for example, spared the death penalty on that score. Mr. Luv-Lyte may have unique characteristics of which I'm unaware such that his loss would be irrecoverable even if I didn't see it that way (or no one did). Neither the sequoia nor Mr. Luv-Lyte can voice their own interests, at least not their *existential* interests. It's also possible that there are some consequences so horrific that trampling the rights, even the existential rights of a thing understood to be both precious and voiceless, may be necessary to avoid that consequence; say, burning down the Louvre´ to prevent a deadly pathogen from escaping. This would certainly be an irrecoverable loss, and we might well conceive the Louvre's interests in the same way we conceive a corporate person's, but compared to the irrecoverable loss of life due to the pathogen, many would mourn the loss of the Louvre, but few would likely balk at the decision.

The climate crisis also presents us with palpable scenarios of irrecoverable loss—though many tend to balk, or at least ignore the warning signs. From vanishing shorelines to critically endangered species, once the Kiribati Islands have been submerged by rising sea waters their capacity to support human communities is vanquished. Once as much as half of the world's nonhuman species have gone extinct due to climate change impacts, they're gone forever.[34] Mitigation, however, has its own high cost. In fact, it's hard to imagine an effective global strategy for the meaningful reduction of greenhouse gases that avoids trampling the rights of those whose voices are already muted by a social and economic order that cannot afford to recognize the moral standing of its resources, labor, and disposable commodities. Anil Agarwal and Sunita Narain argue, for example, that an important environmental think tank, the *World Resource Institute's* (WRI), attempt to "blame developing world countries for global warming and perpetuate the current global inequality in the use of the earth's environment and resources" is not supported by data showing that "India and China cannot be held responsible even for a single KG of carbon dioxide or methane that is accumulating in the earth's atmosphere." In fact, they go on to argue, since "[t]he accumulation ... of these gases is mainly the result of the gargantuan consumption of the developed countries, particularly the United States," it is the developed countries who must set the example by moving to reduce their own carbon emissions first.[35]

That the irrecoverable loss of atmospheric integrity affects everything, living and nonliving, from microcosm to megafauna, on the planet does not imply, in other words, that responsibility for mitigating against its worst effects belongs equally to everyone. According to Agarwal and Narain, the WRI view achieves little more than reinforcement of the structural inequalities responsible for the social and economic divide between the Global North and South— leaving the latter effectively voiceless all the while saddling Global South countries with the unrealistic expectation that their citizens will consume even less than they already do. The prospect that China and India should reduce their carbon emissions is effectively a prescription for the continuing poverty that makes their human populations and natural resources vulnerable to the exploitation and extraction of Global North industrial enterprise. It's thus no surprise that the governments of these countries reject the responsibility to reduce their emissions, and have now become the two most rapidly industrializing countries on the planet with a growing carbon footprint to match.[36]

Agarwal and Narain's "you broke it, you fix it" argument has several significant implications for any mitigation strategy that seeks to preserve the moral standing of those impacted by the climate crisis. They argue that such a strategy must first come to terms with the facts about those most vulnerable and most harmed, and second it must include their voices in articulating solutions that address not only environmental harms but the oppressive social order that perpetuates those harms:

> But to carry out this strategy to improve land productivity and meet people's survival needs, development strategies will have to be ecosystem specific and holistic. It would be necessary to plan for each component of the village eco-system and not just trees... To do this the country will need much more than just glib words about people's participation or wasteland development. It will demand bold and imaginative steps to strengthen and deepen local democracy by creating and empowering democratic and open village institutions. Only then will people get involved in managing their environment. It will mean disman-tling the inefficient and oppressive government apparatus and changing laws so that people can act without waiting for a good bureaucrat to come along... Those who talk about global warming should concentrate on what ought to be done at home.[37]

Although they may phrase it differently, it is the village and its villagers to which Agarwal and Narain attribute moral standing. "Glib words" such WRI's shallow appeal to equality, is merely thin cover behind which the business as usual of "inefficient and oppressive government apparatus" continues to cater to multinational corporations. The solution to both mitigating against the cli-mate crisis and dismantling an unjust social and economic order, they argue, is to "dismantle" that oppressive bureaucracy, change the laws, and work toward "empowering democratic and open village institutions."

What Agarwal and Narain are arguing for is, of course, revolutionary. A vision of democratic institutions that operate in the interest of a desirable pre-sent and future for a specific ecological and moral community, its impetus derives from social, economic, and environmental interests—but in a context of resistance to, as Cronon might describe it, a history of the usurpation of local resources and the violation of (at least) basic human rights. For Agarwal and Narain, the key to successful mitigation lay in providing reasons at the local level for people to become invested in the "management" of the environment, a scenario only possible once government and its wealthy associates are out of the way. This sounds great. Indeed, it's hard to argue—as a matter of respect for (at least) human rights—against more democracy. The problem is that the evidence offers few good reasons to believe affirming the rights of developing world peoples necessarily will result in mitigating against the climate crisis. Indeed, as Sedki Karoui and Romdhane Khemakhem show in their Tunisian study "Consumer Ethnocentrism in Developing Countries," while many factors contribute to the overall growth of product consumption,

> [p]revious research has shown that consumers in developed countries display a high level of consumer ethnocentrism by prioritizing local products over

foreign manufactured ones. It is generally believed that consumers from developing countries, and least developed countries, are more inclined to buy imported goods than domestic ones.[38]

Although the authors go on to hedge this claim to some extent, arguing that better marketing at the national level can deter the consumption of imports and encourage the consumer ethnocentrism they favor, very little mention is made of either the contribution to greenhouse gas emissions made possible by more consumption across the board, or the even greater environmental impacts likely to come from the contribution transport and product preservation make to those impacts. Either way, the race to achieve a standard of living modelled after the high consumption comforts of the Global North little hedge against it.

Once again, we're faced with some very difficult questions about what constitutes the life worth living in the age of climate change. But what we've seen as well is that these questions are unique neither historically nor with respect to the profound effects they can have on human and nonhuman welfare. There's no guarantee that efforts to mitigate against the potentially irrecoverable losses likely to accrue the climate crisis will be necessarily consistent with safeguarding the rights of human, corporate, or nonhuman persons. And there's no guarantee that efforts to mitigate against climate change even at the cost of respect for moral standing can generate future conditions where recovery and expansion of these rights will be possible. But, although the direct impacts are perhaps more immediate and somewhat more measurable, these same disclaimers apply to the next pandemic, the next economic recession or depression—to any catastrophe that stretches out over time. It's no wonder that African American leaders compare the slow but deadly effects of racism to a "pandemic" of social and economic inequality, especially in light of the disproportionately negative effects of the virus on communities of color,[39] or that environmental justice activists like Elizabeth Yeampierrre argue that

> [c]limate change is the result of a legacy of extraction, of colonialism, of slavery. A lot of times when people talk about environmental justice, they go back to the 1970's or 60's. But I think about the slave quarters. I think about people who got the worst food, the worst healthcare, the worst treatment, and then when freed, were given lands that were eventually surrounded by things like petrochemical industries... In our communities people are suffering from asthma or upper respiratory disease, and we've been fighting for the right to breathe for generations, It's ironic that those are the signs you see at these protests—"I can't breathe."... The communities that are the most impacted by Covid, or by pollution, it's not surprising that they're the ones who are going to be the most impacted by extreme weather events. And it's

not surprising that they're the ones targeted for racial violence. It's all the same communities, all over the United States. And you can't treat one part of the problem without the other, because it's so systemic.[40]

In one respect, it's pretty simple: an environmental ethic that makes rights its primary focus without a consideration of consequences, is bound to, in some sense quite literally, miss the forest for the trees. But an ethic that too narrowly focuses on consequences at the expense of rights is bound to trample and potentially destroy the very thing whose happiness it sought to preserve.

Ethics is, of course, more complicated than this given the social and economic injustices still embedded in the bone marrow of access to basic, even existential, resources—clean water and clean air. But it is all about breathing. Breathing clean air, breathing easy, trying to breath with the knee of a police officer on your neck, breathing a sigh of relief that the rent is paid, breathing in terror herded down a conveyor belt to an electric stun gun, taking a last breath on a ventilator alone in a hospital room. Thinking about the values we must preserve for any future worth wanting can help us navigate between moral standing and a consideration of consequences. But it doesn't necessarily tell us what kinds of things actually qualify as morally considerable. Singer, Stone, Regan, Cronon, and many others certainly try to show us who qualifies and why. And equally many in the movements against police brutality, or for animals rights, or in the sciences hold up a stark mirror in front of us whose reflection is a human chauvinism that is racist and speciesist—that has a well-manicured capacity for denial. If corporations can count as persons before the law, so can trees or rivers—or androids, zombies, viruses, or the Internet, but who gets to decide this and to what ends can either challenge the reigning chauvinist status quo or reinforce it. We could adopt a wholly cynical view: if anything can count as a person, perhaps nothing actually counts. In that case, given the prospect of irrecoverable loss, perhaps any strategy to mitigate against the climate crisis is fair game. But this seems sure to be self-defeating insofar as the world at the end of that gambit, one stripped of respect for moral standing and thus vulnerable to every flavor of might makes right, seems a far cry from being able to offer a life worth living.

3.2   Respect for Life: The "Good of Its Own" Extensionism of Holmes Rolston III

3.2.1   Respect for Life and an "Ethic for Species"

This brings us to a last variety of moral extensionism, one developed by Holmes Rolston III, commonly referred to as *Respect for Life*. Contrary to

Regan and Singer, Rolston argues that neither being the subject-of-a-life nor, even more minimally, having the capacity to suffer are necessary to ground the moral considerability of living things. Indeed, what Rolston calls an "ethic for species" offers little regard to qualities like sentience, shifting the focus of moral considerability to the genetic information of which individuals are fleeting instances. Contrary to Stone, however, Rolston excludes nonliving entities from the calculus of moral standing altogether. Distinguishing "purely physical systems" from organisms as "defenders of their own lives," Rolston's preclusion of machines such as missiles would also, presumably, extend to other human-made artifacts like corporations and governments even though particular machines are instances of reproducible design and institutions exemplify ideologies or belief systems.

Living things, argues Rolston, embody "axiological systems," that is, purposeful organic structures. They're sources of value *and* valuing in virtue of being instances of a species, that is, they exemplify unique configurations of genetic information as sentient or nonsentient organisms. Living things exhibit characteristics that even very complex, though inanimate, entities do not, especially the capacity to consume nutrients, self-propel, repair injuries, avoid predators, and reproduce offspring. As Rolston makes the point in "Respect for Life: Counting What Singer Finds of No Account":

> True, plants lack conscious will and intentional pursuit; Singer is right about that... But are there no significant differences between plants, rivers, and guided missiles? No, claims Singer, because they are all purely physical processes. In Singer's dichotomy, there seem to be only two metaphysical levels; conscious experiencers and merely physical processes... Can we be more discriminating? ("Respect for Life," p. 249).

Rolston thinks we can be more discriminating, and that we must:

> Consider plants. A plant is not an experiencing subject, but neither is an inanimate object, like a stone. Nor is it a geomorphological process, like a river. Plants are quite alive. Plants, like all other organisms, are self-actualizing. Plants are unified entities... Plants repair injuries and move water, nutrients, and photosynthate from cell to cell; they store sugars... They can reject genetically incompatible grafts... A plant, like any other organism, sentient or not, is a spontaneous, self-maintaining system... executing its program, making a way through the world, checking against performance by means of responsive capacities with which to measure success. Something more than merely physical causes.... Is operating within every organism. There is information... recorded in the genes, and such information,

unlike matter and energy, can be created and destroyed. That is what worries environmentalists about extinction... In it [information] lies the secret of life, and an environmental ethics will need a discriminating account of such life, and appropriate respect for it. ("Respect for Life," p. 249).

To respect these processes, this "secret of life," is, argues Rolston, to respect what he calls the "good-of-its-kind," that is, the value realized through an organism's endeavor to "actualize" itself as an instance of a particular kind or species of entity. "Good" thus accrues not to individuals *per se*, but to *this* instance of preserving and reproducing a "kind." A living thing is "good" because, left to its own developmental course, it will actualize the species represented in its genes; its value therefore accrues not to its particularity or individuality, but to its realization as a living embodiment of a species whose tenure on the planet is only as secure as its axiological mission, namely, *reproduction*.

Whereas missiles, argues Rolston, can instantiate only the intentions of their inventers—motives external to their creation—plant's realize the information stored in their evolving genetic histories, "motives" internal to their physical state:

> The physical state that the organism defends is a valued state. A life is defended for what it is in itself... Such organisms may have no will or desires, but they do have their own standards. Every organism has a *good-of-its-kind*; it defends its own kind as a *good kind*. [This] is not to be dismissed as mere metaphor. That rather seems the plain fact of the matter. ("Respect for Life," p. 251)

Rolston offers an example distinguishing between two trail signs, one he describes as a representation of Singer's ethic, the other Respect for Life. The message of the first is "Please leave the flowers for others to enjoy," that of the second: "Let the flowers live!" For the first, argues Rolston, the flowers "count only for people," whereas the second "invite[s] a change of reference frame" to the value of the flowers as a species, a unique instance of living information. "Let the flowers live!" demands recognizing the flowers *as* the flowers, whereas "Please leave the flowers for others to enjoy" values only their utility for human purposes. Seeing that difference, he argues, can help us to reorient toward respecting life *as* life regardless whether, say, it's more convenient to just walk through the flowers, trampling them, or rip them out of the ground because they offend our allergies. Indeed, it's just this fundamental difference of perspective that's captured, argues Rolston, in the famous ecologist Aldo Leopold's "*Land Ethic*" axiom: "*a thing is right when it tends to preserve the integrity, stability, and beauty of the biotic community. It is wrong when it tends otherwise.*"[41]

3.2.2   Valuing the Threat of Extinction over the Capacity for Suffering

While Rolston's flower example doesn't appear especially contentious (few would reject the altered signage), the implications of this variety of moral extensionism are in fact colossal. In valuing the species over its instances, Rolston disposes moral considerability to prioritize, for example, the threat of extinction over the prevention of suffering. In valuing "information" over individuals, he extends moral status to nonsentient living things, but he also commits moral decision-making to courses of action that, pitting species against each other, could *generate* conditions for suffering. In advocating Leopold's axiom, he promotes environmental sustainability over sentient experience, but in so doing he invites a calculus of means to ends whose quotient of misery could be immense. Respect for Life thus raises at least three serious questions:

- Is the production of suffering, not merely tolerating its occurrence, consistent with moral considerability? Can such ends-to-means decision procedures be justified regardless the breadth, duration, or sheer ferocity of pain? Does this follow regardless species so long as the ends—preservation from extinction—can be achieved?
- Is the preservation of species from extinction always of greater value than the prevention of suffering? If not, what are the criteria for deciding?
- Can science tell us enough about cases of threatened extinction that we can decide confidently what actions we're warranted to undertake in the name of species preservation?

Consider an example Rolston offers to illustrate his view: a growing population of goats introduced to San Clemente, an island off the coast of California.[42] He argues that because the goats pose a direct threat of extinction to three endangered plant species, and as the goats were not themselves endangered, the right course of action was to remove them, even if this meant killing them, and even if that meant some (or many) of the goats might suffer being shot, but not killed immediately, by helicopter. "The well-being of plants at the species level," he writes, "outweighs the welfare of the goats at the individual level."

Put differently: of course, we want to save endangered species from extinction. But whether that means we should sign on to the knowable *production* of suffering as an acceptable consequence of achieving that worthy goal is not *thereby* made obvious by the fact that the entities who will suffer or even die are not endangered. A utilitarian like Singer might point out that without some additional argument that avoiding extinction is of paramount value, choosing preservation over suffering isn't necessarily justified. Do we want to save Florida's Everglades from invasive Burmese Pythons?[43] Yes; at the cost of killing baby Pythons by bludgeoning? To what lengths should we go to preserve the Western Prairie Fringed Orchid?[44] Perhaps barring the expansion of suburban sprawl doesn't count as suffering, but that doesn't answer the question what does, and for whom. What about a scenario from *The Handmaid's Tale*? In Margaret Atwood's dystopia women are enslaved and raped to save humanity from its own reckless decimation of fertility via environmental pollution.[45] What lengths, and at whose cost in suffering, is it permissible to go to save the human beings of the future from the human actions of the past? Do we really want to preserve every species of living organism? Aren't there some forms of bacterial or viral infection we'd rightly drive to extinction? MRSA? Streptococcus pneumonia? HIV? Ebola? Covid-19?[46]

Rolston's reasoning runs counter not only to Singer's argument for the extension of the principle of utility to the prevention of suffering beyond the human community, it also runs afoul of Stone's commitment both to the moral standing of individuals, living and nonliving. "Running counter" is, of course, not by itself a criticism of Rolston, but it is instructive to see what prioritizing species over individuals actually means for moral considerability in light of these alternatives. With respect to Singer, what if instead of endangered flowers or shrubs, we imagine some species of microbial organism, and instead of goats, golden retrievers? No doubt, we'd *feel* differently; we'd likely be less sanguine about the helicopter slaughter of companion dogs for the sake of preserving a species of microbes even if we do in fact value the nonsentient organisms. Rolston could, of course, counter that our feelings are beside the point, and he'd be right to some extent: feelings make for unsteady moral grounding. But in this case queasiness may point to something more deeply problematic about Respect for Life. Consider: we could swap the goats for any non-endangered species of living thing, including human beings. We could even swap human decision-makers for Martians who determine that because human beings are responsible for the climate change threatening the planet's habitability for any number of species, we're the ones who have to go.

We'd be unlikely to accept the Martian's execution of Rolston's reasoning even if the Martians could zap us out of existence instantly and painlessly, and not just because it's us at the end of a zapper. It's because that queasiness reminds us that the moment we accept any form or quantity of suffering as permissible in the quest to achieve some other end, however good or even noble, it opens the door to other scenarios that take the same form as Rolston's—but that few moral agents would accept. Does the survival of a species of microbes outweigh the suffering of individual golden retrievers? Maybe so; but is the threat of extinction for the microbes sufficient to warrant shooting the retrievers from a helicopter? Would we be more comfortable if the retrievers were removed or killed painlessly? Or if the microbes contained the cure for lung cancer? Does the stability of earth's atmosphere outweigh the psychological suffering of human beings randomly chosen for selective "culling" in the interest of reducing the rate of human population growth? Would we feel better if the CEOs of the hydrocarbon, petrochemical, and animal agriculture companies were "euthanized" first? The point, of course, is that it's one thing to excuse suffering and/or killing when what's at stake are goats and flowers, but it seems a very different thing when the stakes are people and the planet. But the strategy of justification is the same, namely, that there are at least some ends so vitally important that achieving them justifies at least some means—even at the high cost of suffering or extermination. Any question relevant to the existential condition of human beings feels, of course, far more significant than saving a species of microbe; it *is* different, but perhaps not for the reason we think of most immediately. Our first response is likely that human beings just are of greater value than any species of microbe—that nothing could turn us, as it were, into the goats of San Clemente. But what's also true is that the continuing existence of human beings threatens countless species, including Homo sapiens. So, why shouldn't the Martians, following Leopold, determine that an action is right when it promotes biotic integrity, and wrong otherwise—and thus that it would be wrong *not* to remove the single greatest threat to the planet and its atmosphere: human beings?

We also don't need to appeal to extraterrestrials to motivate these kinds of worries. *Guardian* columnist Melissa Davey reports that the risk of spreading Covid-19 during Black Lives Matter protests is substantial, and that, at least in the case of Australia, the Health Protection Principal Committee "has been clear. People should not attend mass gatherings of any kind because even though rates of community transmission of Covid-19 are low [in Australia]… there is still a risk the virus may spread."[47] Preventing the spread of infection, in other words, requires "killing" the protests. This "killing," of course, is intended metaphorically, not literally, but it's easy to imagine a protester arguing that, given that the protest's point is to raise awareness about police brutality—indeed, police murders of African American men—that "killing" the protests is tantamount to allowing the continuing spread of perhaps the most pernicious pandemic in the planet's history, racism. But do considerations of the serious threat posed by Covid-19 to public health outweigh the suffering borne by individual protesters caused by generations of racism? Do considerations of the threat posed to the endangered flower species at San Clemente by the goats outweigh the likelihood that some of the goats shot from helicopters won't be instantly killed, may fall, break legs, suffer tremendously? Should the welfare of the whole outweigh that of its parts, knowing that some of the "parts" will be harmed? Davey reports that although "Australia has made commendable efforts to contain Covid-19, the social and public health consequences of racism have been brought to the fore by the Black Lives Matter Movement … It's clear that protests will go ahead despite the health advice about Covid-19."[48]

Is it reasonable to compare the BLM protesters defending African Americans against gun-wielding police to animal rights activists defending the goats against gun-wielding marksmen?

We might be tempted to regard a conflict between containing the spread of a pandemic and addressing racism simply as a that of two competing but equally important public welfare goals. But the truth is more complicated— and in ways that illustrate important questions for arguments like Rolston's: in choosing a species of endangered flower over the goats, Rolston prioritizes avoiding extinction over preventing suffering. In advising against going to a BLM protest, the Australian Health Committee prioritizes avoiding a viral outbreak over the welfare of a specific group of Australians racially targeted in virtue of their indigenous status (or Americans in virtue of the history of slavery). But this is not merely about whether a particular end—preventing pandemic outbreak—justifies the means—discouraging or even banning protests against racism and police brutality. It's about whether *knowingly* permitting the *suffering* of individuals can be justified under *any* circumstance, to achieve *any* goal. And this, of course, depends not just on the relation of means to ends, but on what unit of value takes priority—the individual capable of suffering, or the preservation of, as Rolston puts it, information at the level of a species. Perhaps, the critic might argue, comparing the prevention of a pandemic to saving a species of nonsentient plant life is morally odious. But this misses the point: the logic of the argument is the same; the difficult question is whether there exist some things or kinds of things that are exempt. But if we're to take Leopold's moral axiom seriously, the answer is clearly *no*. An action is right when it contributes to biotic integrity; it is wrong otherwise.

Indeed, from the point of view of Leopold's axiom, Covid-19 is a *gift* to the planet for at least two reasons: first, in the effort to prevent spread, many countries, including the giant greenhouse gas emitters like the United States, China, and India, imposed "lockdowns," effectively cauterizing emissions from cars, factories, mining operations, and air travel. The sudden appearance of blue skies over cities like Kolkata and Beijing was striking. But if looking into the sky wasn't sufficiently convincing, Benjamin Storrow, writing for *Scientific American*, reports that "[o]n April 7th [2020] global carbon dioxide emissions plummeted to levels not seen since 2006, according to a study … that suggests the coronavirus pandemic might have led to the largest reduction in CO2 ever recorded."[49] That a pandemic can contribute to enhanced biotic integrity, even at the planetary level, via mechanisms like state-mandated lockdowns, stay-at-home orders, and self-preserving individual behavior is, however, only one way a global viral outbreak can achieve this goal. The second way is to simply facilitate viral spread. Left to its own biologic devices, Covid-19 will cull the human population, reducing its rate of growth, thus the rate of consumption, waste, and ultimately greenhouse gas emissions in an even more dramatic and enduring way than temporary lockdowns. Such a project is, of course, morally perverse and self-defeating from the point of view of virtually any construal of the life worth living. The very idea of *knowingly* allowing a virus sans vaccine to run rampant, killing off the elderly, the sick, the immune system-compromised, and those made vulnerable in virtue of poverty, is effectively to convert it into an instrument of genocide. While this may fulfill the fantasy of "want to save the planet? Kill yourself," the very prospect that anyone should be empowered to make *this* kind of decision is well beyond morally odious; it is monstrous. All but the most ecologically fascist would reject it out of hand.

Still, the relationship between the pandemic, the lockdowns, and the reduction in greenhouse emissions, is instructive. Storrow, for example, reports that "few scientists are cheering the sudden change. To the contrary, researchers increasingly view the precipitous drop in emissions as a sign of how much work the world has to do to avoid the worse impacts of climate change." The reason these researchers remain pessimistic despite a 17% reduction in emissions shortly after lockdowns were imposed, is because it turns out that "individual changes in behavior produce limited emissions reductions. Much of the world stopped travelling, eating in restaurants and buying merchandise. It was an unmatched experiment and yet 80% of emissions was untouched." Rob Jackson, earth scientist at Stanford, estimates that "global emissions will fall 4% in 2020 if the world returns to normal this Summer," and "7% if lockdowns persist in parts of the world for the rest of the year." But this still falls short of the "7.6% annual reductions the United Nations said are necessary over the next decade to hold the global temperature rise to below 1.5 degrees Celsius."[50]

While it doesn't take a pandemic and a lockdown to clarify what we need to do in order to avoid at least some of the most devastating implications of the climate crisis, what Covid-19 has shown us is that what's going to be required to motivate any genuine mitigation effort is far more than the temporary suspensions of a lockdown, whatever its hardships. Restraining the rise of global temperature will require a radical shift in our disposition toward the environment, a point certainly foreshadowed by Rolston and Leopold who at the very least encourage us to think in terms of the planet, its atmosphere, its ecologies, its diversity of species, and its human populations as an interactive whole. But even if we adopt ecological holism less as a moral imperative and more as an attitude toward a life worth living, it won't diminish the workload necessary to cut greenhouse gas emissions sufficiently for the long-term. Difficult questions remain concerning how the world's biggest, wealthiest, and most prolific polluters can be held responsible for their overwhelming share of the climate crisis. But these are the questions that lead back to the insight that, given their inherently global nature, environmental crises are always inflected by social, economic and health-oriented realities. Executive Director of the United Nations Global Compact, Lise Kingo, argues that "[t]he coronavirus pandemic is just a 'fire drill' for what is likely to follow from the climate crisis, and that the protests over racial injustice around the world show the need to tie together social equality, environmental sustainability, and health."[51] Given the intimacy of the relationships that implicate the climate crisis in racial inequality, the coronavirus in climate change, and the racially predictive incidents of Covid-19 morbidity, the idea that prioritizing any one of these over the others will be effective in addressing any of the others seems incoherent, if not self-defeating.

3.2.3 Is a "Species Line" a Living System?

It might seem that we're demanding more from Rolston's Respect for Life than what can be reasonably expected to accommodate. The philosopher Ludwig Wittgenstein quipped in an aphorism that at some point in our decision-making we must settle for "this is simply what I do," (*Philosophical Investigations*, para. 109). But the applicability of a moral principle derives not from its capacity to resolve the easy cases, but the complex thorny ones. Deciding to preserve a threatened species of richly festooned parrot against a mite infestation, or Hemlocks against Woolly Adelgid[52] makes it seem easy to think of the endangered species as the "bigger event." But even if we set aside the thorny social and economic issues that inevitably arise for an environmental ethic, thinking of species as "bigger" may still be misleading. Consider Rolston's argument that what is "bigger" is, *by definition*, more important than what is *transient*, regardless other features such as sentience:

> This ethic for species will need a justification in principle, and we can suggest how that might work. The species is a bigger event than the individual, regardless of whether the member individual has interests of sentience...The species line is the *vital* living system, the whole of which individual organisms are the essential parts. ("Respect for Life," p. 261)

For Rolston it's a "plain fact of the matter" that the central unit of value is the species in virtue of its being a "bigger event," that is, a more permanent repository of information that signals a unique configuration of life. But consider: while we've extended that value to include species other than *homo Sapiens*, the value itself is a deeply human one rooted in the significance *we* attribute to qualities like originality, fragility, irreplaceability, rareness. Respect for Life is thus arguably as much an *aesthetic* criterion for determining moral considerability as it is an ethical one. While that fact doesn't necessarily count against it, it does raise the question whether Rolston's moral extensionism is about respect for *life, per se*—or respect for the reproducibility of certain aesthetic qualities we just so happen to find in the species life of organisms.

Is Rolston's bigger event a bigger *moral* event or a bigger *aesthetic* one? If the latter, Stone might interject that we can find these qualities in nonliving and/or human-made things just as well, for example, architectural design, state constitutions, works of literature and art, corporate business plans. True, the "vital" qualities of these things are reproduced by mechanical as opposed to "self-organizing" means. But why should external as opposed to "self-organizing" matter to moral considerability? Rolston says it does:

> In this bigger picture, it's not just plants that are self-organizing, but plants and all living things, sentient ones included, are products of a more comprehensive process of self-organizing, or spontaneous organizing, that characterizes the planet. The generativity is the most fundamental meaning of the term "nature," "to give birth." … The planet as a self-organizing biosphere is the most valuable entity of all, because it is the entity able to produce all the Earthbound values. ("Respect for Life," p. 266).

Although a species of plant comes to be what it is via its "generative" history and a missile is the product of mechanical design, why should these facts consign the missile to the "purely physical" in the case where they share relevantly similar aesthetic qualities? If it's information we seek to preserve, if that defines "vital," the preservation of a newly discovered, highly fragile, ancient missile design would seem just as well to warrant poisoning the mice who'd make a meal of it as the preservation of endangered plants justifies slaughtering invasive goats. What, in other words, privileges "self-organizing" over artifactual design is at least mysterious, and Rolston doesn't make it any clearer by positing "generativity" as the "fundamental meaning" of "nature," or by insisting the earth is the "most valuable entity of all." After all, the same evolutionary generativity that "gave birth" to the planet's species might just as well have given birth to nothing or evolved bereft of the conditions to support life—and absolutely nothing requires that it be otherwise. It can give birth to deadly viruses like Covid-19 via the generativity of zoonotic transmission or it can sustain hardy species like the Tardigrade, arguably "the toughest, most resilient form of life on earth, able to survive for up to 30 years without food or water and endure temperature extremes of up to 150 degrees Celsius, the deep sea and even the frozen vacuum of space."[53] What would *this* species have to endanger such that a decision to exterminate it could be justified?

Lastly, insofar as Rolston's criteria for prioritizing information over individuals doesn't require we draw a distinction between living and nonliving, it doesn't preclude the advent of androids—sentient robots—as candidates for moral considerability. Why couldn't a design for an android command the same respect for life in virtue of the "evolution" of its design specifications, originality, the rarity of its instances? Is there any reason in principle why a race of androids, reproducing mechanically, fully capable of becoming integrated into a community of both mechanical and biotic organisms, some sentient, others not, could not be included in Leopold's axiom that what's right are actions that preserve the integrity, stability, and beauty of the biotic community, and what's wrong tend otherwise? As Stone shows, biologically evolved entities have no principled monopoly on moral standing, and while androids might not have the capacity to feel pain, this excludes them only from Singer's criteria, not from Respect for Life. No doubt Rolston would find the idea that androids ought to be afforded the same respect as species-information unpalatable. But other than the arbitrary appeal to length of time, there's nothing is his claim that "Earth is the source of value" in virtue of "the millennia of natural history" that precludes androids from qualifying for moral considerability under the principle, Respect for Life. Perhaps their possible existence requires we review what counts as "living." But then again, the nearly indestructible eight-legged Tardigrade raises the same question since what constitutes a living organism includes the possibility of its death.

3.3   Summary and Questions

We began this chapter with the observation that while it might seem we've focused our attention on the moral status of nonhuman animals instead of the environment, what we've actually done is avoid prejudicing our discussion of environmental ethics against the role that consciousness, sentience, or intellectual wherewithal likely should play in a life worth living fit to confront twenty-first-century challenges, especially climate change. We then undertook a brief review of Singer and Regan in the interest of providing context to the introduction of our next philosopher, rights-oriented theorist Christopher Stone. Stone retains Regan's focus on the individual, but rejects the claim that sentience, or even being a living thing, is a necessary condition for counting as morally considerable. Stone then extends moral considerability to legal status, arguing that if human-made entities like corporations can count as persons protected by the law, so too nonsentient living things like trees or nonliving things like ecological systems. Both can be said to have an interest in avoiding harm; if moral standing derives from the moral considerability of interests, interests should be able to be represented as litigable. Stone argues that not having the capacity to stake an interests-claim ought not to weigh against the fact of having interests. It's thus not only trees that have moral standing, it's *this* tree, *this* tributary, *this* flock of Mallards, *this* mountain—natural objects, whose standing is predicated on their having (at least) the same rights as those recognized in the entities that endanger them.

One difficulty in Stone's position is that it pits the rights of natural objects against corporate entities most responsible for harm to nonhuman animals and ecosystems, especially the animal agriculture and fossil fuel industries. Defending the interests of Polar Bears against oil and gas drilling in the Arctic or the rights of rivers to be protected from acid mine run-off raises difficult questions about whose interests take priority, and on what grounds. Here too climate change offers perspective. On the one hand, we either act to defend the interests of natural objects toward future sustainability, or we'll all pay a heavy price, some heavier than others. On the other hand, distinguishing the interests of natural objects from those of their human advocates is a slippery business since even framing these issues in terms of future sustainability detracts from the moral standing of natural objects themselves. In short, thinking about the values we must preserve for any future worth wanting can help us navigate between moral standing and a consideration of consequences. But it doesn't necessarily tell us what kinds of things actually qualify as having moral standing. If corporations can count as persons before the law, so can trees or rivers—or androids, zombies, viruses, the Internet.

Contrary to Regan and Singer, Holmes Rolston III argues that prioritizing the individual is not the right route to moral considerability. In his "ethic for species" Rolston shifts our focus to genetic information of which individuals are instances. Contrary to Stone, Rolston excludes nonliving things and ecosystems from moral standing altogether. Distinguishing "purely physical systems" from organisms as "defenders of their own lives," Rolston's exclusion of human artifacts such as missiles implies that entities such as corporations and governments lack moral standing even though they may be instances of reproducible design, ideologies, or belief systems. He argues that living things embody "axiological systems," that is, purposeful organic structures. They're sources of value and valuing in virtue of exemplifying the larger central unit of value, the species, and they exhibit characteristics that even complex, though inanimate, entities do not, especially the capacity to consume nutrients, self-propel, repair injuries, avoid predators, and reproduce offspring. Respect for life is thus respect for what Rolston calls the "good-of-its-kind": value realized as an organism's endeavor to "actualize" itself as a reproducing instance of a particular kind or species of entity. Whereas as human artifacts like missiles realize only the "external" intentions of their inventers, plant's realize information stored in their evolving genetic histories, "motives" internal to their physical state.

Rolston's argument raises a number of thorny issues, but particularly questions about when, if ever, means that include allowing suffering can be justified by ends—even very good ends. In valuing species over instances, he redefines moral considerability to prioritize threat of extinction over prevention of suffering. In valuing "information" over individuals, he extends moral status to nonsentient living things, but also commits moral decision-making to courses of action that pit species against each other, generating the conditions of suffering. Another issue is that valuing the species over the individual is itself anthropocentric. It's rooted in qualities *we* attribute to "kinds" of things. Respect for Life is thus arguably as much an *aesthetic* criterion for determining considerability as a moral one. While this may not count against Rolston's view, it does raise the question whether his version of moral extensionism is about respect for life, or respect for the reproducibility of certain aesthetic qualities we just so happen to find at the level of the species more than the individual.

1. What is Christopher Stone's argument for the legal standing of natural objects like trees? How is his view comparable to or different from Peter Singer's and/or Tom Regan's?
2. What role do concepts like sentience, living/nonliving, natural/humanmade play in Stone's reasoning?
3. How does Stone justify the transition from moral considerability to legal standing? What are the implications of such a view for how we see law?
4. What is Holmes Rolston III's argument for "respect for life?" What key role is played by the concept of "information"? "Species"? Why does Rolston regard the species as "bigger" than the individual?
5. What specific place does Rolston accord to endangered species in his argument? Why is it important?
6. How does Rolston's argument for "respect for life" raise thorny questions about when the ends justify the means—and the means include suffering?
7. What important questions are raised for Stone by a consideration of the history of rights offered by writers such as William Cronon?
8. What important questions are raised for Rolston concerning how we think about the value of species over individuals in light of the climate crisis and its implications for social and economic justice?

Annotated Bibliography

Barry, Brian. "Sustainability and Intergenerational Justice." *Theoria* 45, 89, pp. 43–65.
Barry explores the question whether the principle of utility can be extended to future generations as an argument for the present generation's responsibility to the future.

Cronon, William. "The Trouble with Wilderness or, Getting Back to the Wrong Nature," in William Cronon (ed.), *Uncommon Ground: Toward Reinventing Nature* (W.W. Norton, and Company, 1995), pp. 7–28.
Cronon argues that the concept "wilderness" is a creation or a fiction that captures the desire to escape back to some untouched nature, but that also conceals a violent history of the removal of indigenous peoples from their native lands.

Doremus, Holly. "Environmental Ethics and Environmental Law: Harmony, Dissonance, cacophony, or Irrelevance." *Berkeley Law Scholarship Repository* 37 (1), (2003). https://scholarship.law.berkeley.edu/cgi/viewcontent.cgi?referer=https://www.google.com/&httpsredir=1&article=1874&context=facpubs.
Doremus provides an excellent review of the legal issues and progress (or lack thereof) since Stone's work on the legal standing of natural objects.

Elder, P.S. "Legal Rights for Nature: The Wrong Answer to the Right(s) Question." *Osgoode Hall Law Journal* 22 (2), (1984), pp. 285–95. https://digitalcommons.osgoode.yorku.ca/cgi/viewcontent.cgi?referer=https://www.google.com/&httpsredir=1&article=1935&context=ohlj.
Elder argues that Stone's view of the legal standing of natural objects is mistaken, and that according standing to things like trees is an issue already adequately covered by "conventional ethics and law."

Goodluck, Kalen. "Covid-19 is Sweeping Through the Navajo Nation," *Wired*, May 23, 2020, https://www.wired.com/story/covid-19-is-sweeping-through-the-navajo-nation.

Hettinger, Ned. "Valuing Predation in Rolston's Environmental Ethics." *Between the Species* 5, (1989), pp. 1–10.
Hettinger argues that Rolston's privileging of plant species can be extended to nonhuman animals in a fashion that does not preclude meat-eating.

Jamieson, Dale. "Animal Liberation is an Environmental Ethic," *Environmental Values*, November, 1997, https://acad.carleton.edu/curricular/ENTS/faculty/dale/dale_animal.html.
Jamieson argues that, contrary to much opinion inside and outside philosophy, environmental ethics is a close ally of animal rights—and must be.

Jamieson, Dale, ed. (1999). *Singer and His Critics* (New York: Wiley-Blackwell).
In this anthology, Jamieson includes a number of critical assessments of the
    work of Peter Singer, including that of Holmes Rolston III.
Miller, Peter. "Axiology and Environmental Ethics." *Business and Professional
    Ethics Journal* 19 (1), (Spring 2000), pp. 65–77. https://www.jstor.org/
    stable/27801211?seq=1#page_scan_tab_contents.
Miller argues that psychological theories place "disturbing limits" on the
    value of nature, encouraging the view that, following John Locke, it
    exists solely for human use.
Pavlik, Steve. "Should Trees Have Legal Standing in Indian Country?&#x201D."
    Wicazo Sa Review 30 (1), (Spring 2015), pp. 7–28. https://www.jstor.org/
    stable/10.5749/wicazosareview.30.1.0007?seq=1#page_scan_tab_contents.
Pavlik argues that although Stone's original argument for the legal standing
    of natural objects received a good deal of attention when it was written
    several decades ago, that attention did not result in positive action in the
    United States. It's now time to revisit that argument—"beginning with
    tribal governments."
Rolston, Homes III. (1989). *Philosophy Gone Wild: Environmental Ethics* (New
    York: Prometheus).
This is Rolston's landmark contribution to his view, "respect for life," where
    he lays out ins a series of self-standing essays his vision for an environ-
    mental ethics grounded in the species as opposed to the individual.
Rolston, Holmes III. (1994). *Conserving Natural Value* (New York: Columbia
    University Press).
In this work, Rolston expands his argument from *Philosophy Gone Wild* to
    specific questions concerning biological conservation.
Rolston, Holmes, III. "Respect for Life: Counting What Singer Finds of No
    Account," in *Singer and His Critics* (New York: Wiley-Blackwell, 1999),
    pp. 247–68.
In this essay, Rolston makes out his argument for the value of living things
    at the level of the species, and against Peter Singer's prioritizing of
    individual suffering.
Rolston, Holmes, III. (1999). *Genes, Genesis, and God* (Cambridge: Cam-
    bridge University Press).
Rolston argues that the phenomena of religion and ethics cannot be reduced
    to biological explanation.
Rolston, Holmes, III, ed. (2011). *A New Environmental Ethics: The Next Mil-
    lennium for Life on Earth* (New York: Routledge).
An anthology devoted to the future of confronting 21st century environmental
    crises, edited in light of Rolston's wealth of work in environmental ethics.

Rolston, Holmes III. "How Humans Differ From Other Animals," *Interview,*
Closer to Truth, https://www.closertotruth.com/interviews/2884.
Rolston presents his view of the differences between human beings and nonhuman animals in virtue of what he argues is the superiority of human
intellect or what he calls "synaptic possibility."
Stone, Christopher. (1988). *Should Trees Have Standing? Towards Legal Rights*
for Natural Objects (Palo Alta, CA: Tioga Publishing Company).
In this key work of environmental ethics, Stone argues for the extension of
legal standing to natural objects like trees. He expands on a utilitarian
argument for moral considerability to its implications for law-making
and application.
Stone, Christopher. "Stone Revisits "Should Tress Have Standing?" *YouTube,*
https://www.youtube.com/watch?v=eV9JmQwFXg0.
Stone revisits his original argument for the legal standing of natural objects
like trees in light of a specific case of land development challenged by the
Sierra Club.
Stone, Christopher. "Habeas Corpus for Animals? Why not?" *Washington*
Post, June 12, 2010, http://www.washingtonpost.com/wp-dyn/content/
article/2010/06/11/AR2010061105310.html.
Stone expands his argument for the legal standing of natural objects to include
nonhuman animals, in this case sea lions.
Wittgenstein, Ludwig. (2001). *Philosophical Investigations,* Trans. G.E.M. An-
scombe. Second Edition (Blackwell Publishers).
One of the most significant explorations of language use ever to be undertaken, Wittgenstein argues that "the meaning of a word is its use"—or
rather, its usefulness.

Online Resources

1. Dale Jamieson, "Animal Liberation is an Environmental Ethic," *Environ-*
   mental Values, November, 1997, https://acad.carleton.edu/curricular/
   ENTS/faculty/dale/dale_animal.html.
2. "The Bison: From 30 Million to 325 to 500,000 Today," *Flat Creek Inn,*
   https://www.flatcreekinn.com/bison-americas-mammal.
3. "Cartographic Concepts: Navajo Land Acquisition," http://www.mapmanusa.
   com/cci-exhibit-7.html.
4. M Natalie and M Brianna, "Native American Poverty in Arizona. Story
   Maps," *Story Maps,* January 17, 2020, https://storymaps.arcgis.com/stories/
   b7b09da92c664e0baa5fd375c045cc26.

5. "Indian Health Services: Healthcare Facilities," https://www.ihs.gov/navajo/healthcarefacilities.
6. Raul M. Grijalva, "Chair Grijalva, Natural Resources Committee Launch New Coronavirus Resource Center, Seek Impact Information from Indian Country," *Natural Resources Committee*, https://naturalresources.house.gov/media/press-releases/chair-grijalva-natural-resources-committee-launch-new-coronavirus-resource-center-seek-impact-information-from-indian-country.
7. Kalen Goodluck, "Covid-19 is Sweeping through the Navajo Nation," *Wired*, May 23, 2020. https://www.wired.com/story/covid-19-is-sweeping-through-the-navajo-nation.
8. Kristoffer Tigue, "Covid-19 and Climate Change Threats Compound in Minority Communities," *Scientific American*, April 20, 2020, https://www.scientificamerican.com/article/covid-19-and-climate-change-threats-compound-in-minority-communities.
9. "More Coronavirus Testing Planned at New Mexico Meat Plant," *My High Plains*, May 22, 2020, https://www.myhighplains.com/news/new-mexico/more-coronavirus-testing-planned-at-new-mexico-meat-plant.
10. Eric Klauk, "Environmental Impacts on the Navajo Nation from Uranium Mining," *Impacts of Resource Development on Indian Lands*, https://serc.carleton.edu/research_education/nativelands/navajo/environmental.html.
11. Susanne Berthier-Foglar, "Uranium Mining on Sacred Land," *ELOHI: Indigenous Peoples and the Environment*, https://journals.openedition.org/elohi/304.
12. N. Van Doremalen, "Investigational ChAdOx1 nCoV-19 Vaccine Protects Monkeys Against Covid-19 Pneumonia," *National Institutes of Health* (NIH), https://www.nih.gov/news-events/news-releases/investigational-chadox1-ncov-19-vaccine-protects-monkeys-against-covid-19-pneumonia.
13. Celina Kareiva, "Animal Rights at the University of Washington," Seattle Magazine, June, 2015. https://www.seattlemag.com/article/animal-rights-university-washington.
14. Nancy Heneson, "Live Animals in Car Crash Studies," *The Humane Society Institute for Science and Policy: Animal Studies Repository*, https://animalstudiesrepository.org/cgi/viewcontent.cgi?article=1018&context=acwp_arte.
15. "Monkey Tests Spark Outrage," *Gazette and Herald*, August 3, 2000, https://www.gazetteandherald.co.uk/news/7401030.monkey-tests-spark-outrage.
16. David Sanger, et. al. "Profits and Pride at Stake, the Race for a Vaccine Intensifies," *The New York Times*, May 20, 2020, https://www.nytimes.com/2020/05/02/us/politics/vaccines-coronavirus-research.html.

17. "Retire Imprisoned Monkeys After the Possible Spread of Covid-19," *People for the Ethical Treatment of Animals* (PETA), https://support.peta.org/page/18347/action/1?locale=en-US.
18. David Grimm, "'It's Heartbreaking.'' Labs are Euthanizing Thousands of Mice in Response to the Coronavirus Pandemic," *American Association for the Advancement of Science* (AAAS), March 23, 2020, https://www.sciencemag.org/news/2020/03/it-s-heartbreaking-labs-are-euthanizing-thousands-mice-response-coronavirus-pandemic.
19. Eric Loomis, "Opinion: Spotted Owl Protections Didn't Kill Logging Jobs; Timber Industry Did," *The Oregonian*, September 14, 2019, https://www.oregonlive.com/opinion/2019/09/opinion-spotted-owl-protections-didnt-kill-logging-jobs-timber-industry-did.html.
20. Holloway, Carson. "Are Corporations People?" *National Affairs* 37, (Fall 2018), https://www.nationalaffairs.com/publications/detail/are-corporations-people.
21. Blake Hurst, "The Omnivore's Delusion: Against the Agri-Intellectuals," *American Enterprise Institute* (AEI), July 30, 2009, https://www.aei.org/articles/the-omnivores-delusion-against-the-agri-intellectuals.
22. "2017 Major Criminal Cases," *Environmental Protection Agency* (EPA), https://www.epa.gov/enforcement/2017-major-criminal-cases.
23. Felicity Berringer, "New Battle of Logging Vs. Spotted Owl Looms in West," *New York Times*, October 18, 2007, https://www.nytimes.com/2007/10/18/us/18owl.html.
24. "Summarizing Five Years of NOAA Research on the Impacts of the Deep Water Horizon Oil Spill on Dolphins," *NOAA Office of Response and Restoration*, https://response.restoration.noaa.gov/about/media/summarizing-five-years-noaa-research-impacts-deepwater-horizon-oil-spill-dolphins.html.
25. Margaret Badore, "13 Amazing and Critically Endangered Frogs," *Treehugger*, February 29, 2016, https://www.treehugger.com/slideshows/endangered-species/13-amazing-and-critically-endangered-frogs.
26. "International Climate Impacts," *Climate Change Impacts: Environmental Protection Agency*, January 19, 2017, https://19january2017snapshot.epa.gov/climate-impacts/international-climate-impacts_.html.
27. "Why Lichens Matter," *U.S. Forest Service*, June 16, http://nadp.slh.wisc.edu/conf/2016/pptpdf/159_geiser.pdf.
28. "Bees," *BeeOdiversity*, http://www.beeodiversity.com/en/issue/bees.
29. Stephen Onderick, "Save the Planet, Kill Yourself: A Documentary," *Kickstarter*, 2016, https://www.kickstarter.com/projects/1234068001/save-the-planet-kill-yourself-an-independent-docum.

30. "Human Population Growth and Climate Change," *Center for Biological Diversity*, https://www.biologicaldiversity.org/programs/population_and_sustainability/climate.

31. Robert Goodland and Jeff Anhang, "Livestock and Climate Change," *World Watch*, December 09, http://www.worldwatch.org/files/pdf/Livestock%20and%20Climate%20Change.pdf.

32. Hillary Rosner, "Hordes of Wild Pigs Make Palm Oil Even More Destructive," *National Geographic*, December 21, 2017, https://news.nationalgeographic.com/2017/12/palm-oil-wild-pig-boom-rainforest-environment.

33. "Old-Growth Logging's Last Stand," *BioGraphic*, December 20, 2016, https://www.biographic.com/posts/sto/old-growth-loggings-last-stand.

34. "10 Animals Threatened by Climate Change," *EarthDay.Org*, February 7, 2019, https://www.earthday.org/how-climate-change-is-threatening-our-species.

35. Anil Agarwal and Sunita Narain. "Global Warming in an Unequal World: A Case of Environmental Colonialism," *Oxford Scholarship Online*, 2019, https://www.oxfordscholarship.com/view/10.1093/oso/9780199498734.001.0001/oso-9780199498734-chapter-5.

36. Andrew Freedman, "The Countries that Pushed Carbon Emissions to Record Levels," *Axios*, December 6, 2018, https://www.axios.com/china-india-us-pushed-carbon-emissions-to-record-levels-in-2018-1b1e171a-d46a-49b7-bc4a-7250942a1a7d.html.

37. Ibid. Agarwal, Anil, and Sunita Narain.

38. Karoui, Sedki, and Romdhane Khemakhem. "Consumer Ethnocentrism in Developing Countries." *European Research on Management and Business Economics* 25 (2) (4.2019), p. 63. https://reader.elsevier.com/reader/sd/pii/S2444883418300809?token=3FA4259B42B9E9309099038EF047106DCB41AE4AF7B6BB92ED7956315C00AAA3242517E9B17827E87294A7DDF40B8CCA.

39. Morgan Medlock, "Covid-19 Will Pass. Will We Be Able to Say the Same About the Racism It Illuminated?" *STAT*, April 23, 2020, https://www.statnews.com/2020/04/23/covid-19-will-pass-what-about-the-racism-it-has-illuminated.

40. Gardener, Beth. "Unequal Impact: The Deep Links between Racism and Climate Change." *Yale Environment 360*, June 9, (2020), https://e360.yale.edu/features/unequal-impact-the-deep-links-between-inequality-and-climate-change.

41. John Hayes, "Fracking in Trout Country," *Pittsburgh Post-Gazette*, May 4, 2014, https://www.post-gazette.com/sports/hunting-fishing/2014/05/04/Anglers-divided-new-technologies-extracting-energy-near-trout-streams/stories/201405040092.

42. Christopher McGlade and Paul Ekins, "The Geographical Distribution of Fossil Fuels Unused When Limiting Global Warming to 2 Degrees Celsius,"

Nature, January 8, 2015, pp. 187–90. https://www.nature.com/articles/nature14016.

43. *Earth First!* http://www.earthfirst.org.

44. Andrew Nickels, et. al., "Can Parents Refuse a Potentially Life-Saving Transplant for Severe Combined Immunodeficiency?" *Pediatrics* July, 2016. http://pediatrics.aappublications.org/content/138/1/e20160892.

45. Miller, Peter. "Axiology and Environmental Ethics," *Business and Professional Ethics Journal*, 19, 1 (Spring 2000), pp. 65–77. https://www.jstor.org/stable/27801211?seq=1#page_scan_tab_contents.

46. Leopold, Aldo. (1968). *A Sand County Almanac* (Oxford: Oxford University Press). https://www.aldoleopold.org/post/understanding-land-ethic.

47. Melissa Davey, "Black Lives Matter: Health Experts Assess Risks of Covid-19 Transmission at Australia protests," *The Guardian*, June 12, 2020, https://www.theguardian.com/australia-news/2020/jun/12/black-lives-matter-australia-protest-will-blm-protests-spark-second-covid-19-coronavirus-wave-health-experts.

48. Ibid. Melissa Davey.

49. Benjamin Storrow, "Global CO2 Emission Saw Record Drop During Pandemic Lockdown," *Scientific American*, May 20, 2020, https://www.scientificamerican.com/article/global-co2-emissions-saw-record-drop-during-pandemic-lockdown.

50. Rob Jordan, "Stanford Researcher Envisions Energy and Environment Landscape After Covid-19," Stanford News Service, May 19, 2020, https://news.stanford.edu/press-releases/2020/05/19/environment-energy-covid-19.

51. Fiona Harvey, "Covid-19 Pandemic is "Fire Drill" for Effects of Climate Crisis, Says UN Official," *The Guardian*, June 15, 2020, https://www.theguardian.com/environment/2020/jun/15/covid-19-pandemic-is-fire-drill-for-effects-of-climate-crisis-says-un-official.

52. "Hemlock Wooley Adelgid," *Northern Research Station, United States Department of Agriculture, Forest Service*, https://www.nrs.fs.fed.us/disturbance/invasive_species/hwa/risk_detection_spread/variability_hemlock_decline.

53. "The Last Surviving Species on Earth May Well be the Tardigrade," *Science Daily, University of Oxford*, https://www.sciencedaily.com/releases/2017/07/170714071459.htm.

4

TWO EXAMPLES OF AN ECOCENTRIC ETHIC: ALDO LEOPOLD, ARNE NAESS, AND THEIR CRITICS

4.1 Human-Centeredness, Human Chauvinism, and Ecocentrism

4.1.1 Ecocentrism and the Limits of Moral Extensionism

While moral extensionism seeks to expand well-established moral principles like utility or the Categorical Imperative to nonhuman animals and ecosystems, *ecocentric* thinkers like Aldo Leopold and Arne Naess take what they insist is a very different path toward realizing their vision of an environmentally defensible way of life worth living. Broadly, *ecocentrism* (*ecological holism, biocentrism, or anti-anthropocentrism*) is the view that the only ethic capable of taking nonhuman animals and ecosystems into adequate moral account is one that makes its point of departure the *wholesale repudiation* of human-centeredness and the embrace of an ecologically centered moral compass. For these thinkers, human-centeredness, *anthropocentrism*, just is fundamentally *chauvinistic*, and thus intractably bent to self-interest and material gain.[1] Moral principles crafted to solve human conflicts can offer little more than a model distorted by human objectives likely to preemptively devalue nonhuman beings and ecosystems.[2] The best approach to an environmental ethic is thus to consign these old moral ideas to the landfill of human history and begin anew squarely committed to putting, as Aldo Leopold puts it, the "biotic community" first, next, and last.

It's hard to deny that ecocentrism has a point. How did we arrive at the climate crisis? Why is the next world war likely to be fought over what some call

This is Environmental Ethics: An Introduction, First Edition. Wendy Lynne Lee.
© 2022 John Wiley & Sons, Inc. Published 2022 by John Wiley & Sons, Inc.
Companion Website: https://thisisphilosoph.wordpress.com

"blue gold," that is, potable water? What, besides human excess, accounts for the extinction of the western black rhino? The Yunnan Lake newt? The Xerces blue butterfly? What other than human encroachment can account for the zoonotic spread of viruses like Covid-19? What the evidence points to is a human nature replete with a nearly bottomless capacity for denial, excuse-making, willful ignorance, and short-sightedness, making the prospect of moral rehabilitation unrealistic at least without a radically new *compelling* moral principle to guide judgment and decision-making. Is ecocentrism this new principle? If so, can it offer a way of life? Is such a life likely to be desirable—however, morally binding? How do we convince others to renounce their human chauvinism? Part of what's difficult here is that even if it's true that our traditional moral principles are inadequate, that by itself does not show that ecocentrism is either the best, much less the only, alternative, or that it shares nothing in common with moral extensionism. It also doesn't necessarily count against an ecocentric ethic if it turns out that it does share some common objectives. What matters is that its advocates be able to show *how* an ecocentric ethic can make the central pivot of its moral decision-making the biotic community, how this can produce defensible conditions for a life worth living, in what such a life consists, and whether it's realistic. On the one hand, while each of the moral extensionisms we've surveyed can be incorporated into moral judgment, they're liable to considerable criticism. It's far from obvious that they can promise a sustainable, much less desirable, future. Yet on the other, what "desirable" means from the point of view of an ecocentric ethic is itself unclear given that one's first duty is to displace self-interest in exchange for the interests of the biotic community.

Our first question, then, is "does the disavowal of self-interest, adopting instead an ecocentric perspective, make ecocentrism radically new?" Here the answer is no. Ecocentrism does in fact share a focus on *consequences* with utilitarians, particularly in light of a principle we know well already—Aldo Leopold's: an action is right when it contributes to the integrity and stability of the "biotic community," and wrong otherwise (*A Sand County Almanac*, p. 224). We know that integrity and stability implicitly refer to the future and are thus inherently consequentialist. They aim at an ecosystem's capacity to sustain itself and its species life. From an ecocentric perspective, Leopold exchanges the utilitarian's maximizing happiness and minimizing suffering for maximizing ecological sustainability, minimizing erosion. Unlike Peter Singer, who places high value on impartiality to show us why nonhuman animals must be included in any moral calculus concerning suffering, Leopold effectively eschews concern for suffering and replaces it with whatever actions promote the biotic community's capacity to reproduce itself. But, the critic might respond, suffering *does* matter; consideration for it forms a key aspect of sound moral judgment. To ignore suffering in favor of virtually any other end, no matter how noble, has the potential to invite all manner of violence, cruelty, and neglect in the name of that end.

Leopold offers essentially two responses to this criticism. First, a too-narrow focus on suffering, and therefore on individuals, can miss issues of even greater consequence, at least from an ecocentric point of view. In *A Sand County Almanac*, for example, Leopold gives an oft-cited example of wolves:

> Even without sight or sound of wolf, it is implicit in a hundred small events: the midnight whinny of a packhorse, the rattling of rolling rocks, the bound of a fleeing deer, the way shadows lie under the spruces. Only the uneducable tyro can fail to sense the presence or absence of wolves, or the fact that mountains have a secret opinion about them ... My own conviction on this score dates from the day I saw a wolf die. We were eating lunch on a high rimrock, at the foot of which a turbulent river elbowed its way. We saw what we thought was a doe fording the torrent, her breast awash in white water. When she climbed the bank toward us and shook out her tail, we realized our error. A half-dozen others, evidently grown pups sprang from the willows and all joined in a welcoming melee of wagging tails and playful maulings. What was literally a pile of wolves writhed and tumbled in the center of an open flat at the foot of our rimrock. In those days we had never heard of passing up a chance to kill a wolf. In a second, we were pumping lead into the pack, but with more excitement than accuracy...When our rifles were empty the old wolf was down, and a pup was dragging a leg into impassable slide rocks. We reached the wolf in time to watch a fierce green fire dying in her eyes. I realized then, and have known ever since, that there was something new to me in those eyes—something known only to her and the mountain. (pp. 129–30)

I quote the passage at length to make clear that Leopold is deeply attuned to the wolf's suffering. Looking into her fierce green eyes, it plainly troubles him. He is surely aware that the description of the pup dragging its leg will serve only to emphasize to the reader that the wolves are living suffering beings, each an individual, this pup trying to survive—and we know it won't. But, as he goes on to explain, the "extirpation" of wolves as ranching expands across the country could only mean one thing: growing deer herds. It's in light of this new, human-caused, problem that the meaning of "known to her and the mountain" becomes clear: while suffering is not irrelevant, "pumping lead into the pack" is another kind of wrong: killing the wolves disrupts a biotic community that needs them to maintain ecosystemic balance. What Leopold recognizes that is new, at least to him, is what becomes the centerpiece of an ecocentric ethic: seeing the world not through the eyes of the wolf, but through the "eyes" of what the wolf "knows," that is, not through the wolf's suffering, but through what that suffering *signifies*: all living things, many of them moments of sentience, have a place in the biotic community, but it is the community that defines that place and thus the community that must "decide" what best sustains it into the future, even if what that means is reintroducing wolves and exterminating the deer. Leopold is clear: suffering is not a thing to be sought—pumping lead into a pile of wolves is reckless. But suffering is also not the deciding factor where the sustainability of a biotic community is at stake. What Leopold claims to know is not necessarily *empathy*, but rather *foresight*.

Leopold's second response, then, is that moments of foresight like the one ignited for him looking into the dying wolf's green eyes isn't necessarily the common experience of most folks. That, in any case, is the ecocentric assessment of human nature; it's pretty bleak, and the ecocentrist has a compelling case to make. Quite literally mountains of evidence in the form of coal tailings or landfills, ocean-wandering islands of plastics, radioactive forests, and abandoned cities like Chernobyl or Fukushima, toxin-associated cancers—all before we even arrive at the fraught intersection of social order and the climate crisis—make this case. Consider for example a recent French Citizen's Assembly vote to make Ecocide a crime, indeed, a crime prosecutable at the International Crimes Court at the Hague. Utilizing the concept of "nine planetary boundaries (CO_2 levels, ocean acidification, biosphere integrity) beyond which we cannot go without risking irreversible damage to the planet's capacity to sustain human life," the assembly's aim is to see internationally enforceable laws erected that would "remove the impunity of big polluters" such as big fossil fuel and big animal agriculture from criminal liability.[3] Notice, however, that the intended beneficiaries of such laws are still first and foremost human beings. That is, even if these laws went some ways to protect the plant's "boundaries," and their ancillary effects were a benefit to nonhuman animals and ecosystems, for the ecocentrist this doesn't go far enough in that the chauvinism at their core retains the prerogative to reverse course—returning to our destructive ways, jeopardizing the future.

The only way to tackle issues so impactful and global in scope, argue the ecocentrists, is to get beyond anthropocentrism. While law may well play a significant role, an ecocentrist ethic begins with a transformative personal disavowal of self-centeredness that puts, as Leopold phrases it, "the land" first even at the cost of convenience, money, or comfort. Needless to say, this is no easy undertaking. Thinking our way beyond human interests demands a sustainable *personal* commitment easily displaced by social expectation, cultural traditions, and expediency. Imagine, for example, the effort to sustain a vegan lifestyle when your friends are headed out to a Burger King; we know the lives of factory farm animals are miserable,[4] but cheese-burgers look delicious, and fast food is super-convenient. Consider how difficult it might be to say no to the landman from the fossil fuel company who wants to drill for natural gas under your forested back acres.[5] We know the environmental hazards associated with horizontal slickwater hydraulic fracturing (fracking), but the offer of money that could pay for a child's college education is hard to turn down. How do we say no to that—especially when all our neighbors said yes?[6]

An ecocentric ethic is thus utilitarian is as much as it's about the consequences of human chauvinism even as it radically shifts our focus from individuals to ecosystems, and therefore from suffering to biotic integrity. What this shift of perspective teaches us is that the reform represented by moral extensionism just won't do. Indeed, so long as human interests remain the guiding lodestar, even the force of laws like those proposed by the French Citizen's Assembly can offer no guarantee that the future won't be scarred by greed and waste. As Cronon shows, much in Western culture invites both the denial of our environmental impact and the effective elision of the history that exposes it. We're rewarded for greed, gluttony, dissipation, and apathy. We know that burger tells a story of great suffering, but everything on the menu tells us it doesn't matter. We know that although our child's college education is important, so too the hazards posed to other people's children in the form of polluted groundwater, poor air quality, and greenhouse gas emissions produced by natural gas extraction infrastructure.[7] Indeed, if anything counts against the French Citizen's Assembly despite the willingness to see ecological destruction criminalized, it is that its anthropocentric outlook still doesn't go far enough. For the ecocentrist, reform has plainly failed us. It's time for revolution.

4.1.2   Ecocentrism as Psychic Transformation and Moral Paradigm Shift

The revolutionary transformation toward the adoption of an ecocentric ethic is doubtless a heavy psychic lift. Consider, for instance, our dependence on hydrocarbons.[8] The necessity of petrochemicals, coal, plastics, or other hydrocarbon products to virtually every form of manufacture and transport seems intractable, and virtually everything we do or eat can be traced back to our intimate affiliation with fossil fuels. Though a limited resource, hydrocarbon extraction offers a paradigmatic example of the myth of endless resources; its high value and our capacity to deny its potential exhaustion is made clear by the Herculean technological effort undertaken to extract every last drop from under the planet's surface "Extractivism" is as deeply embedded an aspect of the global North way of life as is driving cars, buying bottled water, fertilizing our lawns, and eating cheeseburgers. It's thus not surprising that expanded protections for wildlife impacted by the Deepwater Horizon disaster in 2010 were scuttled by President Trump in early 2018. They were in the way of a planned re-boot of oil and gas drilling operations in the Gulf of Mexico and along the US Eastern Seaboard.[9] Similarly, President Obama's 2016 *Presidential Proclamation* establishing *Bears Ears National Monument* was rescinded one year later, again by the Trump administration.[10] The gas company, EOG Resources, has proposed drilling operations at the site.[11]

In both cases protections were extended, then withdrawn; species and habitats preserved became again endangered. For the ecocentrist, examples like these illustrate precisely why reformist moralities have failed, and thus why a more radical approach is required. To extend and then withdraw protections reveals human chauvinism at its ugliest in that such actions at once recognize the value of preserving wildlife, but choose human interest and expediency regardless. As William Cronon would likely point out, *Bears Ears* is not only a site valued for its wildlife and beauty, but as sacred to the indigenous peoples of the American Southwest. While ecocentrism may not be as new to environmental ethics as its proponents claim, it's application of the principle of utility is radically different in its shift from a focus on suffering to the sustainability of the biotic community. But whether a shift to sustainability can move us to behave individually or collectively in more environmentally responsible ways remains to be seen. Can a human-centeredness cast as inherently short-sighted and selfish achieve the transformation required to live an ecocentric ethic? That is the next key question.[12] After all, if what we must do cannot be made to cohere with what it's possible for us to do, and if what's possible cannot be made desirable (or at least palatable), it's not clear we've yet arrived at the moral life worth living.

Consider Leopold's "land ethic." It derives its justification not from a view of the natural world that presupposes human domination, but from the premise that morality *per se* has its origins in our environmental, that is, *existential* conditions.[13] "The extension of ethics, so far only studied by philosophers," writes Leopold, "is actually a process of ecological evolution. An ethic, ecologically, is a limitation on freedom of action in the struggle for existence" (*A Sand County Almanac*, p. 202). He then goes to draw an analogy between ecology and human society arguing that the interdependencies that define relationships in either case show that "the individual is a member of a community of interdependent parts" regardless their species, and that therefore "[t]he land ethic simply enlarges the boundaries of the community to include soils, waters, plants, animals, or collectively: the land" (*A Sand County Almanac*, pp. 203–4). It's not surprising that, for Leopold, it's not enough simply to reject human chauvinism in favor of a conventional environmentalism that asks of us little more change than recycling, improved gas mileage, or Meatless Mondays. "A land ethic," argues Leopold, "changes the role of Homo Sapiens from conqueror of the land-community to plain member and citizen of it," and it recognizes the role of conqueror is destined to become "self-defeating" (*A Sand County Almanac*, p. 204). The "cowman who cleans his range of wolves," for example, "does not realize he is taking over the wolf's job of trimming the herd to fit the range. He has not learned to think like a mountain. Hence, we have dustbowls and rivers washing the future into the sea" (*A Sand County Almanac*, p. 132).

To think like a mountain is thus to undertake a *paradigm shift*, a transformation in the way we think about the planet and our place on it, that moves us away from human chauvinism and away from a moral thinking whose narrow range of application serves mostly as a pretext for fulfilling human interests.[14] But what that requires is that traditional forms of moral extensionism not merely be set to the side as inadequate, but unmasked as thinly veiled iterations of self-interest with a "kinder, gentler face." Consider, for example, Singer, Regan, and Stone— the expansion of utility, *subject-of-a-life*, and the extension of rights to nonsentient entities via recognized proxies. Each offers a way in which nonhuman animals and ecosystems come to be recognized as morally considerable modeled after capacities associated with human beings. Their arguments aim to *extend* to nonhuman entities and agents not only principles crafted to solve human conflicts, but after characteristics associated with human being. Singer privileges psychological and intellectual suffering over physical pain. Regan explicitly privileges self-consciousness over "mere" sentience. Stone's appeal to the rights of nonsentient entities may go the furthest to enfranchise nonhuman animals and biotic communities, but it still treats its object of moral consideration as a rights-bearing individual as opposed to prioritizing the relationships that characterize the place of individuals in the biotic community.

From an ecocentric perspective, however, so long as the primary unit of moral considerability is the individual effectively detached from the community, our judgments about what actions should be undertaken will be distorted by an unrealistic picture of the interdependencies of which individuals, including individual species, are a part. Such a distorted focus only reinforces the primacy of the individual over the community, and can, according to the ecocentrist, have disastrous consequences. To focus, for example, on the fate of the spotted owl abstracted from the historical context of logging, the role of unions in conservation, economic decline, or corporate outsourcing offers an incomplete picture of how the owl became endangered. Similar stories can be told for Sumatran elephants, Baleen whales, and Monarch butterflies, but the focus need not be endangered species to make the point that an anthropocentric morality is liable, as it were, to miss the forest for the trees. In *Not for Humans Only*, for example, Singer gives a now famous example of a power station. The question before a community government is whether to build on site A that "would be more expensive because the greater depth of the shifting soil… will require deeper foundations" or site B, a "favored breeding ground for thousands of wild fowl" (Singer, "The Place of Nonhumans in Environmental Issues," p. 142). Singer asks whether the wildfowl should enter into the moral calculus. But the way the example is set up—pitting two sets of individuals against each other—may well ignore other important factors. What if the community is poor, has been waiting for a new power station for a generation, or what if the power station itself poses a significant health hazard in virtue of toxic waste emissions? What if, among the species of wildfowl is an endangered species? What if the site is chosen in part because it can utilize a waterway for waste disposal? What if the station threatens to obscure the view of a favorite scenic vista? What if shifting soil at site A threatens to expose toxic waste at a long-abandoned landfill? What if the station promises jobs to a struggling community trying to climb out from underneath the economic devastation of a pandemic?

The point, of course, is that once we take into consideration all of the factors relevant to the decision about where to build the power station, it is less clear whose suffering counts for more. Singer's aim is to encourage us to see the waterfowl as having an interest that ought to be included in the community deliberations. But the example also implicitly invites us to see the expense of building at site A as less significant than the destruction of the favored breeding ground. It *is* less significant if the community can afford to build at site A without great sacrifice. But it's also not hard to imagine circumstances where the community will suffer substantial harm in choosing to favor the birds. In fact, power stations, landfills, factory farms, and waste incinerators are frequently built in low-income and/or minority neighborhoods precisely because the land is less expensive, the community is unlikely to resist because activism endangers employment, and because there may be a promise of jobs at the site. The extension of this traditional version of the principle of utility, in other words, can encourage us to include the interests of nonhuman beings in our moral calculus, but insofar as it does not demand we prioritize the biotic community as a whole, it offers no guarantee either that the interests of nonhuman beings will receive a hearing outside human prerogatives, or that decisions will be made that place the welfare of the wild fowl breeding ground first. We can also imagine a scenario, where it's not a power station, but rather another species of wild fowl, an invasive species, that endanger the favored breeding grounds. In that case, what the preservation of the biotic community requires is the elimination of the invasive species regardless the possible suffering this might produce, and contrary to the critical moral criteria for the utilitarian. The point is that making our focus the welfare of individuals—whether individual species, human communities, or even power stations—can obscure what's in the long-term interest of an ecosystem as a whole.[15]

Singer's power station example also illustrates the distance between ecocentrism and more conventional, though more popular, brands of environmentalism: better resource management, re-use, less waste, recycling, Meatless Mondays, controlled burns, "cage free" eggs.[16] The nonthreatening vocabulary of "management," however, asks little more from us than that we not toss soda cans out of car windows, and the jingoistic "Meatless Monday" reminds us that Beef Taco Tuesday is right around the corner. Not only do such weak forms of conservation leave our sense of entitlement unchallenged, for thinkers like Leopold they reinforce it:

> To sum up: we asked the farmer to do what he conveniently could to save his soil, and he has done just that, and only that. The farmer who clears the woods

off a 75 percent slope, turns his cows into the clearing, and dumps its rainfall, rocks, and soil into the community creek is still a respected member of society. If he puts lime on his fields and plants his crops on contour, he is still entitled to all the privileges and emoluments of his soil conservation district. The district is a beautiful piece of social machinery, but it is coughing along on two cylinders because we have been too timid, and too anxious for quick success to tell the farmer the true magnitude of his obligations. (*A Sand County Almanac*, p. 209)

Though Leopold doesn't highlight it explicitly, among the reasons the farmer doesn't realize the "true magnitude of his obligations" is because no aspect of the social order of which he's a member asks him to. The conservation district is appreciated as a "beautiful piece of social machinery" because, despite its ecological failings, it reinforces the social and economic order that defines what it means to be the farmer—but also the soil, the cow, the community, and the farm. Each occupies its own functional place in that social machinery, and the objective of all, wittingly or otherwise, is to keep the machinery running regardless its coughing on two cylinders. "One basic weakness of a conservation system based wholly on economic motives," argues Leopold, "is that most members of the land community have no economic value" (*A Sand County Almanac*, pp. 210, 212). If the farmer cannot, as it were, hear the coughing it's because his conscience has simply not been charged with that obligation. But it's also because the sound of the machinery—social and mechanical—chugging along the rails of his economic wherewithal stifles the coughing under the roar of tractors and trucks, firehall carnivals, and bingo games.

"No important change in ethics was ever accomplished without an internal change in our intellectual emphasis, loyalties, affections, and convictions," writes Leopold (*A Sand County Almanac*, pp. 209–10). Still, recognizing this doesn't mean that transformation to an ecocentric worldview is easy. Although some transformations are achieved through confrontation with irrefutable evidence, more aren't. Even the shift from a geocentric worldview to heliocentrism, or from creationism's 6000-year-old Earth to the 4.54 billion years supported by science wasn't settled overnight (there are still holdouts).[17] Perhaps climate change will provide the necessary impetus to ignite this paradigm shift, but we can expect plenty of resistance and even more apathy—all the while the clock is ticking on a climate crisis driven by human excess undeterred, perhaps even normalized, by conventional environmentalism. Can the ecocentrist convince us to eschew our human interests in favor of the future of the global climate? Or, given the magnitude of ecocentric expectation, would it be better to just settle for Meatless Monday? [18] By introducing us to an image not from conservation but from ecology called the "Land Pyramid," Leopold aims to convince us that "[l]and, then, is not merely soil; it is a fountain of energy flowing through a circuit of soils, plants and animals" (*A Sand County Almanac*,

p. 216). The pyramid itself consists of many layers, beginning with a foundation of biota and upon which each succeeding layer is dependent (*A Sand County Almanac*, pp. 214–18). For Leopold, the pyramid forms the conceptual and psychic basis for a genuinely ecocentric outlook, a transformation not only of personal consciousness but collective conscience (*A Sand County Almanac*, pp. 223–6). Offering Moses as his example, Leopold argues that the Decalogue "evolved in the minds of a thinking community," and that the land ethic is an emotionally as well as intellectually evolving process (*A Sand County Almanac*, p. 225). Although Leopold might find fault with the French Citizen's Assembly in virtue of its anthropocentrism, that its objective is to introduce us to the concept of "ecocide" as a crime against the planet captures the central meaning of the land pyramid: being on top does not entitle human beings to rule the planet, but rather reminds us that we're as or more dependent than any other of its living things. The "soil-oak-deer-Indian" may now be the "soil-corn-cow-farmer," but the "lines of dependency for food and other services" are not what changes. What changes are the ways we think and talk about "land."

4.2   Aldo Leopold, Ecological Conscience, and the "Plain Citizen"

4.2.1   The Role of Language in Ecocentric Thinking

As we have seen, the vocabulary with which we approach environmental issues offers a potent illustration of just what are the stakes, a point about which Leopold is acutely aware. Indeed, one way to describe his project in *A Sand County Almanac* is as an effort to get us to see that the vocabulary of "conservation" can be misleading, and that a shift to the more ecocentric conceptual framework of "the land" offers not only a truer account of ecological interdependencies, but one that encourages development of an ecological conscience. Adopting an ecocentrist worldview, for example, requires significant change in the way we think about *how* nonhuman animals and ecosystems intersect with human interests, but also how the way we *refer to* nonhuman animals and ecosystems can reflect and influence the way we think about them. Terms like "resource," for example, implies a "for us" that betrays a chauvinistic worldview; even references to "scarce resources," though encouraging less waste, still invites little deeper reflection about why human beings produce such mammoth waste to begin with. Indeed, even terms like "waste" invite us to reconsider how we understand animal bodies, water, and land. After all, the animal waste produced in factory farms includes the bodies of animals that became sick or were mortally injured in the cruel process of, say, debeaking, or are unfortunate enough to be born male chicks.[19] As the moral extensionist would point out, these examples offer little beyond conventional environmentalism, but from an ecocentric perspective, the situation is more troubling still in that there's little in the expansion of the vocabulary of suffering or rights that propels moral extentionism to think in terms of concepts that are ecocentric as opposed to anthropocentric. For the ecocentrist the very concept of "management" presupposes that "nature" is something apart from human action, something that must be managed or even dominated for the sake of human development and comfort, as opposed to left wild. As we've seen in Cronon's account of "wilderness," what counts as "wild" is itself very much determined by human interests. Language matters: "management" no more counts as genuine conservation than "wilderness" counts as "never touched by human beings." We might decide to take our RVs to the Grand Canyon, but from the point of view of the ecocentrist, this no more signifies the development of an environmental conscience than ordering a veggie burger at a Burger King signifies a revolt against factory farming.[20]

No doubt, human chauvinism is reflected in our language-use, but is language a reflection of a human nature that is inalterably chauvinistic? Leopold seems to worry that this might be the case, but argues nonetheless that we can change, that our view of ourselves and the ecologies of which we're members can evolve. The general form of this question is: what features or capacities characterize human nature, and how fixed are they? There is real debate here that extends well beyond ethics, and it matters greatly because whatever limits what is psychologically, emotionally, or intellectually possible for human beings bears directly not only on our capacity to change, but change in what ways—especially if it involves sacrifice. If chauvinism is a fixed trait, revolutionary transformation in the direction of an ecological conscience would seem to be stillborn.[21] But if not, the ecocentrist call to radical transformation, though certainly moving in the right direction, might itself be liable to modification and require policing to insure our compliance. Neither of these prospects seem very attractive. The first makes revolution a hopeless venture; the second seems like an invitation to an environmental dictatorship, what some critics have called *ecological fascism*. The reformist might argue that while we need to see real change in human perspective, this doesn't demand a wholesale rejection of human-centeredness. We could teach our children to take nonhuman suffering seriously more consistently. The rights of nonsentient entities like trees and rivers could be built over time into their worldview. Just because our initial impulse toward the extension of a moral principle, argues the reformist, is human-centered needn't imply that more gradual change cannot be made enduring. Perhaps we don't need a paradigm shift, just the educated recognition that human-centeredness neither necessitates nor entitles human chauvinism.

It's not hard to see, however, that the ecocentrist has several avenues of response. First, as a practical matter, Singer, Regan, and Stone were all writing in the 1960s and 1970s. Their arguments have had plenty of time to see real change come to fruition. But, while we have seen modest progress both at the personal and at the national policy level, environmental law seems always to be threatened with repeal,[22] and a few more vegans do not a solution to the climate crisis make. Second, although it may be true that the committed human chauvinist will have even less incentive to undertake the demanding shift to an ecological conscience than the less taxing hopes of the extensionist reformist, given what we're now faced with in the form of firenadoes, viral outbreaks, scale-busting hurricanes, and the like, now may be exactly the moment for truly revolutionary change. It's striking that, for Leopold, the language of that change comes in the rather unassuming package of what he calls the *plain citizen*. The central idea is simple: human beings are equal but not superior in value to other beings within a given ecosystem, and we ought to strive to act in accord with that understanding. We're "member[s] of a biotic team" (*A Sand County Almanac*, p. 205), whose first priority is the good of that whole, that biotic community—not necessarily the good of any single member (p. 204). Leopold offers as an illustration the biotic history of the Mississippi Valley:

> Consider, for example, the settlement of the Mississippi valley. In the years following the Revolution, three groups were contending for its control: the native Indian, the French and English traders, and the American settlers. Historians wonder what would have happened if the English at Detroit had thrown a little more weight into the Indian side of those tipsy scales which decided the outcome of the colonial migration into the cane-lands of Kentucky. It is time now to ponder the fact that the cane-lands, when subjected to the particular mixture of forces represented by the cow, plow, fire, and axe of the pioneer, became bluegrass. What if the plant succession inherent in this dark and bloody ground had, under the impact of these forces given us some worthless sedge, shrub, or weed? Would Boone and Kenton have held out? Would there have been any overflow into Ohio, Indiana, Illinois, and Missouri? Any Louisiana Purchase? Any transcontinental union of new states? Any Civil war? (*A Sand County Almanac*, p. 205)

For Leopold what matters to the history of territory, acquisition, and settlement is less about *whether* human chauvinism is the product of culture or human nature. Ecological history is crucial to our understanding of our place in the natural world, but its moral significance hinges on what the "cow, plow, fire, and axe" meant for the transition from cane-land to bluegrass, not on whether chauvinism is inherent to human being. Nature or culture, it's sufficient for Leopold that human actions *are* culpable for environmental commodification and destruction, that human chauvinism *is* the feature of human action that must be supplanted by an "ecological conscience" (pp. 207–10), and that the human penchant for conquering can come to be recognized as self-defeating. Such is the insight that, at least in theory, produces the plain citizen.

There are, however, other histories beside those of conquering from which we can draw inspiration relevant to the idea of the plain citizen. Indeed, as eco-feminist Stephanie Lahar argues, historical evidence exists showing that "styles and types of consciousness that developed in tribal societies were more focused on collective than individual identities… sustainable relations with the nonhuman environment result from a more collective locus of identity and strong, even rigid, customs and traditions that serve to keep the group in a homeostatic relation to its environment" (Lahar, pp. 95–6). Lahar offers a rich example in the Neolithic period, arguing that, far cry from the colonizing excursions of French and English traders, the matriarchal and matricentric traditions and practices of the Neolithic created a social arrangement "not only good for women, but also directly related to positive social characteristics such as peacefulness, cooperation, and benign relations with the natural world" (Lahar, pp. 97–9). For Lahar, the worldview detailed in Leopold's example of the Mississippi Valley is *dualistic*; that is, the French and English traders are disposed to see the land and its native inhabitants as property, obstacle, or waste, but themselves as conquerors separate and unaffected by natural forces. To the contrary, the cultures of the Neolithic suggest that dualistic ways of conceiving the world are actually a *departure* from ecological conscience. If so, the plain citizen needn't be invented—but recuperated.

Both Lahar and Leopold cast the divorce of human beings from nonhuman nature as chauvinistic, but Lahar goes further arguing that "[e]cofeminism sees as destructive not only the perceptual distancing and isolation of different peoples from each other, but also the habits of dualistic thought that separate human society from nature," elevating not only society over nature but also whatever is identified with society over whatever is identified with nature: human beings over nonhuman animals, men over women, white over black and brown, the Global North over the Global South (p. 110). "To consider moral dimensions of responsibility for the flourishing of some people and forms of life and the suffering of others," argues Lahar, "we must add ethical judgments to an understanding of unequal and changing power relations" (p. 110). In other words, if we're to fully appreciate why, for example, unloading buckshot into a pile of wolves should feel immoral, or why we should care about the extinction of Sumatran elephants, or why it matters that people of color are disproportionately affected by Covid-19, we must first understand how dualist forms of thinking authorize domination. Ethical judgment thus becomes the province not of the empowered, but rather of a plain citizen who acts "to the best of one's ability from a sensibility that simultaneously knows and values oneself as an individual; is compassionate through identification with human and nonhuman others and caring about others' lives and well-being; and is creative, undergoing self-transformation through cultivating a relation to collectives ranging from human families to the planetary community" (p. 111). To be clear, Lahar doesn't use the phrase "plain citizen," and Leopold's experience looking into the green eyes of the dying wolf he has shot may not fit exactly Lahar's appeal to compassionate identification—but both seek to disrupt a construction of reality whose consequences have done great harm to our relationships with the biotic and the human community in virtue of the same faulty dualistic reasoning. Lahar's view, however, offers a deeper more nuanced understanding of what it means to develop an ecological conscience, both because the historical context she provides suggests that human chauvinism may be no more a fixed human trait than patriarchy or racism, and because, unlike Leopold, Lahar's plain citizen doesn't demote the value of individuals, but rather seeks to situate that aspect of identity as critical to an ethic capable of compassion.

4.2.2   Scientific Knowledge and the Ecocentric Disposition

Among the important questions relevant to the development of an ecological conscience is what role knowledge—historical, experiential, scientific— plays in the transformative shift from human chauvinism to an ecocentric worldview. Scientific knowledge about Wisconsin songbirds, Sumatran elephants, lowland gorillas, hemlock trees, starfish, humpback whales, etc., the biotic communities they inhabit, and the profound harm human beings have already inflicted upon these communities in the form of habitat appropriation, pollution, species decimation, and, of course, climate change can provide momentum to the struggle for change. But Leopold also clearly has more than scientific knowledge in mind when he prods us to "think like a mountain," or a wolf, or a deer, setting aside our parochial interests in "favor of the perspective of the mountain" who "has lived long enough to listen objectively to the howl of the wolf," or the wolf whose howl tells the story of the mountain itself.[23] Both scientific knowledge and the ecocentric disposition that follows, at least partly, from it epitomize aspects of ecological conscience, supporting Leopold's central moral claim: "a thing is right when it tends to preserve the integrity, stability, and beauty of the biotic community. It is wrong when it tends otherwise."[24] Epistemically, the principle captures the idea that we have a responsibility to *know* in what the integrity, stability, and beauty of the biotic community consist; morally, it encompasses the idea that we have a duty to *act* on what we know. The real thrust of the principle, however, is the claim that *actions that fail to exemplify this responsibility are wrong, knowable as such, ought therefore not to be undertaken, and are worthy of moral condemnation if they are.* The principle applies to people, communities, and institutions whose moral duty, individually and collectively, is to insure through action, enculturation, policy, and law the integrity of the biotic community. Actions that make their first priority the advance of human interests at the expense of the biotic community are to be counted as unethical—even if setting aside those interests is inconvenient or prohibitively difficult. While the commitment to living Leopold's principle doesn't necessarily imply that human interests and welfare are precluded from this moral calculus—we too are plain citizens—it does mean that such interests must be weighed critically against the possibility that acting on them will bode ill for the biotic community.

Given, then, the importance of being able to predict the possible consequences of a particular action (practice, law, or policy), knowing constitutes as much a moral duty for the ecocentrist as does the decision to act since being able to predict whether an action is likely to affect the integrity of the biotic community forms an essential feature of decision-making. Knowing in what integrity consists for a given biotic community effectively determines, at least in an ecologically ideal world, what constitutes the life worth living; it's the life that strives for equilibrium or, at minimum, the least possible disruption consistent with meeting basic needs. Consider, for example, what Leopold's principle might mean in the context of climate change: if our first moral duty is to know in what *future* planetary ecological integrity likely consists, then some forms of climate change denial are wrong because the deniers know better; it's *epistemically derelict*.[25] We know that a warming atmosphere will have profound effects including shoreline erosion, hotter fiercer fires, prolonged drought, more frequent high-intensity hurricanes and tsunamis, disrupted bird migrations, the extinction of endangered species, pollinator population collapse, virulent disease vectors, etc., and in both word and deed our denial actually demonstrates that we know what we deny. Indeed, it seems unlikely that the carefully orchestrated will to cognitive dissonance we see from, say, the Heartland Institute[26] or Climate Depot[27] could have any other basis than to run interference for the industries that fund their "scientific critics." We know that powerful economic and political interests are served by preserving a status quo supported by their epistemic dereliction. It's not hard to see where the hydrocarbon industry would be if its boards of directors began to pay more than lip service to the climate crisis, or if the CAFOs moved to significantly reduce their own greenhouse gas emissions.

But the capacity for denial that lengthens the road to developing an ecocentric conscience is, at least one other kind of case, about more than political or economic expediency. It's about more than preserving the myth of endless resources, more than wealth and power—at least in this world. From the point of view of the ecocentrist, this variety of denial isn't wrong because it's self-serving—or at least narrowly chauvinistic; it's wrong because it refuses to recognize any base of knowledge about which it could be epistemically derelict. In other words, *it denies that there is anything to deny*, and does so in the interest of a worldview radically disconnected from the sciences, or even from most ordinary folks' understanding of the world.[28] This view of the relationship of human beings to nonhuman nature comes cloaked in the garb of religious faith, and casts itself as insight or intuition that preempts and supplants scientific knowledge. A particularly insidious variety of denial, it effectively hijacks our tendency to intellectual laziness and the desire for easy answers, thereby rendering evidence that doesn't conform to it irrelevant. Consider an example: at a June 2020 commissioner's meeting in Palm Beach Florida, a small but vocal group of residents excoriated the commissioners for their unanimous vote to mandate mask-hearing in the interest of reducing spread of the coronavirus. The city had seen the rate of infection, and hospitalization begin to climb steeply after a brief period of "flattening the curve." The climb, unsurprisingly was attributed to Governor DeSantis' decision to permit businesses, recreational facilities, and beaches to reopen after several months of pandemic lockdown, recommending, but not requiring masks and social distancing. One angry Palm Beach resident claimed that wearing masks "killed people." She insisted she was preparing to make "citizens arrests" of any who'd try to impose mask-wearing, decrying mask mandates as "the Devil's laws." Another claimed that mask-wearing amounted to "throwing God's wonderful breathing system out the door."[29] It's easy, of course, to simply dismiss this form of denial as kooky, certainly not aligned with the majority of people whose understanding of Covid-19 is sensible—faith-based or otherwise. Kooky notwithstanding, however, what makes this form of denial a significant obstacle to the development of an ecocentric conscience is that it's not merely epistemically derelict. Rather, it cannot be confronted—at least with any hope of being effective—by evidence contrary to its claims because *evidence* is not what motivates it; faith is. Or rather, a very specific rendition of faith.

This same variety of denial—or the denial that there is anything to deny—has its analogue in the climate crisis. Just as the evidence that mask-wearing is crucial to stemming the tide of a viral tsunami is met with dismissal by those who make absurd claims about "Devil's laws" and "God's breathing systems," so too the scientific evidence for climate change is met with dismissal by some, particularly evangelical Christians who, according to Bernard Daley Zaleha and Andrew Szasz, equate environmentalism with "neo-Pagan-style nature worship" that "might even lead to anti-capitalist sentiments" (Zaleha and Szasz, pp. 20–1). In "Why Conservative Christians Don't Believe in Climate Change," Zaleha and Szasz trace Christian antipathy to the evidence for climate change to its roots in the dualistic thinking that dominates some conservative Christian theology. Crediting environmental historian Lynn White's seminal essay "The Historical Roots of out Ecologic Crisis," Zaleha and Szasz argue that "[r]ecent research seems to confirm White's rather bleak assessment of the relationship between Christian beliefs and environmental attitudes." White argued that insofar as Christian theology was dualistic—rooted in the radical divorce of humanity from nonhuman nature (including that of human bodies)—and anthropocentric, granting to human beings dominion over the earth (White, pp. 1205–6), it cast the die for treating nonhuman nature as a commodity, and for the denial required to continue to do so regardless the consequences—indeed, to deny that treating nature as a disposable commodity has any negative consequences. This toxic form of dualist anthropocentrism is especially well personified in evangelicals like E. Calvin Beisner who, in response to whether he "ever worried that he might be wrong about the non-existence of global warming" said that "even if global warming turns out to be real and harmful, it is of little ultimate importance [to the Christian], because where one is going to spend eternity should be any reasonable human's primary concern" (Zaleha and Szasz, p. 25).

What Beisner's answer reveals, however, is not merely epistemically derelict; it denies that the climate crisis matters *no matter what* the truth is about whether it's real. Even if the climate crisis is real, it can be discounted because the destination of one's soul is what matters. Even if science does offer us an accurate account of the planet, it's of no significance because the planet is merely a way-station on the way to eternity. Still, Beisner at least acknowledges the possibility that human actions impact the planet. To see the denial that there is anything to deny about whether human actions have done harm to the planet and its atmosphere, we turn to radio show host Janet Parshall who may come closest to the more wholesale rejection of reason and evidence evinced by the Palm Beach pandemic-deniers. In Beisner's 2010 "Resisting the Green Dragon" campaign, Parshall narrates a video "striking for its scary music, flashy graphics, and strident rhetoric":

> In what has become one of the greatest deceptions of our day, radical environmentalism is striving to put America and the world under its destructive control. This so-called "Green Dragon" is seducing your children in our class- rooms and popular culture. Its lust for political power now extends to the highest global levels. And its twisted view of the world elevates nature above the needs of people, of even the poorest and the most helpless. With millions falling prey to its spiritual deception, the time is now to stand and resist. Around the world, environmentalism has become a radical movement, something we call the Green Dragon, and it is deadly. Deadly to human prosperity, deadly to human life, deadly to human freedom, and deadly to the gospel of Jesus Christ. Make no mistake about it, environmentalism is no longer your friend, it is your enemy. And the battle is not primarily political or material, it is spiritual. (Zaleha and Szasz, p. 26)

While this form of denial is profoundly anthropocentric, what decisively distinguishes it from the chauvinistic motives of the fossil fuel or the animal body industries is that it is not driven by economic or political objectives, at least in the first place. The primary goal of the Palm Beach pandemic deniers and the evangelical "green dragon" slaying anti-environmentalists is *salvation*, and while this certainly evinces self-interest, because it's not about tangible—*fungible*—objectives realizable in this world, but rather about the status of one's soul heading into the next, little about this world is likely to matter to it other than as an obstacle to attaining eternity.

As White shows, however, the dualism that defines Christian anthropocentrism lays the foundation for the translation of land into property, for examples like Leopold's Mississippi Valley or Cronon's Westward expansion and the creation of "wilderness," itself an escapist kind of property for weary white men trying to "find themselves." The Christian soul-seeker thus has common cause with the industrialist in that both conceive human nature as superior to and apart from a nonhuman nature cast as essentially—fundamentally—*disposable* (White, p. 1206). Put differently: if White, Zaleha and Szasz are correct, the project of developing an ecocentric conscience against this worldview, informed as it is not merely by crass economic motives but by religious commitments immune to reason and evidence, is going to be at least a formidable uphill struggle. White observes that "somewhat over a century ago science and technology... joined to give mankind powers which, to judge by many of its ecologic effects, are out of control. If so, Christianity bears a huge burden of guilt" (White, p. 1206). That may well be, but what the climate crisis and pandemic deniers demonstrate is that it's not guilt that governs resistance to the "green dragon" or the refusal to wear masks; it's the entitlement borne of the belief that conceiving the planet as god's proving ground in the quest to earn points toward eternity makes the planet merely a placeholder, a stage for a test of faith, and therefore nothing of value in itself. Against this history, can an ecological conscience be fostered? Can we come to "think like a mountain"? Can the fierce green light Leopold sees in the dying eyes of the wolf get us to the humility necessary to appreciate the histories, species diversity, and interdependencies of nonhuman nature? This seems like a climb.

4.2.3   Thinking Like a Mountain, or Not

Two questions present themselves at this juncture: whether human beings are outfitted with the epistemic wherewithal to develop an ecocentric conscience and, if so, whether this is the right route to take toward articulating an environmental ethic. If White, Zaleha, and Szasz are correct, the barriers—economic, cultural, and religious—are challenging, but none necessarily impugn the capacity for human disposition and thinking to evolve in light of evidence and a respect for science. It may be that the real issues are simply practical: motivation, time, responsibility, and empowerment. Can the urgency of the climate crisis provide sufficient impetus to develop a genuinely ecocentric worldview? Is there still enough time to undertake it? Who is responsible to lead the way? Who risks being disempowered—or disempowered further? On one hand, perhaps developing an ecocentric conscience needn't be like reinventing the wheel. On the other, it's still not clear whether the answers to any of these questions lend themselves to democratic or collective decision-making.

There do, however, exist ecologically oriented traditions and practices other than those detailed in *A Sand County Almanac*, and it is worth considering whether any of these may offer insight into the virtues and the limitations of Leopold's vision of an ecocentric conscience. Consider, for example, Deane Curtin's exploration of indigenous women's intimate understanding of the relationship between an ecology, responsibilities to family and community, food security, and a specific sense of place. In "Women's Knowledge as Expert Knowledge," Curtin describes the relationship of some women to the land not merely as "experience," "developed sensibility," "insight," and the like, but as a specific kind of *knowledge*:

> Because women have been charged with many kinds of caring labor, *women's knowledge is relational*. Women tend to locate knowledge in the concrete relational space between individuals, not in the abstraction of isolated, autonomous individuals. The relations that define community are broader than the human community. They include the entire ecological community, *this* place. (Curtin, p. 90)

Shades of Leopold's plain citizen certainly color this description, and Curtin lends it yet more depth arguing, first, that *"[w]omen's knowledge is inherently collaborative*...the project of the whole ecological community" (p. 90). She gives as an example cooking, the sharing of culinary traditions, and seed sharing (p. 90). Second, Curtin argues that *"[w]omen's knowledge is ... transparently situated"* (p. 90). That is, "to form an opinion, women need to know the life histories of the people and contexts they are speaking about" (p. 90). Third, *"[w]omen's knowledge is temporal"* (p. 90). Yet "if it grows out of actual contexts and histories, it is also future-directed... [It] operates not only in the spaces between individuals but also in the times between generations" (p. 90). Lastly, Curtin argues that *"women's knowledge is bodily knowledge."* Because cultural dualisms have defined women in terms of the body and nature, women tend to cultivate knowledge that integrates head and hand. Their knowledge consists more in "thoughtful ways of doing" than in "ways of thinking about" (pp. 90–1).

The dualisms Curtin refers to are precisely the same that White credits for the rise of Christian anthropocentrism, but while Curtin is careful to remind her reader that her own account generalizes—practices vary across culture, geography, and ecology—she also insists the ecological and relational quality of women's knowledge offers something vital to developing a more ecologically oriented ethic. Indeed, the very conditions under which many indigenous women engage in subsistence farming may, argues Curtin, offer a reason to take women's knowledge seriously, "Poor Third World women," she writes, "cannot even pretend to escape the temporal reality of life that is demanded by caring labor... Caring labor produces transparent knowledge; such knowledge is superior just because it is transparent, situated between nature and culture. Survival depends on it" (p. 92). For Curtin, the prospect of transparency in the relation between nature and culture evinces an important moral value: honesty or frankness—a value Leopold advocates for the plain citizen. Because caring labor, moreover, is about labor that's collaborative, temporally situated, and bodily, and because it's intimately associated with survival—with life and death—it surely makes sense to characterize it as the work of conscience, ecological conscience.

Whether the expert knowledge Curtin describes is rightly characterized as eco*centric*, however, is an important question whose possible answers shed light on what ecocentric means and what it requires with respect to action. No doubt, Leopold's principle, "*a thing is right when it tends to preserve the integrity, stability, and beauty of the biotic community. It is wrong when it tends otherwise*," is not what's in the forefront of the minds of the Indian women Curtin describes in the performance of caring labor. By the same token that these women cannot pretend to be able to escape the caring labor required of their life conditions, so too such a principle would likely present itself to them as the kind of indulgence—a "way of thinking about"—for which they have neither time nor resources. A knowledge that "integrates head and hand" is, however, perhaps better understood as neither ecocentric nor anthropocentric, but rather as an integrated set of practices that "operates not only in the spaces between individuals but also in the times between generations." That is, perhaps the expert knowledge for which Curtin credits practices most common to indigenous women cannot be, as it were, boxed in by dualist descriptors. Perhaps because such practices are essentially relational, temporal, contextual, and vulnerable to the vicissitudes of environmental change, they are and aren't human-centered; they are and aren't ecocentric. Perhaps this vocabulary just doesn't adequately capture in what such an expert knowledge consists; indeed, perhaps the vocabulary that best captures ecocentrism *as opposed to* anthropocentrism is one in which *relation-with* is replaced with *relation-over*.

What Curtin's analysis of expert knowledge shows is that as a practical matter for communities who don't enjoy the luxury of being able to simply walk away from their conditions or responsibilities, the idea that it's useful to draw a hard and fast distinction between the anthropocentric and the ecocentric is unlikely to gain traction; it will not get the caring labor done, and it's unlikely to add to the knowledge the subsistence farmer and her family already have. Indeed, the dualism presupposed by the directive that we ought to think like a mountain—and not like a woman climbing up to a stream to fetch clean water, or not like the vista outside her house where she sits gazing in appreciation at dusk after the last meal of the day is eaten, dishes washed, children bathed—cannot capture either the labor that colors her days or the sensibility she brings to her own bodily life or her life as a member of a human and nonhuman community. To think like a mountain is likely, for her, nonsense. But this isn't because she doesn't know the mountain and it's not because she understands her place in the world as radically superior to it and all its inhabitants (say, like the Palm Beachers). To think like a mountain is nonsense because her "knowledge of head and hand" is already integrated *with* the mountain, with the generations to come before and after that live in its shadow, and with everything the mountain provides—everything that becomes her own body, the bodies of her children, the bodies of her community. She is and *knows she is* the mountain—not in any mystical sense beyond the reach of the sciences, but simply because the caring labor necessary to survival makes it so, just as the mountain "knows" her insofar as its own contours along well-worn trails, common forks, at overlooks and rest-stops, is altered and reconfigured by generations of people and animals moving through its upslopes and valleys.

The nonsense of assuming that to adopt an ecocentric ethic is to "think like a mountain," but that to think like a human mother, sister, daughter, partner, wife is human chauvinism sheds a different and critical light on Leopold's example of the dying wolf. The idea that unloading rifle fire into a pile of playing wolves should draw no further attention than applause for Leopold's soul-searching, that we needn't worry about the prospect that such activities reinforce violent cultural patterns, suggests that behind the anthropocentrism, lurk other motives and values, namely, maintenance of a social order that authorizes some to carry out acts of violence and harm against others. To be clear, the right comparison here is not that hunting may not form an important feature of many indigenous cultures; it does. The right comparison revolves around the motives for killing the wolf. We can readily imagine killing wolves to protect critical livestock in a community whose survival depends on the milk and meat the livestock produce. But, as Leopold details with some wincing grief, survival is not the motive of the young men who, however lacking in accuracy, simply open fire on the pack. That Leopold appears to feel regret, or at least remorse, however, shouldn't be read as indicating that he recognizes what he's done is wrong—at least not because it's a wasteful disruption of a community that includes wolves, or a needless expenditure of energy better spent in other activities. If the action is wrong for Leopold, it's because it violates what *nonetheless remains separate and apart from human beings*, namely, the biotic community.

While the language of "biotic community" pays lip service to the integration Curtin identifies as the expert knowledge of many indigenous women, the

directive to disavow our human-centeredness and move toward an ecocentric ethic retains the human versus nature dualism that White shows is at the
root of human chauvinism and its ecologically destructive trajectory, especially
in its Christian expression. From the perspective of Curtin's analysis of expert
knowledge, what makes killing the wolf wrong is the harm it exacts against a
community to which people, their own families, and other nonhuman beings
belong, as well as the unnecessary suffering it produces—not merely that the
action fails to contribute to the biotic community. Put differently: shooting the
wolves is an immoral action, not merely the failure to perform the right action.
By insisting that all forms of anthropocentrism are chauvinistic, Leopold misses
alternative incarnations, expert knowledges, whose human-centeredness doesn't
align with the dualism implicit in his ecocentrism, and he effectively reinforces a
chauvinism that not only privileges human beings over nonhuman animals and
the biotic community, but, as Curtin's and Lahar's analyses illustrate, a competitive patriarchal worldview over a more communal egalitarian one.

4.2.4   Ecocentrism, the Principle of Utility, and the Patriarchal Social Order

It's an open question whether it's too much to expect Leopold to have been able
to appreciate the ecologically oriented worldviews of other cultures beyond his
decidedly Western own. Nonetheless, it's also not hard to see that the human
versus nonhuman nature dualism at the root of his argument for an ecocentric conscience manifests itself in other Western discourses of domination:
human versus nonhuman animal, European versus Indigenous, and male versus female, each set posed as opposites, each a hierarchical relation of domination and submission, entitled and resource, privileged and disposable. In
her essay "Acts of Objectification and the Repudiation of Dominance," Chaone
Mallory specifically takes up the role that dualist domination plays in Leopold's thinking, particularly around the practice of sport hunting. She argues
that despite the common defense that good sportsmanship in hunting evinces
respect for the animal hunted, the real point is to buttress a "phallogocentric
and patriarchal" relationship between mostly white affluent men and everyone
as well as everything else: nonhuman nature, nonhuman animals, nonwhite
men, and all women. Hunting is thus "largely an elite activity practiced by
those with privileged cultural and economic status, a status possessed by Leopold as well as the majority of hunters in North America" (p. 62), a fact, argues
Mallory, reflected in the very way Leopold articulates his ecocentric outlook:

> [W]hile the particular insights of Aldo Leopold have, on one level, proven to
> be very useful in getting the debate about environmental ethics "on the table"
> and into scientific and philosophical discourse, environmental philosophers,

ethicists, and professionals should exercise great caution in relying too heavily on the works of Leopold as a source of conceptual guidance, because the work of this "seminal figure" is impregnated with ideas which may be reinforcing of the very notions that have been revealed by feminist and nonfeminist environmental ethicists as damaging to a harmonious nature/culture relationship. (Mallory, p. 65)

It's possible, though perhaps a more cynical judgment than Leopold can bear, that among the reasons his work has received so much applause is *because* it reinforces a patriarchal and economically elitist social order, all the while according to the targets of his criticism, male, affluent, white hunters, the power to undertake the transformation to plain citizen he advocates. Although Mallory doesn't go that far, what she does make clear is that the primary beneficiaries of Leopold's "seminal" work are precisely those who, like Leopold, already enjoy the privileges of sex, race, and economic class.

The problem, Mallory contends, is that there is no way to have the ecocentric cake and eat it too; aspiring to become the plain citizen cannot be reconciled with Leopold's view of sport hunting:

The problem with such a means of augmenting one's moral mettle (and, for that matter, "communing" with nature), however, is that it does so at the expense of another creature, a creature who undeniably has an interest in remaining alive. To persist in deliberately stalking an animal who poses little or no threat to one's person and whom one does not need to kill in order to be assured of being fed is to sublimate the interests of the animal to one's own for a purpose which is justifiable on strictly anthropocentric and self-serving grounds. Killing the animal becomes, in effect, entertainment, a means of escaping the pressures and rigors of civilized life. Or it is done in order to promote or enhance one's own moral development, as Leopold claims, and to refine one's skill at behaving in a manner befitting a "gentleman." Thus, such an action would be, according to the traditional standpoint of an ecocentric environmental ethics, prima facie wrong since these environmental ethicists deny that human beings ought to be permitted to exploit the natural world for reasons such as these. To choose to hunt in the modern era is to assume an attitude of domination over the animal being sought. The hunter in his or her arrogance presumes to decide (with the help of a little luck and skill, of course) whether the animal will live or die. (Mallory, pp. 65–6)

Part of what's remarkable in this passage is that Mallory connects a utilitarian theme, having an interest in avoiding suffering, with Leopold's reinforcement of the dualism that underpins human chauvinism. She shows how the dualism that permits the domination and suffering of nonhuman

animals in sport hunting cannot be reconciled with the position plain citizens adopts for themselves as equal—but not superior—members of the
biotic community.

To stalk and kill an animal for entertainment reinforces a form of domination
that, because, as Curtin might point out, the fact that hunting is unnecessary to
survival in this case cannot be reconciled with any social order other than that
which made leisure for hunting possible, at least for some, in the first place, and
that social order invariably privileges sex, race, and economic class. That stalking and killing the animal creates suffering for it epitomizes at once the dualism
that establishes human chauvinism and the violation of utility enshrined in Leopold's principle that an action is right when it contributes to the stability of the
biotic community. While that stability may also in some circumstances require
the "culling" of a deer population, that objective is so radically different from
that of sport hunting, it leaves the reader to wonder whether appeals to Leopold's
principle can be exploited as expedient cover or excuse. As Mallory makes the
point, sport hunting treats the animal as merely a means to the end of the hunter's
desire for a certain kind of experience, namely, the experience of domination
as a form of entertainment. "Thus, one is viewing the animal as an instrument
to one's pleasure or satisfaction" she argues, and then deploying a concept from
Rolston, "not considering (or is choosing to ignore) the notion that the animal
has a good of its own, and a perception of the world. To do this, the animal must
be objectified, treated as something external to oneself, not as a co-participant
in what Leopold would call the 'circuit' of life… [A] conclusion must be reached
that the animal is lesser than oneself" (Mallory, p. 66).

That Leopold sees sport hunting as consistent with the promotion of an ecocentric ethic becomes less surprising when, as Mallory argues, we see that his view
of human and nonhuman nature is itself dualistic and that it's rooted in the view
that morality is ultimately borne out of conflict. Influenced by a faulty view that
Homo sapiens "evolved primarily as a hunter," Leopold ignores the thesis—available during his lifetime—that early human communities were primarily engaged
in scavenging and gathering in favor of the view that men are hunters and women
gatherers (Mallory, p. 74). What evidence shows is that "hunting and meat consumption are not, and never were, essential to human survival," putting the lie to
this particularly pernicious justification for patriarchy (Mallory, p. 75). The central
point, however, points again to Leopold's appropriation of the principle of utility. Given his claim that an ethic is "a limitation on freedom in the struggle for
survival," that is, that ethics is about struggle—not cooperation, a limit on freedom
as opposed to a realization of community, it perhaps makes sense that Leopold
sees the objective of morality as insuring the conditions where this struggle can
continue. Combined with his view of early human history, it's not surprising that
for Leopold sport hunting epitomizes a quintessential human activity, modeling
an essential human nature as competitive, violent, an end to freedom for some

and affirmation for others. It's also no wonder, as Mallory spells out in the context a family life where Leopold plainly regards his sons as worthy of greater attention than his daughters, especially with respect to activities like hunting and the outdoors, that this essential human being is male (Mallory, pp. 72–3).

If Mallory's analysis is correct, the meaning at the core of "contributing to the integrity and stability of the biotic community" is embodied in whatever actions conform to that community's essential nature, namely, actions that reinforce and replicate the dualistic, hierarchical, and patriarchal nature of "nature." As Mallory shows, if this is how we are to understand ecocentrism and what it means to develop ecocentric conscience, ecocentrism is inconsistent with even the most basic definition of an environmental ethic:

> [S]port hunting of the kind practiced by Aldo Leopold is an act of domination which is inconsistent with what is taken to be a basic claim of environmental ethics: the claim that humans are not morally superior beings who are entitled to subjugate members of the more-than-human world... The hunted animal is being treated as a means and not an end for reasons that do not outweigh the prima facie case against killing other living, sentient beings. In this way the act of hunting differs substantially from say, the cultivation of vegetables and plant products. (p. 75).

Insofar as sentient beings are to be treated by any environmental ethic as ends, and not merely as means, there is no reasonable way to reconcile Leopold's ecocentrism with environmental ethics. As Curtin and Mallory make clear, this is not because killing nonhuman beings is never justified; it is because what is contained in the very essence of sport killing is the epitome of a relationship that objectifies the "other" and therefore cannot see it or treat it as other than an instrument or a commodity.

Could Rolston's *Respect for Life* offer an avenue of response to the feminist critique of Leopold? This prospect also seems unlikely. Like Stone, Leopold regards as morally considerable nonsentient entities like rivers and mountains. For Rolston, however, only species of living things are entitled to respect for life; the central unit of value for Rolston, we recall, is the *species*. Indeed, while both Leopold and Rolston direct our moral attention to the future, and while they'd agree that the futures of species and ecosystems are intertwined, their ultimate objectives are still very different. On the one hand, Leopold's view of biotic integrity could, in theory, sanction the extinction of a species that threatened the "stability, integrity, and beauty" of a biotic community. For Rolston, however, we could imagine the potential for greatly altering a particular ecosystem in the interest of preserving a species from extinction; his goal is not the biotic community *per se*, but rather preserving genetic information—a very different objective we could imagine being achieved, say digitally, without any biotic community at all. Where the stability of an ecosystem is threatened by the presence of an endangered species, and where the option of relocating that species is attended by credible concern over its survival, it's the species that must take priority on Rolston's view, not the biotic community other than insofar as it supports that genetic legacy.

4.3   Arne Naess: Deep Ecology and the Eight-point Platform

4.3.1   The Eight-point Platform

In his landmark essay, "The Shallow and the Deep, Long Range Ecology Movement," Arne Naess offers a sketch of what becomes the *Eight-Point Platform* (1986), a set of ecocentric directives designed to bridge the gap between the more personal moral decision-making we're inclined to associate with Aldo Leopold, and the public, even internationally coordinated, policy required to preserve whole ecosystems from corporate-scale mining, logging, cattle grazing, monocultural agriculture enterprises, and the like. Whether personal or public, Naess takes aim at what he characterizes as a "shallow" form of environmental commitment, arguing that any long range movement for ecological integrity and stability must look beyond human-centered motives toward the adoption of an ecocentric perspective. He thus distinguishes the "shallow" environmental movement from what he calls "deep ecology": "[t]he shallow ecology movement is concerned with fighting against pollution and resource depletion. Its central objective is the health and affluence of people in the developed countries. The deep ecology movement has deeper concerns, which touch upon principles of diversity, complexity, autonomy, decentralization, symbiosis, egalitarianism, and classlessness" ("The Shallow and the Deep," p. 1). We can debate whether the twenty-first-century environmental movement remains primarily about the welfare of Global North peoples, or whether, for example, work undertaken by the army of scientists for the *United Nations Intergovernmental Panel on Climate Change* (IPCC) to produce its most recent report, the *Sixth Assessment Report*, remain in the shallow.[30] But activists like Greta Thunberg might contest this characterization. The Youth Climate Strike for which her work has been instrumental point toward at least some expanding awareness among young people, and her Fridays for the Future (FFF) originated in a consciously global effort to create awareness about the climate crisis in young people for whom the future is jeopardized.[31]

Whether Naess' vision of deep ecology as an ecocentric movement and as a governing set of principles for bodies like the IPCC offers a realistic or desirable environmental ethic depends, of course, on what it implies for real-time decision-making and policy formulation. In "The Shallow and the Deep," Naess spells out his "Seven-Point Survey," a set of arguments intended to ground the Eight-Point Platform. Point one of the survey "rejects the human-in-environment image in favor of the total-field image." Like Leopold's "plain citizen," Naess sees "organisms as knots in the biospherical net or field of intrinsic relations," that is, relations in which the definitions of its members depend on each other, and where separation alters or even destroys them (p. 1). Point Two "accepts biospherical egalitarianism—in principle," but hedges the idea of a basic equality "because any realistic praxis [useful activity] necessitates some killing, exploitation, and suppression." Personified in the image of the "ecological field worker" who acquires "deep-seated respect, or even veneration for ways and forms of life," Naess specifically rejects the "master-slave role" that, he argues, alienates man from himself, yet, like Leopold gazing into the eyes of the dying wolf, seems ambivalent about how far "in principle" goes. This ambivalence is reiterated in Point Three where Naess argues that insofar as Deep Ecology "emphasizes principles of diversity and symbiosis," the struggle for survival should be interpreted as "the ability to co-exist and cooperate in complex relationships, rather than the ability to kill, exploit, and suppress" (p. 2). Naess then draws an explicit comparison between "the annihilation of seals and whales," the domination of human tribes and cultures" (p. 2), and (Point Four), the hierarchy of economic class, rejecting all as incompatible with a fundamentally egalitarian ecocentric worldview.

Yet, as we observed on a closer reading of Leopold, however aspirational is Naess' egalitarianism, an "in principle" that "*necessitates*" "killing, exploitation, and suppression" opens the door to the same wide range of exceptions in the name of preserving biotic integrity and stability, now rephrased as "diversity, symbiosis, and complexity," as did Leopold's "A thing is right..." Naess argues (Point Five) that although deep ecologists are as concerned as shallow environmentalists with issues like pollution, it's the latter who miss the forest for the trees (p. 2). Progress on one front, for example the installation of scrubbers to remove foul and corrosive gases from wastewater treatment plants, can cause harms to other populations—say, if the cost of clean water rises to offset the cost of the scrubbers. What thus distinguishes the shallow environmentalist from Naess' ecocentrim is the deep ecological focus on holistic and long-term goals as opposed to short-term temporary fixes whose primary if not exclusive beneficiaries are human communities. Placing the moral weight squarely on the long-term health of whole systems, human and nonhuman, in this utilitarian calculus, "[a]n ethics of responsibility," writes Naess, "implies that ecologists do not serve the shallow, but the deep ecological movement" (p. 2), an emphasis that does not sit comfortably with Point Seven: "the deep ecology movement supports autonomy and decentralization" (p. 3). On the one hand, it's certainly reasonable to conceive of wholes within yet larger wholes. We think of watersheds, forests, deserts, wetlands, mountains, high plains, villages, towns, and cities in this way, and what applies to preserving the diversity, symbiosis, and complexity of one does not, of course, necessarily apply to another. There's no more a one-size-fits-all in ecology than there is in human culture, and to try to make it so is itself oppressive and corrosive. On the other hand, however, the most significant and ominous issues of our time—environmental, geopolitical, economic, and public health—are not only unlikely to be effectively addressed other than through internationally cooperative governments and agencies, but could become even more potentially catastrophic left to the autonomous and decentralized decision-making of local county and township boards, school boards, chambers of commerce, and faith-based councils.

The issues we likely think of most immediately are the climate crisis, emerging pandemic, and the exploitive relationship between the global North and the global South concerning food security, politically motivated violence, human and nonhuman migration, waste-dumping, and the outsourcing of cheap labor. While we can imagine local ordinances aimed, for example, at barring multinational corporations from using beaches near fishing towns as medical waste dumps, or county boards deciding to bar contracts with vulture-ventures like Monsanto for the use of so-called Frankenseeds to grow rice,[32] we also know who wins when conflicts emerge. We know that appeals to autonomy and decentralization are no more likely to save the Alaskan fishing village from Dutch Royal Shell's plan to drill just off its coast than such ideas, however noble, will save either from calving icebergs gratis the climate crisis.[33] Autonomous decision-making, moreover, is only as morally defensible as are the motives of its board or commission members. A county board made up of climate change deniers only contributes to the crisis when it grants a permit to build another CAFO, gas well, or landfill. A township committee populated by pandemic deniers who refuse to enforce a mask ordinance may be decentralized, but this hardly counts as responsible. Naess acknowledges that the Seven Point Survey is not "derived from ecology by logic or induction," but from the lifestyle and observations of the ecological field-worker, and that its formulations are "vague generalizations, tenable only if made more precise in certain directions" (p. 3). He argues that each point "express[es] a value priority system" aimed at replacing the blunt-edged instruments—threats of environmental catastrophe, hunger, and war—left to ecologists trying to influence policy and law (pp. 3–4). The aim of the *Eight-Point Platform*[34] is thus to supply that necessary bridge between the shallow and the deep, but also between threats of disaster to which policymakers become inured and the creation of law more consistent with an ecocentric worldview.

The philosophical aim of the *Eight-Point Platform* is to provide actionable substance to what Naess refers to as the *ecosophy* he describes toward the end of his *Seven Point Survey*. An ecosophy, argues Naess, is "a philosophy of ecological harmony or equilibrium" (p. 4). "A philosophy as a kind of wisdom," he writes, "is openly normative; it contains norms, rules, postulates, value-priority announcements, and hypotheses concerning the state of affairs in our universe. Wisdom is *policy wisdom*, prescription, not only scientific description and prediction" (p. 4, my emphasis). The practical aim of the *Eight-Point Platform*, then, is to supply the "policy wisdom" for governing bodies to articulate policy and erect law consistent with an ecosophic—ecocentric—ethic. It stipulates goals that must be met in order to achieve not merely a sustainable planetary ecosystem but a Titanic shift from a human-centered world to one premised on the conjecture that all living things have *inherent worth* (or *intrinsic value*) that is, value independent of resource, tool, or disposable, value as *this* specific organism or system. Naess understood the urgency of moving from voluntary private morality to public policy: environmental crises have ever-more devastating consequences, resources have become more polluted or exhausted, ancillary effects including terrorism, war, and human migration more probable. Naess knew that the time for easy recycling and applause for Meatless Mondays had passed, that corporate greed is at the center of environmental erosion, and that global phenomena like climate change necessitate a global response. As fellow ecocentrist Frederic Bender argues in *The Culture of Extinction* (2003): human industry has released at least 160 million tons of CO_2 into the atmosphere, half of that since 1960. Carbon dioxide emissions now exceed five billion tons annually, and this is at least 100 times that of the Earth's volcanoes. It just gets worse from there. Fact is, argues Naess, we're beyond what personal moral resolve can achieve; we need a unified, collective, and global ecological conscience to revolutionize the public sphere, and an ecocentric worldview that can provide the basis for articulating a society consistent with the stability and integrity of the biotic community.

The *Platform* might best be understood as Naess' charter for Leopold's plain citizenship where the focus shifts somewhat from "plain" to "citizen." Naess takes the repudiation of chauvinistic self-interest as foundational to moral agency, but seeks to go further to articulate a framework toward the collective will of whole communities; the plain citizen thus embodies the biotic community not only in his or her private life, but in helping to formulate, enforce, and conform to laws and policies which reflect community-wide ecocentric commitments. Like any ethic, Naess' *Platform* is utopian. He doesn't speak to us as individual decision-makers, but as one variety of living entity among others, of equal but not greater inherent worth, in hopes of engendering a social DNA consistent with the *Platform's* aspirations:

1. The well-being and flourishing of human and nonhuman life on Earth have value in themselves [inherent worth]. These values are independent of the usefulness of the nonhuman world for human purposes.
2. Richness and diversity of life forms contribute to the realization of these values and are also values in themselves.
3. Humans have no right to reduce this richness and diversity except to satisfy vital needs.

4. The flourishing of human life and cultures is compatible with a sub-stantially smaller human population. The flourishing of nonhuman life *requires* a smaller human population.
5. Present human interference with the nonhuman world is excessive, and the situation is rapidly worsening.
6. Policies must therefore be changed. These policies affect basic economic, technological, and ideological structures. The resulting state of affairs will be deeply different from the present.
7. The ideological change will be mainly that of appreciating life quality (dwelling in situations of inherent value) rather than adhering to an increasingly higher standard of living. There will be a profound aware-ness of the difference between bigness and greatness. Those who sub-scribe to the foregoing points have an obligation directly or indirectly to implement these changes.
8. Those who subscribe the foregoing points have an obligation directly or indirectly to participate in the attempt to implement the necessary changes.

One way to think about the *Eight-Point Platform* as a social ethic is to con-sider whether it can offer actionable direction to formulating public policy in response to a crisis, and whether such policy can be made consistent, or consis-tent enough, with other social values such as freedom of movement and freedom of speech. While what Naess has in mind are environmental crises like deforesta-tion, desertification, unchecked pollution, and the climate crisis, a useful way to consider some of the most obvious questions raised by the *Platform* concerning the policies it might authorize, who decides, and what enforcement would entail may be through the lens of a crisis whose impacts are harmful, immediately visible, global, and in need of urgent action: a viral pandemic.

Although the science and technology for tracking the impacts of climate change have improved dramatically over the last several decades, drawing the connections between, for example, extreme weather events and rising global temperature is not as readily observable as looking at a virus under a microscope. This isn't because we can't track the Cat-5 Hurricane or watch news footage of people racing to load their cars in the effort to escape the Paradise, California firenado;[35] it's because while we experience weather, we don't experience climate, thus its impacts on global warming, directly. We understand climate change through many sciences, including a form of predictive modeling we use to predict disease mortality, but we measure the extent to which climate change is a *crisis* less in terms of objective indicators like respiratory failure, neurological damage, and morbidity, and more in terms of what its implications mean for, for instance, food security, fire insurance, or human migration. We also tend to confuse weather with climate, a fact climate change deniers exploit to their advantage.[36] A viral outbreak like Covid-19, however, can be tracked in real time, internationally, and through a cornucopia of different metrics: epidemiology, virology, emergency room occupancy, ICU bed pressure, Personal Protective Equipment (PPE) demand, contact tracing, test-positivity, state health department registry, congregate care living facility reports, funeral home, graveyard, and cremation demand, among others. What becomes clear on even a cursory survey of response to the virus by countries like China compared to the United States is that protocols involving surveillance, behavioral modification (especially mask-wearing), testing, quarantine, and restriction of travel required to curb the spread of the virus are more efficaciously instituted and observed in some countries than in others. But they all have at least two key things in common: the goal is to save human lives, and government—decisively or reluctantly—plays a crucial role in the achievement or failure of that goal.

It's hard to imagine a more human-centered goal than saving human lives from a viral pandemic. Given its ecocentrism, it seems then that the *Eight-Point Platform* would have very little to say toward achieving this goal. Not so: in fact, a pandemic can provide a striking object of comparison that highlights by contrast important features of the *Platform* and the assumptions that inform it. Imagine a country confronted with the possibility of a new pandemic, for example, G4:

> Chinese researchers have discovered a new type of swine flu that can infect humans and has the potential to cause a future pandemic, according to a study released on Monday, though scientists have cautioned that the virus does not pose an immediate global health threat. The disease, which researchers called the G4 virus, is genetically descended from the H1N1 swine flu that caused a pandemic in 2009. G4 now shows "all the essential hallmarks of a candidate pandemic virus," said the study, published in the scientific journal Proceedings of the National Academy of Sciences (PNAS). Chinese researchers based at several institutions... discovered the G4 virus during a pig surveillance program. From 2011 to 2018, they collected more than 30,000 nasal swab samples from pigs in slaughterhouses and veterinary teaching hospitals across 10 Chinese provinces. From these samples, researchers identified 179 swine influenza viruses—but not all of them posed a concern. Some only showed up one year out of the program's seven, or eventually declined to nonthreatening levels. But the G4 virus kept chowing up in pigs, year after year—and even showed sharp increases in the swine population after 2016.[37]

Although no evidence (to date) has shown that G4 can spread human to human, Chinese researchers have already documented cases of pig to human spread, and have warned that "the virus was on the rise among pig populations," and could "pose a serious threat to human health" if not carefully monitored. Transmission of the virus from pig to human could "lead to severe infection and even death..."

If it seems genuinely difficult to comprehend what's at stake in this story from any other point of view besides a human-centered one, it's probably because the prospect of another pandemic on top of Covid-19 is simply paralyzing. Our baseline interpretive disposition swiftly becomes survival; the idea of another viral monster wed to its crushing economic implications overshadows every other aspect of the story, including the emergence of G4 directly from large-scale porcine animal agriculture, the value of novel proto-life forms, and our hand in the creation of both the virus and the potential for zoonotic transmission. Yet, it's precisely these features that form the scaffolding for an ecocentric cautionary tale, albeit a dark one. Consider the first point of Naess' *Platform*: "[t]he well-being and flourishing of human and non-human life on Earth have value in themselves. These values are independent of the usefulness of the non-human world for human purposes." Although there is dispute concerning whether viruses count as living things, they're certainly proto-living things. Like their infectious brethren among the bacteria, we're generally disinclined to accord to them any sort of value beyond utility. We think in terms of "good" and "bad" bacteria depending upon whether it serves some human function, but few if any viruses are counted among the "good." In contradiction to *Platform Point One*, our goal is to eradicate them. But, Naess might respond, isn't our motive for eradicating Covid-19 or G4 rooted in the same human chauvinism we take for granted to justify the manufacture, slaughter, processing, and eating of pigs in the first place? The same mechanisms that create suffering for the pigs and produce greenhouse gas emissions (as well as other forms of toxic waste from the slaughter and processing of pig bodies), are those which create the conditions for the zoonotic transmission, in this case, of G4. But at the root of these, we find human chauvinism the primary driver. It's not merely that had we honored *Platform Point One*, we'd not be in this position—facing the potential for another devastating pandemic. It's that the pig body-eating and the emergence of G4 are the product of the same disrespect for the "flourishing of human and nonhuman life." Still, the prospect that we'll recognize our chauvinism in the causal chain that links the subjugation of nonhuman life to the environmental destruction that follows from it to our own heightened vulnerability to disease remains slight at best. It's just not that hard to imagine someone heading home after two months in a hospital with an oxygen tank and scarred lungs—but stopping by a fast food for a pulled pork sandwich on the way.

The point, of course, is that from the point of view of an ecocentric ethic, what the G4 story illustrates is hypocrisy, specifically the kind of hypocrisy that arises out of the belief that we can dominate and command the resources of the planet as if we were in charge, and do so without consequence. We might also consider this hypocrisy in light of *Platform Point Three*: "Humans have no right to reduce this richness and diversity except to satisfy vital needs." Like other industrial-scale agricultural ventures, pork-producing factory farms contribute to the reduction of ecological richness and diversity in several ways: the pig production is itself monocultural, bred for specific characteristics like accelerated growth, volume of meat, and taste; the CAFO takes up many acres recruited to pork slaughter and processing; the waste, dumped into nearby rivers or spread as fertilizer is ecologically corrosive, destroying wetlands, contaminating waterways, altering soil composition; that greenhouse gas emissions contribute to extinction for non-human animal and plant species is well-established. Although Naess casts *Point Three* in the vocabulary of rights, that little of factory farm production goes to the satisfaction of vital needs also speaks to consequences. We could survive a future denuded of much of the richness and diversity to which *Point Three* refers. But that we behave as if we control whether this reduction will impact us, that we'll be spared disease, demonstrates not the humility necessary to recognizing the rights of others, but the denial that conflates want with need, and then takes us by a fast food on the way home from a hospital.

We could tick through each of the *Platform Points* to essentially the same conclusions. It's perhaps *Point Five*, however, that most succinctly captures what Naess sees as wrong with human chauvinism: "present human interference with the non-human world is excessive, and the situation is rapidly worsening." Covid-19 and G4 each offer straightforward examples of "excessive." The production of millions of pigs for slaughter, consumption, and profit illustrates the kind of interference whose massive scale leaves little room for doubt that its impacts will be as excessive as the callousness, gluttony, and greed that made it possible. Multiply the conditions for the emergence of a new breed of swine flu by a factor of chicken and cattle feeding operations, and the real wonder, at least for thinkers like Naess, is that the situation isn't worsening more rapidly than it is. But what's also true for Naess—clarified in his use of the language of rights—is that what's wrong with our recalcitrance to adopt an ecocentric ethic is not "merely" that the consequences of our human chauvinism will ultimately be bad for future generations of human beings. It's that value in the case of living organisms precedes and preempts our use, in this case, our consumption of these nonhuman creatures. That is, if living things have value independent of human judgment, to refuse to recognize that value constitutes a violation of the living thing that has it. Pigs are living sentient entities, each capable of being terrorized on its way to the slaughter house stun gun. But, of course, so too are wolves, and if all that distinguishes the pig from the wolf is the manner of its death or the terror it experiences before it dies, it seems at best arbitrary to see one killing as justified and the other not. It won't do, in other words, to find the slaughter of the pig somehow more condemnable because the pig is bred to be eaten; that fact alone doesn't make the consumer more chauvinistic, especially (following Mallory) if shooting the wolf for sport is really just another kind of consumption: entertainment. Moreover, many a consumer of pork might see the slaughter of pigs as less condemnable precisely because the circumstance of their existence is as "food animals." Point being, once again, that "intrinsic value" is a slippery notion that, arguably, is itself asserted to achieve human ends or at least to excuse human actions. The effort to eradicate viruses reduces the diversity and richness of the biotic community—by definition. But it's hard to imagine even the most ecocentric of plain citizens refusing a ventilator.

4.3.2   The Ecocentric Dichotomy

A difficult issue with which the *Eight-Point Platform* must deal is the possibility that people simply will not willingly accede to policies or laws that endanger their current ways of life, that they'll see the implementation of laws designed, for example, to protect an endangered wetland or save a species of owl from extinction as ecocentric tyranny. We might compare this particular variety of objection, however, to the refusal to wear masks during a pandemic: once we understand the extent to which the benefits outweigh the costs, it's hard to see such objections—even if they do require modest inconvenience—as legitimate. The critic might respond, of course, that saving the owl from extinction has cost jobs, that this is far more than inconvenience. But, as we have seen, this story—like many about species extinctions—is more complicated than owls versus jobs, and we can reasonably expect that to be true of protections for wetlands as well. A more serious objection, however, is that its motives needn't be especially chauvinistic to spark resistance to the imposition of ecocentric policies. We could agree in principle with a deep ecological worldview *and* strongly oppose its involuntary imposition just as we could oppose abortion *and* oppose outlawing it. Both may seem to invite the long hand of the law too far into our personal lives and decision-making. Many might fear an ecocentric future "deeply different from the present" not because the present is entrenched in unearned privilege, but simply because the prospect of giving up the power to make decisions when they conflict with respect for inherent worth (however that comes to be defined) doesn't obviously square with democratic institutions like the vote or free speech rights. Others might be leery of policies implemented to reduce the rate of growth for human population, or of what "vital needs" may not include, or whether ecocentrism precludes any use of nonhuman animals for human purposes (for example, Covid-19 vaccine research). Who, moreover, is to be authorized to determine how the ecocentric society is to function, and how? By what mechanism should such authority come to power? With what checks and balances?

Gaining a clear idea of these important issues requires an understanding of what we'll call the *ecocentric dichotomy*, and it returns us once more to the "shallow" and the "deep." Recall that shallow environmentalism is human-centered and assumes that human-interests can be made fully consistent with the needs of the planet's ecologies and nonhuman citizens; this, Naess argues, has plainly failed, and the proof is in the deterioration of the planet's ecosystems. The deep ecologist attributes our current environmental dilemmas to a human chauvinism that permeates not just our social institutions, but our very psyches. For thinkers like Naess, the formation of an ecological conscience is a matter not only for personal moral decision-making but the kind of collective action that can generate enduring social change codified as policy and law. Personal commitment is certainly desirable, but insufficient to the crises we now face precisely because such crises are global by their very nature. The ecocentric dichotomy can thus be defined as a dilemma borne out of the shallow environmentalist's desire to see some environmental goals accomplished—even at the expense of reinforcing a chauvinistic system of values—and the inevitable clash with deep ecological commitments to the integrity of the biotic community as a whole that cannot be squared with a chauvinistic system of value. Recycling is fine, but it will not mitigate the impacts of climate change; going vegan is great; but it won't put an end to animal agriculture. The dichotomy is personified, Naess argues, in the actions of professional ecologists, say folks who work for the American Bureau of Land Management (BLM), who compromise their environmental principles in the face of market-driven pressures and their government lobbyists only to ultimately contribute to ecosystem erosion. He laments that "[e]stablished corporate interests—the fossil fuel companies and the pampered large banks…do not wish to see downward redistribution of wealth and power, nor the economic annihilation of all the sunk capital that is the fossil fuel economy." Surely, in other words, there's some hypocrisy in accusing deep ecology of a tendency to fascism when "established corporate interests," especially in their relations with government, already wield so much power. Corporate lobbyists and donors who buy environmental deregulation seem to be the real fascists. Whatever the professional ecologist's environmental beliefs, they seem to be preempted by the timber industry and the fossil fuel corporations.

Put simply: for Naess, there is no way to make this system of chauvinist exchange value and short-sightedness work. What's required if we're to see a future for human beings and the planet's biotic communities is a revolutionary—civilizational—transformation to societies grounded in deep ecological principles like those outlined in the *Eight-Point Platform*. If human interference with nonhuman nature is the thing that's "excessive," only substantive change at the level of policy and law will be able to address it. No one can combat climate change alone, so it's our collective understanding of the planet's ecologies and atmosphere that must change. *We* must change. Environmental philosopher Frederic Bender makes a similar point rhetorically when he asks:

> [w]hy continue to sacrifice ecospheric integrity to preserve business-as-usual growth? Why refuse to consider deliberate change, based on the best science currently available, rather than wait to have changes thrust upon us by deteriorating circumstances? Why not consider the ethics of voluntary simplicity and start developing elegant, minimal impact technologies consistent with an ecologically sustainable, postindustrial economy? (*The Culture of Extinction*, p. 90)

In referencing voluntary simplicity, Bender clearly hopes that transformation to an ecocentric conscience can be achieved without the coercion of law. Yet, by posing this hope in the form of "why not?" questions, he affects a tone that's more shaming than encouraging, suggesting that perhaps people aren't ready to adopt voluntary simplicity of their own accord.[38] Put differently: few would deny it's good to develop low-impact technologies, or that we should teach our children "a profound awareness of the difference between bigness and greatness." But can we be *made* to do any of these things? Do we have a right to vote for climate change deniers? Can we withdraw our children from ecocentric schools? Can we drive Dodge RAMS? Will there *be* Dodge RAMS? "Policies," Naess argues, "must therefore be changed," and this change will "affect basic economic, technological, and ideological structures." What's the force of this "must"? Who pays for it? What's the cost of violating statutes created to ensure my respect for inherent worth? Do I have good reason to think the burden of this shift to an ecocentric postindustrial society will fall equally on all human beings? Or will it fall with greater disadvantage and suffering on those least able to evade its enforcement?

These are difficult questions, and it's not hard to see how Naess' use of imperatives raises the specter of an authoritarian version of an ecocentric society. After all, we can be made to do (or not do) *lots* of things already, almost all of them in the interest of the safety and welfare of others. Speed limits, airport screening, laws governing public urination, property, marriage, child support, mask-wearing—these are all impositions on our freedom to do as we wish; but who'd raise serious objection to any of these other than the way they're enforced? Consider, for example, police brutality in the murder of George Floyd and the subsequent call to defund police departments.[39] Although the call for significant restructuring of policing, particularly the use of chokeholds and other violent restraint measures, challenges the way in which government executes some of its most basic obligations to public safety, few if any were calling for the end of policing, *per se*. It's not the coercive aspect of the law itself to which we object—all law is coercive by definition; it's that so long as we regard a law as defensible—in the public interest—our objections are almost always to the way law enforcement is carried out. Similarly, we might not object to the implicitly coercive aspect of the *Platform* any more than in other governing structures—so long as we regard the *Platform* as defensible in itself.

The challenge is that the *Platform* isn't *just* about the welfare and safety of human beings or whether their conditions are conducive to these objectives; exposure to pollution, the unavailability of healthy food, fishery collapse, can all jeopardize the conditions of human well-being. The Platform, however, isn't really *about* these issues; it's about radically transforming the very way we conceive human and nonhuman beings, and their place as plain *citizens* in the biotic community. Deep ecology is *ecocentric*. The structure of any government can "affect basic economic, technological, and ideological structures." But a government formed on the basis of the *Eight-Point Platform* would surely have to have powers to enforce, for example, laws to control whatever might be regarded as threatening to the biotic community, present and future. In its most fundamental incarnation, ecocentric policy must make its primary focus things like human overpopulation, consumption, interference in the nonhuman world; the aim is to revolutionize the character of our moral decision-making on the premise that "vital need" only makes sense in the context of a stable planetary ecology. But it's interference, namely, interference in some of the most intimate aspects of human life, especially reproduction, that incite the specter of regimes that, at least with respect to their instruments of enforcement, resemble governments that look more like Saudi Arabia than like anything compatible with *voluntary* simplicity.

It might seem at this juncture that we're putting the cart before the horse—that because we've not witnessed the rise of any such government, worries about whether it could become as oppressive and authoritarian as the autocratic regimes we know aren't really warranted. But even prior to the *Eight-Point Platform*, worries about whether, given its subordination of the welfare of individuals to that of the community, ecocentrism could become a fascist realization of Leopold's land ethic had already begun to gain some traction. "It's holism is the land ethic's principal strength," writes J. Baird Callicott, "but also its principal liability" (Callicott, p. 124), especially since its central principle, a thing is right when it contributes to the biotic community and wrong otherwise, "makes no reference at all to 'fellow members.' They have gradually dropped out of account as 'The Land Ethic' proceeds to its climax" (Callicott, p. 123). Citing fellow environmental theorist Michael Zimmerman, Callicott argues that one defense against this charge is that the Land Ethic is without any of the other characteristics typical of fascism: militarism or nationalism (p. 125). But that has not been sufficient for Leopold's critics who, for example Kristin Shrader-Frechette, argue that the subordination of all creatures, human and nonhuman, to the integrity of the biotic community constitutes a form of unjust domination (Shrader-Frechette, 1996, pp. 15–25). Callicott counters that among the reasons

> Leopold refers to the various stages of ethical development ... as "accretions" [is because] [a]ccretion means "increase by external addition or accumulation." The land ethic is an accretion—that is, an addition—to our several accumulated social ethics, not something that is supposed to replace them ... [T]he duties attendant upon citizenship in the biotic community ... do not cancel or replace the duties attendant on membership in the human global village (to respect human rights). (Callicott, p. 125)

The land ethic, in other words, is not intended to supplant the moral compasses we have already developed, but rather augment those values and commitments with the addition of a pledge to act in accord with ecocentric principles. Callicott goes on to offer a guide for prioritizing our multiple community memberships in the hope of resolving conflicts among and between them (pp. 125–8).

But there remain other issues, and these are not restricted to whether the land ethic can be translated democratically into policy or law, or whether treating it as an addition to our moral thinking can be reconciled with our traditional ways of solving conflicts. Throughout the *Eight-Point Platform*, Naess makes it clear he rejects the idea that transformational change at the level of a society can be achieved solely through the actions of individuals acting on their own—and he's right about that. But Naess also neglects the fact that some individuals are empowered in ways that other are not, and empowered in ways that depend on the structurally subjugated labor of those others. In other words, Naess' characterization of human chauvinism misses the extent to which chauvinism is not one-size-fits-all, but rather as sexed, gendered, and racialized as is the society he targets for revolutionary change. Philosopher Kathryn Yusoff argues that when terms like "we" are deployed in a fashion blind to the ways in which their uses are imbued by race, prescriptions for change in the direction of greater justice are bound to be distorted; indeed, they're likely to reproduce the same racialized forms of injustice, including environmental injustice, typical of the original social order. In *A Billion Black Anthropocenes or None*, Yusoff argues that insofar as the *Anthropocene*, the current human-centered era, is conceived in terms of the fortunes (or misfortunes) of relatively affluent white people, themselves the beneficiaries of hundreds of years of black and brown slavery and subjugation, what will count as an environmental crisis will be conceived in terms of what harms white people:

> If the Anthropocene proclaims a sudden concern with the exposures of environmental harm to white liberal communities, it does so in the wake of histories in which these harms have been knowingly exported to black and brown communities under the rubric of civilization, progress, modern-

ization, and capitalism. The Anthropocene might seem to offer a dystopic future that laments the end of the world, but imperialism and ongoing (settler) colonialisms have been ending worlds for as long as they have been in existence. (p. xiii)

From the point of view of Yusoff's argument, the Eight-Point Platform epitomizes precisely the "dystopic future that laments the end of the world," but is empowered to do so only because it ignores, as Cronon might also argue, the colonialisms that function to erase the black and brown bodies whose labor is subjugated to the same extractivist chauvinism as is the "body" of the planet.

When Naess claims, for example (Point Five), that "[p]resent human interference with the non-human world is excessive, and the situation is rapidly worsening," he ignores the fact that this excessive interference is neither the product of all human beings—but rather a small subset of the privileged—nor are the effects of this excess borne exclusively by the nonhuman world. Situating her discussion of a racialized Anthropocene in the context of the science of geology, Yusoff argues that "[g]eology is a relation of power and continues to constitute racialized relations of power, in its incarnation in the Anthropocene and in its material manifestation in mining, petrochemical sites and corridors, and their toxic legacies—all over a world that resolutely cuts exposure along color lines" (Yusoff, p. 10). In other words, to whatever extent the science of geology is implicated in ventures like mining—coal, diamonds, natural gas, precious metals—it's implicated in the history of the back-breaking exploitation of black and brown bodies conscripted to a labor whose beneficiaries were not and are not these indigenous or imported peoples, but rather white capitalists. The interference, as Yusoff puts it, that is "white geology" instantiated in extractivist capitalism is indeed excessive. But to hold it liable as "human interference" as opposed to the interference of those systemically benefitted by the racialized structure of labor is not only to erase the history of the black and brown lives whose bodies supplied that labor, but to do so for the sake of advancing authority. Naess, Point Six: "Policies must therefore be changed. These policies affect basic economic, technological, and ideological structures. The resulting state of affairs will be deeply different from the present."

Because the "policies that must therefore be changed" reflect a "history" stripped of its racialized roots, the prospect that the "basic economic, technological, and ideological structures" that subjugate black and brown bodies will face interrogation with respect to their role in the production of environmental destruction is unlikely. In fact, it's as buried beneath the rubble of privileged "white geology" as do these laboring bodies remain consigned to disposable commodity. Naess' claim that the "resulting state of affairs will be deeply different from the present" should policy be made to conform to deep ecological principles is, at least from Yusoff's point of view, no more plausible than that this history of subjugation won't continue to fertilize resistance movements for racial justice; it has and it will. "Seeking to monumentalize Anthropocene history," writes Yusoff, "is an attempt to reclaim an 'innocence' around this geohistory" (Yusoff, pp. 11–2). But movements like Black Lives Matter are no more likely to let that claim to innocence go unchallenged than Jim Crow era monuments to the Confederacy. The same kind of challenge applies, however, to the *Eight-Point Platform*. Insofar as Naess universalizes blame, spreading out the responsibility for damage to the environment as if all human beings had an equal hand in it, he effectively reclaims "innocence" for those actually culpable; he absolves them with the cover of "all." But the effect is to reinforce a racialized chauvinism whose "resulting state of affairs" is not "deeply different" now than during, for example, slavery, segregation, or red-lining. As Yusoff makes the point, "[I]f the Anthropocene is viewed as a resurrection of the impulse to reestablish humanism in all its exclusionary terms of universality, then any critical theory that does not work with and alongside black and indigenous studies… will fail to deliver any epochal shift at all" (Yusoff, p. 18). No doubt, Naess would object to the idea that his deep ecological project bore any relation to the Anthropocene. The point, after all, of the *Eight-Point Platform* is to undermine human chauvinism. But if Yusoff's analysis is correct, insofar as the Platform reproduces the same exclusionary humanism, the same authorized male whiteness, as does the Anthropocene, it undermines its deepest ecological aspirations, and can deliver no "epochal shift" at all.

4.4   The Authoritarian Politics of the Eight-point Platform

4.4.1   Ecocentric Tyranny and Human Population Control

While many questions remain about how we should understand Naess' *Eight-Point Platform*, especially as a framework for policy or law, certainly one of its more incendiary claims is Point Four: "[t]he flourishing of human life and cultures is compatible with a substantially smaller human population. The flourishing of non-human life *requires* a smaller human population." That flourishing is compatible with a smaller human population—few would argue with that; that it *necessitates* a smaller human population—this opens a Pandora's Box with respect to what means might be regarded as justified to achieve that goal, imposed by whom, even on the most charitable interpretation we might offer, namely, to reduce the rate of population growth (as opposed to, say, genocide). It's not difficult to imagine policies whose enforcement would be monstrously oppressive—especially as they'd be imposed primarily (if not exclusively) on women, for example, compulsory use of birth-control pills or devices, mandatory abortion after a first child, compulsory sterilization. Although Naess' motives are certainly different, the very idea of imposing controls on human reproduction raises the specter of the Eugenics movement, a dark episode in American history defined by the involuntary sterilization of thousands of women and men in the United States according to vaguely defined qualities like "imbecility," "criminality," and "feeble-mindedness" which were almost always associated, as writers like Yusoff would point out, with race and economic class.[40] That Naess' aims are, like Leopold's, the integrity and stability of the biotic community does not expunge the coercive element of Point Four; it merely raises the question whether these ends, noble though they may be, can justify whatever means might be required to achieve them.

Of all the points included in the Platform, then, Point Four likely comes closest to the prospect of ecofascism simply because "required" invites the use of force. On this point, ecofeminist philosopher Ariel Salleh observes that

> The phenomenon of "overpopulation" does need to be seriously examined. However, given the ethical issues of eugenics-genocide and of a woman's right over her own body, the targeting of "population control" by white male environmentalists in the North has both racist and sexist dimensions. Observe how many Americans opposed to abortion in the United States endorse population control programs in Asia and South America... Such programs originated in a post-World War II middle-class urban desire to protect the quality of life—that is, high levels of consumerism. These days the argument for population control is formulated more prudently in terms of protecting the Earth's "scarce" resources. Even this injunction, however, as it is applied to the Third World exclusively, is patently hypocritical. Each infant born into the so-called advanced societies uses about fifteen times more global resources during his or her lifetime than a person born in the Third World... What much of this talk about population control may express is a projection and displacement of guilt experienced by those who continue to live comfortably off the invisible backs of working women in the Third World. (Salleh, "Class, Race, and Gender," pp. 232–3)

Salleh's is an acutely harsh assessment of the deep ecological argument for population control. In "Class, Race, and Gender Discourse in the Ecofeminism/ Deep Ecology Debate," she takes aim at its substance, proponents, and its audience. That the argument is now "formulated" in the "more prudent" vocabulary of resource protection in no way alleviates the burden of its past association with eugenics, nor does its superficially ecological justification address the hypocrisy personified by white abortion opponents in the United States who "endorse" population control programs for the black and brown women of the developing world. The deep ecological argument also largely ignores, argues Salleh, the radically different levels of consumption that would seem to make the predominantly white women of the Global North far more suitable candidates for compulsory birth control than their African and Asian sisters.

The argument implicit in the Eight-Point Platform's appeal to population control is thus, according to Salleh, hypocritical, oppressive, and patriarchal. In "Deeper than Deep Ecology: The Ecofeminist Connection," she argues that Naess' argument for the rejection of anthropocentrism on the grounds that what is implied by inherent value is "biological egalitarianism," his argument is "cancelled" by his failure to grapple with the "master-slave role" implicit in the fact that anthropocentrism positions men over women by the same logic it empowers human beings over nonhuman nature ("Deeper than Deep Ecology," p. 340). Similar to Yusoff's analysis of how the Anthropocene both erases and reproduces race as a subjugated class, Salleh argues that Naess' uninterrogated view that "anthropocentrism" signifies an *equality* of domination of human beings over nonhuman nature both erases and reproduces sex as a subjugated class, one long identified through the processes of pregnancy, birth, and child-care with notions like "Mother Nature" ("Deeper than Deep Ecology," p. 340). Thus, the hypocrisy implicit in Naess' formulation of "man's" alienation from nonhuman nature—the alienation that the adoption of an ecocentric ethic is intended to remedy—is bound to run deep:

> The deep ecology movement, by using the generic term *Man* simultaneously presupposes the difference between the sexes in an uncritical way, and yet overlooks the significance of this difference. It overlooks the point that if women's lived experience were recognized as meaningful and were given legitimation in our culture, it could provide an immediate "living" social basis for the alternative consciousness which the deep ecologist is trying to formulate and introduce as an abstract ethical construct ... As Naess rightly ... points out, the denial of dependence on Mother/Nature and the compensatory drive to mastery which stems from it, have only served to alienate man from his true self. Yet the means by which Naess would real-ize this goal of species equality is through artificial limitation of human population ... [This] is quite at odds with the restoration of life-affirming values that is so fundamental to the ethic of deep ecology. (p. 340)

By reproducing "the difference between the sexes" without examining the way in which this difference is taken to position the alienation of "man" from nonhuman nature against "women's lived experience," particularly with respect to pregnancy, childbirth, and child care, Naess blinds himself to what he needs to avoid the necessity of appealing to "artificial" and oppressive, even fascist, means for controlling human population: women's experience as a "living" foundation for a social—ecocentric—conscience. As Salleh makes clear, it's not the goal of developing a more ecologically oriented society to which she objects, it's that insofar as deep ecology resorts to the oppressive strategies it must defeat to achieve it, the goal itself is bound to remain elusive ("Class, Race and Gender Discourse," pp. 243–4).

4.4.2   Does Environmental Crisis Justify Ecocentric Policies or Laws?

Point Eight of the *Eight-Point Platform*: "those who subscribe to the foregoing points [of a deep ecological ethic] have an *obligation* directly or indirectly to implement these changes." Like "require" with respect to the reduction of human population, the force of "obligation" raises the specter of emergent governing institutions for whom such binding moral ideas could function to justify authoritarian policies or laws that, in the interest of biotic community future stability, impose substantive restrictions on individual behavior and action. Depending on factors like geography, economic wherewithal, class status, racial and sexual identity, or education, life in a society governed in accord with the *Eight-Point Platform* (or something like it) could be radically different than what we have come to expect, especially in the Global North; or not, as we've seen in parts of the Global South. Though, to be clear, to the extent that Global South communities conform to ecocentric ideals, this is not likely due to the adoption of any *Platform*, much less laws or regulations formulated according to it, but simply as a matter of cultural practice and subsistence. It's important, however, to remember this cautionary: that Naess treats as universal a Global North, capitalist, consumption-driven disposition to nonhuman nature is bound to distort and misrepresent facts about the relationship between human communities and the ecologies with which they interact. Even Global North communities vary widely according to factors like economic class, gender, and race. Hence questions about who is authorized to "implement changes," what entitles them to do so, upon whom, with what justification, to precisely what ends, at what cost, and to whom—these are as vulnerable to misrepresentation as is responsibility for the impacts of human chauvinism bound to be unjustly blamed on those least able to defend themselves or their ways of life. This, at least in part, is what the critics mean by ecofascism.

Who is responsible to take up the task of implementing change is complicated in part by factors absent in Naess' implicit universalizing, and in part because ignoring these factors effectively reinforces the "we" that is not a "we," but rather a Global North affluent white "he" targeted, but at the same time ratified as authoritative, by the *Platform*. There is another factor, however, that complicates Naess' ethic, one that's vitally important to its credibility *as* an ethic, and that bears directly on the question of who is responsible to implement change: *urgency*. That is, how urgent need an environmental crisis be, *and with respect to what or whom*, to justify policies, regulations, or other measures that restrict the behavior of individuals and communities to some greater extent than current law? While the obligation to act to implement change for thinkers like Naess and Leopold derives its force from a moral argument about "our" place as plain citizens in the larger biotic community, and therefore does not need an event or a state of affairs to justify it, crises like climate change can serve to bring that obligation into sharp focus. But should urgency be accorded moral weight? In what kinds of cases? Who is authorized to decide? According to what reading of the *Eight-Point Platform*?

On the one hand, if Naess' argument for the *Platform* is well-reasoned, moving to implement change on the basis of it shouldn't need anything more than the force of that argument. The conditions under which the argument is made, paradise or apocalypse, should be treated as irrelevant to whether disavowing human chauvinism is good or bad. If the ecocentric life worth living is a good life, it is so regardless whether in living it we're made particularly happy, so long as abject misery (since it could produce a disruption in ecosystemic stability) can be avoided. The obligation to strive to live that life derives simply from its being the right way to live, and would continue to be so whether the world embodied ecocentric integrity, diversity, and stability, or not. On the other hand, it's hard to ignore the role urgency plays in formulating the arguments for deep ecology (or any environmental ethic), and it's certainly possible to produce good reasons why urgency should count as a factor in evaluating whether ecocentrism offers a better environmental compass than its moral extensionist competitors. First, it seems unlikely that Naess would have articulated the *Platform* in the way he did, with pointed references to issues he saw as pressing, except that he himself saw urgency as an important element in the formulation of its points. If each of the points contains an implicit call to action, Point Eight, is explicit; the obligation to implement change doesn't mean the change is urgent, but given each of the preceding points in the *Platform*, it surely implies it. Second, setting aside supposition about Naess' motives, ethics is *about* action. Unlike metaphysics (theories about the nature of reality) or epistemology (theories about what counts as knowledge), theories in ethics are specifically about what rational agents ought to do, how they ought to behave, what they ought to avoid, and what should count for such agents as morally good or bad, right or wrong. So, if "urgency" is rightly understood as a way of *qualifying* the significance of performing or not performing an action, then it belongs to ethics, including ecocentric ethics. To claim, in fact, there are some actions whose performance is imperative because a moral principle demands it, such as rights that must be observed (a prisoner's right to clean water), or consequences that must be avoided even at high cost (global nuclear holocaust) is to stake a claim on the urgency of adhering to that principle and acting in accord with it.

Urgency, however, takes on a particularly important, though not necessarily clear, direction with respect to Point Eight of the *Platform* in virtue of Naess' specific reference to "obligation." Adherence to an ecocentric ethic obligates its subscriber to implement, at least insofar as it's possible, the *Platform's* program. Although Naess provides some examples of what he regards as urgent, human overpopulation for example, the question "How urgent need an environmental crisis be, *and with respect to what or whom*, to justify measures that restrict behavior to some greater extent than current law?" seems difficult to answer at best, in light of (1) objections to the *Platform* raised by critics like Salleh (2) the imperative phrasing of Point Three, "[h]umans have *no right* to reduce this richness and diversity except to satisfy vital needs, and (3) the range of interpretation, and what factors should count as relevant to it, of Point Seven, "[t]he ideological change will be mainly that of *appreciating life quality...* rather than adhering to an increasingly higher standard of living. There will be a profound awareness of the difference between bigness and greatness." Despite what is too often *de facto* denial, few disagree that in virtue of its global, indeed, planetary implications, the climate crisis is the Motherlode of all crises. But equally few would defend the claim that "planetary threat" is the only "urgent" that counts. So—what, short of threat to life on planet earth, counts as sufficiently urgent that responding to it justifies implementing restrictions on human individual and collective behavior above and beyond extant laws and regulations? What justifies "authoritarian," if anything? And how should we evaluate whatever case that may be in light of factors that contest a human chauvinism taken to be "universal"?

These are genuinely difficult questions because they're about what we're willing to live with, but they're also about what others may be forced to live with. We rightly fear overreaction to crisis, or worse: the imposition of restrictions in cases where a threat is inflated or misrepresented in order to affect a consolidation of power unachievable through legitimate means. We have reasons to find government and its law-enforcement agencies suspect. The Patriot Act may have justified roots in the September 11th terrorist attack on the World Trade Center, but it's also been deployed to less transparently legitimate ends such as the surveillance of Americans engaged in First Amendment protected protest; some argue that President Trump's 2020 Independence Day Speech decrying protests against police brutality as a "Leftist, Marxist, Communist, Anarchist" plot to take down the country is an attempt to create a sense of urgency in order to distract us from the Covid-19 pandemic and bolster his reelection bid. Still, it's surely possible that "urgent" rightly describes crises that, though they may not encompass the magnitude of the climate crisis, nevertheless demand decisive, coordinated, rational, effective, and timely action, perhaps even at the cost of having to impose restrictions many will find onerous, and some may rightly find oppressive. So, what might these look like? Consider conservation biologist Vickie Boult's account of at least 400 elephant deaths in Botswana, Spring 2020:

> Worrying news has recently come to light: hundreds of elephants have been found dead in Botswana, and as yet, there is no clear cause of death. But as an <u>expert in elephants and their conservation</u>, I believe we can at least rule out a few possible answers. Here's what we do know: the first deaths were reported in March, but significant numbers were only recorded from May onwards. To date, it's thought that the death toll stands at nearly <u>400 ele-</u>

phants of both sexes and all ages. Most of the deaths have occurred near the village of Seronga on the northern fringes of the Okavango Delta, a vast swampy inland region that hosts huge wildlife populations. Many of the carcasses have been found near to water. Of those discovered so far, some lay on their knees and faces (rather than on their side), suggesting sudden death, although there are also reports of elephants looking disoriented and even walking in circles. The tusks of the dead elephants are still in place and, as yet, no other species have died under similar circumstances.[41]

Among the explanations ruled out are poaching "since the tusks of the dead elephants have not been removed," killing by local farmers frustrated by elephant-caused crop damage. "[T]he sheer number of dead elephants, and the lack of reports of gunshot or spearing wounds, does not support this hypothesis." Ditto for intentional poisoning since no other species in the region have been reported as suffering the same fate. Also ruled out are natural causes such as drought. The remaining possibility is disease, potentially an Anthrax outbreak similar to one that killed 100 elephants in Botswana as recently as 2019.

Given the possibility that the right explanation for this massive elephant die-off is disease outbreak, and given that, though rare, it is possible for Anthrax to transmit from nonhuman animals to human beings,[42] would some variation of the martial law the Chinese government imposed on Wuhan, locking it down as the number of Covid-19 cases began to escalate and the body count began to rise, be warranted for Botswana's Okavango Delta region to contain the spread to other elephants and prevent the possible transmission to people? Can the *Eight-Point Platform* offer actionable guidance? From its point of view, it matters less whether elephant to human transmission is possible; it's sufficient to count it as at least a regional crisis in virtue of the die-off's negative effects on the ecosystem, especially if any of its species are endangered (*Platform*, Point Three). The die-off also exemplifies Point Five: whatever the cause of the die-off concerning, excessive human interference is likely to play some role. Still, human interference caused by, for example, corporate negligence is a different thing than the efforts of farmers to plant subsistence crops. Assuming Anthrax is the right diagnosis, the likelihood that this outbreak could become a global pandemic is very small. Human to human transmission is possible, but rare, and elephant range is confined to ever-smaller regions of the world. The Platform does not require "urgent" to imply "global," but the question still remains: does this kind, scope, nature, duration, or affected population, human and nonhuman, of a crisis qualify as urgent? Sufficient to warrant the imposition of regulatory statutes aimed at preventing spread, transmission, or environmental hazard? Does it matter whether farmers in the nearby village have comparatively little say—even if suspicion falls on them—about the possible causes or best course of action given the far greater power of, say, the corporate coal mining facility thirty miles away, but in the same region or province? To be clear, these are not just questions about whether or when laudable ends justify morally repellant means; they're not even just about who gets to decide—though this is critically important. They're about what and who ought to be prioritized in the evaluation of what and why a crisis counts as urgent. Put differently: questions of urgency remind us that ethics is about right and wrong, but it is also about power.

Whether the Botswanan elephant catastrophe counts as urgent enough to justify authoritarian intervention to address it is not made evident by appeal to the *Eight-Point Platform*. It's not the elephants or their likely suffering that count, at least first. It's not the near-by villagers' suffering or livelihoods, and it's not the planet unless the impacts of a presumed Anthrax outbreak threaten the planetary ecosystem, itself unlikely. It's plausible that the Botswanan regional ecosystem might be improved if the farming villagers were moved out. But whether that can be justified—whether the die-off counts as urgent enough to justify that—depends on the causes of the deaths, although human encroachment is a likely factor. The status of the farming villagers is also likely to come under scrutiny from quarters like Salleh, Yusoff, Mallory, and Curtin. We could consider other cases, for instance, the United Nation's *Reducing Emissions from Deforestation and Forest Degradation Program* (REDD) whose aims are global—reforestation to offset carbon emissions—but whose impacts on the human populations it displaces in the Amazon Basin are troubling, to say the least (Bayrak, Ten Years of REDD +). We could consider the Kenyan war against massive crop-destroying locust invasion,[43] or the exponential spread of Covid-19 in the United States due to noncompliance with masking policies. What these all have in common in one way or another is not only excessive human interference in local, regional, or global ecosystems, but the interplay of factors relevant to economic wherewithal, geographical location, and lack of decision-making power—Botswanan farmers, Amazon Basin indigenous populations, Kenyan pastoralists, and a segment of the American citizenry. Each is an example of crisis for a biotic community—elephant range, rainforest, crops, cities, and neighborhoods. None, however, are the climate crisis. None threaten the capacity of life on the planet to regenerate itself, though each in its own way is very likely experienced as apocalyptic by some, human and nonhuman beings. So, the question whether they credibly authorize the use of force to prevent more damage to an ecosystem as a whole, including villages and cities, remains an open one. Moreover, because the causes of a crisis are not always known (was it Anthrax?), because the intentions of a program may themselves be defensible (reforestation in the massively denuded Amazon basin), because the impacts may be nearly irretrievably devastating to human and nonhuman beings (plague of Locusts), because there may be perceived issues of rights (mandatory mask policies)—*because urgency is rarely if ever the only morally relevant factor we must consider*—what Naess' argument for "obligation" comes to is likely to remain a matter of ambivalence even for the committed ecocentrist. Except, perhaps, when it comes to the climate crisis. But even here there's reasonable worry that the imposition of authoritarian laws, programs, and penalties in the interest of mitigating global warming is in danger of throwing out the baby with the bath water—that is, producing conditions that, though good for the biotic community, are experienced as unlivable by some in the human community, a possibility that threatens to produce self-defeating forms of resistance.

In the end, the *Eight-Point Platform* seems to present us with more questions than answers. If we're the chauvinists Naess makes us out to be, ecocentric authoritarian rule may be the only viable strategy that can save us from ourselves, and thus from global calamite. If, however, human-centeredness isn't necessarily fated to narrow self-interest, there may yet be democratic avenues for combating environmental deterioration, even if climate change doesn't afford us much time. By conflating "human-centered" with "chauvinistic" Naess defines human beings as creatures bound to fail to appreciate the inherent worth of nonhuman nature. It's thus surprising that he also sees this failure as remediable through a radical transformation of conscience—even if the only plausible means for producing that transformation requires force. While the ecocentric dichotomy depicts human chauvinism as if it were an ineradicable feature of human nature, even the most tyrannical program of restoring integrity to the biotic community assumes that human nature is malleable, *transformable*, under the right conditions. That view of human beings is neither new nor deep. Rather, what history shows is that it too often operates to justify despotic forms of rule that, like the critics of the REDD program argue, result in the reinforcement of an existing social order that manifests its chauvinism as racism, patriarchy, and speciesism.

4.4.3   Summary and Questions

Ecocentrism is the view that the only environmentally responsible ethic is one that begins with the *wholesale repudiation* of human-centeredness. Such *anthropocentrism*, argues the ecocentrist, is essentially *chauvinistic*. That is, while we may be capable of extending moral principles built to attain human-centered goals and solve human conflicts to other human beings, they make poor models for the moral considerability of nonhuman beings and ecosystems. Better policies, technological improvements, and more eco-friendly regulations won't do. What we need, argues the ecocentrist, is to radically transform our relationship to nonhuman nature and create an ecologically centered way of life. What we need, in other words, is a *paradigm shift*. Here, however, arises a dilemma: if human-centeredness is *inalterably* chauvinistic, the transformation to what Leopold calls an "ecological conscience" would be precluded by this fact. If human-centeredness isn't inalterably chauvinistic, the call for a paradigm shift is blunted by the *malleability* of human interests. Perhaps, the moral extensionist might argue, we need a substantive change in human perspective but not a wholesale rejection of human-centeredness. We could develop convincing arguments for taking nonhuman suffering seriously; perhaps the rights of nonsentient entities like trees and rivers could be built into an expanded anthropocentrism. Do we need a paradigm shift, or do we simply need to recognize in enduring actionable ways that human-centeredness neither necessitates nor entitles human chauvinism?

Aldo Leopold argues for a radical transformation of worldview according to which human beings come to understand themselves as *plain citizens* or members of "biotic teams." Our first priority is the good of that whole—not any single privileged member of the biotic community. As he makes the point in *A Sand County Almanac*: the *land ethic* changes our role "from conqueror of the land-community to plain member and citizen of it." In addition to the question *whether* we're capable of making the transformation from chauvinism to ecocentrism, Leopold also needs to show us *how*. For the chauvinist who sees conservation solely in terms of economic gain, the value of land is property, a vehicle for accumulating wealth. For the ecocentrist, value derives not from exchange, but from the biotic community. Songbirds may have little value for the chauvinist but, for the ecocentrist, their right to exist is of equal value to our own. For Leopold, what's required of an ecological conscience is not merely that human chauvinism becomes supplanted in favor of ecosystem integrity, but that "plain citizenship" becomes naturalized to the consciousness of human agents. But by what avenue other than models provided by moral principles already familiar to us can we make this transition?

Leopold responds to human chauvinism by prodding us to "think like a mountain," but he insists that this is more than the transformation of human conscience. Scientific knowledge forms a key part of the ecocentric disposition, providing *epistemic* substance to Leopold's central moral principle: "a thing is right when it tends to preserve the integrity, stability, and beauty of the biotic community. It is wrong when it tends otherwise." This principle captures the idea that we have a responsibility to *know* in what the integrity, stability, and beauty of the biotic community consist; we have a duty to *act* on what we know. Actions that fail to exemplify this responsibility are wrong, knowable as such, ought not to be undertaken, and are worthy of rebuke. The principle applies to persons, communities, and institutions whose moral duty, individually and collectively, is to insure the integrity of the biotic community. While human interests and welfare aren't necessarily precluded from this moral calculus, they must be weighed critically against the possibility that acting on them will bode ill for the biotic community. Consider climate change: if our first moral duty is to know in what *future* planetary ecological integrity likely consists, climate change denial isn't wrong just because it's self-serving; it's wrong because it's epistemically derelict. The question for Leopold, then, is whether I need to be able to think like a mountain in order to develop and ecological conscience. We do, after all, want to know and understand the world even if we think it's *our* world. Do I need to be able to think like a mountain to know and appreciate what the mountain is as a rich and diverse ecology? No doubt, the way we represent what we know can be skewed to rationalize human chauvinism. But knowledge is neither human-centered nor ecocentric necessarily.

We might see Leopold as a bridge between moral extensionism and ecocentrism. The land ethic is consequentialist, with some significant modifications: Leopold doesn't make the capacity to suffer central to moral evaluation, but rather whatever is conducive to preserving biotic communities even if this means, for example, hunting to reduce the size of a deer population or eradicating a population of a non-endangered species to save from extinction an endangered one. On this point, then, Leopold aligns more closely with Rolston's *Respect for Life* than with Singer. But this comparison also has its limits. Like Stone, Leopold includes nonsentient entities like rivers and mountains as morally considerable. For Rolston, however, only species of living things are entitled to respect for life; his central unit of value is the *species*. While both Leopold and Rolston direct our moral attention to the future, Leopold's view of biotic integrity could, in theory, sanction the extinction of a species that threatened the "stability, integrity, and beauty" of a biotic community. "Endangered," in other words, isn't the critical moral value; biotic diversity and integrity are, and this can be consistent with extinction if an endangered species threatened diversity in a particular biotic community. For Rolston, a very different scenario prevails: we could imagine altering an ecosystem to preserve a species from extinction because the unit of value isn't the integrity of the biotic community, at least in the first place, but preserving genetic information.

In his landmark essay, "The Shallow and the Deep, Long Range Ecology Movement," Arne Naess sketches what becomes the *Eight-Point Platform*, a set of directives designed to bridge the gap between private morality and public policy. The aim of the *Platform* is to supply a conceptual framework for governing bodies to articulate policy and erect law consistent with an ecocentric worldview. It offers goals that must be met not merely to achieve sustainability but a paradigm shift from anthropocentrism to an ecocentrism. For Naess, the key moral driver of this shift is that all living things have *inherent worth* (*intrinsic value*). The *Platform* offers a charter for Leopold's plain citizenship. Naess takes the rejection of human chauvinism as foundational to moral agency, seeking instead to develop a framework for the ecocentric conscience of whole communities. Plain citizens embody this community not only in their private lives, but in laws and policies that reflect their commitment to preserving the inherent worth out of which biotic integrity is made possible. But there are many problems with the *Platform* and its imperative directives, some that reflect back on Leopold, and some that raise serious questions about power, who wields it, and with what justification. One difficult is the possibility that if a particular people or population won't accede to policies or laws that endanger their current ways of life, an ecocentric society could require a kind of tyranny to achieve its sustainability objectives. Some may fear an ecocentric future not because it will remain steeped in the unearned privilege of the present, but because it authorizes the same unearned privilege in the future. Others might be leery of Naess' specific goals, for example, instituting policies aimed at reducing the rate of human population growth, banning the use of nonhuman animals for things like Covid-19 vaccine research, or moving villagers out of their homes under a program of reforestation. Who decides how the ecocentric society is to function, and how?

Getting a clearer picture of these issues requires understanding what I'll call the *ecocentric dichotomy*. Embodying Naess' division between what he calls the "shallow" and the "deep," shallow environmentalism assumes that human-interests can be made consistent with the needs of the planet's ecologies and nonhuman citizens. This, Naess argues, has plainly failed. Deep ecology sees human chauvinism as culpable for our current environmental crisis, but enduring social change cannot be left to the moral transformation of individuals; rather, it's the province of collective action codified as policy and law. One difficulty is that while I can be made to do (or not do) *lots* of things in the interest of a biotic community that includes human society, the *Platform* is about far more than safety and welfare. It's about radically transforming the way we conceive nonhuman entities and ecosystems. A government formed on the basis of the *Eight-Point Platform* might have powers to alter these institutions in ways we rightly regard as repressive, or worse: that laws ostensibly created to preserve biotic integrity in fact reinforce a racist, patriarchal, and speciesist social order.

Assuming that a society imagined in accord with the general outline of the *Eight-Point Platform* is desirable, how do we achieve it without sacrificing the liberty to make our own decisions, individually or collectively, about what counts as the life worth living? When do the ends—a sustainable future premised on the concepts of inherent worth and biotic integrity—justify the means if the means involve the forfeiture of at least one value we hold dear, the right to conceive of nonhuman animals and nature as I wish—even against a prevailing ecocentric social order? The central question, however, may still be about human nature: if we just are human chauvinists, ecocentric tyranny may be the only way to save us from the environmental crises we cause. If, however, we're capable of seeing beyond self-interest, there may yet be democratic avenues to pursue for combating environmental deterioration, even if climate change doesn't give us much time. Then again, if we're truly human chauvinists, it may be that no volume of force can compel us to behave in ways that are environmentally responsible—no matter how oppressive or authoritarian. For those already made vulnerable by factors of economic class, race, sex, geography, and indigenous status, ecocentrism may seem like just one more avenue of disempowerment.

1. What argument for the Land Ethic does Aldo Leopold intend to convey through central concepts, "plain citizen," "thinking like a mountain," and "ecological conscience"?
2. How is Leopold's moral principle, "A thing is right when…" essentially utilitarian? How does this potentially provide a bridge between moral extensionism and ecocentrism?
3. How does the concept of inherent worth (intrinsic value) play a key role in the ecocentric arguments of Leopold? Arne Naess?
4. What is Arne Naess' Eight-Point Platform? How does it exemplify Ecocentrism as a program for articulating policy and law?
5. What is the ecocentric dichotomy, and how is it exemplified in Naess' distinction between shallow and deep ecology?
6. Why is Naess' version of ecocentrism subject to the criticism that it legitimates authoritarian forms of government or policy?

Annotated Bibliography

Abram, David (2010). *Becoming an Animal: An Earthly Cosmology* (New York: Vintage Books).
In this excellent example of deep ecological thought in action, Abrams argues that he "strive[s] to discern and perhaps to practice a curious kind of thought, a way of careful reflection that no longer tears us out of the world of direct experience in order to represent it, but that binds us ever more deeply into the thick of that world."
Abram, David (1997). *The Spell of the Sensuous: Perception and Language in a More Than Human World* (New York: Vintage Books).
A distinctively philosophical work, Abrams draws our attention to the experience of nonhuman nature in the effort to develop a deep ecological argument for understanding human life in the larger world of nonhuman animals and nature.
Bayrak, Mucahid Mustafa and Lawal Mohammed Marafa. "Ten Years of REDD+: A Critical Review of the Impacts of REDD+ on Forest Dependent Communities." *Sustainability* 8 (2016), pp. 1–22.
Bayrak and Marafa argue that the impacts of the United Nations reforestation program, REDD, on forest dependent communities in the Amazon Basin has not produced the climate change mitigating results intended

and has meant additional hardships for local human communities displaced by the program.

Bender, Frederic (2003). *The Culture of Extinction: Toward a Philosophy of Deep Ecology* (Humanity Books).

Bender offers a defense of deep ecology, especially Naess' Eight-Point Platform in light of Bender's thorough-going critique of capitalism as the primary driver of environmental deterioration.

Callicott, J. Baird. "Holistic Environmental Ethics and the Problem of Ecofascism," in *Beyond the Land Ethic: More Essays in Environmental Philosophy* (State University of New York Press, 1999), pp. 116–29.

Callicott defends deep ecology from the accusation that it justifies ecofascism by arguing that Aldo Leopold's land ethic is intended as an addition to environmental ethics, but not as a replacement.

Cavazza, Elisa. "Ecosophy at the End of Nature." *The Trumpeter* 30 (2) (2014), pp. 115–40.

Cavazza offers a striking compare and contrast between the works of deep ecologist Arne Naess and Bruno Latour with a specific focus of how each aims at a reinterpretation of the concept of "humanity."

Cryer, Paul. *"Why Ecocentrism is the Key Pathway to Sustainability,"* The Millennium Alliance for Humanity and the Biosphere (MAHB), https://mahb.stanford.edu/blog/statement-ecocentrism.

After providing an excellent overview of ecocentrism, Cryer argues that adopting the ecocentric perspective is the "key" to mitigating climate change.

Curtin, Deane. "Women's Knowledge as Expert Knowledge: Indian Women and Ecodevelopment," in Karen J. Warrren (ed.), *Ecofeminism: Women, Culture, Nature* (Indiana University Press, 1997), pp. 82–98.

Curtin argues that the kind of knowledge women attain through their direct interaction with nonhuman nature has value environmental ethicists ought to take more seriously.

Devall, Bill. "The Deep Ecology Movement: Reformist Environmentalism." *Humboldt Journal of Social Relations* (Fall/Winter 1979). https://theanarchistlibrary.org/library/arne-naess-and-george-sessions-basic-principles-of-deep-ecology.

Devall argues that, unlike what he calls reformist environmentalism, deep ecology "questions the fundamental premises of the dominant social paradigm," and that the reform movement will eventually have to come to terms with its more radical alternative.

Devall, Bill. "Applied Deep Ecology." *The Trumpeter* 10 (4) (1993). http://trumpeter.athabascau.ca/index.php/trumpet/article/view/367/577.

Devall describes a conference where the principles of the rising deep ecology movement transformed the lives of its participants, including many reform-minded environmentalists.

Fox, Warwick (1995). *Towards a Transpersonal Ecology: Developing New Foundations for Environmentalism* (New York: SUNY Press).

Fox develops a spiritually-oriented deep ecology grounded in the philosophical insights of writers like Arne Naess and Bill Devall, but also in transpersonal psychology.

Frechette, Kristin Shrader. "Individualism, Holism, and Environmental Ethics." *Ethics and the Environment* 1, pp. 15–25.

Frechette levels criticism at environmental holism on the grounds that an ecocentric ethic is liable to ecofascism.

Lahar, Stephanie. "Roots: Rejoining Natural and Social History," in Greta Gaard (ed.), *Ecofeminism: Women, Animals, Nature* (Temple University Press, 1993), pp. 91–117.

Lahar argues that the traditional distinction between natural and social history is an artificial one, and that what ancient human history shows is that we might be better off to reconsider its usefulness.

Lee, Wendy Lynne (2010). *Eco-Nihilism: The Philosophical Geopolitics of the Climate Change Apocalypse* (Lexington: Rowman and Littlefield). ch. 2, pp. 102–15.

Lee argues that Arne Naess' Eight-Point Platform is vulnerable to the criticism that it legitimates authoritarian forms of government in the name of saving the environment.

Leopold, Aldo (1949). *A Sand County Almanac* (Oxford: Oxford University Press).

In this landmark work, Leopold lays out his seminal argument for the "plain citizen" and an ecocentric—as opposed to anthropocentric relationship to the land.

Leopold, *"Thinking Like a Mountain,"* http://www.eco-action.org/dt/thinking.html.

Here, Leopold expands on concepts central to making out the argument for the important place of knowledge in our responsibility to foster the biotic community.

Mallory, Chaone. "Acts of Objectification and the Repudiation of Dominance: Leopold, Ecofeminism, and the Ecological Narrative." *Ethics and the Environment* 6 (2), (2001), pp. 59–89.

Mallory takes Leopold's ecocentrism to task for its reproduction of the forms of domination that an ecocentric worldview claims to repudiate.

McPherson, Guy. *"Resources and Anthropocentrism."* Resilience, October 12, 2009, https://www.resilience.org/stories/2009-10-12/resources-and-anthropocentrism.

McPherson argues that to understand how our language itself resists the move to a more ecologically sustainable perspective, we should look at how we use anthropocentric words like "resource."

Naess, Arne. "The Shallow and the Deep, Long Range Ecology Movement. A Summary." *Inquiry* 16, pp. 95–100. https://iseethics.files.wordpress.com/2013/02/naess-arne-the-shallow-and-the-deep-long-range-ecology-movement.pdf.

In this seminal essay, Naess sketches what later becomes the Eight-Point Platform, arguing for a variety of ecocentrism that is as much about policy and law as it is about private moral decision-making.

Naess, Arne, and George Sessions. *"The Eight-Point Platform,"* Foundation for Deep Ecology, http://www.deepecology.org/platform.htm.

The Eight-Point Platform comprises a set of principles and goals a society must seek to embody in order to realize itself as ecocentric. This follows on Naess' "The Shallow and the Deep" as a mature expression of Naess' ecocentric philosophical argument.

Naess, Arne, and George Sessions. "Basic Principles of Deep Ecology." *The Anarchist Library.* https://theanarchistlibrary.org/library/arne-naess-and-george-sessions-basic-principles-of-deep-ecology.

Naess and Sessions lay out the Eight-Point Platform with substantial annotation and explanation of each of its points.

Salleh, Ariel Kay. "Deeper than Deep Ecology: The Ecofeminist Connection." *Environmental Ethics* 6, (1984), pp. 339–45.

Salleh offers an ecofeminist critique of the deep ecology of Arne Naess. She argues that deep ecology reproduces the man versus nature and man versus women hierarchical dualisms it claims to reject.

Salleh, Ariel Kay. "Class, Race, and Gender Discourse in the Ecofeminism/Deep Ecology Debate," *Environmental Ethics* 15, (1993), pp. 225–44.

In this essay Salleh continues to develop her critique of the deep ecology of Arne Naess, responding to specific claims of Naess' defenders.

Sessions, Robert. "Deep Ecology Versus Ecofeminism: Healthy Differences or Incompatible Philosophies?" *Hypatia* 6 (1), (Spring 1991), pp. 90–107.

In this essay Robert Sessions lays out a defense of deep ecology against the ecofeminist criticism that the arguments contained in the Eight-Point Platform lend themselves to a variety of environmental fascism.

Sessions, George and Bill Devall (2001). *Deep Ecology: Living as if Nature Mattered* (Layton UT: Gibbs Smith).

Deep ecologist George Sessions explores the possibility of human consciousness expanded to counter what he perceives as a centeredness responsible for environmental crisis. Like Naess, Sessions embraces inherent worth and the notion that all nonhuman animals and ecosystems are of equal worth.

Sessions, George, ed. (1994). *Deep Ecology for the 21ˢᵗ Century* (Boulder, CO: Shambhala Publishers.
This edited anthology offers a wide array of deep ecologist thought, including Leopold, Naess, Sessions and a number of others.
Singer, Peter. "The Place of Nonhumans in Environmental Issues," in William Shaw (ed.), *Social and Personal Ethics*, 8th edn, pp. 142–6.
Singer argue that it's morally imperative that we consider the effects of human actions on nonhuman animals and their ecosystems, for what affects them also affects us.
White, Lynn. "The Historical Roots of Our Ecological Crisis." *Science* 155 (3767), (March 10, 1967), pp. 1203–07.
In this groundbreaking essay, White shows how the rise of Christianity gave rise both to the Industrial Revolution and, as a consequence, the devastation to the planetary environment.
Yusoff, Kathryn (2018). *A Billion Black Anthropocenes or None* (University of Minnesota Press).
In this groundbreaking work, Yusoff traces the history of racism though the science of geology showing that there are likely no sciences exempt, but that the sciences upon which extractivist ventures are premised may be even more vulnerable.
Zaleha, Bernard Daley, and Andrew Szasz. "Why Conservative Christians Don't Believe in Climate Change." *Bulletin of the Atomic Scientists* 71 (5), pp.19–30.
Following Lynn White's "The Historical Roots of our Ecological Crisis," Zaleha and Szasz argue that climate change denialism and anti-environmentalist sentiments common to fundamentalist Christianity stem from the fear that environmentalism will klead to pagan worship.

Online Resources

1. Haydn Washington, et.al., "Statement of Commitment to Ecocentrism," *Ecological Citizen*, https://www.ecologicalcitizen.net/statement-of-ecocentrism.php.
2. Jonathan Padwe, "Anthropocentrism," *Oxford Bibliographies*, May 6, 2016, http://www.oxfordbibliographies.com/view/document/obo-9780199830060/obo-9780199830060-0073.xml.
3. "French Citizens' Assembly Votes to Make Ecocide a Crime," *Team Ecohustler*, https://ecohustler.com/culture/french-citizens-assembly-votes-to-make-ecocide-a-crime.

4. John McKenna, "Factory farms: Misery on the Hoof," *Irish Times*, March 4, 2014, https://www.irishtimes.com/life-and-style/health-family/factory-farms-misery-on-the-hoof-1.1711296.

5. John McFarland, "Dealing with Landmen," *Oil and Gas Lawyer Blog*, December 7, 2011, https://www.oilandgaslawyerblog.com/dealing-with-landmen.

6. Wendy Lynne Lee, "Why Fracking Epitomizes the Crisis in American Democracy: Profiteering and the "Good American," *Raging Chicken Press*, March 17, 2012, https://ragingchickenpress.org/2012/03/17/why-fracking-epitomizes-the-crisis-in-american-democracy-profiteering-and-the-good-american.

7. Gary Fuller, "How Fracking can Contribute to Climate Change," *The Guardian*, May 29, 2016. https://www.theguardian.com/environment/2016/may/29/fracking-contribute-climate-change.

8. "The End of Fossil Fuels," *Ecotricity*, https://www.ecotricity.co.uk/our-green-energy/energy-independence/the-end-of-fossil-fuels.

9. Darryl Fears, "Trump Ends Obama-Era Policy to Protect Oceans, Created in Response to Deepwater Horizon Oil Spill," *Chicago Tribune*, June 20, 2018, https://www.chicagotribune.com/news/nationworld/science/ct-trump-ends-ocean-protection-policy-20180620-story.html.

10. Christina Wilkie, "Trump Rescinds National Monument Protections on 1.8 Million Acres of Utah Canyon Land," *CNBC*, December 4, 2017, https://www.cnbc.com/2017/12/04/trump-rescinds-national-monument-protections-on-1-point-9-million-acres-of-utah-canyon-land.html.

11. Steve Horn, "Federal Research Has Been Stoking Oil, Gas Interest in Bear's Ears Monument for Years," *DeSmog Blog*, June 7, 2017, https://www.desmogblog.com/2017/06/07/bears-ears-national-monument-oil-gas-trump.

12. Jennifer Kobylecky, "Understanding the Land Ethic," *The Aldo Leopold Foundation*, May 29, 2015, https://www.aldoleopold.org/post/understanding-land-ethic.

13. "The Land Ethic," *The Aldo Leopold Foundation*, https://www.aldoleopold.org/about/the-land-ethic.

14. Aldo Leopold, "Thinking Like a Mountain," *University of Kentucky Archives*, http://www.uky.edu/OtherOrgs/AppalFor/Readings/leopold.pdf.

15. Paul Cryer, "Why Ecocentrism is the Key Pathway to Sustainability," *The Millennium Alliance for Humanity and the Biosphere* (MAHB), https://mahb.stanford.edu/blog/statement-ecocentrism.

16. "How to Decipher Egg Carton Labels," *The Humane Society*, https://www.humanesociety.org/resources/how-decipher-egg-carton-labels.

17. Eric Hovind, "Evidence for a Young Earth," *Creation Today*, May 6, 2010, https://creationtoday.org/evidence-for-a-young-earth.

18. *Meatless Monday*, https://www.meatlessmonday.com.

19. "Chick Culling," *Wikipedia*, https://en.wikipedia.org/wiki/Chick_culling.

20. *CAFO: The Tragedy of Industrial Animal Factories*, http://www.cafothebook.org.

21. Guy McPherson, "Resources and Anthropocentrism," *Resilience*, October 12, 2009, https://www.resilience.org/stories/2009-10-12/resources-and-anthropocentrism.

22. Nada Pavlovic, "The Trump Administration is Reversing 100 Environmental Regulations," *New York Times*, May 20, 2020, https://www.nytimes.com/interactive/2020/climate/trump-environment-rollbacks.html.

23. Ibid. Aldo Leopold, "Thinking Like a Mountain."

24. Ibid. Jennifer Kobylecky, "Understanding the Land Ethic."

25. John J. Piccolo, et. al., "Why Conservation Scientists Should Re-Embrace Their Ecocentric Roots," *Conservation Biology*, December 15, 2017, https://onlinelibrary.wiley.com/doi/full/10.1111/cobi.13067.

26. *The Heartland Institute*, https://heartland.org.

27. *Climate Depot*, https://www.climatedepot.com.

28. Lee, Wendy Lynne. "Dewey and Climate Denial²," *Philosophy Now*, Issue 135, 12, 2019, pp. 16–20.

29. "Angry Residents Erupt at Meeting Over new mask Rule," *CNN*, June 2020, https://www.cnn.com/videos/politics/2020/06/24/mask-mandate-florida-anger-erupts-coronavirus-vpx.cnn).

30. *United Nations Intergovernmental Panel on Climate Change*, https://www.ipcc.ch.

31. James Margolin, "I'm Not Only Striking for the Climate." *New York Times*, September 20, 2019, https://www.nytimes.com/2019/09/20/climate/global-climate-strike.html.

32. Tom Laskawy, "Frankenfoods: Good for Big Business, bad for the Rest of Us," *Grist*, May 9, 2013, https://grist.org/food/frankenfoods-good-for-big-business-bad-for-the-rest-of-us.

33. Erica Martinson, "Shell Calls Off its Multibillion Dollar Mission in Alaska's Arctic," *Anchorage Daily News*, September 28, 2016, https://www.adn.com/energy/article/shell-drops-arctic-drilling-plans/2015/09/28.

34. Arne Naess, "The Eight-Point Platform," *Deep Ecology.Org*, http://www.deepecology.org/platform.htm.

35. Michelle Robinson, "Firenado: Massive Tornado of Swirling Flame Whirls Over Butte County Town," *SFGate*, September 9, 2018, https://www.sfgate.com/california-wildfires/article/firenado-fire-tornado-butte-paradise-devil-13378650.php.

36. Mark Maslin, "The Five Corrupt Pillars of Climate Change Denial," *The Conversation*, https://theconversation.com/the-five-corrupt-pillars-of-climate-change-denial-122893.

37. Jessie Yeung, "China Researchers Discover New Swine Flu with 'Pandemic Potential,'" *CNN*, June 30, 2020, https://www.cnn.com/2020/06/30/asia/china-swine-flu-pandemic-intl-hnk-scli-scn/index.html.
38. "What is Voluntary Simplicity?" *The Simplicity Collective*, http://simplicitycollective.com/start-here/what-is-voluntary-simplicity-2.
39. Nick Reilly, "Minneapolis Vows to Disband Police Department in Wake of George Floyd's Death," NME, June 8, 2020, https://www.nme.com/news/music/minneapolis-vows-to-disband-police-department-in-wake-of-george-floyds-death-2683554.
40. "Unwanted Sterilization and Eugenics Programs in the United States," *Public Broadcasting Service*, January 29, 2016, https://www.pbs.org/independentlens/blog/unwanted-sterilization-and-eugenics-programs-in-the-united-states.
41. Vicky Boult, "Hundreds of Elephants are Mysteriously Dying in Botswana—A Conservationist Explains What We Know," *The Conversation*, July, 2020, https://theconversation.com/hundreds-of-elephants-are-mysteriously-dying-in-botswana-a-conservationist-explains-what-we-know-142004.
42. "Anthrax: How People are Infected," *Centers for Disease Control*, https://www.cdc.gov/anthrax/basics/how-people-are-infected.html.
43. "Kenya ramps up Fight Against Desert Locusts," *Daily Sabah, Reuters News Wire*, June 7, 2020, https://www.dailysabah.com/world/africa/kenya-ramps-up-fight-against-desert-locusts.

5

FROM THE ECOCENTRIC ENDGAME TO ECO-PHENOMENOLOGY

5.1 The Radicalized Ecocentrism of Derrick Jensen

5.1.1 Blow up the Dams

Appreciating the full range of implication stemming from adopting ecocentrism as a way of life probably has no better representation than writer Derrick Jensen's 2006 *Endgame*. Translated into the terms of the twenty-first century's ecological crises, and directed to the young and disaffected, Jensen takes a particularly dark version of human chauvinism as a given feature of human nature, and argues for an ecocentric worldview equipped to confront and conquer the human excess he identifies *as* "civilization." Key ideas from works like Naess' *Eight-Point Platform* are adapted to *Endgame*'s "eco-primitivist" argument for a world "deeply different from the present" (*Point Six*). Yet Jensen takes a decisively more uncompromising view of the strategies required to achieve that world, raising not only issues like whether achieving a sustainable ecocentric future justifies authoritarian policies but whether, given the toxic brew of environmental urgency, human chauvinism, the failure of policy to generate effective change, and never-ending corporate excess, such goals justify the use of violence to bring "civilization" to an end. For Jensen it does:

> The primary reason [to maintain civilization] is to gain, maintain, and use resources—oil in the first case (as well as to provide a staging area for further invasions), trees in the second. Further, both invading and clear-cutting damage landscapes, damage our habitat. They further enchain the natural

This is Environmental Ethics: An Introduction, First Edition. Wendy Lynne Lee.
© 2022 John Wiley & Sons, Inc. Published 2022 by John Wiley & Sons, Inc.
Companion Website: https://thisisphilosoph.wordpress.com

world. The primary motivation for liberating a river, on the other hand, isn't selfish, except insofar as it benefits oneself to live in an intact, functioning natural community (duh!), and insofar as doing good feels good. This all leads to probably the most important question of this book so far: with whom or what do you primarily identify? A way to get at that question is to ask: whom or what do your actions primarily benefit? Whom or what do you primarily serve? (*Endgame*, Vol. I, p. 216)

Jensen advocates blowing up dams to liberate rivers and their fish populations, but this is merely the prelude toward achieving the revolution he envisions, a clearing out of the polluted detritus of human greed, replacing it with communities grounded on principles like those embodied in the *Platform*. From Jensen's ecocentric perspective, the real violence isn't "liberating" a river; it's maintaining a civilization that would dam the river in the first place.

The primary point of departure for Naess and Jensen is the fact that the planet's capacity to sustain life is on an accelerating collision course with resource-destroying human activities. But whereas Naess makes the main locus of change *policy* (especially *Platform Point Six*), Jensen argues that insofar as the institutions responsible for policy-making are themselves irreparably compromised by interests incompatible with biotic integrity, real change must come from those less committed to maintaining that *status quo*. Indeed, it must come from quarters committed to putting an end to the "civilization" that brought us the climate crisis, or at least from those who have the capacity to weather the revolutionary turbulence that would presumably accompany actions like blowing up the dams. "You cannot use the master's tools to dismantle the master's house," argued the feminist theorist Audre Lorde in response to the question how we ought to bring about the end of patriarchal institutions like marriage and the traditional male-headed family.[1] Similarly, Jensen's radicalized ecocentrism holds that we cannot take up the struggle to found sustainable ecocentric communities from within a civilization whose institutions remain dependent on the myth of endless resources and the inevitable ecological destruction that it produces. Put simply: Naess and Jensen share similar *ends*, namely small human communities built on deep ecological values like "appreciating life quality" and the "profound awareness of the difference between bigness and greatness." But they differ substantially on the *means* to achieve these ends. Jensen takes ecocentric principles not merely as aspirational, but as *directives to action*. His implicit appeal to utility is not about developing policies that, however otherwise authoritarian, might serve to mitigate suffering on the way to a more ecocentric reality. Nor is he especially sensitive to minimizing suffering for individual creatures *per se*—as Peter Singer would have it. For Jensen, the *ecocentric imperative* to end civilization provides marching orders more in the spirit of Malcom X's "by any means necessary" or Rolston's ecological holism without the hand-wringing over what constitutes the primary unit of value—it is the species and the ecosystem.[2] Jensen treats it not merely as laudable, but as imperative that "civilization" comes to an end for the sake of the future biotic stability of the planet and its capacity to support life—including, but not as privileged, human life. Like other forms of ecocentrism, Jensen privileges the planetary over the individual, biotic integrity over the sufferings of human and nonhuman individuals. But unlike Naess and Leopold, Jensen makes it clear he's looking to organize the guerrilla army that can conquer "civilization," make ecocentric principle into actionable ways of life, and preempt back-sliding into the morass of human chauvinism.

Our primary responsibility as moral agents is, at least in the first place, to facilitate the endgame, in effect, a radicalized version of Naess' *Platform Point Eight*: "[t]hose who subscribe to the foregoing points have an obligation directly or indirectly to implement the necessary changes." There are many ways we can read this. We might read "directly" as a reference to the policy-making Naess advocates, as well as indirectly in terms of the coordinated activism of the *Sierra Club*[3] or the *Environmental Defense Fund*[4]—recognized environmental organizations. Or we might read "directly" in the terms Jensen proposes in *Endgame*, as action orchestrated as much to confront the policies, institutions, laws, and corporate powers responsible for environmental crisis as the first crucial step in addressing the crises themselves. Naess, Jensen, and Leopold, Rolston—all enlist us as specific sites of environmentally relevant action; all strongly advocate for an ecologically oriented conscience. But Jensen goes a significant step further arguing in effect that what "obligation" entails is not only the effort to imagine a "state of affairs deeply different from the present," but to implement actionable strategies toward realizing it *outside* the agencies of government, and in direct resistance to capitalist ventures. It's not hard to see, however, that even gesturing in the direction of blowing up dams raises very important questions about when, or even whether, the use of violence can be justified as a means to achieve laudable ends—any laudable ends. Do any moral principles license the use of violence—under any circumstances? If so, what violence, to what ends, justified according to what criteria, carried out my whom, under what conditions?

For Jensen, the conditions are a "civilization" that is unsalvageable, the first salvo of its undoing the *Twenty Premises* that introduce us to *Endgame: Volume I: The Problem of Civilization*, "Premise One: civilization is not and can never be sustainable." This is especially true of industrial civilization... "Premise Six: Civilization is not redeemable... If we do not put a halt to it, civilization will continue to immiserate the vast majority of humans and to degrade the planet until it... collapses" (*Endgame*, Vol. I, p. IX). The language here is clear and uncompromising, and it paints a picture of a world on the brink of calamite. Fast-forward fourteen years, and, if anything, Jensen has sought only to reinforce his central position:

> Here's a story that I hope will make things clearer. When I was a kid, my mum told me to clean my room, and I didn't do it. She told me again, and I didn't do it. She kept telling me to clean it, and I didn't do it. And finally, she said to me, look, either you clean your room, or I'm going to do it for you, and you are not going to like it, because I'm going to throw everything away. So what I wish we would do is start cleaning up the room on our own. Because if we don't do it, nature is going to do it for us, and we are not going to like that at all. The first thing we do is recognize that the room's actually dirty. Part of the problem is that we are addicted to the system. This is why we are not going to have that voluntary transformation that I really want, because we are not going to give it up...[5]

Although Jensen doesn't mention climate change or Covid-19 as examples of how nature is going to "clean up our room for us," in response to a question concerning the "collateral damage" to human life that would come from a return to "pre-Civilization," he remarks that the world would not really be "dog-eat-dog" because nature would be able to provide for a smaller human population, and in a May 2020 interview Jensen describes cities as perfect "factory farms" for pathogens like the coronavirus. In other words, while Covid-19 might "clean up our room for us" (at least for city-dwellers), the resulting smaller human communities would be benefitted. To be clear, Jensen's not (necessarily) arguing that it would be permissible for the pandemic to continue to shred human populations unabated, he expresses wry dismay at the hypocrisy evinced in our feigned surprise that Covid-19 is such an effective killing machine.[6]

The important moral issue here, however, is not about whether Jensen is right; he *is* right: cities and their systems of transport *are* highly effective disease vectors. Human-caused environmental destruction, particularly the encroachment on nonhuman habitat, *is* intimately connected to the zoonotic transmission that make pandemics possible. Our feigned surprise at the sheer virulence of Covid-19 does reflect hypocrisy about the fact that we know what zoonotic transmission is; we know that a warming climate accelerates it, and we know that our own bodies have themselves been weakened by the polluted and denuded environmental conditions that millennia of planetary abuse has created. The issue is what to *do* about these crises, and what it is morally permissible to do. For Jensen, what passes for "environmentalism" is rarely more than a "green" version of the civilization that must come down. At best, more honest "[e]nvironmentalists… pretend that symbolic victories translate into tangible results. We hold great protests, make great puppets, and witty signs to carry, write huge books… but the salmon still go extinct, phytoplankton populations still plummet, oceans still get vacuumed, factories still spew toxins…" *(Endgame*, Vol. II, p. 778). At worst, faux-environmentalists actually help facilitate more planetary destruction behind the green sloganeering of "sustainability."

Consider, for example, Michael Shellenberger whose activities as the founder of the *Breakthrough* Institute,[7] and more recently *Environmental Progress*,[8] function, at least from an ecocentric perspective, to "green" highly profitable corporate ventures for forms of energy that are at least controversial (nuclear power) or significant contributors to greenhouse gas emissions (hydraulic fracturing for natural gas). That Shellenberger is praised by far right disinformation machines like the *Daily Caller*[9] might be enough to give any thoughtful reader a pause. But whether Shellenberger speaks for the political Left or the Right is not, at least from the point of view of the *Twenty Premises*, the relevant point; it's that Shellenberger epitomizes the civilization Jensen seeks to end, and worse—that he embodies that civilization *in the name of* environmentalism. While there may be legitimate arguments to be made about the utility, safety, and environmental benefits of nuclear energy, the dangers of nuclear accidents, the hazards of depleted uranium, *(Endgame*, Vol. I, p. 61), or radioactive nuclear waste, for ecocentric writers like Jensen, the real issue is that the nuclear power industry fuels, quite literally, the industrial scale mass production and consumption that is killing the planet. To defend it, as does Shellenberger, is to defend the civilization responsible for that harm.

Still, what distinguishes Shellenberger's defense of nuclear energy from his promotion of the natural gas industry is not merely that he downplays hazards; it's that he misrepresents facts. In 2015 Op-Ed for *USA Today*, for example, Shellenberger and colleague Ted Nordhaus argue that the main reason environmentalists moved away from support for the natural gas industry was not environmental, but economic: "[g]as became cheap and abundant thanks to fracking… fearing that cheap gas would slow down the transition to renewable energy, environmental leaders now claim that fracking is contaminating wells and depleting aquifers, and that leaking natural gas makes fracking worse for global warming than coal."[10] Shellenberger and Nordhaus effectively accuse the anti-fracking movement of lying, and then go on to defend the many technologies involved in hydraulic fracturing. They point out rightly that natural gas burns cleaner than other fossil fuels. But their promotion also involves the kind of sleight of hand that, at least according to writers like Jensen, epitomizes the degraded values that taint civilization. Shellenberger and Nordhaus ignore, for example, the destruction generated in producing extraction-ready well-pads, the potential for the release of radioactivity from deep under the earth's surface during the fracturing process, the pollutants spewed by the produced-water tankers, drilling equipment tractor-trailers, and leaking pipelines. They ignore the fact that fracking releases methane, a far more potent greenhouse gas than carbon dioxide.[11] To claim the mantle of "environmental-ist" on a misrepresentation and, as part of that strategy, to try to impugn the motives of those whose activism may endanger the profitability of the industry you promote is—from the point of view of any ethic—morally suspect. But for an ecocentrism whose vision of the future is propelled by the wholesale repu-diation of capitalism, the wrong is particularly egregious and speaks to a kind of human chauvinism run amok.

5.1.2   The Environmentalism of the Civilized

What Shellenberger as his corporate colleagues count on is that the answer to Jensen's question, "Do we want to keep our cars and computers and lawns and grocery stores even at the expense of life on the planet?" (*Endgame*, Vol. II, p. 781), is one we either won't get around to asking, or if we do we'll see that this was the wrong question altogether. In an Op-Ed promoting his book, *Apoca-lypse Never*, Shellenberger rejects the claim that climate change is a crisis more serious than other crises. He then apologizes "[o]n behalf of environmental-ists everywhere ... for the climate scare we created over the last 30 years."[12] As the *Guardian's* Graham Readfearn reports, this downplay includes denying that climate change is at least partly responsible for extreme weather events like firenadoes: According to Shellenberger, writes Readfearn, "climate change was not making natural disasters worse, fires have declined around the world since 2003, and the more dangerous fires beings experienced in California and Australia were because of the build-up of wood fuel and more houses near forests."[13] But like Shellenberger's argument for natural gas production, this is only partly true, and what's left out might make for a very different moral judg-ment. As Readfearn points out, "[a] review of the academic literature produced earlier this year in response to Australia's devastating bushfire summer found 'human-induced warming has already led to a global increase in the frequency and severity of fire weather, increasing the risks of wildfire.'" But even more to the point for Jensen's ecocentrism is that Shellenberger's "apology" illustrates the extent to which environmentalism has been debauched by civilization's corrupting capitalism. Environmentalists coopted by climate change denial aren't environmentalists; they're apologists for civilization.

In an eerily prescient passage from *Endgame*, Jensen muses that "[m]ost of the people I know recognize that their choice really is between life and civ-ilization, and if they could snap their fingers and make civilization go away they'd do it in a heartbeat... Some would not be unhappy if a virus took us all out. Anything to stop civilization's gross destructiveness" (Vol. II, p. 781). The contrast with industry advocates like Shellenberger could not be starker, but while it serves to highlight civilization's "gross destructiveness" all

Shellenberger really needs is that we want to keep our cars and computers. So, while the people Jensen claims to know might make civilization go away in a finger-snap if they could, ordinary environmentalists—though still offended by Shellenberger's coopting of the title—are likely to remain true to the human chauvinism he counts on. From the point of view of Jensen's radical ambitions, this is the far harder mountain to scale because the environmentalism of the civilized—policy change, regulatory statute, agency creation—is safer, easier, requires less commitment, and rarely raises questions about the use of violent means to achieve just ends. The environmentalism of the civilized is, however, doomed to failure not only "because the global economy is incompatible with life" (*Endgame*, Vol. I, p. 369), but, on Jensen's account, because the means we have within this system—recycle, reuse, organics, boycotts, scheduled protests, electric cars, and the like—can only reinforce it by making its destructiveness possible, if regulated. A slower pace of destruction is no less destructive than a cancer treated with chemotherapy is still cancer, and still likely to recur. So long as consumption remains uninterrogated, nothing really changes:

> There are problems with attempting to spend or boycott our way to sustainability. The first is that it simply won't work. Spending won't work because within an industrial economy nearly all economic transactions are destructive... even buying "good things" isn't really doing something good for the planet so much as it is doing something not quite so bad... For an act to be sustainable it must benefit the landbase...Rare indeed within our culture is the economic activity that improves the landbase... The problem is not our humanity. The problem is this culture—this *entire* culture—and slight changes in spending habits won't significantly stop the destruction. (*Endgame*, Vol. I, pp. 409–10)

For Jensen, the environmentalism of the civilized poses a greater danger to the future than the faux-activist's effort to greenwash dirty capitalist ventures. The hypocrisy of the "Shellenbergers" is relatively transparent. We call it out without guilt. But calling out the hypocrisy of the environmentalist who really is buying organic, driving an electric car, going vegan—who is making some sacrifice—seems uncharitable. Yet that is precisely what Jensen argues we must do, or face the "endgame" that a civilization rooted in the myth of endless resources and the vice of relentless consumption has made for us.

Consider, for example, former Vice President Joe Biden's "bold climate plan." Endorsed by Noah Smith, *Bloomberg* business writer, the plan focuses on "clean energy and investment in new technology" to affect a shift to "100% clean electricity by 2035."[14] The plan epitomizes an environmentalism of the civilized. Contrary to critics who deride it (and Biden) as "far Left," Smith argues that

[t]his is the right idea for a number of reasons. Because solar-power prices have dropped so much more than expected, it's now economical to tear down existing coal plants and replace them with solar. Natural gas will be harder to replace because solar is intermittent; storage is still expensive and wind is only a partial solution… but just as with solar power, storage technology will become cheaper the more of it is deployed… Biden's plan focuses on providing direct government employment, creating a Climate Conservation Corps that echoes on of FDR's more popular programs. Having government give people jobs isn't always a good idea, especially when it cannibalizes jobs from the private sector. But the U.S. will emerge from the coronavirus pandemic with a huge pool of unemployed workers who need jobs.[15]

What makes this, for Smith, the "right idea" is that it preserves the basic institutions and industrial mechanisms of capitalist production and consumption, all the while advancing sustainability—at least as an aspiration. It implies that we can stave off at least some of the most devastating effects of the climate crisis, provide jobs, relieve our dependency on coal, and salvage our national honor without having to sacrifice our high level of consumption or the country's status as a Global North center of power. We can have our cake and eat it too, and we can make "clean" energy patriotic, all the while keeping the engines of the "free" market whirring.

The trouble, of course, is that what we know from history and science is that for as attractive as Biden's plan sounds, the evidence is on Jensen's side. At best the results of Biden's environmentalism of the civilized are merely "less bad," and the dose of self-deception required to see this as truly sustainable is quite high. Nowhere does the plan actually challenge the worldview that produced a civilization that led us into the climate crisis, the grotesque economic disparity of the Global North compared to the Global South, or the next pandemic. To be sure, Biden's plan isn't the "bold" of Shellenberger's apology, but for the ecocentrist, its failure to probe the institutions that will continue to reward a few, including the *Breakthrough Institute*, at the immense expense of the many makes its potential for substantive environmental improvement no more than "slight changes in spending habits." Perhaps its most telling feature is that, other than closing the coal mines, little in Biden's boldness aims to improve the landbase without which, argues Jensen, the plan doesn't advance biotic integrity, much less an ecocentric vision of the future. Among the common features of consumer civilization, argues Jensen, is the "deeply and most-often-invisibly held beliefs that there is really only one way to live, and that we are the one-and-only possessors of that way," and that it's "our job to propagate this way, by force when necessary, until there are no other ways to be" (*Endgame*, Vol 1. p. 22). While Biden's plan doesn't evince that belief explicitly, it also doesn't question whether the most polluting, consuming, and wasteful way of life on the planet, the "American way," is sustainable. While it seeks to substitute dirty fossil fuels for cleaner solar and wind, it does so without recognizing that the latter come with costs of their own, or that without significant conservation we're likely to make little real headway—except for the stock-holders and CEOs of "green" energy companies. Most importantly, nothing in Biden's environmentalism of the civilized demands the psychic paradigm shift from an anthropocentric to an ecocentric worldview.

According to Jensen it must all come down. "Bringing down civilization," he writes,

> first and foremost consists of liberating ourselves by driving the colonizers out of our own hearts and minds: seeing civilization for what it is ... [It] then consists of actions arising from that liberation, not allowing those in power to predetermine the ways we oppose them, instead living with and by—and using—the tools and rule of those in power only when we choose ... [It] is not about being morally pure—morality define, of course, according to those in power—but is instead about defending our own lives and the health and lives of our landbases. (*Endgame*, Vol. I, p. 252)

Two things are especially notable here; first, Jensen gives his revolutionary a bit of wiggle room to use the master's tools, arguing in effect that so long as the ends remain liberation, whatever means are necessary to achieve them may be justified. Second, given this wiggle room, being an ecocentric revolutionary is not about being morally pure. How can it be if achieving its ends permits the use of the master's tools—like guns? Indeed, as the point is to destroy "the capacity of those in power to exploit those around them," the means may "in some circumstances... involve education," in others "destroying physical infra-structures," and in yet others "it involves assassinations," raising again the issue whether the use of violence can ever be morally justified, and what it would mean to say that it could. Jensen also insists, however, that "[a]ll morality is particular, which means that what may be moral in one circumstance may be immoral in another," and that we must keep at the forefront of our decision-making that the morality of civilization is compromised, potentially beyond reclamation, by the fact that it's used to justify "killing the planet." The duty, then, of the ecocentric revolutionary is to act to put a halt to that atrocity, "to stop the grotesque and ultimately absolute violence of civilization" (*Endgame*, Vol. I, p. 253), and if it turns out that using the master's tools to dismantle the master's house offers the most efficacious means, so be it. To fail, he argues, "is by far the most immoral path any of us can choose" (*Endgame*, Vol. I, p. 253). Put differently: failure is not an option because the stakes are life on earth. If the use of the master's explosives is therefore the only or even simply the most efficient way to bring it all down, then the use of the master's tools is just, even righteous. Even imperative.

Setting aside for the moment questions about the use of violence, at least two other significant issues haunt this argument: first, Jensen clams that the most *immoral* path is the one that *fails* to cleave to the objective of ending civilization. In other words, for Jensen it's not enough (whether or not we deploy the master's tools) to merely work, however diligently, in the direction of putting an end to civilization; it is *imperative* to do so. Yet "imperative" conflicts with the idea that "what may be moral in one circumstance may be immoral in another" unless we take "killing the planet" to be so "particular," as Jensen puts it, that what is justified in that case would not necessarily be so in any other. Perhaps the fact that this case is about *existential* conditions does distinguish it from every other, but if so Jensen must show why the existential conditions of potentially all life on the planet outweighs the existential conditions of, for example, the villagers drowned after the dam was blown. Why, in other words, do *numbers* of lives, the *diversity* of lives—a planet full of lives—matter more when those numbers are greater, especially when the lives of some will be sacrificed? Few would dispute that the ends—saving life on the planet—are plainly defensible, but does that mean, or at least mean obviously, that the use of means that will produce suffering and death for the few is justified? Does it matter that the few (or, more likely, quite a few) will probably number among the most vulnerable—the least likely to be able to get out of the way? If it's life that concerns Jensen so much that we have a duty to prevent the "killing of the planet," why it is morally permissible to sacrifice some lives for others? Is Jensen's reasoning self-defeating? Hypocritical? What does "imperative" countenance?

Second, if morality is itself polluted by civilization how do we know whether the choice to use the master's tools in a particular circumstance is not a self-deceptive excuse to do what we wanted to do anyways? (How, in fact, do we know what count as the Master's tools?) It seems this risk would be high given that while Jensen reminds us that "we should always remember who makes the rules" (*Endgame*, Vol. I, p. 252), he also allows for the kind of wiggle room that, in theory, could make announcing the choice of an Impossible Burger at a Burger King a revolutionary act—though still dining out at Burger King. One could lecture about the evils of capitalism at a college in a foreign country, but fly on an airplane to get there. What are the rules for deciding compromise? Perhaps the clearest examples are simply the most transparent—using the master's megaphone to call out a message of resistance, or the master's gun to kill the master. But while these examples may satisfy "imperative," the latter raises again hard questions about the use of violence and whether the appeal to "imperative" functions as an excuse for deploying it. To be clear, the point is not that hypocrisy in using the master's tools isn't inevitable. Hypocrisy *is* as inevitable as the fact that none live or can live without civilization. Even the Unabomber, Ted Kaczynski, was part of a civilization where he could earn a PhD in mathematics at the University of Michigan and own property with his brother.[16] The point is that insofar as we're required by an imperative to choose which hypocrisies we're willing to brook in realizing it, Jensen offers precious little short of quoting a fellow insurgent's "I will do whatever it takes" to *limit* the violence he thinks we should be willing to deploy—and therefore whether *any* hypocrisies are off the table—to end civilization.

The question isn't then merely about whether violence is ever morally justified, but whether even in the service of an imperative some forms of violence remain condemnable—no matter what. According to Jensen, civilization is at the rotted root of brutality dealt to the planet, its ecosystems, and its lives. Perhaps only violent means can bring it down. But what comes after? A return to a simpler "eco-primitivism"? Jensen argues that "if industrial civilization doesn't come down soon—very soon—there is no future for us" (*Endgame*, Vol. II, p. 883). Yet in response to the criticism that he's "only interested in tearing things down" as opposed to providing alternatives, Jensen insists that he "does not provide alternatives because there is no need," that American "Indians" don't ask that question, and that "they" can "teach us how to live" along with "the land" (*Endgame*, Vol. II, p. 889). Even setting aside romanticized stereotype about the many, some of them ancient, civilizations of the indigenous peoples of the Americas, it's hard to see how "there is no need" inspires confidence in the prospect that what comes after will be anchored to moral constraint against the violence believed to have been required to get to that point. In the *Communist Manifesto* Karl Marx agitates for a revolution grounded in a critique of capitalism not altogether unlike Jensen's, and Marx is often criticized for offering too little to what comes next, especially given the sacrifice and violence required to take down the owners of the means of production.[17] But even Marx offers more to sketch the kinds of communities *that make that sacrifice worth it* than a "there is no need" that punts to "Indians" to teach "us." What post-ecocentric revolution communities might look like brings us full circle back to the question of the master's tools: if we cannot know with confidence what counts as a just use of the Master's tools in the course of fomenting revolution, how can we know what counts as an unjust use afterward? If we blow up dams to save rivers, can we retain execution for unreconstructible polluters? Can we selectively utilize viral strains to the ends of human population control? Jensen worries that if civilization doesn't end soon, there will be no future for us. But who is the "us"? Who pays to save this "us"?

5.1.3   The Ethics of Human Population, of Life and Death

What counts as a morally defensible strategy (much less a way of life worth living—or dying for) consistent with Jensen's radicalized ecocentrism raises some of the thorniest moral questions we're likely to face. But these have their roots in earlier thinkers whose call to arms against environmental deterioration has only been made louder and more urgent with the advent of crises like increasing global food insecurity, clean water scarcity, the emergence of pandemic viral infection, and the climate crisis. As we've seen, questions about the use of coercive or even autocratic means for the purpose of human population control arise in Naess' *Platform Point Four*: a "flourishing human life requires a smaller human population." Jensen, however, also takes up this issue, making the point in an even more forceful way—in response to the observation that his ecocentrism is "heartless":

> Consider our utter disregard for overshooting carrying capacity—our belief that somehow these ecological principles don't apply to us. Consider also our denial of death and our deification of humans, especially civilized humans, most especially rich white civilized humans. All of this has to stop. The truth is that I'm going to die someday, whether or not I stock up on pills. That's life. *And if I die in the population reduction that takes place as a corrective to our having overshot carrying capacity, well, that's life too. Finally, if my death comes as part of something that serves the larger community, that helps stabilize and enrich the landbase of which I'm a part, so much the better.* (*Endgame*, Vol. I, p. 123, my emphasis)

Whether "corrective" refers to the environmental consequences of the planet's exhausted carrying capacity,[18] or to actions more deliberate and more consistent with "all of this must stop," is unclear—at least in this passage. But what is clear are the ecocentric values reflected in the idea that a person's death can serve the larger community—that dying can be a morally defensible means to these larger ends regardless the cause insofar as "that's life too." What would human agency look like if we took the environment to be *the* preeminent value, the value that sets our moral compass and directs *all* of our decision-making? What would it mean for our most basic, often wrenching, decisions? Should I have children? Abort a pregnancy? Get a vasectomy? If I'm diagnosed with cancer, should I undergo chemotherapy? Should I refuse to wear a mask to protect myself and others from a viral outbreak? Are there forms of work I should refuse? Should I drive a car? Become vegan? Opt for a carbon-neutral tiny house? Where should I live?

These are difficult and important questions for any environmental ethic, but they become particularly pressing—and complicated—when human population is identified as the root cause of the planet's deteriorating ecosystems. That "we" ask these questions, as opposed to others, and the way we pose them, reflects the privilege that accrues to the ability to secure services like abortion, vasectomy, chemotherapy. Each is connected one way or another to human life and death, and thus to population. But each is also deeply inflected by economic class, social position, cultural mores, gender, race, geographical location, and religion. The appeal to human population growth as justification to end civilization is thus not as straightforward as it may seem—or as Jensen makes it out. There is, for example, no necessary connection between population and consumption. Some of the most densely populated countries, regions, and cities on the planet have relatively low rates of consumption, including fossil fuels.[19] In addition, some people (or even whole communities) occupy positions where these are, or aren't, decisions that *can* be made, where economic and social wherewithal make "should I have children?" into a *decision*; others are not so empowered. Having access to critical social services like reproductive health care clinics, health insurance, bank loans, cars, healthy food markets, or personal protective equipment are what make what is possible into what is do-able. Some of these questions, moreover, are unlikely to have meaningful, much less actionable, answers outside particular traditions, or as Kathryn Yusoff might put it, outside specific incarnations of the Anthropocene, forms of power, and instantiations of knowledge or expertise (Yusoff, pp. 11–12).

"The histories of the Anthropocene," argues Yusoff, "unfold a brutal experience for much of the world's racialized poor and without due attention to the historicity of those events (and their eventfulness)" (pp. 11–12). A key aspect of that history is population. Consider, for example, the relationship between human populations, the mineral extraction made possible by geology, and the silver mining history of Potosi, Bolivia, especially in the sixteenth and seventeenth centuries. As the planet's voracious appetite for silver grew along with its human population, the number of indigenous whose families have lived in Potosi for generations began to plummet. An environmental and human tragedy by any measure, Potosi illustrates the complex relationship between the geology of rich silver deposits, the exploitation of unscrupulous silver mining companies, brutal and back-breaking labor, mercury and lead poisoning, flagrant racism and sexism, the valuation of silver as currency, the complicity of the church, and the ambitions of the Spanish Empire (Robbins, *Mercury, Mining and Empire*). It shows in brutal detail that human communities can be decimated right along with the ecosystems upon which they and their conquerors depend.[20] In light of examples like Potosi, the contrast between Yusoff's characterization of the Anthropocene and Jensen's "civilization" is striking. For Jensen, "civilization" is an essentially monolithic malefactor responsible for the destruction of the planet's carrying capacity. "Civilization" signifies a "we" whose members across the globe stand equally guilty for environmental destruction. Jensen's "we" is reminiscent of the "our planet" in Naess' declaration that "[n]ow is the time to share with all life on our maltreated earth through the deepening identification with life forms and the greater units, the ecosystems, and Gaia,[21] the fabulous, old planet of ours." Naess' reference to "ours" seems to imply some equitably shared world whose peoples have had an equal hand in its maltreatment. Each of "us" must be equally alienated from

Gaia to be in need of "deepening identification with the earth's life forms." But it's hard to reconcile this assignment of blame with the experience of Potosi's effectively enslaved indigenous population. Not only were many of its laboring human bodies as scarred by mining as was the environment razed in the conversion from mountain to silver-factory, the idea that a suffering laborer's identification with "the earth's life forms" is deeper than the deadly effects of mercury on his brain seems unlikely, if not insulting.

Naess is right that the "fabulous old planet" is endangered like it has never been before. But, as Yusoff makes clear, there is no universal "we," no "our" fabulous old planet. Some would find it nonsense, even offensive, to be told that their identification with Gaia needed deepening. Quite unlike the white American hunter who unloads a hail of bullets into a pack of wolves for fun, the South American indigenous woman may find her miles walk to pump water and gather firewood doesn't need a moral evaluation for which she has little time and less leisure. Responsibility for maltreatment of the fabulous old planet neither distributes itself equally, nor does "fabulous old planet" situate the real lives of real people; many don't enjoy the luxury of contemplating their alienation; some don't need to make a special effort to form deep identifications with other life forms. Indeed, the comfortable "we" of affluent white men like Naess and Jensen cannot describe the realities of the vast majority of the world's people, though, as Yusoff shows, utilizing the reference to "we" does help spread out, and thus effectively erase, the guilt of the actually culpable: "[i]f the imagination of planetary peril coerces an ideal or 'we,' it only does so when the entrappings of late liberalism become threatened. This 'we' negates all responsibility for how the wealth of that geology was built off the subtending strata of indigenous genocide and erasure, slavery and carceral labor, and evades what that accumulation of wealth make possible in the present" (Yusoff, p. 106). Exchange "civilization" for "late liberalism," in other words, and the claims made by ecocentrists like Naess and Jensen reveal the privilege of the social positions they occupy, positions precisely the same as the capitalists and policymakers who they can be assured will take them seriously because the social "strata" to which they belong is the same: the ecocentric radical arrested and charged with blowing up dams and sentenced to three years in federal prison is still not George Floyd who dies under the weight of a chokehold for allegedly trying to pass a counterfeit twenty dollar bill.[22]

What Yusoff makes clear is that whatever radical change thinkers like Naess and Jensen aspire to see realized depends for its authority and audience on the maintenance of the civilization that empowers them—the civilization they argue must come down. This is the fact that must be concealed, for which deploying the universal "we" provides cover, allowing them to hide their privilege behind the bodies of those whose labor makes that privilege possible. Their disavowals of human chauvinism are legitimated through the implicit authority which attends the "strata" of the late liberalism to which they belong, that insures, at least for them, against the distractions of starvation, the expectations of child or elder care, or the viral exposure that comes with wage labor. These things need not be their worries. The "we" that negates responsibility for how the wealth of, say, geology's intimate relation to the fossil fuel industry is built just as well negates responsibility for how the *Eight-Point Platform* or the *Twenty Premises* are themselves built on the wealth geology makes possible in the form of the corporate extractivist enterprise that quite literally fuels a world they oppose, but that also grants them the leisure to mount their opposition. To be clear, it's not anyone's fault, including Naess and Jensen, to be born privileged by ethnicity, nationality, or geography. But what is not fault can still bestow responsibility, at a minimum not to turn away from what else might be destroyed in liberating the fish from a dam blown up. To presume that the woman carting water home a mile both ways needs to be told about the "fabulous old planet" reflects the same insolence reflected in "our" penchant for ignoring the history of Potosi. What arguments like Yusoff's show is that the erasure of that "subtending strata," the *people* whose muffled voices put the lie to that "we," is the necessary condition of the imperative that fortifies the "we" Jensen needs to make out the argument for the end of civilization: the readers to whom the *Twenty Premises* likely look the most compelling are, after all, those most likely to have the wherewithal to survive. Except for tokenized "Indians," the "strata" are only in the way. Jensen can tell a thousand stories about listening to the oppressed; he can give fatuous expression to the relative insignificance of his own life. But little evinces privilege more than being in a position to forfeit it.

For Jensen saving the fabulous old planet evokes a fairly simple calculus: where the ends are nothing less than avoiding ecological apocalypse, the means by which to avert that tragedy must be calibrated accordingly. There will be casualties, but the stakes are that high and the hour that late. How we arrived at this point matters less than what "we" must do to restore biotic integrity; what our dreams might be matters just as little:

> To reverse the effects of civilization would destroy the dreams of a lot of people. There's no way around it. We can talk all we want about sustainability, but there's a sense in which it doesn't matter that these people's dreams are based on, embedded in, intertwined with, and formed by an inherently destructive economic and social system. Their dreams are still their dreams. What right do I—or does anyone else—have to destroy them? At the same time, what right do they have to destroy the world? (*Endgame*, Vol. I, p. 125)

Our dreams may be our dreams, but the world's right to exist unmolested takes priority: "How do I want the land where I live to be in a thousand years?"

Jensen asks. "The answer to that question depends of course on answers to: How does the land want to be in a thousand years? And those answers depend on answers to: How was the land prior to civilization?" But the land, argue writers like Cronin and Yusoff, is never just the land—at least not unless we retreat back in time millions of years. "To be included," she writes, "in the "we" of the Anthropocene is to be silenced by a claim to universalism that fails to notice its subjugations..." (p. 12). Jensen's universal attribution of blame for the destruction of "the world" ignores, in other words, the very histories of "land" whose subjugations explain our arrival at this junction, and without which "we" will be destined to recreate precisely that civilization he'd lump together with those to whom the land does speak.

In example after example, *Endgame* details the systemic institutionalized violence perpetrated, according to Jensen, by a global social and economic system, a *civilization* dependent on ecological destruction. The only strategies capable of addressing this violence are therefore those that aim at putting an end to the system itself, returning the "maltreated earth" to a state where it is self-sustaining and self-recuperating. Jensen refers to this rather contrived appeal to history as "deep green resistance."[23] His aims are to recruit not only adherents but agents willing to blow up dams in the interest of restoring the land "prior to civilization." Naess would not likely have been comfortable with deploying violent means to achieve these ends. But that's not really the point. Insofar as the *Eight-Point Platform* authorizes a specific set of ecocentric objectives acutely discordant with the status quo, it paves the way for the kinds of means Jensen argues are justified and even necessitated by the urgency of our present state of environmental crisis. By conflating human-centeredness with human chauvinism, and then insisting we disown our anthropocentric ways, Naess effectively makes the case that the only way to make the break is through actions that decisively signify embrace of an ecocentric worldview and the resolute rejection of civilization. Among the ways that must be, if not rejected, radically modified, however, are the mechanisms of human population growth, reproductive sexuality. What better way to signal embrace of an ecocentric worldview than to voluntarily limit the making of offspring? And, what more terrifying and odious a prospect than the imposition of statutes that invade the most private of human activities?

Of all the moral dilemmas that connect human agency to ecological consequence, we'd be hard-pressed to locate one more pressing, fraught, or intimately a feature of human self-conception than the creation, pregnancy, birthing, and rearing of children. We can be persuaded to give up driving big cars, eating animal bodies, and living in Mansions—but to be told we cannot have or must limit the number of our children cuts very close to the bone of what many think it means to be human. That Naess and Jensen occupy the privileged positions of white Western men pronouncing on the necessity of human population reduction might rightly seem offensive, except that, with important caveats, it's impossible to ignore the fact that the planet is in fact not an endless fount of resources. Although a world population nearing eight billion is likely not as meaningful a number as the number of gallons used to fuel our cars, the number of pounds of animal body we consume, or the number of acres we put to golf courses and shopping malls, it's also no trivial fact that the policies and politics of human population control affect the world's women and girls in specific, often despotic ways. It's also difficult to imagine what the world might look like after we blow up the dams without the swift erection of laws whose punitive enforcement could resemble the autocratic regimes of the present—especially with respect to reproduction. Whether our points of departure are one-child policies of China's recent past or extreme restrictions on access to abortion in states like Texas, Mississippi or Georgia, the very idea of laws that invade a woman's bodily autonomy seem inconsistent with virtually any of our moral principles. What could overrule so essential a human right? What ends could justify such invasive and oppressive means? Yet, because the climate crisis *is* an existential crisis, perhaps what that means is that all options are on the table.

5.2   Worth: A Value Intrinsic to Living Things or a Weapon of Consent?

5.2.1   "We Are at War."

Standing on the steps of a state capitol building wearing comfortable shoes and khakis at lunchtime on a Tuesday while hoisting signage depicting the blue marble earth and its iconic slogan "Save Our Mother!" while elected representatives politely file out around you doesn't cut it—at least for Jensen. Guerrilla warfare gets closer to what he has in mind:

> If you are driving to a dam with liberation on your mind, do not speed. Do not have a broken taillight. Do not have an expired tab on your license plate. Do not tell your friends about it. Do not tell your girlfriend, the daughter of a deputy sheriff. Do not tell anyone about it. Do not tell anyone who does not need to know. Do not tell anyone who isn't directly involved. Do not tell anyone except those you know will keep quiet even if it means they go to prison for forty years. (*Endgame*, Vol. II, p. 642)

It's hard to imagine a starker disavowal of the precautionary principle, and yet for Jensen there's a sense in which the violence potentially required to hit the planet's reset button enacts a kind of ultimate precaution: it wipes clean the taint of human excess and thereby returns us to a world dictated by ecologically informed caution. The trouble, of course, isn't merely the casualties—human and nonhuman—that might have to be sustained to recuperate the planet in some more pristine form; it's that the climate crisis genie is already out of the bottle. There is no return to the Garden of Eden. The likelihood that any "civilization destroying" action would achieve anything like what Jensen envisions is unrealistic no matter what means we deploy to realize it. There is, however, a more charitable reading, one that suggests an avenue that, while it won't return us to the Garden, may come closer: enculturating the ecocentric worldview from the cradle in order to insure the people who come after the revolution will embrace the ecocentric imperative Jensen (and Naess) advocate. Even this would take generations to achieve, and how close it gets us (and who is "us") is fraught at best. It is nonetheless this world that Jensen's *Twenty Premises* and his advocacy of guerrilla warfare is for, and it's this world that's implied throughout Naess' *Eight-Point Platform*. The questions, then, are these: with what concept or concepts could the enculturation of an ecocentric worldview be made effective? What ideas would need to be internalized and operationalized in order to achieve and sustain a functionally animated ecocentric worldview? Can enculturation of an ecocentric worldview be internalized sufficiently by enough people to avoid having to resort to more authoritarian forms of enforcement? And, of course, is such a worldview morally defensible? Is this the route to the life worth living?

The concept that fits this description, may have the most practical utility, and has currency among environmentalists, especially ecocentric thinkers like Jensen, Naess, and Holmes Rolston III, is the concept of *inherent worth*. The ecocentric worldview derives its legitimating force from the idea that value exists *inherently* in organisms and ecosystems as a defining property of a thing, like being a mammal or having a blood type. Recognizing such worth is for Naess the necessary first step in the project of turning away from our human-centeredness because it compels us to recognize value that transcends utility, cannot be commodified, and thus must be respected. So too for Jensen: the fact of a thing being *that* thing constitutes an inalienable source of worth. Yet for Jensen, unlike Naess (at least it's not as clear in Naess), civilization makes the recognition of inherent worth difficult, if not impossible. How do we embrace Aldo Leopold's, "think like a mountain," or sea birds, or factory farm cows from within a "civilization" that systematically classifies nonhuman animals and their biotic communities as instruments or commodities? We can't, argue Naess and Jensen. Indeed, it is the embrace of inherent worth that's at the core of repudiating human chauvinism and embracing an ecocentric ethic. In *A Language Older Than Words*, Jensen offers a graphic and disturbing example of what the failure to recognize inherent worth has come to:

> Inside the chute, facing a blank wall, stands a steer. Until the last movement he does not seem to notice when a worker places a steam-driven stunner at the ridge of his forehead. I do not know what the steer feels in those last moments, or what he thinks. The pressure of the contact triggers the stunner, which shoots a retractable bolt into the brain of the steer. The steer falls, sometimes stunned, sometimes dead, sometimes screaming. (*A Language Older Than Words*, p. 5)

He then compares the slaughter of factory farm animals to his own experience of childhood abuse to that of rape victims and lastly to developing world children in factory sweat shops:

> My father, in order to rationalize his behavior, had to live in a world of make-believe. He had to make *us* believe that the beatings and rapes made sense, that all was as it should, and must, be... Here's what I think: it's a sham. It's a giant game of make-believe. We pretend that animals feel no pain, and that we have no ethical responsibility towards them. But how do we know? We pretend that other humans—the women who are raped, for example...or the one hundred and fifty million children who are enslaved to make soccer balls, tennis shoes, Barbie dolls, and the like—are happy and unaffected by it all. We pretend all is well as we dissipate our lives in quiet desperation. (*A Language Older Than Words*, pp. 5–6)

For Jensen, it's scenes like these that distinguish Naess from Jensen, and for the latter, put the lie to mere policy reform. Jensen's turn of phrase, "make-believe" evokes the chauvinism responsible for the pretense that "anything we do not understand—anything that cannot be measured, quantified, and controlled—does not exist," and that value is exclusively the function of that control: "We pretend that animals are resources to be conserved or consumed when, in reality, they have purposes entirely independent of us." Another name for that purpose is inherent worth.

The same goes for "human resources," women's bodies, children, and ecosystems; however otherwise violated, each is a site of inherent worth—has a purpose of its own. Jensen remarks similarly in *Endgame* six years later:

> We are at war. War was declared against the world many thousands of years ago. War was declared against women. War was declared against children. War was declared against the wild. War was declared against the indigenous. (*Endgame*, Vol. II, p. 543)

What ending this war demands for Jensen are whatever means are necessary to bring down the civilization that permits such atrocities, and then a reintroduction of human culture and society to the belief that cows and kids, women's bodies and planetary biota, are all sites of value independent of their utility. An entrenched and calcified human chauvinism cannot be overcome from within the civilization that depends on it. It must be overthrown from without by insurgents for whom inherent worth is as much a battle cry as it is a governing moral principle. Put differently: the concept of inherent worth functions as a justifying premise for the use of violence; it's this concept of value that serves as the foundational presupposition of the *Twenty Premises*. It's this concept that, for Jensen, substantiates the idea that the ends—restoring the planet's biotic integrity—justify the means—blowing up the dams.

For Jensen, whatever has inherent worth is owed as a matter of moral duty the defense and protection of its existential, hence ecological, conditions. Inherent worth isn't merely a value like, for instance, aesthetic or instrumental value; it is the preeminent value that overrides all others and can therefore demand adherence. Buttressed by this concept, it's no wonder the *Twenty Premises* reads like a manifesto for eco-warriors sufficiently provisioned with access to weapons and staples; their mission may not be ordained from on high, but the charge to defend inherent worth feels righteous. There are, however, serious moral and practical issues with this argument—with respect to what can be justified in executing the revolution, what the post-revolution world looks like and how it functions, and with respect to what strategies are morally defensible in the enculturation of the ecocentric ethic necessary to maintain that world. The call to end civilization doesn't necessarily tell us how to determine in what inherent worth consists in the execution of the revolution, and it offers little guidance about the transition to the post-revolution world other than that ending civilization is necessary to restore respect for inherent worth. Jensen's right that capitalist industry is unsustainable, but while this fact may commit us to the ecocentric revolution, can it be justified as a *strategy* to treat civilization as a monolithic whole? While we acknowledge, in other words, there is no such thing as "civilization," that this notion evinces the same unearned privilege empowering those the revolution would presumably replace, can it nevertheless be justified as a weapon of war given the stakes are the capacity of the planet to support life?

- Premise One: Civilization is not and can never be sustainable. This is especially true for industrial civilization.

Art, music, architecture, science, and medicine are parts of civilization, but they're also human-made artifacts, so perhaps they cannot be said to have inherent worth. Does this mean that adherents to Premise One should be prepared to forego chemotherapy for cancer, antibiotics in case of infection, vaccination against Covid-19? Human beings are sites of inherent worth but, as Jensen points out, we all die and this benefits the biotic community. In other words, the issue is not merely how we determine in what inherent worth consists, but—in the case of competing sites of value—what site is worth *more*, how we determine that, and *who* is authorized to make that call. This is truly a Pandora's Box in that it raises many of our earlier questions concerning the structural inequalities often implicit in arguments for the application of moral principle. Indeed, we have little good reason to believe that, especially pre-revolution, such determination won't be made by the same class of people authorized in the present: mostly white, Western(ized) affluent men like Jensen.

The issue here is not that Jensen fails to recognize the structural inequalities that govern ignoring the inherent worth of, for example, the land base and its conversion into the merely instrumental value of resource; he does. The issue is that such inequalities only matter when they serve to advance the goal of bringing down civilization:

- Premise Two: Traditional communities do not often voluntarily give up or sell the resources on which their communities are based until their communities have been destroyed. They also do not willingly allow their land bases to be damaged so that other resources—gold, oil, and so on—can be extracted. It follows that those who want the resources will do what they can to destroy traditional communities.

This claim is faulty in at least two ways: first, traditional human cultures have contributed to their own demise or migration by destroying their land bases.[24] To romanticize them as if they avoided environmental destruction undervalues the complexities of traditional cultures, glosses over significant intersection with ethnicity, sex, gender, and species, and paints a picture of "traditional" that provides only illusory scaffolding for adopting an ecocentric worldview. Second, though there's truth to the claim that "those who want the resources will do what they can to destroy traditional communities," because this over-simplifies the relationship between traditional culture and potential usurper, it leaves wide open the question to what inherent worth applies. To what exactly is owed defense of its inherent value? A traditional community—that willingly sells its land to the capitalist? The landbase before the arrival of any cultural imposition? The people, including those who work for the coal company? Jensen defends a version of "traditional" that fits his ecocentric narrative, but however much that version seems to recognize structural inequality, because what it depicts is an overly simplistic *caricature*, the effect is to reinforce the inequality it eschews. "Traditional culture" is as much a monolith for Jensen as is "civilization."

To oversimplify the complex and always evolving relationship between culture, ecologically destructive corporate enterprise, a landbase, its people and the nonhuman animals that inhabit it in order to assign blame may make the defense of inherent worth *appear* just. But in this case inherent worth cannot be understood as *inherent* at all; it is a tool fabricated for the pursuit of ending civilization. We know this in part because the primary purpose it serves for Jensen is as a vehicle for eco-warrior recruitment, and in part because unless these relationships are oversimplified, recruitment to the ecocentric worldview is unlikely to be successful. Put differently: the call to bring down civilization needs a clear unequivocal enemy. The best candidate for that position is the ecologically exploitive capitalist who converts all value into value that can be defined as the opposite of inherent value, namely, instrumental, resource, or commodity value. But in order for that opposition, and the recruitment of eco-warriors that depends on it, to be effective, there must *be* such a thing as inherent worth—whether there is or not. Whether things *actually* have such worth is thus immaterial. What matters is the work the concept can deliver to the *Twenty Premises* narrative for ending civilization, and whether the performance of that work has the muscle necessary to secure a guerrilla army.

The dualist logic Jensen deploys pitting inherent against instrumental value in traditional community versus civilization also contains an ahistorical element that has the potential to distort our moral judgment. Although he offers the appearance of an historical narrative emphasized in the use of words like "traditional," this turns out to be more window-dressing than substance. As Cronon and other environmental historians show, history is not only important to ethics, but vital to understanding what the moral issues are. This is especially true at the juncture of moral, environmental, and social justice issues, and could not be more insightfully illustrated than in Nicholas Robin's *Mercury, Mining, and Empire*. Robins shows how silver mining in the Andes gave rise to a capital enterprise powerful enough to determine the course of nations, control its own military, and conscript its own armies of laborers. Silver currency is at the epicenter of this story, yet it's the product of mining and refining processes whose human and environmental toll was (and is) devastating. Robins' story is very much about how the forced labor of indigenous peoples produced silver at devastating cost to their native ecologies, their health, and their cultures. But it's also about how religious dogma, nationalist conquest, and barely concealed greed produced immense wealth. "The belief in the unending flow of silver from the Americas," writes Robbins, "also encouraged profligate spending by the [Spanish] crown, underwrote Spain's military and political ambitions, and reinforced its commitment to Catholic orthodoxy.... This unprecedented flow of New World silver was not only the catalyst for the development of a global economy; it also sustained the world's economy for centuries" (*Mercury, Mining, and Empire*, p. 5).

In other words, the story of silver mining isn't reducible to an oversimplified recipe for defending traditional communities against the incursions of "civilization." Jensen might respond that he's speaking in general terms to make his conceptual point in the defense of inherent worth, but this doesn't suffice since

what's true in Robbin's story of capital conquest is that the conscription of labor from traditional communities involves not only outright enslavement, but
a more nuanced and seductive brew of religion, family structure, the roles of
women and children, and the place of those who collaborate with the invaders.
To reduce this complex and agonizing history to a caricatured dichotomy of
civilization versus traditional community does neither justice. But worse, to
offer such a reduction as justification for the use of violence in the interest of
defending one of its fabricated rivals—that is more troubling still. Hence, it is
darkly ironic that among these rivals, Jensen opposes the violent—identified
as civilization—against the non-violent, implicitly cast as the post-civilization
ecocentric community:

- Twenty Premises, Three-Five: Our way of living—industrial civilization—is
  based on, requires, and would collapse very quickly without persistent and
  widespread violence. Civilization is based on a clearly defined and widely
  accepted yet often unarticulated hierarchy. Violence done by those higher
  on the hierarchy to those lower is nearly always invisible, that is, unnoticed.
  When it is noticed, it is fully rationalized. Violence done by those lower
  on the hierarchy to those higher is unthinkable, and when it does occur
  is regarded with shock, horror, and the fetishization of the victims. The
  property of those higher on the hierarchy is more valuable than the lives of
  those below. It is acceptable for those above to increase the amount of property they control—in everyday language, to make money—by destroying
  or taking the lives of those below. This is called production. If those below
  damage the property of those above, those above may kill or otherwise
  destroy the lives of those below. This is called justice.

There is certainly truth here, particularly with respect to Jensen's recognition
that violence often occurs in the interest of preserving a socially stratified status
quo, and that institutionalized violence is typically rationalized and concealed
behind a thin veneer of legitimated authority. But I say "thin" because the potential for the veneer to be torn away becomes greater in direct proportion to the
crises a people are forced to confront. As Poppy Noor reports for *The Guardian*,
for example, while many American governors and mayors appear to be willing to volunteer their residents as potential casualties of Covid-19 in order to
meet President Trump's demand that public schools open despite the pandemic,
many (and especially) citizens less privileged by class or race can see that this is
a charade to protect the markets. Missouri Governor Mike Parson offers a case
in point when he insists that "When they go to school—they're not going to the
hospitals. They're not going to have to sit in doctor's offices. They're going to go
home and they're going to get over it ... We gotta move forward."[25]

Governor Parson's claims are simply false. Although children rarely suc-
cumb to Covid-19, they're not immune; though children under ten years old

transmit the virus less frequently, asymptomatic spread is still quite possible. They might "get over it" and still have infected grandma. Multigenerational households, more common in the United States for African American and Latinx families for cultural and economic reasons, are also made more vulnerable for these very reasons. Echoing Texas' Lieutenant Governor Danial Patrick's claim that older Americans should be willing to sacrifice themselves for the economy, that being willing to die to keep the markets open is a patriotic act, we know what Governor Parson's means by "move forward." Few would dispute the claim that prevailing upon any group of citizens to risk death in order to preserve a faltering economy is perverse. Implying that to do otherwise is unpatriotic exemplifies the kind of violence Jensen identifies as civilization; in this case a violence draped in the flag. That some of those expected to make this "ultimate sacrifice" were World War II (even World War I) veterans makes the appeal to patriotism a veneer as thin as tissue paper. But while the violence illustrated by Governor Parson's view of the pandemic make the call to end civilization seem obvious, clear-cut cases like this remain the outliers. Cases like Potosi are far more the norm because the complexity of history is far more the norm.

Although silver mining at Potosi and Huancavelica offers a potent metaphor for the human and environmental cost of the extractive industries, this is because it puts faces, histories, cultures, and specific ecological and geographical conditions to that cost. This dark chapter of human and environmental history is about the callous disregard for human welfare characteristic of colonial silver mining in the Andes, As Jensen would no doubt agree, but it's also about gender, religion, disease, water, the world history of slavery, how silver became a medium of exchange, the aspirations of the Spanish Empire, and far-flung wars. Jensen's right that there exist invisible (or not) hierarchies defining who counts as a beneficiary and who a commodity of "civilization," but without a more nuanced understanding of how each of these interact under specific conditions, the call to end civilization has no obvious target. Or worse: everything becomes its target and everyone other than those outfitted to survive the ensuing tumult become its casualties.

In Potosi some of the most intimate of relationships were the most deadly. Wives cooked food for families with contaminated water and utensils, unwittingly poisoning their husbands and children. Corrupted priests took advantage of hierarchical, but also trusted, relationships to sell their parishioners into a system of wage slavery. Single men from outside the community sought solace in the arms of local prostitutes, interactions mediated through the exchange of silver. In premise six, Jensen claims that "civilization is not redeemable" and that if we "do not put a halt to it... civilization will continue to immiserate the vast majority of humans and to degrade the planet until it (civilization, and probably the planet) collapses." Premise Seven: "the longer we wait before we ourselves bring it down—the messier will be the crash, and the worse things will be for those humans and nonhumans who live during it, and for those who come after." He might be right. But how do "we" decide who is the "we" charged with bringing civilization down? Isn't it likely to be those who occupy the least vulnerable positions with respect to arrest and prosecution, or who have avenues available which enable them to flee? Doesn't that fact reproduce the very hierarchy Jensen seeks to undermine? How can "we" know who will live and who will die, except that the latter will be those human beings, nonhuman animals, and plant species least able to protect themselves from the violence that will surely ensue as part and parcel of the endgame? In other words, *we do know.*

5.2.2   After the End

Among the pressing ethical dilemmas that confront Jensen's ecocentric ethic, that pits hard questions about what is morally defensible against what is ecologically significant, perhaps even crucial, given the climate crisis, is that a recruiting cry to end civilization can as easily be deployed by a despot ready to commit genocide as by a righteous eco-warrior with a sense of decency and forbearance. Can we tell the difference between them other than in hindsight? We'd like to think so, but we know from human history that this is not always apparent. The end of civilization doesn't necessarily imply the construction of a just society after the rubble is cleared, and there's no mechanism or decision-making criteria implied by the concept of inherent worth that by itself supplies direction for how survivors will organize society after the end. It was commonplace to "justify" enslaving Africans in the US South by appeal to the notion that the slaver knew better what was in the interest of the enslaved than the slave.[26] What prevents the post-civilization leaders from appealing to the same bigotries to justify a social order that privileges them at the cost of others—the same "others" who bear that expense now? Perhaps the inherent worth of the slave is realized in serving her master; perhaps the woman's is in sexual service; maybe nonhuman animals just are food.

No doubt, Jensen would find this characterization of the post-civilization world distasteful. But distaste doesn't address the fact that human societies *did* produce the social, environmental, and viral crises we now face. Without a clearer accounting of how we arrived at this juncture, it seems cold comfort to suggest that adopting an ecocentric ethic will avoid it in the future; that is, short of the enforcement undertaken by autocratic regimes. And, of course, it's far from clear that this world would be more desirable than the one we already have; indeed, it could merely compound racist and sexist institutions with autocratic oppression. Given these many questions, it's not surprising that Jensen is often asked what comes after the end:

> People often ask me what sort of culture I would like to see replace civiliza-
> tion, and I always say that I do not want any culture to replace this one. I want
> 100,000 cultures to replace it, each one emerging from its own landbase, adapted
> to and adaptive for its own landbase, each one doing what sustainable cultures
> of all times and all places have done for their landbases: helping the landbase to
> become stronger, more itself, through their presence. (*Endgame*, Vol. II, p. 887)

"Helping the landbase to become stronger" can be made perfectly consistent with the institutions of slavery, patriarchy, autocracy, religious persecution, and the slaughter of nonhuman animals. We could, in fact, imagine a dystopia where any or all of these are necessary to make the landbase stronger, and thus justified as such. Nothing, moreover, precludes the emergence of the voracious forms of capitalist culture adapted to its landbase through the same forms of denial and self-deception that animate the myth of endless resources. As Lynn White shows, it's not that Christians didn't care about the landbase; it's that they believed that, as an endless provision of God, its purpose was to serve the growth of the Christian Kingdom. One thing seems clear: the most waste-ful and exploitive civilizations of the Global North didn't arrive at the climate crisis through some decisive break in the historical trajectory of their cultures. The Industrial Revolution of 1750 marks a turning point in human and envi-ronmental history, but this isn't because human beliefs about the world (or the planet) had changed; it's because our technologies caught up with a worldview already deeply anchored in the human psyche of that time.

In *The Uninhabitable Earth*, David Wallace Wells argues that the climate crisis could result in a planet unfit for human life. We needn't merely imagine, he argues, a planetary landbase so degraded that none but the most miserable human culture could survive it. The evidence is right in front of us in the form of a warming atmosphere and the implications that affect every organism and species, every ecosystem and geography. We could imagine Jensen's 100,000 cultures before we reach that tipping point, emerging from water wars, the next pandemic, or out of the rubble of a scaled-up Fukushima. But regardless Jensen's tendency to romanticize the post-civilization world, every culture, however violent, wasteful, and exploitive *is* "adaptive and adapted" to its land-base; it could not survive to the status of "culture" otherwise. Destruction is a form of adaptation limited by time, suffering, and resources; it's as adaptive as are neurotic or psychotic forms of coping for people. Cultures and people cope, even if poorly, even if the end result is demise. That environment-de-stroying forms of adaptive behavior may produce disastrous consequences for human and nonhuman populations implies neither that a particular cultural configuration wasn't adaptive in the past, nor that pockets of its population won't survive, carry on with the same worldview, and perhaps become more mercenary in the future.

Moreover, if we just are the chauvinists Naess and Jensen make us out to be, it's hard to see how we avoid repeating the same errors of self-interest and greed moving forward. Perhaps we can avoid this unpleasantness and uncertainty by ending civilization now. Perhaps the daunting crises humanity faces will teach us the lesson that an ecocentric ethic is the best, most the adaptive strategy for 100,000 new cultures. But this too is human-centered. For whom other than ourselves would we make the kinds of sacrifices an ecocentric adaptation would require? Even human chauvinism can be directed at ends that help the landbase—are superficially ecocentric, but actually serve the purposes of maintaining a particular social order. It's not hard to imagine, for example, cultures for whom helping the landbase "justifies" institutions like slavery, brutal forms of reproductive control, "euthanizing" the elderly, or righteous crusades to conquer one of the other 100,000 that fail to tow (or reject) the ecocentric worldview. This isn't, of course, what Jensen has in mind at all. But what in the ecocentric worldview actually precludes these atrocities so long as the "help the landbase"?

Whether the new world Jensen envisions is really as radically different from the old one—whether it's worth the monumental volume of suffering and death required to achieve it—remains an open question. In fact, it remains an open question for Jensen who offers a glimpse of what the world of 100,000 cultures would look like ideally for him. The surprise (or not) is that it's no culture, and no people, at all:

> There's a place I go when the sorrow gets to be too much for me, when I feel I just cannot go on. It's only a few miles from my home, and coincidentally only a couple of miles from a couple of different sites where in the nineteenth century the civilized massacred hundreds of Totowa Indians. In the 1960s a corporation started to put a housing division there too. The corporation laid out paved roads in neat squares. But then because of environmental concerns it was never able to get permission to build the houses. So, for the last forty years the housing division has sat. And the forest has begun to reclaim its own. Trees push through pavement, roots making ridges that run from side to side of the street. Grass comes up in every crack. Wind, water, sand, and bacteria make potholes that grow year by year. Or maybe we should switch perspective and speak of the ground beneath finding its way back to the surface. Trees and bushes reach from each side of the road to intertwine limbs, at first high above the ground, then lower and lower, until sometimes you can't even see where there used to be a road. (*Endgame*, Vol. II, pp. 887–8)

Drafted near the end of *Endgame's* Volume II, it at first seems a bit jarring that—after so much effort and pages of text—it turns out that the best culture is the one erased by the forest, grown over by a biotic integrity fully restored. Where there are no human beings, there is no risk of an emergent human culture that could come to resemble civilization. But it also wholly undermines Jensen's claim to want 100,000 cultures each cleaving in its own way to its own landbase. Perhaps even Jensen worries that the end of civilization could generate the conditions of civilization, or worse: a society faced with a profoundly degraded planet and atmosphere that could thus become even more violent, more brutal than the one it replaced. We could cast his musings as misanthropic, but whatever the case, a world with no people is a world in need of no ethic at all, not even an ecocentrism.

5.3   Why Experience Matters: John Dewey, David Wood, and Kath Weston

5.3.1   What Is Eco-phenomenology?

It's hard to miss the importance of experience to Derrick Jensen's theorizing about our relationship and responsibilities to the environment. Indeed, the context of the earlier passage where Jensen confronts the claim that the ecocentric imperative is "heartless" is his own struggle with Crohn's disease,[27] and he frequently references moments from his childhood—good and bad—not merely as background, but as substantively involved in the formation of his environmental conscience. In that same passage, Jensen says he's comfortable with the prospect that his death may "serve the larger community," and he chastises a woman, going as far as to call her "narcissistic," because she wants to keep her access to drugs to treat diabetes and heart disease. Jensen argues that because such access is premised on a "Western culture" he casts as "the root of our trouble," we should forego "Western" medicine for the sake of the larger community (*Endgame*, p. 123). This is, of course, a pretty bitter pill to swallow (no pun intended), requiring a great deal of self-sacrifice, and it's not very clear what counts as "Western Medicine." Kidney Dialysis? Tylenol? Sex reassignment surgery? Knee replacements? Therapeutics or a vaccine for Covid-19? Whatever else we think of Jensen's response, we can be sure it's drawn from a deep well of experience woven both helpfully and "heartlessly" throughout *Endgame*. Important here, however, is that descriptors like "helpfully" or "heartlessly" hint at the strengths and weaknesses of appeals to experience especially, as is the case with Jensen, as part of the criteria for moral decision-making.

Experience does matter *greatly* to moral reasoning. Yet the *idea* that experience is important to the quest for an environmental ethic remains under-theorized in much of its major figures and arguments. No doubt the value of experience lurks just below the surface of countless examples of the rights of trees, piles of wolves, poisoned silver miners, or in Jensen's wrenching description of the terror experienced by factory farm animals. If we did not feel wonder in the forest, horror in the prospect of suffering, or disgust at the conditions of slaughter, we'd likely not be concerned with notions like "rightness" or "wrongness" at all. It's because we care—we're capable of *empathy* in addition to reason—that we struggle with ethical quandaries. Yet experience, human or nonhuman, is rarely prioritized as a *criterion* of moral decision-making in its own right. To be clear: few would argue that appeal to experience provides a foundation for an environmental ethic on its own, or that it's an alternative to good reasoning. But experience may have something to offer to moral thinking more than mere color, or distraction, or an obstacle; indeed, it may turn out to be a critical element of a life worth living precisely because our experience solicits emotions like empathy (among others) that we value and regard as worth cultivating. Some argue that it's experience, especially of moral failure, that lends depth, particularity, context, humility, forthrightness, courage—that is, *propulsion* to our moral discourse. So, it's fortunate that there are theorists willing to take the role of experience in moral thinking about environmental issues seriously, namely, the *eco-phenomenologists*. A youthful sub-discipline of environmental philosophy, eco-phenomenology has come into its own in late twentieth- /early twenty-first-century thinking. Some argue that the ideas and the arguments that link experience specifically to environmental ethics can't have arrived too soon as an alternative to moral extensionism or ecocentrism. After all, they point out, it's the experience of falling ill to a virus, of going without food, of being exposed to the chemical toxins used in hydraulic fracturing, of watching a culturally vital monument become degraded, of having no access to clean water, and of extreme weather events caused by the climate crisis that are the important issues of this century. They're important not merely because of measurable damage exacted against human and nonhuman populations and their ecologies, but because living in and through that damage so vitiates the prospect of living a good life, and of hope for a good future, is unlivable.

David Wood and Kath Weston, each in original but quite different ways, exemplify the eco-phenomenological approach to ethics. Each explores the experience of human and nonhuman nature in a fashion that, while not aimed at developing an ethic *per se*, nonetheless offers valuable and probing insight. The question both face is whether eco-phenomenology can *ground* moral decision-making beyond what is "merely" felt to be right. As we'll see, this is a difficult question indeed. It's one thing to take experience seriously as an occasion for personal reflection or even deeply significant self-review concerning one's behavior toward the environment. No doubt powerful experiences of the natural world's capacity for the beautiful and the ravaged, the sublime and the terrifying can provoke us to think long and hard about what we eat, wear, and drive, where we live, and what we *do*. Moving experiences can be life-changing. But, whether, and for all the reasons we find it arresting, compelling, repellant, dull or shiny, experience can *by itself* ground an ethic—that should generate some real moral anxiety for us. Whose experience matters? Matters the most? Is the feeling that a particular experience (or even kind of experience) is good sufficient to say that it *is* good? Experience is inflected by sex, gender, ethnicity, culture, religion, class, history, geography, and previous experience in ways that can alter how we comprehend our own and that of others. Do these factors undermine the prospect of good judgment? If we feel compelled to step outside our own experience to make judgments more objectively, is there any good reason to consult it at all? Aren't there good reasons to distrust our experience as a barometer of what count as the facts?

The challenge for Wood, Weston, or any eco-phenomenologist who seeks to move beyond merely recounting experience, is that while we can *describe* our own experience as meaningful, even morally compelling, this doesn't necessarily entitle us to *prescribe* what ought to characterize the actions of others on that basis alone, however much it feels to us like we should. Sometimes we do feel like we "just know" right from wrong—it's intuitive. But, difficult as it is to see, the feeling of certainty *by itself* doesn't entitle us to infer that our experience can function as moral criteria for that of others.[28] We cannot derive an *ought* from an *is*, especially an "is" that's subjective, that we can only share with others by telling them about it. I might feel deeply committed, for instance, to a vegan way of life, and this might be grounded in my experience of nonhuman animal suffering, say videos I've seen of factory farms. Certainly, I can try to persuade others to follow me into veganism; I can decide not to date carnivores; I can advocate for animal rights. But can my experience get me any further than this, for example, to demanding vegan school lunch programs? A ban on animal agricultural operations in my county? Can I insist my partner avoid working for companies whose product, or even vaccine research, involves animal trials? Surely, I need more than my experience to rely on for direction. Plus, my view of my own experience might change. What if a future experience, say, witnessing starvation, is felt to be so compelling it supersedes the one that originally drove my veganism? Is there a right or wrong judgment of my past experience to be made if I change my mind about what my experience tells me to do?

Another example: Jensen is as entitled as anyone to reject "Western" medicine. He can try to convince us, as he does, that we should do the same. He can even resort to shaming tactics to dissuade us from using the prescription medications he derides as "Western" medicine. But insofar as he's appealing, at least implicitly, to the ecocentric imperative to justify his efforts to persuade us, he *is* appealing to a moral principle by which he interprets his experience as ethically relevant. Wouldn't I be doing the same if, as a vegan, I deployed arguments like pointing to the consequences in animal suffering of factory farming (Singer) or the notion that the concept of rights applies to all entities capable of sentience (Regan)? Yes, and Jensen would agree. The point is to get us to embrace the right moral principle, ecocentrism in Jensen's view, and then interpret our experience in light of it. On one hand, principle provides a framework for judgment but it's experience that gets us to care. On the other, getting us to care doesn't tell us what to do; it's principle that tells us why we ought to care, at least when it's grounded in relevant facts and an argument for why its application to those facts can, for example, produce a greater balance of good over harm or suffering, defend some set of valuable rights, or especially important here, protect the ecological conditions of a livable future.

Consider, for example, a claim made by Dr. Stella Immanuel that the medication hydroxychloroquine is an effective and safe treatment, even a cure, for Covid-19. At first, we might be tempted to take this claim at face value given that Dr. Immanuel is a physician, and thus occupies a position of relevant authority. It's easy to see why we ought to care about whether her claims are true—Covid-19 is a potentially deadly virus for which treatment, much less cure, has been elusive at best. It's also not hard to assign the principle of utility to the question whether hydroxychloroquine should be offered to patients since her claim is that the ends—a treatment for the virus—justify the means, the use of hydroxychloroquine. The difficulty, then, isn't the absence of either a moral principle or the experience that makes appeal to utility meaningful; people are dying, and treatment is desperately needed. The problem is that Dr. Immanuel's claims about the efficacy of hydroxychloroquine are false. As leading expert on infectious disease and National Institutes of Health (NIH) director Anthony Fauci makes clear: "We know that every single good study… has shown that hydroxychloroquine is not effective in the treatment of Covid-19."[29]

That Dr. Immanuel makes a number of other claims about the use of alien DNA in medical treatments for various forms of disease, or the activities of supposed witches and demons also, of course, raises important questions about her credibility. But what matters here is that the introduction of experience—especially experience inflected by urgency, fear, need, and suffering—as a factor into moral reasoning should not be taken as a substitute for the weight of the evidence. Sober judgment of hydroxychloroquine makes clear that it cannot treat coronavirus, and that it can contribute to more harm; administering it without informed consent may violate a patient's rights; the future its use forebodes offers very little to combat the Covid-19 virus. Indeed, given that Dr. Emmanuel's claim for the drug's efficacy is false, it's not really surprising that its use fails the judgment of virtually every principle of moral judgment, whatever else their differences. There's also no depth of commitment or number of sincere expressions of belief that this agent works to treat Covid-19 that can make it true that it does treat Covid-19. Experience can supply morally relevant propulsion, but if this isn't accompanied by respect for fact over self-interest, what we're left with is just another example of human chauvinism.

5.3.2   John Dewey and the Aesthetic *in* Experience

That experience—perceptual, psychological, somatic, social, and spiritual—can afford us insight into the intimacy of our relationships in and to the natural worlds inside and outside our bodies is not a new idea. In his philosophical psychology, *de Anima* (*On the Psyche*) the ancient Greek philosopher, Aristotle, argues that the soul or psyche just is the principle that governs the organization of the bodies of living things.[30] At every level, nutritive, perceptual, and intellectual, the realization of a living thing is facilitated via its relationships with objects in its internal and external environment; it's no stretch to characterize Aristotle's conception of organisms as essentially ecological (Lee, 2007, pp. 72–4). More ancient still is Socrates "the unexamined life is not worth living" which, as I've argued, is readily translated into a governing principle for modern times, especially as we come face-to-face with the consequences of our individual and collective action in the age of climate change, and the many issues that characterize a constellation of crises: growing food insecurity, extreme weather events, more frequent and more virulent virus outbreaks, human and nonhuman migration, and the greater likelihood of war or acts of terror to secure clean water. If the examined life is understood to consist *essentially* not only in the dispassionately rational, but also the personal and experiential, this is surely only in part because it is *one's own life* where the effects of such crises are felt. The other key feature of our lives, however, is the presence of others, human and nonhuman, some of whom we love, and to whom we are intimately and experientially attached. The value of these others prods us to reflect on the decisions we make because the experience of a moral failure that impacts them is what we must live with.

Thus, it's no surprise that there are specific kinds of things we desire from our experience, individually and collectively, not the least of which is that it's meaningful, that it doesn't merely happen to us, that we're active participants in its formation, and that it includes elements sufficiently desirable that we can imagine repeating it, sharing it, and that the future makes it, or something like it, possible for others. Perhaps something like this was what the American philosopher John Dewey had in mind when he introduces us to the concept of the aesthetic *in* experience:

> [W]e have *an* experience when the material experienced runs its course to fulfillment … A piece of work is finished in a way that is satisfactory; a problem receives its solution; a game is played through; a situation, whether that of eating a meal, playing a game of chess, carrying on a conversation, writing

> a book, or taking part in a political campaign, is so rounded out that its close is a consummation and not a cessation. Such an experience is a whole and carries with it its own individualizing quality and self-sufficient. It is *an* experience. (*Art as Experience*, p. 205)

Eating a memorable meal, finishing a long-worked manuscript, or listening to sorrowful Lake Loons[31] in the moonlight on a still pond—each comprise *an* experience in virtue of the satisfaction we derive from their particularity, their "wholeness." This isn't, argues Dewey, because we abstract them from the "situation" in which experience transpires, but, quite to the contrary, because they remind us of the relationship between our own capacities for seeing, tasting, hearing, feeling, and the objects of that perception. The very intimacy and richness of that relationship is what, for Dewey, comprises what he calls the aesthetic *in* experience.[32] Something more than "beautiful," though surely that's included, the aesthetic is that which is "able to be appreciated," an experience that has "qualities that render a thing or phenomenon memorable, unique, distinctive." Not only is the object or phenomena of our experience of value, but so too the place, locale, or situation to which the experience directs further attention—the context that makes the aesthetic *in* experience possible.

Eating a meal, playing a game of chess—these events don't occur in a vacuum, but rather, as Dewey puts it, in a *situation* that makes possible experience that's memorable, distinctive; it offers *consummation* as opposed to merely an end. It includes an element of the deliberate and the desirable. However fleeting or prolonged, it offers opportunity for appreciating what *in* experience we want to make sure remains possible for ourselves and for future others. "For life," writes Dewey, "is no uniform uninterrupted march or flow. It is a thing of histories, each with its own plot, its own inception and movement towards its close ... A flight of stairs, mechanical as it is, proceeds by individual steps, not by undifferentiated progression" (*Art as Experience*, pp. 205–6). The very character of experience, in other words, is on this view aesthetic in the sense that experience forms the context within which the kind of value we want to preserve to the future is made possible. *An* experience, for Dewey, is what we keep, what stays with us, what we recall with joy or anxiety, what we sometimes share with others, whether comfort or fear, joy or terror. It directs us to the conditions we must work to preserve in order to make future opportunities for the aesthetic *in* experience possible. That our experience can be made richer or poorer depending on factors such as ecological stability, biodiversity, fresh air and clean sparkling water—or the anxiety associated with their potential loss—forms the essential warp and woof of the "flow" that ultimately comes to describe histories personal, cultural, even civilizational. That experience can inform us of abilities we share across a wide spectrum of species, sentient and not, reminds us that we too are animals dependent as are all living things on the planet's resources and recuperative capacity.

For Dewey "[e]xperience in this vital sense is defined by those situations and episodes we spontaneously refer to as being 'real' experiences; those things of which we say, in recalling them, that *was* an experience" (*Art as Experience*, p. 205). The "real," of course, can be the stuff of many things, but it's more likely to become the stuff of *an* experience, under conditions that offer some sense of stability, diversity, opportunity, joyfulness, safety, control, and a sense of wholeness. Why else pursue the mountain climb? The surfing? The new spicy food? Why hope for a vaccine for coronavirus? Why return to the Paris Climate Accord? For many, of course, the "real" can just as readily generate anxiety or even fear: hiking the water back down to the village from further and further away because clean water is scarce, navigating a rocky and perilous gorge to graze animals, eating rice tainted by pesticides, heading home after a long, perhaps ventilator-dependent, hospital stay with an oxygen tank to recover from Covid-19. There's likely no way to fully address the range and meaningfulness of *an* experience without addressing it at the level of the least fortunate first—especially in the global South. This isn't merely because it seems certain that if the aesthetic *in* experience is possible here, it's possible anywhere, but because the experience of the vulnerable and the subjugated often cleaves the most closely to issues that affect the human existential condition most directly: food and water scarcity, exposure to pollutants, toxins, and disease, flood, fire, drought, and the brutality of those systemically empowered over the lives of ourselves and those we care for.

The aesthetic *in* experience isn't, in other words, significant to environmental ethics because it's comfortable or easy. It's significant because it affords an opportunity for us to ask about what kind of experience we hope will come to characterize our own lives, but also those who come after, and thus what conditions we must strive to insure to the future. It is, of course, a fair question to ask whether we have any such moral responsibility to the future, especially since we cannot predict it with any precision. But this is actually the easy question: all moral consideration is directed at the future insofar as morality itself is about what criteria should govern not merely this judgment and action, but judgment and action *generally*. Such consideration is all the more crucial to an environmental ethic insofar as the ecological conditions of the only planet we have form the existential conditions of our lives and the lives of those who come after. As Brian Barry makes this point in his essay "Sustainability and Intergenerational Justice," the prospect of justice distributes itself not merely within generations, but between them, (pp. 96–101). The "vital interests of people in the future" he writes, "have the same priority as vital interests of people in the present" (p. 99). That is, while there may be ultimately little other than our desire that the experience of future others be able to be as rich and meaningful as is our own—that we recognize that our own vital interests are not *to us* greater than theirs will be *to them*—the fact that the realization of such a desire comes with no guarantee does not imply that our moral duty is any more *only* to the present than it is *only* to ourselves. "Place and time," writes Barry, do not themselves "provide a morally relevant basis on which to differentiate the weight to be given to the interests of different people" (p. 100), or even different people at different times. The hard question, then, is less whether we can justify a moral duty to the future, but rather what we're willing to do, to work at, to forfeit in order to make a future of realizing vital interests possible given the destruction we have waged and are still waging against the planet and its atmosphere. If our past is any guide, we have not learned much, but it's also no stretch to interpret Barry's reference to vital interests in light of Dewey's *an* experience. Indeed, Barry gives us a compelling example modeled after an earlier thought experiment hailing from Henry Sidgwick:

> Let us imagine one world exceedingly beautiful...[P]ut into it whatever on this earth you most admire—mountains, rivers, the sea, trees, and sunsets, stars and moon. Imagine all these combined in the most exquisite proportions so that no one thing jars against another but each contributes to increase the beauty as a whole. And then imagine the ugliest world you can possibly conceive... simply one heap of filth, containing everything that is most disgusting to us ... without one redeeming feature... The only thing we are not entitled to imagine is that any human being has or ever...can live in either...Still is it irrational to hold that it is better that the beautiful world should exist than the one that is ugly? (pp. 113–4)

If it's not irrational to wish the beautiful world to exist—even if no human being ever experiences it—this is surely because the experience of what can be aesthetically appreciated as beauty, as "exquisite proportion," in addition to color, diversity, variation, and the like, is precisely the stuff of *an* experience we'd hope to be possible for *anyone*. This is not to say, as Barry recognizes, that the repellant world is not sustainable; it may be. It is to say that to whatever extent, as Dewey argues, experience forms a crucial feature of our moral thinking, it does so because a future worthy of sacrifice and hard-won change in the present must be one in which we would ourselves be willing to live. Barry makes a similar point, if more stoically, writing that "virtually everybody who has made a serious study of the situation ... has reached the conclusion that the most elementary concern for people in the future demands big changes in the way we do things" (p. 118). Barry and Dewey are, however, advocating for more than simply elementary concern. "We must respect the creativity of people in the future" (p. 104), writes Barry. The value of experience, in other words, cannot be conceived as merely *intra*generational but rather *inter*generational; anything else is hypocrisy (pp. 114–5).

Whereas Barry seeks to extend moral responsibility to ecological sustainability and restoration beyond the present by grounding duty in a framework for the kind of world any rational being would likely hope to inhabit, Dewey gives substance to the character of that world through the provision of rich experiential examples which have the effect of demonstrating in what that duty consists, namely, in sustaining the possibility for the aesthetic *in* experience. What must the planet and its atmosphere be like to make this experience—a pond, a river, a flow—possible?

> In such experience every successive part flows freely, without seam and without unfilled blanks, into what ensues. At the same time, there is no sacrifice of the self-identity of the parts. A river, as distinct from a pond, flows. But its flow gives a definiteness and interest to its successive portions greater than exist in the homogeneous portions of a pond. In *an* experience, flow is from something to something ... The enduring whole is diversified by successive phases that are emphases of its varied colors. (*Art as Experience*, p. 206).

Rivers and ponds both involve water and flow, yet they're different kinds of phenomena and it's in their differences, their varied colors, their variable flow, what we might know about their hydrology, the creatures who inhabit them, their point of termination, that the possibility of *an* experience takes shape. The aesthetic value of *an* experience is, for Dewey, not *about* an object, *per se*. It's about the sense we have of a situated whole, the sense that nothing more is needed for the experience to be complete. Yet, as Barry argues, in not every world are experiences like those Dewey describes here possible; if we can make predictions now, in light of the climate crisis for example, that the future may have little to offer as clean water, as a pond that can support life, as a flow safe to wade, we have plainly not made the "big changes" necessary to meet our moral duty to the future.

Dewey's point, however, is not necessarily that *an* experience is replicable; the point is a world where *an* experience is possible. We could be experiencing the slow crawl of a sea turtle,[33] a guerrilla making her night bed of leaves and branches,[34] or a Sumatran elephant delicately snapping off twigs from an acacia tree.[35] The value of experience isn't necessarily that it can be repeated—it likely can't. It's that the world is configured in such a way that the experience is possible, that such events can continue to occur, that others may be able to witness them. Such configurations cannot be divorced from their ecological conditions. Far more than mere background, the "real" lay in what we see, smell, hear, feel. *An* experience is a composition of these phenomenal qualities, but even more importantly, it's a sum that's far more than its parts. An experience intimates a complex and diverse world whose moral worth lay in the prospect that its loss is unthinkable. Indeed, whichever principle stands the greatest chance of staving off that loss is at least a compelling candidate for the life worth living. *An* experience, in other words, raises the prospect that we do have a moral responsibility to preserve conditions that make it possible for future generations of experiencers. The idea, in fact, that *an* experience should be (as philosopher Ludwig Wittgenstein might have put it) "for use on only one occasion" seems either paradoxical or apocalyptic—it either just is not ever the case or, if it is, it's because the world has ended. *An* experience, in other words, is an inherently social as well as intergenerational concept; *an* experience becomes an experience in sharing it—even if only with ourselves. It's an experience because the prospect of its repeatability is desirable; because in remembering it, we can relive it, at least a little. And while the question whether we have any responsibility to people and/or nonhuman entities not yet born, grown, or otherwise created is a difficult one, it falls well within the parameters of any moral discourse that recognizes that a world where ethical agency depends on something more than environmental stability, namely, stability in *a world worth preserving*—a world whose loss is unimaginable.

When the utilitarian appeals to consequences, they're referring to what happens after an action is undertaken. When we appeal to the concept of having and exercising a right, we implicitly assume it's not for one occasion or one rights-bearer only. When Rolston talks about respect for life, he means the "life" of the species, not just one instance of it. The ecocentrist doesn't revalue just today's ecological integrity; the imperative is meant for tomorrow and the next day and the next. The prospect of a future that makes *an* experience possible is what makes living according to principle sometimes hard, but it's also what makes living worth the next day and the next. While experience may itself be fleeting, it also reminds us of something far larger and more enduring: the ecological conditions that make it possible; the conditions without which the point of moral action may itself become an endangered species. What Dewey then shows us is that while experience may not by itself be sufficient grounding for moral action, insofar as it can remind us what moral action is for, it may be more than supplement to moral judgment; it may in fact be its necessary impetus.

5.3.3   David Wood's Eco-phenomenology

However ecologically reckless our behavior often seems, John Dewey took it at face value that witnessing a Grand Canyon ridgeline at dusk is something we want our children and grandchildren to have an opportunity to experience; that California sequoias, Sumatran elephants, polar bears, white rhinos, killer whales, and bald eagles are worth the environmental work and regulatory initiative to spare them from extinction. It's thus all the more disappointing that our expressed commitment to that future—even our laws and policies—are often betrayed by actions that continue to endanger sensitive habitat and the creatures who depend on it. Hence, it seems clear that the desire for the aesthetic *in* experience is not by itself sufficient to ground an actionable environmental ethic. Even if, as Dewey and Barry remind us, the prospect of a future bereft of the experiential qualities that make life worth living provide valuable substance to the moral ideas and arguments we've explored, phenomenological accounts still remain more descriptive than prescriptive. Perhaps this is how the myth of endless resources penetrates into the bone marrow of our disposition to the planet: despite copious evidence to the contrary, we still take for granted that future access to the Grand Canyon, Sumatran elephants, and bald eagles will resemble the present, and that we needn't do anything to preserve the conditions that can promise the opportunity. For that experience. What's surely needed, then, is an argument that shows the *prescriptive* relevance of experience to principled moral decision-making. One possibility: the *eco-phenomenology* of Wood.

While Wood isn't focused on developing an environmental ethic *per se* in his ground-breaking essay, "What is Eco-phenomenology?" his view of the relationship between our perceptual experience and the tangible world offers important insight that might help us see our experience in a prescriptively relevant light; indeed, his work invites us to flip the question "how do we get from experience to moral principle?" on its head: where appeal to principle so often fails, might there be something in experience that can move us to more ethically defensible action? Can a *deliberate* turn to the content and value of our experience of nonhuman nature move us to act more *deliberately* on behalf of the planet's ecosystems, respect its species-life, and restore its biotic diversity? Among the things we do know is that the principle of utility, the Categorical Imperative, Respect for Nature, and ecocentrism (even at its most visceral) haven't prevented us from behaving in highly destructive ways toward the environment, other human beings, and nonhuman animals. Even the sense of guilt and remorse the appeal to principle can solicit hasn't slowed our tendency to treat the planet's oceans and atmosphere like a latrine or interrupt our denial of the climate crisis. Wood, however, takes a different approach to the integration of experience into decision-making, effectively casting it as the critical ingredient that makes possible the translation of abstract principle into a meaningful framework for comprehending experience as morally significant, as a directive for action.

For Wood, a deeper, more acute comprehension of our relationships with human and nonhuman others offers value to human life inaccessible by other means, including through the sciences or through the reductionistic lens of marketable commodities. He characterizes *eco-phenomenology* as "the pursuit of the relationalities of worldly engagement, both human and those of other creatures" (Wood, p. 3), arguing that while "naturalistic" accounts of our interactions with human and nonhuman nature tend to focus on its scientifically relevant elements (*how* the eye sees, *how* the ear hears) phenomenological accounts tend to be more wholistic, focusing less on the causal or mechanical and more on the experiential or *intentional*:

> Seeing (and hearing and touching) is made possible by there being discrete bodies, including ourselves, that occupy distinct places at particular times, bodies endowed with a mobility that reflects their needs and desires. These are not just natural facts *about* the world, but fundamental *dimensions* of the world, dimensions that structure the very possibility of there being facts at all. And they certainly structure perception, insofar as perception is essentially perspectival, bound to surfaces of visibility, limited by things that stand in our way, and tied powerfully to our embodiment—in our having two eyes, two ears, two hands, and muscles that give us mobility in various dimensions. And that embodiment appears in more complex ways, in our having various somatic and social desires that shape and direct perception, and in the temporal syntheses in which it is engaged. (Wood, p. 2)

Our experience, in other words, is always *about* something; it's *perspectival*—not merely reactive. The conditioning framework of that experience isn't (merely) ideas, moral or otherwise, but an experience-able world made possible by a particular planet and its ecosystems. We might call experience essentially aesthetic in the sense that perception isn't governed merely by the mechanics of our sensory organs, but by our needs and desires—our *intentions*, our point of view, our aspirations, hopes, fears, anxieties—even our denials and ignorance. When we experience the world, we organize it; we make it sensible, appreciable, rational. Even when our capacity to tell fact from fiction becomes hijacked, for example, by conspiracy theories, racist or sexist stereotype, the recurrence of trauma, addiction, or poor education, we still have to live, to care for others, to work, to eat, to sleep. These existential facts remain the constant that informs even the most distorted moral reasoning.

Consider, for instance, the apparent worldview of a Covid-19 anti-masker, Chris Sky, laid out over the course of an interview with writer Jorah Kai. After a discussion over the fact that widespread cooperation with mask-wearing in Japan obviated the need for a pandemic lockdown (Sky denies that the Japanese wear masks at all), compared to Sweden's high body count due to a failure to mandate mask wearing as national policy (Sky insists the Covid-19 deaths are over-counted), the interview turns to the substance of Sky's anti-mask worldview:

Sky: Masks are fine if you wanna wear one. It becomes an issue when it's a mandate bc then you get mandated contract tracing and vaccines. (sic, unintelligible). *Also a fact, and freedom is essential.*

Kai: Even the freedom to die?

Sky: Masks and lockdown are not essential.

Kai: Even the freedom to kill your grandma?

Sky: Now you're being ridiculous

Kai: Or your niece with cancer?

Sky: How about facts, not what-ifs. Pathetic (sic, unintelligible)

Kai: Am I? Let's say you get COVID. But you're strong, don't get sick. But you see your gran, and she does. And she dies. Was it ok? If she gives it to 100 older people and they all die for your freedom, was that ok?

Sky: If she's old or sick, it's her responsibility to wear a mask if you think that helps or protects herself by distancing or staying home. The entire world is responsible for their own personal health. You are not responsible (sic, unintelligible) for me or my mother or your mother.

Kai: Was your freedom worth 100 old people? Our most vulnerable? Our children?

Sky: And once again, bullsh*t. You haven't used one fact. Emotional hyperbole is not an argument dummy. Lol.

Kai: But science says if she wears a mask and you talk to her, and you have it it's 30% protection. If you both wear a mask, it's 99% protection. That's a fact I read.

Sky: Ya, if you're sick, which 99% of people are not. Lol.

Kai: So, that means if we care about our old and sick. We should all wear them, right?

Sky: No, that's not what it means. Not at all, so please stop.[36]

What we discover here is that, although deeply distorted by denial and willful ignorance, Sky nonetheless makes a moral argument intended to bolster and preserve his way of life. Among the "fundamental dimensions" of his world that "structures the possibility of there being facts" are values Sky holds deeply—however untethered to the science of viral transmission. Despite the fact that his behavior plainly endangers other people and himself, we understand Sky's appeal to "freedom" and "personal moral responsibility" as the ideas governing what constitutes the aesthetic *in* experience for him, ideas he's unwilling to reconsider even temporarily in virtue of the value he assigns to them—and to an identity that depends on them. That his identity as too strong or too manly to be struck down by coronavirus is faulty and misplaced. Yet, this is beside the point to the extent that epidemiological facts gain little traction against a worldview so recalcitrant. Sky is wrong, but his experience is his experience.

Sky's wrong about the facts, but such is precisely what illustrates the difference between a phenomenological account and, as Wood puts it, a naturalistic one whatever our moral judgment about Sky's reckless behavior. Naturalistic accounts of experience often enough stand in conflict with perspective, especially when identity (or its loss) is at issue. A naturalistic account can tell us how the *seeing* eye construes the dimensions of an object, but only a phenomenological one can tell us why we're *looking* at, whether our relationship to that object has meaning to us, whether we want to keep looking. As Sky makes clear by the end of the tense interview, he doesn't want to "keep looking." He turns away at the challenge of fact to his identity as a freedom-defending warrior. What Sky's interview shows us in stark relief is that whatever are the natural facts about the world, they're always subject, as Wood argues, to the perspective-forming dimensions and limitations of creatures whose experience is governed by the eyes, ears, organs, limbs, and skin we do have, and not what we don't, but also by the values and principles that inform our *attention*, including that form of attention called *denial*. To be clear: this is not to say that facts are subjective or dependent on the perceiver—far from it. It is to say that to ignore the phenomenological component of our comprehension and appreciation of fact is to ignore the extent to which experience is itself *prescriptive*, and therefore an element of moral judgment we ignore at least at the risk of a significant distortion of our more considered judgment. Wood's phenomenology is *eco*-phenomenological precisely because it seeks to give voice to the embodied, epistemically and ecologically situated conditions that give rise to the actions that inform experience. On this account, we don't *have* experience. We *experience*, and that activity cannot be divorced either from the facts relevant to it, the values inflected in it, or the morally evaluable direction it takes. Why? Because whatever is that direction, the actions experience informs can affect for good or ill the conditions that situate and influence future experience—that become the drivers of self-reflection or denial, of humility in the face of conflicting fact or willful ignorance that, in the case of Sky, can kill grandma and her family, her friends, her nursing home staff, her physicians, her grandchildren.

Because eco-phenomenology includes this fundamentally prescriptive element, it makes sense for Wood to argue that the naturalistic and the phenomenological needn't be opposed. Or, rather, while phenomenology opposes "naïve" naturalism's reduction of the world to its mechanical substructure, it needn't be opposed to the basic relationships that characterize our dependence on the nonhuman world, engaging us as organisms in the processes of natural objects and their ecologies. Eco-phenomenology seeks to spell out that engagement, and thereby bridge the gap between merely describing the aesthetic *in* experience and theorizing it as an essential component of a viable environmental ethic. Eco-phenomenology reminds us that for as much as we rightly value cool-headed reason and the objective judgment to which moral principle presumably appeals, what moves us to act is that we *want* to. Science, however, remains the critical anchor. As Wood, Barry, and Dewey argue, understanding what makes the experience of a rich and diverse planet possible falls not to idiosyncratic desires that preserve any one worldview, but to the preservation of planetary conditions as they're spelled out for us by credible evidence and authority. Given the value Wood assigns to articulating a mutually reinforcing relationship between the naturalistic and the phenomenological, it seems clear the sciences must play a key role in moral discourse concerning, for example, what we should do about the increasing potential for forest fires in California, or how we ought to remediate red algae blooms off the coast of Florida.[37] If we want to see the mighty forests of California return; if we want to preserve the biodiversity of Florida coastal sea life, if we want to prevent or at least be in a position to mitigate the next pandemic, we must pay close attention to what the relevant sciences are telling us about the conditions that produce infernos, suffocates sea turtles and manatees, or can multiply in human lung tissue. Wood hints at something like this when he writes that

> I may be an embodied being, and the object of my awareness may be a tiger or a mountain. But the relation between us—seeing, fearing, hoping, admiring—is not a causal relation, not a physical relation, but an intentional one. When I admire the mountain, the mountain is not affected, and even if rays of light passing from the mountain to me are necessary for this admiration to take place, the admiration is something of a different order. I may be dreaming, say of an imaginary golden mountain, making a causal account of the relation even harder to sustain. And yet the absence of proximate cause does not refute causality. Think of finding a giant rock half way down a valley. Or sea-shells in a farmer's field. To understand intentionality to be opposed to causality is important if we associate causality with determinacy, with linearity, and with a certain kind of automatism. But if the realm of causality were to be expanded in way that overcomes these prejudices, what then? (Wood, p. 12)

Causality, in other words, needn't be narrowly construed according, at least exclusively, to a planetary mechanics that takes little account of the evolving organic relationships that characterize its many and diverse ecosystems. The life sciences have grown beyond metaphors that cast the planet as a machine that can be damaged but not harmed and, for Wood, beyond "a certain kind of automatism" that absolves us of responsibility for that harm. Our understanding of living things and their relationships has expanded to include facts concerning nonhuman animal sentience, the effects of pollutants and toxins on species of living things, and the dependence of planetary life on a stable atmosphere. "What then?" is thus an important question that can likely only be answered in that case where, for example, there continue to exist tigers—a prospect we can no longer afford to take for granted. As Wood says, my relationship to the tiger isn't (merely) causal; it's intentional. I don't merely see the tiger, I look at it and appreciate it. Facts about the conditions of my experience can radically alter the character of that experience. "What then?" This is a different question about a different relationship were our experience of the tiger tainted by the anxiety we might feel standing in front of a zoo enclosure whose descriptive placard read "critically endangered."

Wood's "What then?" in other words, does have an answer: if we value the experience of seeing tigers, we will act to preserve the possibility of that experience. It's the aesthetic *in* that experience—the wonder, the hope, the intention—that would be lost were we to fail to heed the meaning of "critically endangered," and we have science to thank for informing us about the status of this species. For Wood, the bridge that spans the gap between the phenomenological and the naturalistic, just is that ethical dimension of our experience that moves us to a deeper and more acute understanding of species critically endangered, an atmosphere increasingly compromised, migration patterns, the causes of food insecurity, zoonotic transmission. Because eco-phenomenology takes seriously human intention, it can offer a window into some of the darker drivers of human action: science-denial, willful ignorance, or the willingness to be suckered by false claims and false prophets. In this way, eco-phenomenology can help us to connect real harms with faulty judgment.

5.3.4   Kath Weston: The Feel of Experience versus the Force of Principle

Whereas Dewey and Wood provide good if cautious reason to integrate experience into a principled, science-grounded, environmental ethic, fellow eco-phenomenologist Kath Weston takes a different approach, one that raises anew the issue whether including experience in moral decision-making is worth the risk of making it central as opposed to significant—but supplemental. The danger is always that experience is subjective, and thus prone to idiosyncrasy, bias, denial, and the like. Invoking experience as justification for moral action can make us liable to judgment more self-interested than principled, driven more by our emotional states, good or bad, than by reason. Another danger is that because experience is always informed by culture, political ideology, religion, and personal history, it can make us liable to bigotry, racism, classism, human chauvinism, and misogyny. A sanctuary for the aesthetic in Dewey, a valuable counterweight for science in Wood, there's little doubt that taking experience seriously is crucial to the calculus of the life worth living. Nonetheless, its subjective nature is both its greatest asset and its most serious liability—so we must be very careful with respect to *how* we integrate it into an environmental ethic. The risk is substantial: mistaking the capacity of our experience to prod us, sometimes forcefully, to action in the place of good *reasons* to act can lead to bad, even disastrous, decisions. Feelings aren't justifications; feeling certain isn't the same thing as *having good evidential grounds* for being certain. At a time in human history where so much hangs on getting it right, the prospect that decisions about climate change, deforestation, desertification, pollution, species extinctions, disease outbreak, and the immense toll on the habitability of the planet for human and nonhuman beings might be made on the basis of anything less than well-informed science and sober principled reflection—that is a truly terrifying proposition.

This isn't to say, of course, that appeal to principle will always make transparently clear what we should do; moral extensionism and ecocentrism have both advantages and limitations. Nevertheless, one advantage of appeal to principle is that we can know these limitations. We can know why the question to what all does the principle of utility apply matters; we can probe what constitutes the rights of trees or what respect for life means. We're in a position to give hard thought to questions like when the ends do or don't justify the means, whether sentience is required to be a rights-bearer, or whether there are some forms of life we are not obligated to respect. We can ask whether it's plausible or even possible to adopt a fully ecocentric disposition. We can examine these principles objectively, and we can assume that anyone suitably equipped with a good set of critical thinking skills can do the same. Experience doesn't lend itself to any such examination because we can't investigate any other than our own (even that can be pretty murky). People can share their experience with us—but they can also lie about it, and often enough do. We're thus at a distinct disadvantage when we seek to answer questions such as why someone, for example, denies climate change even though it's as well-established as that cigarette smoking causes cancer, or HIV causes AIDS—yet some folks deny these too. Why, for example, do folks like Chris Sky continue to deny the effectiveness of mask-wearing nearly a year into a pandemic? Why do so many ignore the implications of bee-colony collapse despite the fact that the consequences for crop production are potentially calamitous? The issue isn't that these folks don't believe what they're saying when they evince denial; presumably they do. The issue is that belief is no substitute for evidence—even if they think so. It's that however convinced any of us might feel that our experience has led us aright, experience is not by itself evidence of truth. And it matters because being wrong about crises global in scale can be hugely consequential.

It's easy to see then why we might dismiss experience as having any useful place in moral reasoning. But, as Dewey and Wood show, this likely goes too far. So—what's *not* too far? Dewey's view of the aesthetic *in* experience offers important insight into its role in motivating environmentally responsible action; Wood offers a way to bridge the gap between the phenomenological and the scientific. But both are cautious, and certainly stop short of asserting that experience constitutes a variety of knowing *in itself*. But are they right about that? It's on just this issue that Weston's eco-phenomenology is instructive, even if in ways she might contest. Weston's view is, I'll argue, mistaken, but in ways that shed valuable light on the limits the role experience can play in ethics, perhaps especially in the development of an ethic that takes the future of the planet, its ecosystems, and its inhabitants as its primary focus. By advancing a role for experience as an avenue for knowledge that gives it too much authority, I'll argue that Weston shows, however unwittingly, why only *principles* (epistemic and moral, knowing and doing) can occupy the position of backbone of moral decision-making.

5.3.5   Animate Planet and the Menace of Moral Relativism

No doubt, Weston's on to something important when she argues we should strive to incorporate bodily sensations and perceptions into the ways in which we "register" empirical phenomena, (pp. 107–8, p. 119). Describing her view as "embodied empiricism," she argues that our perceptual, tactile experience provide the instruments of scientific investigation in that it "choreographs a bio-intimacy of detection and assessment, which registers conditions through membrane, skin, and retina, then uses reason to sort out the results" (p. 119). Rightly understood, in other words, "[i]n the sense that it matters little whether your 'environment' embodies you, or you it, or both," experience recognized in the terms of *bio-intimacy* can be counted not only as a subjective register of phenomena, but as a variety of scientific inquiry (p. 119). Membrane, skin, and retina aren't merely organs of sensation embodied by a species of creature, but tools through which empirical claims can be assessed, confirmed and refuted. In a marked departure from Dewey and Wood, Weston argues that we can treat "the body as a technology for adjudicating truth claims about the world" (p. 108), and that even where experience stands in clear conflict with the scientific consensus, there may be no good reason to abandon the former for the latter, (p. 115). "Arguments that cite bodily sensations as a reason for doubt," she writes, "are not necessarily antagonistic to science" (p. 115), but even where they are, we might be better-off to go with experience over the science.

Skepticism about phenomena like climate change may thus, on Weston's view, count as scientific *because embodied empiricism counts as doing scientific research*. Climate change skepticism is thus not necessarily as misinformed or just wrong, but rather the product of another kind of scientific knowing. Such, she argues, is fully consistent with the history and meaning of empiricism:

> When skeptics try to understand what, if anything, is changing by noting the conditions that prompt them to reach for an extra sweater or run their wrists

under water to cool off, *they effectively adopt an empiricist stance.* From a philosophical standpoint, the idea that sense experience is the source of all knowledge can be problematic. Yet the conviction that knowledge derives from experience ... also conferred value upon observation and experimentation as tools for understanding the world. Without that conviction European science would have never become European science. (p. 115, my emphasis)

Were Weston's argument essentially a moral plea for us to practice tolerance with respect to the climate change denier until they could be appropriately educated or, failing that, left to their willful ignorance we'd likely understand her argument in terms similar to Dewey's and Wood's—as an attempt to incorporate the value of experience into that bigger epistemic picture not as acquiescence, but as forbearance. But a plea for tolerance is manifestly *not* Weston's argument. Rather, she seeks to efface the distinction between ordinary experience (I'll go get a sweater), and the conduct of investigation (what are the relevant factors in this measurable drop of temperature?). The goal is to elevate the status of experience as a legitimate tool of scientific investigation. The trouble, of course, is that going to get a sweater and measuring temperature aren't the same: the first is not the adoption of an empirical stance because it's not the conduct of an investigation. I'm not trying to see whether the sweater will make me warmer; I *assume* it will. Running my wrists under cold water to cool off on a hot day isn't performing a controlled experiment. It doesn't involve eliminating variables or insuring repeatable experimental conditions; it doesn't adhere to scientific method unless we define "science" so broadly that any claim like "whoa! That's better!" gets to count. Just because all claims—even the most abstract mathematical claims—have some relation to experience does not imply that all claims are part and parcel of a potential scientific investigation. And while Weston may insist she's not taking "embodied empiricism" that far, it's not at all clear where, given the central role played by sensation and perception in making judgments, we'd draw the line concerning what does and doesn't count as doing science.

The "conviction that knowledge derives from experience" and "confers value upon observation and experimentation as tools for understanding the world" is indeed where the project of science begins, but it's not where it ends. After all, "derives from" does not mean "reducible to." Weston herself acknowledges that "the idea that sense experience is the source of all knowledge" is not "unproblematic." But insofar as embodied empiricism effectively subsumes empirical investigation into experiential response, it invests experience with the power to subjugate fact to feeling, truth to "truthiness." Such a view reduces knowledge claims to mere opinion, and the moral claims premised on them to mere expressions of taste or preference. This is *epistemic relativism*, and it gives us little reason to try to convince the climate change skeptic that they're wrong.[38] But this isn't tolerance; it's resignation. In whatever way their view of their own experience may conflict with the science, there's no principled reason the embodied empiricist can offer to challenge it. More troubling still: the climate change denier could deny they're in denial. They could insist that climate change is a "Leftist" conspiracy aimed at creating a one-world dictatorship.[39] Where there's no need for testing theories against the weight of potentially falsifying evidence, the "science" offered at on-line sites like InfoWars[40] or Climate Depot[41] is fully convincing of just this view. Indeed, a primary goal of such websites is to make the denier feel vindicated, confirmed, *knowledgeable*, even though they're simply, perhaps even dangerously, *wrong*. Still, Weston's right about one thing—we should not dismiss such folks as cranks.

The trouble is that Weston is right for the wrong reasons. We should no more dismiss the climate change denier than we should dismiss *InfoWars'* Alex Jones' claim that the children who attended *Sandy Hook Elementary* were child actors staging a massacre to extort the country into instituting more stringent gun control laws,[42] or White House Coronavirus Taskforce pseudo-science proponent, Scott Atlas' claim that herd immunity is a credible scientifically grounded strategy for dealing with the Covid-19 pandemic.[43] But we must take such claims seriously not because they're right, but because allowing them to simply stand without challenge is too often exploited by their proponents as confirmation. Knowledge claims have consequences; *false knowledge claims also have consequences*. Consider for example the claim that if enough people become infected with Covid-19, and assuming they are immune on recovery (itself a dubious claim), that this "herd" immunity can help prevent spread of the virus. Such a claim might seem intuitively plausible. After all, the majority of people who contract the virus don't die from it, and those who do are often compromised by "co-morbidities" that make them more vulnerable. In theory, then, the more people who get the disease and recover from it, the fewer there are to spread the virus. This seems as sensible as reaching for a sweater when we're cold, and so it's no real wonder that many people buy it. The trouble, however, is not merely that herd immunity is dangerously false—requiring potentially millions of infections and therefore deaths before even a semblance of wide-scale immunity could be achieved,[44] it's that adopting the empiricist stance in such cases is very likely less about the pursuit of knowledge, and more about excusing or rationalizing some set of actions (or inaction) to which we're already committed (or to which at least those in decision-making position of power stand to gain). It's easy to imagine, for example, Chris Sky promoting herd immunity. It fits a view of freedom that condones the refusal to wear a mask. It reinforces a worldview where the strong survive and the weak perish as a matter for the order of nature.

Such a "nature" is not, however, the one given to us by the sciences, the one where human encroachment on nonhuman animal habitat makes zoonotic transmission more possible, or the one where the sheer volume of plastic produced for personal protective equipment contributes to greenhouse gas emissions at an ever higher rate. As Tanveer Adyel reports for the AAAS journal *Science*:

> During the pandemic, personal protective equipment (PPE) has driven increased plastic pollution. In response to high PPE demand among the general public, health care workers, and service workers, single-use face mask production in China soared to 116 million per day in February, about 12 times the usual quantity. The World Health Organization has requested a 40% escalation of disposable PPE production. If the global population adheres to a standard of one disposable face mask per day after lockdowns end, the pandemic could result in a monthly global consumption and waste of 129 billion face masks and 65 billion gloves. Hospitals in Wuhan, the center of the COVID-19 outbreak, produced more than 240 tons of single-use plastic-based medical waste (such as disposable face masks, gloves, and gowns) per day at the peak of the pandemic, 6 times more than the daily average before the pandemic occurred. If the increases observed in Wuhan hold true elsewhere, the United States could generate an entire year's worth of medical waste in 2 months.[45]

In short, it's precisely *because* having the right science is crucial to articulating an enduring environmental ethic that we cannot dismiss those who'd claim "alternative science" on the basis of their "embodied empiricism." Weston's eco-phenomenology appears to sanction the worst kind of human chauvinism, namely, the one where science is largely displaced by self-interest, and where self-interest directs experience to self-serving and self-justifying ends—regardless of fact and consequence. A reckless pandemic strategy like that of the Great Barrington Declaration whose signers advocate allowing "those who are at minimal risk of death to live their lives normally to build up immunity to the virus through natural infection, while better protecting those who are at highest risk," "profoundly underestimates the suffering that would result if this strategy were to be enacted."[46] But even beyond that quotient of unnecessary misery, the volume of infection produced by the effort to achieve herd immunity would likely generate the conditions that require the mass production of the personal protective equipment. This, in turn, leads not only to the expansion of plastic disposal islands,[47] but an escalation of the greenhouse gas emissions that drive the climate crisis that, in turn once more, produces the conditions for future encroachment onto nonhuman animals habitat to grow food—and thus the prospect of future zoonotic transmission. Whatever its "sciency" appearance, however, the Great Barrington Declaration is a political/economic document, not a scientific one. Its origin is the American

Institute for Economic Research—a libertarian think tank. And that's just the point: Westin's view of experience as a variety of knowledge can no more filter out the self-interested, the ideologically directed, or even the deliberately weaponized from the self-interested conclusions the empirical stance sanctions. Yet, plainly, these are not as innocuous as putting on a sweater.

However much we dress up "I'm cold" in references to the body as a "technology for adjudicating truth," we're sliding down a slippery slope where every body counts as its own truth-tribunal, including those whose bodies are positioned to impose their will on the rest of us, for example, the bodies of corporate-sponsored climate change deniers or herd immunity economists. If moral decisions are as readily justified on the basis of bodily experience as variable-eliminating experiment, how do we adjudicate conflicts? Is skepticism about climate change warranted just because we don't experience it directly? Weston thinks so, arguing that while climate change is occurring and anthropogenic, the "intransigence" of "progressives" who insist that skepticism reflects nothing more than invested interests and/or willful ignorance says more about the prejudices of class-privilege than about the skepticism of those whose experience doesn't support the scientific consensus, (Weston, p. 107). In other words, progressives are just stubborn and clinging to their lattes. But this isn't an argument for an alternative view of science. This is a moralizing accusation, namely, that to deny that the climate skeptic could have legitimate grounds for their skepticism is *unfair*. Westin's isn't a quest for reinterpreting the quest for knowledge, but rather an expression of indignance over the prospect that the climate skeptic (or any other naysayer) could be wrong, or at the very least isn't afforded a hearing *as* science. Her claims are, in fact, moral claims, and as such can be evaluated with the same attention and scrutiny we might apply to, say, the utilitarian, the rights-theorist, or the ecocentrist.

Weston argues, for example, that the important issue is not just about what "knowledge" is worth reclamation—but *who's*:

> [l]ong before climate change skepticism appeared on the North American scene, long before the fossil fuel industry paid lobbyists to spin credible research on environmental damage into "junk science," people like my Aunt Elsie were accustomed to consulting their bodies in order to decode shifts in both weather and climate. They also looked to the skies, of course, as well as the horizon and, eventually, to a new crop of college-educated professionals called meteorologists ... Like my great Aunt Elsie, some had proved highly skilled readers of corporeal signs. They were close observers of variations, large and small, in the way their bodies felt at work or in repose under different conditions, and they used those observations to make predictions. Secretions from the pores of the skin, pounding headaches, frizzy hair, creaking joints, and popping ankles found their way into debates about

the meaning of changes in cloud cover, annual snowfall, foggy dampness, or the desiccation shared by tongues and rose bushes after too many relentlessly sunny days. (p. 105)

The difficulty with Weston's account is that Aunt Elsie likely takes herself as neither doing science (Embodied Empiricism) nor as making any morally actionable claim. She's simply evincing her particular take on common sense: like Elsie, we consult experience in the ordinary course of assessing conditions and making predictions. Little would compel us to do otherwise precisely because we're not doing science and we're not rendering judgment, at least in any fashion that requires significant deliberation, generates anxiety about consequences, or worries about things like rights. We're just *talking* as people do— through a mix of impression, past experience, know-how, griping, guessing, and the like. There's not a great deal that hangs on such talk, and it's rare that the parties to it expect more from it than common sense. There's no "who's knowledge" to reclaim here, and we're not diminishing Aunt Elsie if we turn to a meteorologist, for example, to find out when a hurricane is likely to make landfall, its category strength, how much rainfall we can expect, and whether hurricanes are going to become more frequent and ferocious. That there's some guesswork with respect to modeling weather patterns doesn't make meteorologists merely "highly skilled readers of corporeal signs." And thank goodness— otherwise we'd likely see far more death and destruction.

In short, there are good reasons why we turn to meteorology and not Aunt Elsie to determine the path of a hurricane, and it's not, as Weston puts it, simply "disdain for a presumptively irrational public." Can science be arrogant? Sure. But arrogance is not itself evidence of truth or falsity, and that "there might be something to be learned from generation of aunts and uncles" is not discounted by science. It's simply *not* science. Indeed, it's when we're confronted with the prospect that our common sense is mistaken (hydrocarbons aren't inexhaustible), that we've missed something important (perhaps nonhuman animals have rights), or that our actions, however unwitting, produce harm (greenhouse gas emissions are warming the atmosphere), that our talk turns from talk to deliberation and debate about what we ought to do. And it's at these moments that we ought to consult what the sciences have to tell us about "clean coal," nonhuman animal consciousness, wearing masks, or greenhouse gas emissions. In other words, it's when our so-called common sense is challenged by evidence that shows we're getting it wrong that the capacity for good moral reasoning becomes essential—that appeal to moral principle displaces sweat and headaches, frizzy hair and creaky joints.

Sometimes we ignore the relevant science at no great cost. But sometimes the cost is catastrophic. Many of the folks who stayed behind to "ride out" Hurricane Florence (September, 2018) likely now wish they'd heeded the warning offered by meteorologists who, far more than readers of signs, made abundantly clear through images, graphs, and copious data precisely what was at stake if they stayed in their homes.[48] Similarly, TikTok influencer "Larz," likely has plenty of regret to offer from his Covid-19 hospital bed after having taken a "coronavirus challenge" that involved licking a toilet seat.[49] And willful ignorance is not, of course, left to the young: retired Texas congressman Rand Paul's article "The Coronavirus Hoax" not only encouraged reckless behavior that may have led to infection and potentially even death, his behavior ultimately ensnared his own son, congressman Rand Paul who continued to refuse to wear a mask or social distance while he awaited his own Covid-19 test results—which were positive.[50] The point is that the excuses father and son gave for their reckless behavior are not really different than Aunt Elsie's reliance on reading "corporeal signs," except for the consequences. Ignoring fact entails risk. Aunt Elsie can deny climate change because it's snowing in Buffalo, but we don't attribute such claims to a knowledge afforded by embodied empiricism; she's just wrong. Uncle Buck can ignore the link between his bacon-burgers and his coronary artery disease, but we'd be derelict if we didn't try to convince him otherwise. Rand Paul's behavior is despicable; it endangers others, some of whom may not have been able to combat a virus with little treatment and no vaccine. Even philosophy isn't exempt from failure borne of, for example, the desire to protect some cherished ideology. The philosopher René Descartes claimed that the screams of tortured animals were simply autonomic nervous system reactions, that only human beings had souls. But science has made clear that this is gross misjudgment. Indeed, we make sure our children never make these kinds of mistakes, and we insist that Descartes wasn't right until he was wrong. He was always wrong.[51] So, Weston's eco-phenomenology is neither a viable alternative view of knowledge nor, for the same reasons, can it be counted as a practicable ethic. The reason? Neither ethics nor science can be reduced to experience even if, as Dewey and Wood show, experience and especially the prospect of future experience can illuminate just why moral principle and objective knowledge matter. This latter is not a small thing—but it's no substitute for informed reason and principled judgment.

5.4   Eco-phenomenology and the Problem of Pseudoscience: Why Ethics Must Be Rooted in Knowledge

However else we interpret Weston's applause for science, in the end it really functions as an honorable-looking placeholder helping her make what is essentially a moral argument for defending the claims of those whose knowledge claims, she insists, have been ignored because of their class status. It's unfair, argues Weston, not to take Aunt Elsie's claims seriously, and our failure to do so derives not from the fact that, say, she's just wrong that a hurricane storm surge could swallow up her beachfront cottage; rather, we fail to take her refusal to leave seriously because we don't take her seriously—and that's unjust. While it's tempting, argues Weston, to dismiss climate change denial as the "misguided rejection of scientific findings that were otherwise abundantly clear," that "[o]n closer inspection… the appeal to bodies to evaluate predictions of ecological catastrophe [make] a certain cultural, historical, and *scientific* sense" (emphasis in original, p. 106):

> Could it be that at least some strains of climate change skepticism in North America owe their inspiration to science, rather than being hostile to scientific analysis? The only way to answer such a question is to set aside mythologies of the United States as a country filled with climate change "deniers," figured as irrational and anti-science, locked in combat with climate change "believers," portrayed as reliable reasoning subjects with the best interests of the planet at heart. Class tensions shadow this facile division into an "us" and a "them." (pp. 106–7)

The first mistake Weston makes is that it is false to claim that the United States is filled with climate change deniers. Fact is, according to a 2014 New York Times analysis, the United States boasts more deniers than any other industrialized country.[52] That there's an element of class in this high number of deniers owes itself to a number of factors, including poor environmental education. But that fact does not lend credence to the claim that we ought to take this variety of skepticism seriously. Whether folks understand the anthropogenic contribution to climate change or not, and whether this lack of understanding includes a class element does not make climate change any the less real or any less anthropogenic. The number of climate science deniers is certainly politically relevant; an ill-informed electorate tends to vote for ill-informed and too often self-aggrandizing representatives. But popularity of belief is not evidence of truth.

The second mistake Weston makes owes itself to a misunderstanding of what is basic to scientific method, namely, that there exist no claims science regards as beyond the pale of skeptical inquiry. Science is a fundamentally open-ended process whose most important epistemic and moral virtue is its deep-going commitment to review and revise even its most cherished premises and theories. That some strains of climate change skepticism are owed to science just is scientific method in action, and does not detract from the fact that over 97% of scientists working on these issues agree that climate change is occurring and is anthropogenic. But maybe we're being unfair. Perhaps Weston can bridge the gap between embodied empiricism and scientific method by showing that scientists themselves engage in both, thereby effacing the distinction between Aunt Elsie and the meteorologists.

Weston profiles several scientific experimenters such as Marie and Pierre Curie who withstood self-inflicted radiation burns, (p. 108),[53] Yamakawa Yukio who deliberately consumed irradiated crops, (p. 109),[54] and J.B.S. Haldane's experiment with the effects of drinking hydrochloric acid, (pp. 110–11).[55] She even entertains the possibility that "the radical acceleration of greenhouse gas emissions from burning fossil fuels amounts to a collective global self-experiment." But while each of these scientists doubtless added something of value to their understanding of the effects of a causal phenomenon, it seems unlikely in the extreme that any would count their experience itself in the *scientific* findings. That the Curies understood something about the experiential qualities of radiation burns doubtless motivated them to further explore the causal relationship of radiation to its ill-effects. But what's also true is that the facts about radiation were fully discoverable whether or not they had undertaken to irradiate themselves. And the same holds for each of the other cases Weston profiles. In other words, while a scientist may be inspired to use themselves as an experimental subject, and while this may afford them insight for future exploration, such self-experimentation is neither a necessary nor a sufficient condition for doing science, and it could just as well be misleading. Weston mistakes experience relevant, but not necessary, to science for doing science.

The pseudoscientific character of Weston's embodied empiricism is made even clearer when she entertains the prospect that the consequences of our failure to curb greenhouse gas emissions amount to a kind of "global self-experiment." She grants that "[a]ny such experiment would amount to an unplanned madcap design rather than a trial inflicted with the deliberation of a J.B.S. Haldane" (p. 111). But she then goes on to insist that there remains "another well-established way of wielding the body as technology in the history of science," and that this more deliberate strategy lends itself to a climate change skepticism we must take seriously beyond merely the ignorant denier versus the educated believer. She argues that "[w]hen placed in the service of scientific investigation, the body's senses can become a sensory apparatus as integral to obtaining results as any crucible, astrolabe, or barometer," and she gives several examples of weights and measures, the smelling of wounds, and the use of instruments like telescopes as extensions of the body, but not replacement given its potential sensory foibles. (pp. 111–13). There's much to be said here, but perhaps most obviously is that had these tools of embodied empiricism been as accurate and effective as Weston claims we'd not likely have developed instruments like barometers and astrolabs.

Still, it's the morally consequential implications of Weston's argument that should give us the greatest pause: while it may well be true that consulting with our bodies can direct us to a correct evaluation, this can also lead us horribly astray—*and there is no principled way to determine the difference*. History is littered with examples of these sorts of mistakes, many informed not merely by experience but by prejudices, preposterous assumptions about the planet and its inhabitants, religious preoccupations, and just plain stupidity. For examples, we need look no further than the false and morally decrepit beliefs that informed the Eugenics movement,[56] NAZI experimentation,[57] the forced removal of indigenous children from their parents to "kill the savage,"[58] Japanese "scientific research" whale hunting,[59] or Li Meng Yan's politically motivated conspiracy theory that Covid-19 is a Chinese biohazardous weapon.[60] That science has been utilized toward nefarious purposes is not the thing that's surprising. What's surprising, at least in Weston, is the prospect that we'd have to accept theories whose motives are plainly not knowledge, but often the maintenance of power, on the grounds that the experience of their proponents has to be accounted as legitimating. Among the purposes of good science is to liberate us from theories anchored in insupportable premises—regardless their motives. Thus, science itself must work from morally defensible premises, regular self-reflective as well as external and unbiased review, and open publicly available research results. It's scientific method with its demand for rigorous, falsifiable and repeated experiment that frees us from false beliefs that can cause irreparable harm. While science claims no perfect track record, skepticism with respect to its theories is at the end of the day less about class than whether the pursuit of knowledge will remain unfettered, socially supported, and valued.

That class status has been and remains a potent factor along with ethnicity, sex, and gender in access to good science education—that is a critically important moral, political, and environmental issue. But it won't be adequately addressed by erecting a straw argument that seeks to elevate lack of education to the status of an alternative avenue to knowing. Aunt Elsie's embodied empiricism will not help her when she denies that Hurricane Florence is likely to be made a more violent storm because of climate change. She should evacuate, and if she's unable because she's poor and has nowhere to go, that is a horrific moral and social tragedy. Surely any effort to comfort Aunt Elsie by affirming her climate skepticism in the wake—literally—of her demolished home would find at least disdain if not moral condemnation. If it's the job of a sound environmental ethic to help Aunt Elsie, it's first job is to tell her the truth about hurricanes—not humor her as a concession to her social and economic class when it would be better to insult her—and save her life.

5.5   Summary and Questions

Taking an especially dark incarnation of human chauvinism as his point of departure, Derrick Jensen argues for an ecocentric worldview equipped to confront the human excess he identifies as "civilization." *Endgame* is Jensen's sweeping condemnation of human institutions and practices, and it offers a roadmap for a radicalized adoption of Arne Naess' *Eight-Point Platform*, perhaps especially Point Six which direct us to envision a world "deeply different from the present." However, whereas Naess makes his focus policy and law, Jensen takes a far more uncompromising view of the strategies required to achieve a sustainable world. Jensen effectively disavows the precautionary principle, and thus raises anew question like "Can the quest for sustainability justify authoritarian policies or even the use of violence to bring the civilization responsible for our current environmental crisis to an end?" Naess and Jensen agree that the planet's capacity to support life is on a collision course with resource-destroying human activities. But while Naess sows the seeds for revolution, Jensen advocates for it as a moral duty, one that will not be realized by the beneficiaries of the status quo, but by those ready to overthrow it.

Naess and Jensen share aspirations for a sustainable future comprised of small human communities built on deep ecological values like "appreciating life quality" or the "profound awareness of the difference between bigness and greatness." But, Jensen argues, the struggle to establish such communities can't come from the civilization that's the cause of environmental collapse; it must come from those whose ecocentric moral compass prepares them to, as he puts it, "blow up the dams." But what counts as a morally defensible strategy to realize this aspiration raises some *very* thorny moral questions, for example, Naess' Platform Point Four: a "flourishing human life requires a smaller human population." Characterizing his own version of ecocentrism as "heartless" Jensen argues that our "deification" of human beings "has to stop," and that if his own death serves to reduce the human population, "well, that's life too." Death "serves the larger community, that helps stabilize and enrich the landbase."

Few dispute that human activity is responsible for crises like climate change, but what Jensen's example illustrates is the larger question: what would the world look like if we took the environment to be *the* preeminent value, the value that sets our moral compass and directs *all* of our decision-making? What if, in other words, we took *inherent worth* to be our moral lodestar? What would the recognition of such worth *as equal* across the spectrum of living and nonliving things mean for the concept of a life worth living? Here too, Naess and Jensen share a critical ecocentric concept. Yet, while Naess sees inherent worth as a governing ethical premise that can inform policy, Jensen offers *Twenty Premises* intended to justify its use as righteous weapon wielded by the ecocentric insurgent to take down civilization.

Despite the fact that Jensen is right to characterize our current environmental condition as urgent, one serious difficulty with his view is that arguments that target "civilization" can just as easily be deployed by despots to justify genocide as by righteous eco-warriors to justify "saving the planet." Can tell the difference other than in hindsight? The end of civilization, moreover, doesn't necessarily imply the emergence of a just society, and there's no mechanism or decision-making criteria offered by inherent worth that can supply direction for how survivors are to be treated after the apocalypse. Can noble ends sometimes justify violent means to achieve them? If we resort to violent means are we in danger of "throwing out the baby with the bathwater"? Can we build a morally defensible life worth living out of the rubble left after ending "civilization"?

These are very hard questions. Still, it would be rash to dismiss Jensen citing our discomfort with the prospect of utilizing violence to achieve sustainability. There's much more to Jensen's ecocentrism, including his view that experience has a valuable role to play in assessing what matters to an environmental ethic. Distinct from Naess' more abstract approach, Jensen's often beautiful, and sometimes terrifying accounts of his own experience (or that imputed to others), introduce us to the possibility that experience may play a more significant role in our moral reasoning than we've considered so far. Jensen offers a glimpse into a relatively new pursuit among environmental philosophers: *eco-phenomenology*. We canvas this new tradition through the work of several writers, John Dewey, David Wood, and Kath Weston. Wood and Weston, each in different ways, exemplify an approach to environmental theorizing that, while not aimed at developing an ethic *per se*, offer valuable insight to the question: can eco-phenomenology *ground* moral decision-making beyond what's felt to be right? Moving experiences, after all, can be life-changing. But, whether experience can *by itself* ground an ethic—that's a harder question to answer. Whose experience matters? Matters the most? Is the feeling that a particular experience (or even kind of experience) is good sufficient to say that it *is* good? Experience is inflected by many factors: sex, gender, ethnicity, culture, religion, class, history, geography, and previous experience. Do these aid or impede good judgment? If we step outside experience to make more objective judgments, is there any good reason to consult it at all?

To gain some better foothold on the relationship between experience and ethics, we turned first to philosopher John Dewey's *Art and Experience* discussion of what he calls the aesthetic *in* experience. Dewey argues that the kind of experience we regard as the most valuable is that which we see to be memorable—experience we would perhaps revisit and repeat, that we hope is possible in the future. Such experience, argues Dewey, includes an element of the aesthetic. Critically, however, the aesthetic *in* experience isn't significant for Dewey because it's necessarily comfortable or easy. It's significant because it affords an opportunity to query what are the necessary conditions that make it possible for future generations of creatures perceptually and cognitively equipped to appreciate the beautiful, the sublime, even the terrorizing. The aesthetic *in* experience prods us to question for whom it's the most possible, and whether this necessarily precludes nonhuman animals (it does not). It directs us beyond our own circumstances to those of others for whom experience of "the world" may be radically different. It prods us to consider the vital role of species diversity, ecological integrity, and whether we owe it to the future to preserve these values. What are the conditions that make memorable experience, possible? Is it the hope that it will remain possible in the future?

While Wood's aim is "What is Eco-phenomenology?" isn't an environmental ethic *per se*, his view of the relationship between our perceptual experience and the tangible world may help us see experience in a morally fresh light. Instead of "how do we get from experience to moral principle?" we might ask whether, "where appeal to principle fails, is there something in experience that can inspire more ethically defensible action? Can attention paid to value of our experience move us to more ecologically sustainable decisions?" After all, we've had thousands of years of hand-wringing application of moral principle to environmental issues—and we've still managed to produce climate change. Could taking our experience more seriously while not ignoring the relevant science offer fresh direction? Wood argues that the experience of our relationships with human and nonhuman others offers value to human life inaccessible by other means, and that while "naturalistic" accounts of these relationships tend to focus on their scientific elements, phenomenological accounts tend to be more holistic, focusing less on the causal or mechanical and more on the qualitative or *intentional*. Our experience, in other words, is always *about* something; it's *perspectival*—not merely reactive, and not necessarily objective. When we experience the world we organize it, make it sensible; we make it appreciable and rational.

Naturalistic accounts of experience might seem opposed to phenomenological ones. A naturalistic account can tell us how the *seeing* eye construes the dimensions of an object, but only a phenomenological one can tell us why we're *looking* at. According to Wood, however, while phenomenology opposes "naïve" naturalism's reduction of the world to its mechanical substructure, it needn't oppose the relationships that "engage" us as organisms, ourselves dependent on the natural world. Eco-phenomenology is the effort to spell out that engagement. Its moral relevance derives from the idea that it's one thing to *know* what is the right thing to do, but another to *feel* it. Perhaps it's one thing to examine one's life to determine its worth, but another to experience it. Maybe that's what being accountable to the future means, or could mean. For as much as we rightly value cool-headed reason and objective judgment, what moves us to act other than that we *want* to? Yet, while both Dewey and Wood see experience as a supplement to knowing, both treat experience's subjective character with caution. Not so for Weston who argues for an "embodied empiricism" that incorporates bodily sensations and perceptions into the ways in which we "register" empirical phenomena. In what she calls *bio-intimacy*, Weston argues that experience provides the basic instruments of scientific investigation, and then "uses reason to sort out the results." In a marked departure from Dewey and Wood, Weston argues that we can treat "the body as a technology for adjudicating truth" and that even where experience stands in conflict with the scientific consensus, we may right decide not to abandon the former for the latter.

One difficulty with Weston's approach to eco-phenomenology is that the view that knowledge derives from experience may be where science begins, but it's not where it ends. Weston's embodied empiricism collapses empirical investigation into experiential response, and thus invests experience with the power to subjugate fact to feeling, truth to "truthiness." Such a view reduces knowledge claims to mere opinion, and the moral claims premised on them to expressions preference. Epistemic relativism, in other words, leads to moral relativism—pretty shaky ground for an ethic. It gives us little reason to try to convince, for example, the climate change denier they're wrong. We tend to dismiss such folks as cranks, and Weston's right that this is a mistake. But she's right for the wrong reasons. We should not dismiss the climate change denier because denial too is a knowledge claim, and as such has the potential to do tremendous harm. No matter what principle we adopt, if we think we have a moral responsibility to challenge the climate change denier, we can't leave knowledge to experience; we can't swap the objective for the subjective. Yet it's Weston's effort to valorize the subjective that makes her view *about* moral considerability: whatever the science, to deny the climate change denier could have legitimate grounds for their denial is *unfair*. But why? According to Weston, among the reasons we dismiss the denier's claims are included elements irrelevant to scientific investigation—such as class or ethnicity. Yet, while Weston is no doubt right to point out that science can be elitist, this does not validate the claims of the denier any more than the parent who refuses to vaccinate their child. There just are facts of the matter here regardless our criticism of science as an institution. So, in the end what's troubling about Weston's argument for treating would-be knowers fairly is that she's made out an essentially moral claim, but one detached from any criterion of evaluation that could accord it moral force. In short, a moral compass that points in the direction of all "truths" are equal, even if for the sake of treating others fairly, points nowhere at all, except, perhaps, to the catastrophe of wasted time and vanishing options.

1. How does Derrick Jensen embody a radicalized version of Arne Naess' *Eight-Point Platform*? What is the ecocentric imperative?

2. What are the *Twenty Premises*? Why does Jensen call for the end of civilization? How do the Premises raise the issue of what ends justify what means?

3. What does John Dewey's discussion of the aesthetic *in* experience bring to the development of an eco-phenomenological approach to an environmental ethic?

4. What does David Wood's attempt to bridge the chasm between experiential and naturalistic approaches to knowledge offer to developing an environmental ethic? What role is played by "naïve naturalism"? "Engaged organisms"?

5. How does Kath Weston's eco-phenomenology differ importantly from either Wood's or Dewey's? What larger role does she accord to experience? What's "embodies empiricism"?

6. How is Weston's approach a cautionary tale about just how much we can invest in the subjective if what we aspire to in the end is a viable environmental ethic?

Annotated Bibliography

Barry, Brian. "Sustainability and Intergenerational Justice." *Theoria* 45 (89), (June 1997), pp. 43–65.

Barry argues that achieving environmental sustainability must include taking seriously the notion of justice across generations.

Bigwood, Carol (1993). *Earth Muse: Feminism, Nature and Art* (Philadelphia: Temple University Press).

Taking the phenomenological approach of Martin Heidegger as her inspiration, Bigwood argues that the feminine has been suppressed in much of Western culture and that his mirrors harm done to nonhuman nature.

Brown, Charles and Ted Toadvine, eds. (2003). *Eco-Phenomenology: Back to the Earth Itself* (New York: SUNY Press).

In this anthology, the reader is introduced to a wide range of eco-phenomenological approaches to our relationship with and experience of nonhuman nature.

Dewey, John (1934). *Art as Experience* (New York: Perigee Books).

Though ostensibly about works of art or architecture, Dewey's argument for the aesthetic *in* experience offers not only an avenue for translating from ordinary experience into experience of a work of art, but also for the aesthetic appreciation of nonhuman nature grounded in the ecological conditions that make experience worth remembering possible.

Jensen, Derrick (2016). *The Myth of Human Supremacy* (New York: Seven Stories Press).

Building on arguments from Endgame, Jensen takes on the common presupposition that human beings are culturally and intellectually superior to nonhuman beings. He argues that this view is a myth that, insofar as it facilitates a divorce of human beings from nonhuman nature, will likely result in self-defeat.

Jensen, Derrick and Aric McBay (2009). *What We Leave Behind* (New York: Seven Stories Press).

Jensen and environmental activist Aric McBay argue for a vision of sustainability premised on the claim that waste is also food, and that this critical cycle of decay and regeneration must be restored.

Jensen, Derrick (2006). *Endgame, Volume One: The Problem of Civilization* (New York: Seven Stories Press).

In this landmark work of ecocentric philosophy, Jensen effectively radicalizes the vision captured by his predecessors, particularly Arne Naess. Jensen argues that the only avenue for realizing a morally defensible world is to end "civilization," replacing it with small human communities that live in harmony with nonhuman nature. Jensen's "Twenty Premises" lay out the argument as a manifesto for revolution.

Jensen, Derrick (2006). *Endgame, Volume Two: Resistance* (New York: Seven Stories Press).

Following directly on *Endgame, Volume One*, "The Resistance" builds on Jensen's argument for bringing down "civilization" and expands it to include a number of broad-ranging proposals for how this task might be accomplished—blow up the dams—and what an ecocentric future might look like.

Jensen, Derrick (2000). *A Language Older Than Words* (New York: Context Books).

Essentially autobiographical, the ecocentric arguments of *Endgame* are foreshadowed in the analogy Jensen draws between the suffering he experienced as a child via an abusive father and the destruction of the planet by "civilization."

Kennedy, Tara. "*Heidegger and the Ethics of the Earth: Eco-Phenomenology in the Age of Technology*," Doctoral Dissertation, 2014, University of New Mexico Digital Repository. http://digitalrepository.unm.edu/phil_etds/7.

Kennedy argues against what she defines as the "ontotheological" conception of living and nonliving things that converts them into "nothing more than meaningless resources," a view responsible, she argues, for our current environmental crisis. She offers an eco-phenomenology modeled after the work of Martin Heidegger in place of this view.

Lee, Wendy Lynne. "Aristotle's Ecological Conception of Living Things and its Significance for Feminist Theory." *Diametros* 13, (grudzień 2007), pp. 68–84.

Lee argues that what careful scholarly excavation of Aristotle's *de Anima* shows is that his view of living things—entities whose capacity for motion is internal to their bodies—is essentially ecological. This reading of Aristotle can offer new insight for feminist theorizing about the intimate relationship between human beings and nonhuman nature capable of countering, for example, Cartesian conceptions of human separation from nonhuman nature.

McBay, Aric, Lierre Keith, and Derrick Jensen (2011). *Deep Green Resistance: Strategy to Save the Planet*, (New York: Seven Stories Press).

In this anthology, the authors expand on ecocentric strategies for the resistance Jensen sketches in *Endgame*.

McDonald, Hugh (2003). *John Dewey and Environmental Philosophy* (New York: SUNY Press).

McDonald offers unique insight into the field of environmental ethics, including Holmes Rolston III, Baird Callicott, and Tom Regan, arguing for a reading of John Dewey that situates him against anthropocentrism and with the main stream of ecocentric thinkers.

Robins, Nicholas A. (2011). *Mercury, Mining, and Empire: The Human and Ecological Cost of Silver Mining in the Andes* (Bloomington, IN: Indiana University Press).

In this excellent work of ecological history, Robins details the very real costs of silver mining to human health, geopolitical conquest, and ecological integrity—across geography, religion, politics, and the back-breaking labor of the indigenous peoples of the Andes.

Scarce, Rik (1990). *Eco-Warriors: Understanding the Radical Environmental Movement* (New York: Routledge).

In this manifesto, Rik Scarce introduces us to a moral argument for rejecting mainstream environmentalism, and embracing radicalized ecocentrism.

Wallace-Wells, David. (2019). *The Uninhabitable Earth: Life After Warming* (New York: Penguin, Tim, Duggan Books).

Wallace Wells argues that the climate crisis could result in a planet unfit for human life. We needn't merely imagine, he argues, a planet so degraded that none but the most miserable human culture could survive it—we are nearing that reality.

Weston, Kath. (2017). *Animate Planet: Making Visceral Sense of Living in a High-Tech Ecologically Damaged World* (Durham, NC: Duke University Press.

Weston's eco-phenomenology captures both some of the most compelling features of taking experience seriously as a guide to judgment and some of its pitfalls, especially with respect to our understanding of the role of science in assessing the impacts of climate change.

White, Lynn. "The Historical Roots of our Ecological Crisis." *The American Association of the Advancement of Science* 155 (3767), (March 10, 1967). https://science.sciencemag.org/content/155/3767/1203.

Wood, David. "What is Eco-Phenomenology?" *Research in Phenomenology* 31 (1), (2001), pp. 78–95.

Wood argues that eco-phenomenology offers a way to reconcile significant differences between phenomenological accounts of experience and scientific ones. Utilizing time as a kind of connective tissue, he argues that it is possible to build a bridge between two very different approaches to the natural world.

Yusoff, Kathryn (2018). *A Billion Black Anthropocenes or None* (Minneapolis, MN: University of Minnesota Press).

Yusoff offers a compelling analysis of what she calls "white geology," that is, the history of extractivist practices from the point of view of deep-going structural inequalities of race.

Online Resources

1. Audre Lorde, "The Master's Tools Will Never Dismantle the Master's House," https://collectiveliberation.org/wp-content/uploads/2013/01/Lorde_The_Masters_Tools.pdf.
2. X Malcolm, "Malcolm X's Speech at the Founding Rally of the Organization of Afro-American Unity," *Blackpast.org*, https://blackpast.org/1964-malcolm-x-s-speech-founding-rally-organization-afro-american-unity.
3. *Sierra Club*, https://www.sierraclub.org/home.
4. *Environmental Defense Fund*, https://www.edf.org.
5. Derrick Jensen, "Interview: Radical Environmentalism: 'We Need to be ready to Risk Our Lives,'" *DW*, September 6, 2020, https://www.dw.com/en/radical-environmentalism-we-need-to-be-ready-to-risk-our-lives/a-53729503.
6. Derrick Jensen, "This [Coronavirus Panic] is Going to Make Our Hatred for Nature even Stronger," *YouTube*, March 23, 290, https://www.youtube.com/watch?v=ZMvROk6jivw.
7. Michael Shellenberger, *The Breakthrough Institute*, https://thebreakthrough.org.

8. Michael Shellenberger, *Environmental Progress*, https://environmental-progress.org/founder-president.
9. Thomas Catenacci, "Environmentalist Issues Climate Scare Apology, Forbes Removes Article," *Daily Caller*, June 30, 2020, https://dailycaller.com/2020/06/30/michael-shellenberger-environmentalist-climate-scare-apology-forbes-article.
10. Michael Shellenberger and Ted Nordhaus, "Campaign to Stop Fracking Sacrifices Nature for Ideology: Column," *USA Today*, July 16, 2015, https://www.usatoday.com/story/opinion/2015/07/16/natural-gas-renewable-fuels-fracking-column/27089397.
11. Adele Peters, "The Destructive havoc that Fracking Has Caused to the Environment, by the Numbers," *Fast Company*, April 14, 2016, https://www.fastcompany.com/3058901/the-destructive-havoc-that-fracking-has-caused-to-the-environment-by-the-numbers.
12. Graham Readfern, "The Environmentalist's Apology: How Michael Shellenberger Unsettled Some of His Supporters," *The Guardian*, July 3, 2020, https://www.theguardian.com/environment/2020/jul/04/the-environmentalists-apology-how-michael-shellenberger-unsettled-some-of-his-prominent-supporters.
13. Graham Ibid. Readfern, "The Environmentalist's Apology: How Michael Shellenberger Unsettled Some of His Supporters," *The Guardian*, July 3, 2020.
14. Noah Smith, "Biden's green Plans Put the Best Ideas of his Rivals to Work," *Bloomberg*, July 15, 2020. https://www.bloomberg.com/opinion/articles/2020-07-15/biden-s-green-plans-put-sanders-warren-s-and-best-ideas-to-work.
15. Noah Ibid. Smith, "Biden's green Plans Put the Best Ideas of his Rivals to Work," *Bloomberg*, July 15, 2020.
16. Alston Chase, "Harvard and the Making of the Unibomber," *The Atlantic*, June, 2020, https://www.theatlantic.com/magazine/archive/2000/06/harvard-and-the-making-of-the-unabomber/378239.
17. Karl Marx, *The Communist Manifesto*. https://www.marxists.org/archive/marx/works/1848/communist-manifesto.
18. "What is Carrying Capacity?" *The Carrying Capacity Network*. https://www.gdrc.org/uem/footprints/carrying-capacity.html.
19. Ritchie, Hannah, and Max Roser. "Fossil Fuels." *Our World in Data*. https://ourworldindata.org/fossil-fuels.
20. Kris Lane, "Potosi Mines," *Oxford Research Encyclopedia: Latin American History*, May 4, 2015, https://oxfordre.com/latinamericanhistory/view/10.1093/acrefore/9780199366439.001.0001/acrefore-9780199366439-e-2.

21. "Gaia Hypothesis," *Courses at Harvard*. https://courses.seas.harvard.edu/climate/eli/Courses/EPS281r/Sources/Gaia/Gaia-hypothesis-wikipedia.pdf.
22. Evan Hill, et al. "How George Floyd was Killed in Police Custody," *New York Times*, May 31, 2020, https://www.nytimes.com/2020/05/31/us/george-floyd-investigation.html.
23. Derrick Jensen, *Deep Green Resistance*. https://deepgreenresistance.org/en.
24. Adam Vaughn, "Humans Have Destroyed a Tenth of Earth's Wilderness in 25 years—Study," *The Guardian*, September 8, 2016, https://www.theguardian.com/environment/2016/sep/08/humans-have-destroyed-a-tenth-of-earths-wilderness-in-25-years-study.
25. Poppy Noor, "The U.S. Politicians Volunteering Other People's Lives to Fight Covid-19," *The Guardian*, July 22, 2020, https://www.theguardian.com/world/2020/jul/22/us-reopening-politicians-volunteering-peoples-lives-coronavirus.
26. "The Southern Argument for Slavery," *U.S. History: Pre-Columbian to the New Millennium*, https://www.ushistory.org/us/27f.asp.
27. "What is Crohn's Disease?" *Crohn's and Colitis Foundation*, http://www.crohnscolitisfoundation.org/what-are-crohns-and-colitis/what-is-crohns-disease.
28. Robert Burton, "The Certainty Bias: A Potentially Dangerous Mental Flaw," *Scientific American*, October 9, 2008, https://www.scientificamerican.com/article/the-certainty-bias.
29. Dickens Olewe, "Stella Immanuel: The Doctor Behind the Unproven Coronavirus Cure Claim," *BBC News*, July 29, 2020, https://www.bbc.com/news/world-africa-53579773.
30. Aristotle, *de Anima*, trans. J.A. Smith. *Digital Commons*, http://classics.mit.edu/Aristotle/soul.html.
31. Gary O. Grimm, "Loon Calls and Malamute Howls," *YouTube*, https://www.youtube.com/watch?v=Qj554TW6F2U.
32. T Leddy, "Dewey's Aesthetics," *Stanford Encyclopedia of Philosophy*, September 29, 2006, https://plato.stanford.edu/entries/dewey-aesthetics.
33. *Sea Turtle Conservancy*, https://conserveturtles.org/information-about-sea-turtles-their-habitats-and-threats-to-their-survival.
34. Kristin Conger, "Why do Gorillas Build New Nests Every Night?" *How Stuff Works*, https://animals.howstuffworks.com/mammals/gorilla-nests1.htm.
35. Jonathan Watts, "Sumatran Elephants Upgraded to Critically Endangered Status," *The Guardian*, January 24, 2012, https://www.theguardian.com/environment/2012/jan/24/sumatran-elephant-upgraded-critically-endangered.

36. Jorah Kai, "Lighthouse Diaries: Interview with an Anti-Masker," *Chong-qing*, August 18, 2020, https://www.ichongqing.info/2020/09/03/the-lighthouse-diaries-interview--withan-anti-masker.

37. Brian Resnick, "Why Florida's Red Tide is Killing Fish, Manatees, and Turtles," *Vox*, October 8, 2018, https://www.vox.com/energy-and-environment/2018/8/30/17795892/red-tide-2018-florida-gulf-sarasota-sanibel-okeechobee.

38. Markus Seidel, "Epistemic Relativism: A Constructive Critique," *Notre Dame Philosophical Reviews*, October 29, 2014, https://ndpr.nd.edu/news/epistemic-relativism-a-constructive-critique.

39. Graham Readfearn, "More Terrifying Than Trump? The Booming Conspiracy Culture of Climate Change Denial," *The Guardian*, December 6, 2016, https://www.theguardian.com/environment/planet-oz/2016/dec/06/more-terrifying-than-trump-the-booming-conspiracy-culture-of-climate-science-denial.

40. *InfoWars*, https://www.infowars.com.

41. *Climate Depot*, https://www.climatedepot.com.

42. Elizabeth Williamson, "Judge Rules Against Alex Jones and *Infowars* in Sandy Hook Lawsuit," *New York Times*, August 30, 2018, https://www.nytimes.com/2018/08/30/us/politics/alex-jones-infowars-sandy-hook-lawsuit.html.

43. Zack Budryk, "Infectious Disease Expert Calls White House Advisors Herd Immunity Claims Pseudoscience," *The Hill*, October 18, 2020, https://thehill.com/homenews/sunday-talk-shows/521605-infectious-disease-expert-calls-white-house-advisers-herd-immunity.

44. "Herd Immunity," *Association for Professionals in Infection Control and Epidemiology* (APIC), https://apic.org/monthly_alerts/herd-immunity.

45. Tanveer Adyel, "Accumulation of Plastic Waste During Covid-19," *American Association for the Advancement of Science* (AAAS), September 11, 2020, https://science.sciencemag.org/content/369/6509/1314.

46. Gigi Kwik Gronvall and Rachel West, "We Cannot Rely on Magical Thinking: herd Immunity is Not a Plan," *STAT*, October 16, 2020, https://www.statnews.com/2020/10/16/we-cannot-rely-on-magical-thinking-herd-immunity-is-not-a-plan.

47. Shashank Bengali, "The Covid-19 Pandemic is Unleashing a Total Wave of Plastic Waste," *Los Angeles Times*, June 13, 2020, https://www.latimes.com/world-nation/story/2020-06-13/coronavirus-pandemic-plastic-waste-recycling.

48. "Hurricane Florence, September 14, 2018," *National Weather Service*. https://www.weather.gov/ilm/HurricaneFlorence.

49. Poppy Noor, "If I Get Corona, I Get Corona: The Americans Who Wished They'd Taken Covid-19 Seriously," *The Guardian*, March 28, 2020, https://www.theguardian.com/lifeandstyle/2020/mar/28/americans-who-dont-take-coronavirus-seriously.

50. Poppy Ibid. Noor, "If I Get Corona, I Get Corona: The Americans Who Wished They'd Taken Covid-19 Seriously," *The Guardian*, March 28, 2020.

51. René Decartes, "René Descartes: *How to Do Animal Rights*, http://www.animalethics.org.uk/descartes.html.

52. Paul Krugman, "Donald and the Deadly Deniers," *New York Times*, October 15, 2018, https://www.nytimes.com/2018/10/15/opinion/trump-climate-change-deniers-republican.html.

53. Nancy Froman, "Marie and Pierre Curie and the Discovery of Polonium and radium," *The Nobel Prize*, https://www.nobelprize.org/prizes/themes/marie-and-pierre-curie-and-the-discovery-of-polonium-and-radium.

54. "Is Food Irradiation Dangerous?" *McGill Office for Science and Society*, https://www.mcgill.ca/oss/article/health-you-asked/food-irradiation-dangerous.

55. "J.B.S. Haldane," *ThoughtCo*, https://www.thoughtco.com/about-jbs-haldane-1224843.

56. Andrea Denhoed, "The Forgotten Lessons of the American Eugenics Movement," *The New Yorker*, April 27, 2016, https://www.newyorker.com/books/page-turner/the-forgotten-lessons-of-the-american-eugenics-movement.

57. "Nazi Medical Experiments," *Holocaust Encyclopedia*, https://encyclopedia.ushmm.org/content/en/article/nazi-medical-experiments.

58. Charla Bear, "American Indian Boarding Schools Haunt Many," *National Public Radio*, May 12, 2008, https://www.npr.org/templates/story/story.php?storyId=16516865.

59. Chris Baynes, "Japan Slaughters 122 Pregnant Whales for "Scientific Research," *The Independent*, May 29, 2018, https://www.independent.co.uk/news/world/asia/japan-whale-hunting-scientific-research-minke-whales-antarctic-southern-ocean-a8374291.html.

60. Bruce Y Lee, "Whistleblower Claiming China Created Covid-19 has Ties to Steve Bannon," *Forbes*, September 176, 2020, https://www.forbes.com/sites/brucelee/2020/09/17/whistleblower-claiming-china-created-covid-19-coronavirus-has-ties-to-steve-bannon/#685c87bb22d5.

6

ENVIRONMENTAL JUSTICE: ECOLOGICAL FEMINISM, SOCIAL JUSTICE, AND ANIMAL RIGHTS

6.1 Climate Change and Environmental Justice

Among the questions that have guided this introduction to environmental ethics has been "When is a planet a *world*?" My hope is that it's clear that what makes a planet a world has to do with all of the ways living and nonliving entities interact on its surface, dwell its depths, inhabit its inclines, canopies, and atmosphere. Like all living things, we human beings are dependent on the planet, its resources and its atmosphere. But the ways we navigate that dependence, creating a multitude of worlds, that is, cultures, religions, forms of government, and systems of moral decision-making, as we go, vary greatly. Geography, proximity to potable water, food security, exposure to heat, cold, disease, and the potential for conflict, as well as factors like sex, gender, race, and class, all play a role in the making of worlds whose benefactors and beneficiaries, winners and losers, impact not merely the future of these worlds, but that of the planet that sustains them. The one thing that binds us all, human and nonhuman, is a planetary environment jeopardized not only by reckless actions, but by inaction, inertia, and denial, especially of the effects of greenhouse gas emissions for the planet's atmosphere.

Worlds are more than planets and, at least according to the ideas, theories, and arguments we've considered thus far, more than human entitlements. We have no other home, and that bodes quite ill if we continue to do damage to this one. Even those who see the planet as merely a repository of resources know that a future without access to clean water, clean air, one that's free from resurgent viral outbreak, firenadoes, tsunamis, hurricanes, and tornadoes is bound for loss, suffering, and violence. Whether these crises take the form of war, terrorism, survival migration, or disease, what we know is that the most vulnerable of the

This is Environmental Ethics: An Introduction, First Edition. Wendy Lynne Lee.
© 2022 John Wiley & Sons, Inc. Published 2022 by John Wiley & Sons, Inc.
Companion Website: https://thisisphilosoph.wordpress.com

present will likely be all the more so in that future dystopia. Yet, we still traffic in nihilistic fictions like the myth of endless resources, the possibility of achieving herd immunity, and the delusion that so-called free markets can address our environmental problems. The many worlds of our cultures, governments, religious traditions, and institutions are composed of diverse, complex, synergistic, and evolving relationships, all of which have the planet as their existential core, most if not all of which remain distorted by human chauvinism in its racist, sexist, and speciesist incarnations. Thanks to the structural inequalities and bigotries built into virtually every human society, the worlds of a fortunate few are secured at the expense of those inhabited by the very many. But social and environmental injustice is as vital a part of environmental ethics as are questions about, for example, the place of experience in moral decision-making or whether moral extensionism is a viable route to the life worth living.

The first priority for any national or global movement in the direction of environmental justice is the explicit recognition that climate change is *anthropogenic*, and that the crisis human activity combined with denial has created is urgent. Now more than ever, what we need is an ethic that helps us to see not only how our many worlds, just and unjust, depend on the planet, but one that can offer direction for evaluating the social and economic institutions culpable for the disproportionate harm the climate crisis imposes on the most vulnerable. Similarly, the Covid-19 pandemic isn't merely a health crisis; it shines a highly revealing light on social and economic inequality. Researchers Caitlyn Brown and Martin Ravallion argue, for example, that "many of the risk factors associated with the severity of Covid-19 are correlated with income. Poor people often have a harder time isolating as a means of protecting themselves from infection,"[1] and according to the United Nations report, "Coronavirus Vs. Inequality," while pandemic "exposes the weaknesses in every society," it's unsurprising that "[d]eveloping countries, and those in crisis, will suffer the most." The report reserves, however, its most sobering assessment for the effects of the pandemic for women who make up the majority of first responders across the globe:

> Women are particularly exposed during health crises. They make up the bulk of the first healthcare responders. If they are working from home, they will likely shoulder an even greater burden of housework and childcare, and they are, in too many cases, in greater danger with their partners. Mounting evidence suggests domestic violence is surging worldwide as a result of lockdowns.[2]

What's clear, in other words, is that the structural inequalities that characterize the status quo of the global order are brought into stark relief by health crises that know no borders geopolitical or geographic. The current pandemic, however, will eventually be able to be tamed through the use of therapeutics and vaccines. A far more daunting, if less tangibly visceral catastrophe confronts us in the potential of the climate crisis to alter the very conditions of life on earth—and it has no vaccine other than radical change in human behavior.

Although many similarities with respect to impacts on vulnerable populations characterize the Covid-19 pandemic and the climate crisis, the challenge posed by the latter is different and, short of a plague for which no vaccine is possible, ultimately greater. There are many reasons for this ranging from our disposition to evade and deny the fact of climate change, to the relative unpredictability inherent in its implications, to rising forms of "vulture" capitalism that seeks to take advantage of the fear and anxiety created by the crisis. An eco-phenomenologist might note that while we can experience in real time the effects of the virus in the faces of the sick and the dying, the effects of the climate crisis are more gradual, less tangible, and thus more readily evaded or denied. A positive test for Covid-19 is presented to us as an indisputable fact. The ferocity of a California wildfire can be diminished by references to poor forest management. The fact that this latter is a bad faith excuse to deny the scientific reality in the interest of oil and gas development, coal mining, animal agriculture, and other greenhouse gas disgorging enterprise only reiterates our commitment to the myths that endanger us.

Neither pandemic nor the climate crisis poses a danger to the planet *itself*. Far from it; Earth will remain long after human beings have vanished in the course of vanquishing so many others. "We," however, do not endanger the planet's capacity to recuperate. In fact, it's a tiny few who are disproportionately culpable not only for destabilizing the planet's ecological integrity, but for encouraging the rest of us to believe that there is no damage that cannot be remediated through the right technology, the right policy, the right political and social order. Captains of industry, heads of state, heirs of largesse, themselves mostly male, white, wealthy, and Western(ized), so depend on our conceiving of ourselves first and foremost as consumers that even when we're presented with moral atrocity like the murder and dismemberment of the journalist Jamal Khoshoggi,[4] the government's failure to locate the parents of 545 migrant children separated at the US–Mexico border,[5] or a proposal for a "herd immunity" that would require the deaths of millions to achieve,[6] we're more likely to seek out scapegoats than confront our own complicity in injustice. Our leaders, themselves beholden to interests directly responsible for the climate crisis, are more likely to evoke slogans like "energy independence," "national security," or economic necessity to "justify" ignoring a murder, a parentless child, or potentially preventable deaths. But such leaders are also emboldened by constituents willing to be persuaded to cry foul on the truth-tellers in order to double down on the myths that preserve their own aspirations for a piece of an ever dwindling pie.[7] Crucial to recognize is that everything in this fictional world of endless resources, endless consumption, and technological fantasy depends on the planet that sustains it. However horrific the murder of Jamal Khashoggi, and the crass expression of value for our oil-driven relationship with the Saudi government over his life, it's arguably cut from the same cloth as, say, our relentless assault on rhino and elephant populations for their tusks,[8] ignoring melting Arctic ice sheets that threaten polar bears,[9] or demanding that meat-processing plants remain open despite cases of viral outbreak.[10] A few benefit, but many suffer. According to the ecofeminists, these keepers of the status quo bear an unequal share of the blame for despoiling the planet, jeopardizing its ecologies in what is an inevitably nihilistic bid to retain the comforts of power.

6.2   Ecological Feminism: Intersectional Analysis and Environmental Justice

6.2.1   Environmental Crisis and Structural Inequality

Incorporating many of the insights and ideas of earlier chapters, we'll now examine a last suite of arguments that share in common not only the commitment to environmental integrity and respect for nonhuman animal life, but the conviction that if we're going to make good on the *worth* of the life worth living, we must pay equal attention to matters of political, social, economic, and environmental justice. That we're unlikely to effectively address any of these without addressing them all wherever they intersect is the key premise of *ecological feminism—ecofeminism* for short.[11] These arguments seek to show that a *sustainability* that ignores matters of social justice, retaining instead the patriarchal and racist social order responsible for environmental damage, offers a future survivable for the few but hardly desirable for the many.[12] Once we see that the beneficiaries of policies that ignore the implications of the climate crisis are largely the same as those culpable for exploitive labor practices, expanded forms of oil and gas extraction, weak environmental law, poor public health policy, and ecologically destructive deregulation, it becomes clear, argue the ecofeminists, that an environmental ethic *is and must be* an ethic of social, economic, political *and* ecological integrity premised first and foremost on the critique of institutions responsible for injustice at every level of the global order.

Each from a specifically feminist *and* environmental perspective, theorists like Karen Warren, Carol Adams, Chaone Mallory, Val Plumwood, and Wendy Lynne Lee—among a wide and varied array of others—take their lead from Audre Lorde's seminal insight: *we cannot dismantle the master's house with the master's tools.*[13] We can't, in other words, expect institutions that depend on the oppression of women, human slavery, the commodification of nonhuman animals, the myth of endless resources, and the belief that our oceans and atmosphere can function as toilets in perpetuity, for their very survival to be willing participants in an environmental ethic that challenges their hegemony. While *British Petroleum* may try to downplay its contribution to climate change by changing its name (briefly) to *Beyond Petroleum*,[14] and while *Smithfield Farms* boasts a project for converting manure to natural gas, referring to itself as a "protein company" instead of a factory farm,[15] neither are likely to take sustainability beyond what sustains the profit-margins of their shareholders. As the makers of the documentary *Cowspiracy*, Kip Anderson and Keegan Kuhn, show, even the Big Green environmental organizations such as the *Sierra Club*, the *World Wildlife Federation*, or the *Environmental Defense Fund* are institutionally averse to the potential for alienating financial gifts from donors whose wealth derives from environmentally harmful and socially unjust practices— but whose donations help to green their public image.[16] In short, we shouldn't be surprised that at the corporate level, green-washing is no more green than counterfeit dollar bills can buy food. But we can't necessarily count on non-governmental organizations to challenge the *status quo* either—not when their donors are patrons of the very institutions responsible for environmental destruction and social injustice.

Common to much ecofeminist critique is the effort to identify the root archetypes, that is, the origin of practices that become enduring institutions. They argue that the legacies of patriarchy, systemic racism, speciesism, and unchecked capitalism reveal patterns of oppression across axes, social, political, economic, and environmental. What each of these institutions have in common most importantly, however, is the capitalist idea that *everything* is a potential *commodity*, that is, a marketable good or service whose value lay not in its ecosystemic contribution, its beauty, or its vulnerability—but simply in its capacity to be exchanged for other things.[17] This idea is cemented into the bedrock not only of capital pursuits, but of military conquest, government, and social status. As ecofeminist Karen Warren puts it, because the self-preservation of these institutions depends on their capacity to take advantage of already existing *hierarchies of value*, their commitment to combat climate change is likely to take a backseat to the patriarchal, racist, and capitalist imperatives that sustain them. Nonetheless, however effectively the beneficiaries of such social structures sustain the illusion that the social order privileging them is fixed, natural, or ordained, theirs' is a house built on shifting sand. Simply put: environmental sustainability is incompatible with the logic of commodifiability because it's irreconcilable with the assumption that the planet is a repository of endless resources as well as a bottomless waste receptacle.[18] Some resources are renewable; some are not. Some resources are renewable, but only at great cost to environmental integrity and, often enough, to human health and welfare.

Consider, for example, the manufacture of solar panels, and the companies that advertise themselves as environmentally conscious such as *Ethical Electric* (*Clean Choice Energy* who purchases solar energy on the open market).[19]

> [H]owever good the conversion to wind and/or solar may sound, the facts are that, first, because companies like *Ethical Electric* ignore the *ecological costs* of industrial scale manufacture of solar panels and wind turbines and second, because they *ignore the cost to developing world laborers* exploited in the process, their ... promotion of Big Solar and Big Wind is as much beholden to the myth of endless resources as is Chevron's. Their resources are no different—marginalized workers and their commodified ecologies. (Lee, *Eco-Nihilism*, p. 31)

While solar and wind turbine powers are renewable, many of the resources they depend on are either not renewable, or they require environmentally destructive mining practices, or their manufacture process is itself polluting, producing greenhouse gases and exposing workers, especially in the developing world, to toxins and carcinogens:

> In addition to reinforcing a system—centralized corporatized utilities—that re- produces an economic and class system [in the U.S.] within which some benefit while others are likely to continue to struggle to pay their utility bills, still others—out of sight and apparently out of mind [in the developing world]—remain vulnerable to labor exploitation and to exposure to harmful toxins in the manufacture of these panels. As reported by *National Geographic*, although solar panels are certainly an improvement over coal-fired power plants because they produce renewable energy: "[f]abricating the panels requires caustic chemicals such as sodium hydroxide and hydrofluoric acid, and the process uses water as well as electricity, the production of which emits greenhouse gases. It also creates waste. These problems could undercut solar's ability to fight climate change and reduce environmental toxics. (How Green Are Those Solar Panels, Really?)" Among these chemicals is cadmium: "OSHA estimates that 300,000 workers are exposed to cadmium in the United States. Worker exposure to cadmium can occur in all industry sectors but mostly in manufacturing and construction. Workers may be exposed during smelting and refining of metals, and manufacturing batteries, plastics, coatings, and solar panels." (Lee, *Eco-Nihilism*, p. 30)

Far from raising key questions about whether an economic system dependent on the idea that everything qualifies as a potential commodity, and that the primary issue confronting humanity is whether demands of growing consumption is itself sustainable, companies like *Clean Choice* effectively seek to cash in on a species of consumption that makes us feel better, but does not, in fact, really ask us to *do* better: solar and wind. This is not to say there are no benefits shifting from fossil fuels to the alternatives; there are. But the benefits are significantly attenuated by the costs to the quest for environmental and social justice. Even a cursory look beneath the thin green surface of *Clean Choice's* business model reveals an enterprise whose focus on industrial-scale profit-generation leaves fully intact the economic system responsible for rising greenhouse gas emissions and the structural social inequalities that provide cheap labor to the manufacture of solar panels and wind turbines.

6.2.2   Threads of Moral Extensionism and of Ecocentrism

Given these realities, it's not surprising that, like the more radical positions adopted by their ecocentric allies, ecofeminist arguments contain an indelible element of resistance, with an important caveat: unlike the ecocentrists, ecofeminists reject the assumption that human beings are *equally* culpable for environmental deterioration. They argue that while there's plenty of blame to go around, there's more to be borne by those who value the marketable of the present over the sustainable for the future.[20] For ecofeminists, social and environmental justice are two sides of one coin. Environmental issues are about more than recognizing our short-sighted human chauvinism; they're about the consequences of social and economic inequality. Inequality, moreover, is certainly about economic class, but it's also about the role sex, gender, and race play in the production and consumption of commodities. It's structural inequality that makes the short-sighted possible and largely invisible—at least to those whose standard of success is deriving the greatest profit from the least investment.[21] Consumers of *Clean Choice's* solar panels are effectively given license to ignore the impacts of cadmium-exposure for workers in China by the sheer moral affirmation that attends their shift to renewables for Westerners. By externalizing the costs of maintaining a high level of energy consumption onto "others," Western consumers can claim environmental consciousness without having to make any substantial change in toward conservation.

Ecofeminists take it as given that there's no adequate response to environmental crises like climate change without at the same time attending to its social, political, and economic aspects,[22] and there's no morally defensible response, for example, to food and water insecurity, human and nonhuman migration, disease, or political violence without a simultaneous evaluation of the ways these events are driven, impacted, and worsened by environmental conditions. Most ecofeminist arguments are inherently *utilitarian* in the sense that they aim to extend the duty to maximize happiness and minimize suffering well beyond human agents.[23] But they also reach well beyond Peter Singer to show that merely expanding institutions that depend on taking advantage of patriarchal and racist social structures won't be sufficient to address suffering, much less mitigate against its causes. Many ecofeminist arguments also include an implicit notion of what it means to be a bearer of rights. Like Christopher Stone, many would endorse the extension of rights to nonsentient entities like trees. But moving beyond Stone, they offer keen insight into what kinds of entities have counted as paradigmatic rights-bearers, and why many women, indigenous peoples, and nonhuman animals as well as trees have been excluded. Many ecofeminists, moreover, find value in the arguments of ecocentric thinkers like Arne Naess and Derrick Jensen who argue that environmental reformist programs fail to address the underlying human chauvinism that privileges the anthropocentric over the eco-systemic. An analysis of human chauvinism without, however, a parallel analysis of its incarnation as heteropatriarchy is destined to be incomplete and distorted. Indeed, ecocentric prioritizing of ecological subjugation over all other forms of oppression finds little support in ecofeminists like Karen Warren whose work lays bare the mutually reinforcing relationships between human chauvinism, heteropatriarchy, and racism.

6.3   Groundbreaking Frameworks: Karen Warren and Carol Adams

6.3.1   Laying Bare the Logic of Domination

In her 1990 landmark essay, "The Power and the Promise of Ecological Feminism," Karen Warren argues that "ecological feminism is the position that there are important connections—historical, experiential, symbolic, theoretical—between the domination of women and the domination of nature, an understanding of which is crucial to both feminism and environmental ethics" (p. 123). Ecofeminism, she argues, offers a "distinctive framework" for the development of an environmental ethic that can take these connections seriously in the effort to address both environmental deterioration and social injustice. Critical to this understanding is the role played by the *logic of domination*, that is the ordering of relationships according to a hierarchy of value that systematically empowers some over others (pp. 123–4). Consider:

A1: Humans do, and plants and rocks do not, have the capacity to consciously and radically change the community in which they live.
A2: Whatever has the capacity to consciously and radically change the community in which they live is morally superior to whatever lacks this capacity.

A3: Thus, humans are morally superior to plants and animals.

A4: For any X and Y, if X is morally superior to Y, then X is morally justified in subordinating Y.

A5: Thus, humans are morally justified in subordinating plants and rocks. (p. 123)

The importance of laying out this hierarchy *as* an ordered hierarchy, argues Warren, is to (a) make its foundational assumptions evident, and (b) move the discourse concerning the relationship between feminist theory and environmental ethics beyond the merely descriptive. If having the capacity to consciously and radically change a community can substantiate the claim to moral superiority, it's a short step to justifying subordinating whatever is deemed inferior. As Warren shows, patriarchy is a natural fit:

B1: Women are identified with nature and the realm of the physical; men are identified with the "human" and the realm of the mental.

B2: Whatever is identified with nature and the realm of the physical is inferior to ("below") whatever is identified with the realm of the "human" and the realm of the mental; or, conversely, the latter is superior to ("above") the former.

B3: Thus, women are inferior to ("below") men; or, conversely, men are superior to ("above") women.

B4: For any X and Y, if X is morally superior to Y, then X is morally justified in subordinating Y.

B5: Thus, men are morally justified in subordinating women.

If we take it as given the assumptions imported from (A2) concerning what counts as morally superior, and then map these onto value dualisms that identify women with the physical/natural/emotional and men with consciousness/mentality/reason, it follows that not only are men superior and women inferior human beings, but that men are justified in subordinating women toward the realization of objectives identified as "human," but that in fact serve heteropatriarchal ends. The logic of domination establishes heteropatriarchy according to precisely the same reasoning as the original argument lays out the structure of human chauvinism. Both depend on "the assumed [value] dualism of the mental and the physical," subordinating the latter as inferior and elevating the former as superior, and both "sanction the twin dominations of women and nature" (p. 124).

Some, of course, will hasten to point out that with the success of the feminist movement, it's only a few ideological dinosaurs and a handful of religious relics who hold such antiquated ideas about women's place. Maybe; but, it's also not surprising that, in the interest of protecting their "petro-masculinity," we have recently witnessed a close alliance between climate change denial and a resurgence of anti-woman, anti-gay, anti-trans—heterosexist—pop-cultural personalities and organizations. Consider, for example, that the American Alt-Right's Proud Boys advertise themselves as "Western Chauvinists,"[24] whose hyper-masculinity takes the form of a vitriolic misogyny, anti-Semitism,[25] and violent white nationalism that has infiltrated even some of our most vital institutions.[26] Reporter Emily Atkin argues that the group embodies "petro-masculinity,"[27] evinced as climate change denial as well as in their members' refusal to mask in the interest of protecting themselves and others from Covid-19 infection.[28] The Proud Boys are neither outliers to American society, nor are they alone with respect to their ambitions. What the evidence "overwhelmingly" shows, argues Atkin, is that climate crisis deniers tend to be "conservative white males" trying to protect their cultural identity as "big strong fearless men."

Consider, for instance, self-professed "skeptic" Bjorn Lomborg whose ridicule of climate activist Greta Thunberg betrays the struggle to preserve a masculinity rooted more deeply in the dual myths of endless resources and male entitlement than in scientific fact, hence: *petro*-masculinity.[29] For men like Lomborg, argue Jonas Anshelm and Martin Hultman, the issue isn't whether the environment is threatened by the climate crisis; it's whether "a certain kind of modern industrial society built and dominated by their form of masculinity" is threatened by efforts to address the climate crisis. *New Republic* writer Martin Gelin captures the point succinctly:

> As conservative parties become increasingly tied to nationalism, and misogynist rhetoric dominates the far-right, Hultman and his fellow researchers at Chalmers University worry that the ties between climate skeptics and misogyny will strengthen. What was once a practical problem, with general agreement on the facts, has become a matter of identity. And fear of change is powerful motivation.[30]

The reason, in other words, we shouldn't be surprised at the endurance and ferocity of climate change denial is because it supports and is supported by an entire suite of long-established bigotries, structural inequalities, and entitlements which define a rapacious masculine identity against a planet and atmosphere that cannot sustain it. What the Proud Boys personify in their violent reaction, for example, to the Black Lives Matter movement for racial justice,[31] their applause of President Trump's nationalist "stand back and stand by" shout out,[32] their defense of "Stop the Steal" conspiracies about alleged fraud in the 2020 presidential election,[33] their insistence that Covid-19 deaths are inflated,[34] and their support for other white supremacist militias like the Boogaloo Bois, [35] is, at least according to Anshelm and Hultman, fear of change—but more specifically, fear of change that undermines their presumptive authority to dominate non-white men, all women, nonhuman animals, and the planet itself as a birthright.

As Warren would likely point out, groups like the Proud Boys may personify the logic of domination, but they also epitomize the losing battle to defend an incarnation of "Western values" inconsistent with a sustainable planet and atmosphere. Their armed displays, climate change denial, and association with violent militias evokes a mythical past that never existed for the vast majority of human beings in the forlorn effort to create a future their own destruction of resources makes impossible—even were it desirable; and it's not. What Warren's account of the logic of domination clarifies is that the reasoning that animates racism, heterosexism, and speciesism is not only functionally the same in each case, it underwrites the subjugation, commodification, and exploitation responsible for environmental, social, economic, and species injustice. Consider, for example, Carol Adam's *Neither Man nor Beast: Feminism and the Defense of Animals*. Expanding the logic of domination to nonhuman animals, Adams argues that if we substitute "animal" for women in (B), 1–5, it becomes apparent how a heteropatriarchal status quo is also speciesist. As Adams makes the point:

> The emphasis on differences between humans and animals not only reinforces fierce boundaries about what constitutes humanness, but particularly what constitutes manhood. That which traditionally defined humans from animals—qualities such as reason and rationality—has been used as well to differentiate men from women…We have inherited a Western philosophic tradition that posits women as closer to animals and as maintaining the animal functions… Historically…women were positioned between man and the other animals, so that women, and especially women of color, were traditionally viewed as neither man nor beast. (pp. 11–12)

Like Warren, Adams argues that it's not sufficient to simply insist that women are human beings and not animals since, first, while such claims may assert the equality of men and women, they do so by reinforcing the "malestream culture's contempt for animals within feminist theory," and second, human beings *are* animals. Merely elevating women's status fails to challenge the value dualisms responsible for the domination of nonhuman animals and nature and, as both Warren and Adams argue, is unlikely to result in the emancipation of either women or nonhuman animals since domination itself remains taken for granted as a natural aspect of nature and society. "This dualistic thinking is part of the problem," argues Adams; it "results from a patriarchal framing of the discussion" (p. 12). Just as Warren counters the classical liberal position that what feminism is about is limited to social and economic equality with men, insisting that "all feminists must oppose the logic of domination," Adams goes further, arguing that the only way to end any form of oppression is to end all; hence ecofeminists who challenge the logic of domination must challenge it in all of its incarnations, including speciesism.

6.3.2   The Naturalized Fictions that Imperil Us

The logic of domination only works so long as we take it for granted that there is a natural order which necessitates its hierarchies of value and status. Yet we have good reason to find such a view of the natural order suspect. That planetary resources are endless, that the atmosphere provides a limitless vault for pollutants and greenhouse gasses, that nonhuman animals lack sentience, that human activity can't alter the planet's capacity to support life—these are all fictions and falsehoods. We can add to the trash pile of false belief the view that race and/or sex bear on the capacity for reason and that the value of everything is reducible to exchange. These beliefs all serve the same set of beneficiaries, and for ecofeminist theorists, it's no surprise that these are mostly white, Western(ized), wealthy male captains of industry and heads of state—or their envious analogues among the working-class white men who fill the ranks of groups like the Proud Boys. Each of these fictions is built into the logic of domination, reinforcing a worldview as human chauvinistic, speciesist, heteropatriarchal, and racist as it is ultimately unsustainable. Applying Warren's critique of the logic can shed light on oppressive relationships of "feminine" to "masculine," "straight" to "gay," or the geopolitical domination of autocrat to subject, conqueror to indigenous, capitalist to laborer, consumer to consumed. But this is really just to stress the point that, for ecofeminist ethicists, what's at the root of *all* forms of domination is not only human chauvinism, but toxic or hegemonic masculinity—petro-masculinity.[36] The same worldview that permits rape turns a blind eye to environmental destruction. The same logic that turns human beings into slaves turns away from the suffering that is factory farming. If Warren and Adams are right, it might be more concise to call anthropogenic climate change, *masculinist* climate change. This, of course, would likely generate considerable backlash. Millions of women drive big cars, eat nonhuman animal bodies, wear fur, and do so as thoughtlessly as many men; and some men, of course, become vegans, care deeply for their children, agitate for animal welfare reforms, and seek lives worth living devoted to more sustainable worlds.[37]

Nevertheless, as Warren and Adams would likely point out, the fact that gender doesn't have a monopoly on environmental conscience does not imply that the logic of domination isn't deeply enculturated. A vegan coal miner, a wealthy heiress who gives up her millions to support an anti-whaling project, or a transgender senate candidate are notable, but exceptions rarely pose an effective challenge to a system of reified inequality. The very possibility of groups like the Proud Boys shows that the logic of domination survives as more than a vestige and, although we may rightly applaud it as progress, women who rise to positions of relative power in corporate culture or in government remain atypical or tokenized. A female CEO of Chevron may well scorn the Proud Boys' Neanderthal sexism, but we have little reason to think that she'll act to move the company away from fossil fuels. The Vegan coal miner can be applauded for taking a principled stand in his personal life, but given the potential danger to his job and his paycheck, we can hardly expect him to counsel his fellows to rise up against the mine owners if—like their counterparts at Tyson Chicken—they discover a bet pool to see how many mine workers contract the coronavirus.[38] Will the twenty-first century make progress on vital matters of social, racial, gender, and environmental justice? This is far from clear. From President Trump's decision to cancel US participation in the Paris Climate Accord[39] to the weakening of the *Endangered Species Act*,[40] to an escalation in the developing world's greenhouse gas emissions,[41] it seems the logic of domination is operating in full vigor—whatever strides vulnerable populations or their champions have otherwise made.

It's clear that the beneficiaries of the logic have no intention of forfeiting their unearned privilege, especially when climate change denial remains so lucrative.[42] It's thus not surprising that many of these are the same voices heard calling for the return to a racist and patriarchal social order thinly disguised as "traditional Western values."[43] That the denial of climate change is a self-defeating proposition is, of course, well beyond dispute from the point of view not only of science but *any* plausible environmental ethic. While Peter Singer might miss the extent to which a moral extensionism aimed at the inclusion of nonhuman animal suffering needs to account for the structural inequalities that subjugate (and feminize) not only animals but women, indigenous peoples, and non-white men, his argument that we must take suffering seriously opens an important door to its causes, and thus to the short step from factory farm misery to animal agriculture's greenhouse gas emissions. While Arne Naess' Eight-Point Platform solicits the criticism that its pitch to population control smacks of fascism, his ecocentrism also makes plain the urgency of our current environmental dilemma, and the kinds of measures we might be compelled to consider for confronting it. It's ecofeminism, however, that spells out the critical ligature connecting human chauvinism, speciesism, and heteropatriarchy, laying bare the *logic* that entrenches an unsustainable *status quo*, making the creation of more ethical and enduring institutions and practices so difficult.

6.4   The Logic of Domination, Nostalgia, Resentment, and Privilege: Jordan Peterson

6.4.1   Antithesis of "The Unexamined Life Is Not Worth Living"

The world where climate change denial can be made to appear rational is the antithesis of Socrates' "the unexamined life is not worth living." Divorced from the realities of the planet and hierarchically ordered according to the logic of domination, such a worldview relieves us the responsibility of having to reflect on the consequences of our actions; for its true-believers, the planet and its inhabitants just is a storehouse of commodities ready-for-disposal by a fortunate few for whom "examined life" need mean little more than what satisfies self-interest or reinforces unexamined privilege. Climate change denial is thus both a necessary condition and an unsurprising consequence of a logic that, once we expose its dependency on the myth of endless resources, is laid bare as the pathologic quest to justify the domination of women, nonhuman animals, the planet, and its atmosphere. From the point of view of ecofeminist thinkers like Karen Warren and Carol Adams, such quests aren't merely misguided, they're self-defeating. Subjugated human populations and "Mother" nature push back. Insofar as the quest to commodify everything requires what the planet cannot, in fact, supply, such quests are even more than self-defeating; they're nihilistic.

What is surprising is how tightly many continue to cling to the "world" the planet cannot support—even when confronted with the undeniable effects of climate change. While some forms of denial are easy to dismiss as ill-informed; say, a president who insists that had the forest floor been "raked" Paradise, California would not have been decimated by the "Camp Fire,"[44] others take a more nimble route, preferring the language of "skepticism" to "denial," integrating the myth of endless resources into the logic of domination, making "skepticism" about climate change, its anthropogenic contribution, or even whether it's good for the planet to appear as if such inquiries had not been fully addressed by the science.[45] The appearance of sophistication isn't, however, necessarily evidence of intellectual integrity; the effort to naturalize climate change denial as part of the public discourse no more means that there remain lingering questions about whether it's occurring or is substantially accelerated by human activity than up means down. Up does not mean down.

One such example of a highly sophisticated incarnation of the logic of domination is University of Toronto Professor Jordan Peterson, beginning with what he eats. Despite its obvious health-hazards, Peterson claims to eat nothing but red meat, water, and salt as the cure for a varied array of illness.[46] As Adams might put it, Peterson says he eats only cow corpses, and while he insists he's not "giving dietary advice," he also fairly chirps in a now-famous interview with the intrepid Joe Rogan that "[s]ince he changed his diet, his laundry list of maladies disappeared," including "depression, anxiety, gastric reflux (and associated snoring), inability to wake up in the mornings, psoriasis, gingivitis, floaters in my right eye, numbness on the sides of his legs, [and] problems with mood regulation."[47]

Nowhere in the interview does Peterson discuss the connection between factory farming and greenhouse gases; nowhere does he raise the prospect of nonhuman animal suffering; nowhere does he entertain the well-established science that makes an all-meat diet a recipe for a health disaster. Peterson appears to assume that his maladies entitle him to eat nonhuman animal bodies, and while few would deny his right to pursue good health, the fact that such a diet is demonstrably unhealthy doesn't seem to deter him or move him to consider whether science has something to say about it. Questions like whether the obligation to avoid being party to unnecessary suffering includes nonhuman animals, or whether factory farm greenhouse gas emissions should bear on our food choices get short shrift from Peterson, except for on the general question of animal rights. He tweets that "animals don't have rights" that "[r]ights are by definition reciprocal." Peterson claims that

> [a]nimals don't have rights. Human beings have rights. Rights aren't "inside" or part of a person. They are part of the complex agreements that make up civilized society... each of your rights is my obligation... Animals cannot shoulder obligation. Thus, they cannot participate in the complex social contract that structures rights.[48]

Peterson situates this view as part of a broadside against what he calls the "Leftist agenda."[49] But, as we've seen, the defense of animal rights has a much longer history including deep roots in expansions of the principle of utility, as well as the categorical Imperative. While we certainly find moral ideas at the center of political agendas, none have any monopoly on the defense (or denial) of animal rights. Indeed, whole branches of the Christian conservatism Peterson seems to favor espouse veganism as consistent with religious obligation.[50]

But even were Peterson right that persuading people to become vegans was part of a "Leftist agenda," it won't help him out of the critical dilemma his claim about rights-reciprocity creates. As Singer and Stone have shown, unless we're prepared to exclude a large number of human beings as rights-bearers, including all infants and small children, the claim that rights-bearing requires reciprocity is just false. Indeed, as Peterson would doubtless agree, if rights were *necessarily* reciprocal, intellectually disabled people, the comatose, Alzheimer's patients, and babies wouldn't count as rights-bearers since they're not capable of the requisite reciprocity. But we, and presumably Peterson, do treat all such human beings as having basic rights, *especially a right not to suffer unnecessarily*. Is there something about just being a human being that makes all human beings rights-bearers and all nonhuman beings not? If so, claiming that the defense of animal rights is part of a "Leftist agenda" isn't an argument for it, and this makes it difficult to avoid the conclusion that his claims about rights have some other goal that drive his demonizing of "the Left." Whatever the case,[51] if Peterson's going to successfully argue for the denial of rights on the grounds that nonhuman animals lack the capacity to reciprocate, he must show what *exactly* it is that distinguishes nonhuman animals from human beings. And he must show that whatever *that* is, it rightly excludes nonhuman animals from the category "non-reciprocal rights-bearer." For at least some nonhuman animal species such as gorillas, chimpanzees, African parrots and cockatoos, this will be difficult at least insofar as the capacity to use a language is a hallmark feature of reciprocity.[52] Then there's Stone's argument for the rights of natural objects like trees. If consciousness doesn't preclude permanently comatose people from the right not to be euthanized, why don't trees, or rivers, or mountains have some right not to be harmed without good reason?

Peterson doesn't address these questions. Instead, he opts for charged references to the "bloody intellectual Leftists" who decry the impact of human activity on the planet,[53] or to the "anti-theist environmentalists" who deny that the planet is a "garden" for human use.[54] The trouble, is that Peterson is in fact deploying straw fallacy in place of argument. That is, he sets up an opponent he can easily knock down—avoiding the necessity of giving reasons—as opposed to addressing the arguments of actual opponents. Singer or Stone, Warren or Adams, after all, might raise real challenges to a worldview that makes a meat-only diet seem plausible. As *Dreamflesh* writer "Gyrus" succinctly puts is, "straw-manning is an important Peterson tactic."[55] Yes, but why? Fortunately, the answer isn't hard to find. Straw arguments help Peterson protect his implicit appeal to the logic of domination. Yet in deploying one fallacy to dismiss his fictional opponents, he also commits another: the fallacy of *begging the question*.

Let's return once more to the all-meat diet and the claim that nonhuman animals don't have rights. Peterson *assumes* what he needs to show, namely that nonhuman beings can't have rights because there's something that relevantly distinguishes them from non-reciprocal human beings *other than merely being members of different species of animal*, and that that thing makes a *morally* relevant difference. This "thing" cannot be "being members of different species" because insofar as there are multitudes of different species, and because it's possible that there exists some species (say, Martians) smarter and stronger than *Homo sapiens*, such an appeal amounts to no more than "because we say so" or "might makes right." "We get to be on top because we say so" is, however, not an argument; it's a proclamation. While Peterson's concern for his health (however misguided) may trump his concern for nonhuman animal suffering, it doesn't follow from that assertion of self-interest that nonhuman animals don't have rights, or that rights require the capacity for reciprocity.

6.4.2   Sophism in Defense of Climate Change "Skepticism"

Peterson appeals to the logic of domination as if it were itself a fact of nature relieves him of the moral duty to investigate whether its implicit human chauvinism is natural or natural*ized*, given or created. The dominance hierarchy puts us on top; therefore, we're on top. The problem here isn't, at least in the first place, that Peterson is a carnivore; it's that his position with respect to what it is to have a right assumes *without reasoned justification* that some just do rightly dominate others, *and* that to question this makes one fair game for dismissal, name-calling, or straw fallacy vilification. Dare to question whether nonhuman animals have a minimum right not to suffer unnecessarily? Leftist! These are the dishonest strategies that Socrates attributed to the Sophists, "teachers" whose aim was to equip their young (male) pupils to win debates not because their arguments stood up under scrutiny, but because winning helped to secure their privileged social status.[56] We might find it amusing to imagine the "take down" Peterson would likely suffer at the hands of the ancient Greek philosopher, but one thing's certain: whatever the best view of rights, Peterson's decrees about reciprocity do not embody "the unexamined life is not worth living," but rather a rendition of the logic of domination for which he gives no argument. In the end, Peterson's reasoning is simply nihilistic. His all-meat diet isn't just a dietary choice; the faux argument he makes for it epitomizes precisely the world the planet cannot support.

All-meat diets depend on an industry that contributes mightily to climate change. It's thus not surprising that Peterson's a global warming "skeptic." Lots of folks eat bacon-burgers without recognizing the connection. But Peterson can't plausibly claim to be one of them, so he opts instead for a strategy aimed at obscuring what's not actually a debate. According to Peterson, it's impossible *for scientists* to "separate the science from the politics." Therefore, he insists the science is "unreliable."[57] If science can't "solve" climate change, what on earth are the rest of us going to do? As Peterson puts it: "how in the world are you going to solve a problem when you can't even measure the consequences of your actions?" This sounds reasonable, but let's think about it: even if we set aside the fact that in science the inability to make precise predictions is virtually never a bar to recommending possible courses of action (in epidemiology, oncology, meteorology, for instance), *and* we also set aside the fact that no one claims to be able to "solve" climate change (the goal is to mitigate its effects and *slow* its progress), Peterson's claims are still false. Climate scientists have no more trouble separating the science from the politics than any of us find it difficult to consider courses of action even when we rarely (if ever) know the precise outcome. The many sciences that comprise the study of climate change (geophysics, biology, chemistry, botany, zoology, vulcanism, meteorology, and dozens more) are as reliable here as they are in the study of virtually any phenomena, that is, *highly reliable*, if not crystal balls of prognostication. Climate science is governed by regular review and subject to rigorous testing and/or modeling. Yet these facts don't seem to be relevant to Peterson; why? Because climate change "skepticism" is not only a predictable feature of the logic of domination, but a necessary condition for preserving the myth of endless resources. A fixed natural and, according to

Peterson, social order requires a fixed set of planetary and atmospheric conditions; nothing less can adequately secure the relation of superiority to inferiority that defines the logic. We must assume the myth of endless resources is true because the alternative requires we review the social structure that exploits it, endangering the ongoing profit to its beneficiaries. The prospect that the myth is false, and that pretending otherwise is nihilistic, cannot be permitted to outweigh the privilege it insures. Like the all-meat diet, climate change "skepticism" embodies the rejection of almost *any* environmental ethic. Peterson may put it best: "Well, what are we going to do? Are you going to stop having heat? You're going to stop having electricity? You're going to stop driving your cars? You're going to stop taking trains? You're going to stop using your iPhones? You're not going to do any of that, and no wonder." In other words, whatever the planet's future capacity to reproduce life, what matters is that the entitlement of the present remain in its full force and vigor—truth be damned.

6.4.3   *12 Rules for Life*: **Human Chauvinism, Speciesism, and Heteropatriarchy**

However disheartening, it's this sort of willful discounting of fact that makes especially toxic forms of contemporary human chauvinism important. To recap: part of what makes any reasonable defense of the logic of domination difficult is that there's no obvious way to divorce its human chauvinism from its speciesism from its heteropatriarchy; they're mutually reinforcing, and mutually dependent. Any weakening of one of the legs of this three-legged stool and it collapses. We began with Peterson's red meat diet, but what we soon discover is that his diet is really just an invitation to his diagnosis of what he thinks has gone awry in Western civilization. The diet symbolizes the toxic heteropatriarchal reclamation of a social order threatened by feminists, environmentalists, "postmoderns," "Leftists," and "Marxists." It signifies everything from threats posed to the heteropatriarchal order by those who'd reject the male-privileging gender pay gap,[58] to "Postmodernism's" critique of gendered pronouns.[59] The all-meat diet elicits Peterson's offer of tough love to young mostly white men he depicts as victims of an emasculated system of Western values.[60]

Peterson speaks in fact to precisely the worldview embraced by the Proud Boys—or at least such is the consensus of some popular Reddit readers:

> Western exceptionalism, bashing up the Left, anti "Marxist-Postmoderninst," and anti-fascist. Although JBP [Jordan Peterson] probably wouldn't take ownership there appear to be a large overlap between his audience... and many other right-wing or anti-Leftist social commentators. Off the top of my head, Gavin McKinnes, Steven Crowder, Charlie Kirk, Milo, and Dave Rubin have

all associated or guested on each other's shows, they're the kinds of people these guys listen to to justify their worldview, whatever you think of it.[61]

The anonymous poster may be right, Peterson wouldn't likely "take ownership" for encouraging the likes of the Proud Boys, but, as Matt Sheedy reports for *The Edge*, some wear Proud Boy T-Shirts to Peterson talks,[62] while others like Matt Languedoc, student writer for the *Amherst Wire*, pen Op-Eds about falling down a right-wing "rabbit hole" populated by far right figures like Peterson (among others, some identified as Neo-Nazis).[63] At such talks, Peterson speaks at length to matters of human frailty and desire. He talks about violence and suffering. The cause of this suffering, however, isn't, according to Peterson, the logic of domination but rather in the refusal of those dominated to accede. As he argues in *12 Rules for Life*, order (masculinity) is not to be overwhelmed by chaos (femininity): "Order is where people around you act according to well-understood social norms, and remain predictable and cooperative. Chaos is what emerges more catastrophically when you find yourself suddenly without employment, or are betrayed by a lover. As the antithesis of the symbolically masculine order, it's presented imaginatively as feminine … Order is the white masculine serpent; Chaos, it's black, feminine counterpart" (Peterson, *12 Rules for Life*, "Overture"). What is morally defensible, in other words is a particular form of *conformity*, namely, to the gender roles of a political order "handed down from our shared past," that is, our shared heteropatriarchal past.[64]

We might be tempted to dismiss Peterson's masculine order-versus-feminine chaos as so much pop-psychology, but if our objective is to articulate an environmental ethic that takes account of the relationship between environmental integrity and social justice, excavating the ways in which the logic of domination embedded in this claim may shed some significant light. For just as order must come to dominate chaos, the masculine the feminine, so too advises Peterson, we must adjust to the "dominance hierarchy" that is nature (or God), (*12 Rules for Life*, p. 21). Humans dominate nonhuman animals; men dominate women, but "mother nature" dominates all. Indeed, "[i]f mother nature wasn't so hellbent on our destruction, it would be easier to exist in simple harmony with her dictates."[65] "She" occupies the helm of a dominance hierarchy as fixed both internally and externally to our bodies as is the Sun fixed in its firmament. The dominance hierarchy, argues Peterson, isn't capitalism or heteropatriarchy; it's "not a human creation," but rather a "near-eternal aspect of the environment" (*12 Rules for Life*, p. 31) from which these other institutions flow as realizations of the order of a nature that cannot be altered, and that by extension *cannot be destroyed* (*12 Rules for Life*, p. 82).

That little of Peterson's literary venture actually conforms to the science doesn't deter him from making claims that are, in fact, empirically testable.[66] One such claim has to do with whether human beings can alter the environment in such a way as to threaten our existential conditions. Climate change science makes clear that we can and we have, regardless of what's required to maintain the dominance hierarchy. It's not then surprising that Peterson dismisses "eco-activists," feminizing them as naïve "idealists" "envisioning nature as "harmoniously balanced and perfect" (*12 Rules for Life*, p. 27). Even a cursory look at Warren's and Adam's arguments, however, make it clear that this is another straw argument. Such dismissal is either willfully ignorant of the ecofeminist literature or intentionally aims to misrepresent it. Both strategies are morally indefensible: the burden of proof to defend a claim is on the one who makes it. Such a mischaracterization of eco-activists may seem to reinforce Peterson's negative disposition toward women, but that only follows if eco-activists really are naïve idealists—and that is demonstrably false.

It's no surprise that Peterson defends his climate change "skepticism" by tweeting a shout-out for a YouTube video produced by the far right-wing *PraegerU*. The video features MIT atmospheric physicist Richard Lindzen, a well-known climate change denier who argues that global warming is a plot by "those who want increasing state control over society," that "added CO_2 will be a net benefit for the earth," and that climate change science is nothing more than the "environmental movement's…war on fossil fuels."[67] The trouble isn't just that Lindzen's view has been thoroughly debunked as bad science by credible scholars, including Penn State climate scientist Michael Mann.[68] It's that this is readily discoverable. Yet Peterson recommends the video anyways to his legions of adoring fans, a pattern of at least willful ignorance promoted in the interest of protecting a key strut of the dominance hierarchy, namely, that human activity cannot harm the atmosphere—that human activity cannot alter the fundamental structures of human or nonhuman nature. As Katie Herzog of *The Stranger* puts it:

> [W]hen someone like Jordan Peterson, who has legions of fans and an outsized influence in this world, cites Richard Lindzen and Prager U as a reputable source, he does a disservice to himself, his viewers, and everyone who doesn't want to watch Miami disappear into the Atlantic. Most of Jordan Peterson's platitudes are, I think, ultimately harmless, but denying the connection between fossil fuels and climate change perpetuates an ideology that is, right now, increasing human suffering. There is something deeply wrong with that.[69]

The lessons here are simple and important—if not offered to us but by contrast with Jordan Peterson: first, truth matters; facts matter; beliefs have consequences. Second, there's an intimate moral relationship between belief and action, and third, the consequences of that relationship reach well beyond any one of us acting on behalf of our own self-interest. That's what Socrates is telling us when he says the unexamined life is not worth living.

We can debate whether Peterson's claims are harmless, but the fact that he has a substantial following suggests otherwise if his fans are convinced that they're entitled to all the animal bodies and fossil fuel that factory farms and gas wells can produce. That these "victims" are also the world's most affluent and wealthy class should give us pause: white Western(ized) men sit at the helm of almost every multinational corporate venture responsible for the climate crisis. Peterson can't afford to acknowledge what 97% of all scientists do. That is, climate change cannot be made to fit what Peterson apparently takes to be the necessary conditions of male-dominated human social life, the dominance hierarchy. Hence, he's willing to bite some pretty tough bullets—distorting the claims of potential critics, recommending denial cloaked as skepticism about the science of climate change, and all of this in order to maintain a worldview in which "chaos," that is, women and "Mother nature" are the eternally identifiable enemy. The possibility that climate change is real and anthropogenic threatens to expose Peterson's version of the logic of domination as an artifact of human chauvinism, not an inalterable fact of nature. If human activity can affect such consequential change, "Mother Nature" isn't so dominating after all, opening the door to the prospect that "the order within the chaos and the order of Being" is no more fixed than human interests need it to be.

6.5   Inseparable: Environmental Ethics and the Quest for Social and Economic Justice

6.5.1   The Deep Roots of the "Dominance Hierarchy"

Figures like Jordan Peterson offer important insight into the question why the logic of domination has persisted for so long even in the face of the planet's future capacity to support life. Understanding how the logic systemically advantages some at expense of others is vitally important to formulating an ethic capable of addressing the intersection of racism, sexism, and speciesism in light of the environmental consequences of that advantage. According to ecofeminists like Warren and Adams, the logic governs a social order that naturalizes ecological destruction, the commodification of nonhuman animals, and social injustice, *for the same reasons*. Hence, they argue, we must address every front if we're to make progress on any. This is a tall order. But history, in this case the insight of Karl Marx' s colleague, Friedrich Engels, can help us. In *The Origin of the Family, Private Property and the State*, Engels argues that the primary beneficiaries of institutions like private property, the commodification of women's reproductive sexuality, and marriage (compulsory monogamy) are men whose control of women's bodies act as a conduit of inherited wealth to male offspring through male bloodlines.[70] He argues that just as land

and livestock came to signify human domination of nonhuman nature, so too women's reproductive capacities came to signify another kind of property: the progeny in which future labor, property, and wealth could be invested and consolidated.

While Engels, however, condemns the rise of patriarchal human chauvinism as "the world historical defeat of women," Peterson embraces it. Where Engels sees that these archetypal forms of commodification foreshadow the machinations of capital that became the Industrial Revolution, Peterson argues that capitalism mirrors the order of nature, and is good on that count.[71] While both Engels and Peterson recognize that capitalist commodification is closely correlated with social inequity, Engels (following Marx) decries the rise of capitalist forms of value as repressive and dehumanizing whereas Peterson insists that the logic of domination is so intractable a feature of our evolutionary heritage that any effort to significantly alter it destroys our "freedom."[72] This is, however, a very curious notion of "freedom" since, at least for women, it appears to mean "free" to surrender to the dictates of a body bound to the "inevitability of pregnancy," and of being "locked into a reproductive cycle from which they [women] had no practical escape."[73] While Peterson acknowledges the 1960s advent of access to birth control, he argues that the freedom the pill offers is more chimera than real since what women want fundamentally is to be cared for by strong assertive males to whom women willingly submit as a matter of evolutionary psychology.[74]

The difficulty here, one that Peterson doesn't acknowledge, is that evolutionary psychology is a highly contentious field in the sciences that includes a cornucopia of competing theories aiming to take full account of facts themselves open to interpretation and new significant finds provided by paleoanthropologists. For example, *Scientific American's* John Horgan argues that whether hunter-gatherer societies conformed to the logic of domination is at least contentious if not false.[75] Gathering, argues Horgan, was generally a more effective and less dangerous way to secure food, and it required all hands on deck to secure enough food, suggesting a more egalitarian social order. Peterson nevertheless persists against the weight of the evidence entertaining the idea that compulsory monogamy offers a solution to men "victimized" by women who reject their sexual advances (and presumably women's own real desires) and are thereby condemned to the status of the "incel" or involuntary celibate. Setting aside the contradiction concerning women's alleged desire to submit (why would we need *compulsory* monogamy if women freely acceded to men's sexual desires?), what could Peterson's aim here be other than to shore up the logic of domination against the prevailing winds of sexual equality? As writer Tabatha Southy explains:

> [Peterson] endorses the idea that some men are being denied sex because other men are taking all the sex from women who are allowed to choose to give them that sex, and that if something could be done to prevent all this

"having sex with people of your choosing" nonsense, some unlucky women would eventually have to settle for the incels. If we could just make that happen, these men would not have to be so "angry at God" and commit mass murder, the argument goes.[76]

What's perhaps particularly perverse in Peterson's reasoning here is that, in the interest of reinforcing the dominance hierarchy, he not only effectively resorts to blaming women for male violence, but bolsters men already feeling stung by the loss of free access to women's bodies by not so subtly reassuring rejected men that they're entitled to use violence. It's hard to imagine any system of ethics for which such rationalization could ever be made morally defensible, or any modern society where we'd regard this form of violence as just. What Peterson's proposal does show, however, is the marathon effort to which one apologist for heteropatriarchal human chauvinism will go to maintain a worldview whose central premises have become harder and harder to support. Perhaps this analysis seems far afield from environmental ethics. It isn't. The premises of arguments like Peterson's are not merely false, they're *nihilistic*. The same logic that "justifies" violence done to women "justifies" violence done to non-human animals—like the unfortunate victims of Peterson's meat diet—and to the planet's capacity to sustain life. Which ethic, moral extensionism, ecocentrism, eco-phenomenology, ecofeminism, some combination of approaches, or something new turns out to be best-suited to address the intersection of ethics and justice remains open to changing conditions and a growing body of scientific knowledge. This much, however, seems certain: a future whose planetary ecosystem and atmosphere is sustainable, but whose institutions remain governed by unexamined structural inequalities, may be worth the struggle to sustain it for some—but it will hardly seem so for the legions of others whose experience of the present points in the direction of revolution, not surrender. Moreover, such limited vision is self-defeating: the kind of ethic the future will require to confront issues potentially devastating as well as global by their very natures are rightly described neither as national nor international; they are planetary. They require an ethic that can transcend boundaries, prejudices, and unearned privileges recognizing that the alternative, *given what we know and can thus work to mitigate*, is effectively genocidal, even suicidal.

6.5.2   Environmental Ethics and the Quest to De-naturalize the Logic of Domination

It's precisely the point of an ecofeminist approach to show that institutions and practices that may seem only trivially connected to environmental issues are in fact crucially relevant because their operative logics are the same: if men need the planet to support their colossal appetites, the planet must support it.

If men need nonhuman animals to sustain their desire to consume flesh, non-human animals must provide it. If men need women's bodies to satisfy their need for sex and offspring, women must supply it. The problem is that nothing requires us to concede to this proscribed harm. Domination is written neither in the stars nor in our evolutionary heritage. Nothing compels rational creatures capable of producing science, art, and ethics to forfeit our quest for a way of life worth living against a dark and cynical determinism. Indeed, it's in virtue of its stark contrast with an ecofeminist approach to ethics that arguments like Peterson's can show us five critically important things:

- The development of a sound moral compass is essential to life in the twenty-first century.
- Given the facts about our current environmental dilemma, especially the urgency presented by the climate crisis, the prospect of future pandemic, human and nonhuman migration, food and water insecurity, and the geopolitical instability that accompanies all of these, ethics and environmental ethics are for all practical purposes the same project.
- Paying attention to science regardless of whether a particular theory or discovery conforms to our favored worldview is one of our most important *moral* charges.
- Understanding the logic that structures all forms of domination and their many intersections is key to making morally defensible change toward a sustainable future desirable to those most vulnerable to the harm dominance hierarchies seek to naturalize.
- The value of principles such as moral extensionism and/or ecocentrism lay in the extent to which they can provide insight into realistic courses of action consistent with the commitment to address environmental deterioration, but also economic and social injustice.

Upshot: whether there exists something in our genes, our evolutionary history, or our brain chemistry that situates us in a dominance hierarchy—*it doesn't matter*. It cannot afford to matter if we're going to make a meaningful stab at articulating a future that's better than mere survival for a tiny few who can afford to outfit themselves with the weapons and provisions to ride the high seas of climate change even for a short time.

We can understand our history *and* refuse to be either bound or excused by it. Indeed, we must if there is to be a morally defensible future worth fighting for. Consider, for example, the pseudo-science argument for herd immunity offered as a remedy for the infectious spread of Covid-19 by neuro-radiologist Scott Atlas. Atlas argues that allowing the virus to spread unchecked throughout a population will create a barrier of immunity to the disease. The argument is patently bad science—but it also reflects a truly obscene neglect of history. First, the bad science: promoted in a document widely circulated, but scientifically unsubstantiated, on the fringes of the far right called the *Great Barrington Declaration*[77] the thrust of Atlas' argument is ostensibly to protect the "most vulnerable" by permitting the healthy to go about their business without masks or social distancing, who then become infected, recover, and are no longer able to infect those less able to fight off the virus.[78] Even a cursory look at the *Declaration's* claims and assumptions make clear, however, the speciousness of its reasoning: it requires our willingness to assume that reinfection is highly unlikely, that the vulnerable are readily identified and can be entirely isolated; and it requires us to accept a staggering incidence of mortality:

> A new, large study found fewer than 1 in 10 Americans have antibodies to SARS-CoV-2, the virus that causes COVID-19. Even in the hardest-hit areas, like New York City, estimates of immunity among residents are about 25%. To reach 50% to 70% immunity would mean about four times as many people getting infected and an "incredible number of deaths," said Josh Michaud, associate director of global health policy at KFF [*Kaiser Family Foundation*]. Even those who survive could suffer severe consequences to their heart, brain and other organs, potentially leaving them with lifelong disabilities … "It's not a strategy to pursue unless your goal is to pursue suffering and death," Michaud said. What's more, some scientists say natural immunity may not even be feasible for COVID-19. While most people presumably achieve some degree of protection after being infected once, cases of people who recovered from the disease and were reinfected have raised questions about how long natural immunity lasts and whether someone with immunity could still spread the virus.[79]

The *Great Barrington Declaration* is not, however, merely bad science. In its willingness to capitulate to mass casualties—particularly in vulnerable populations—it is immoral as well as unjust. Even a cursory examination makes plain who will live and who will die. The Declaration is silent with respect to the role ethnicity and economic status play with respect to vulnerability to infection, illness, and death, even as the evidence makes clear that structural inequality is the key metric for predicting mortality. As reported by Stephanie Soucheray for the *Center for Infectious Disease and Policy* (CIDRAP):

> Black Americans are infected with COVID-19 at nearly three times the rate of white Americans, according to a new document from the National Urban League. The report, based on data from Johns Hopkins University, also shows black Americans are twice as likely to die from the virus. According to the "State of Black America," the infection rate for blacks is 62 per 10,000, compared with 23 per 10,000 for whites. Latinos see even more infections: 73 per 10,000. During the early months of the pandemic, the report asserts

that blacks were more likely to have preexisting conditions that predispose them to COVID-19 infection, less likely to have health insurance, and more likely to work in jobs that do not accommodate remote work. Both black and Latino Americans are also more likely to live in multigenerational housing, which places older, at-risk adults in close contact with younger people who may not know they have the virus.[80]

Scott Atlas' defense of herd immunity appeals, in other words, not only to dominance hierarchies to justify allowing the virus to spread, but at least implicitly to a long history of exploiting the vulnerable to protect the advantaged—a history we ignore at our peril because we know that being less vulnerable to infection in no way means invulnerable.

Bad history, in other words, is ignored history. The point is not merely that we pay for our arrogance when we fail to heed the lessons history can teach, but that ignoring the structural inequalities of our past can now insure that the future of human history writing may itself be at stake. Perhaps it goes too far to suggest that the *Great Barrington Declaration* bears an eerie family resemblance to the American Eugenics Movement of the early twentieth century. Nonetheless, there are several points of likeness that shed light on what history, arguments for dominance hierarchies, and the structural inequalities they help to sustain can teach us about the consequences of bad science. For example, although herd immunity remains a fringe theory (fortunately) aimed ostensibly at halting the reproduction of disease and compulsory sterilization, the hallmark of the American Eugenics movement, aimed at preventing the reproduction of so-called maladaptive behavioral traits such as "laziness," "imbecility," or a disposition to alcoholism, both seek to rid humanity of some form of affliction *solicited by behavior*. That the behavior in question is, for the eugenicist, socially maladaptive and a matter of genetic disposition while, for the advocate of herd immunity, the significance of behavior is simply that it produces high vulnerability to viral infection is certainly a difference, but one largely beside the point. What's important is that whether social or economic conditions—*or the entrenched structural inequalities that generate those conditions*—have any bearing on behavior, adaptive or maladaptive, good or bad, is ignored both in the eugenicist's judgment that improving the human condition requires neutralizing maladaptive genes and in the herd immunity advocate's willful ignorance concerning the conditions that produce the behavior that makes someone vulnerable to disease.[81]

That the eugenicist holds that race is a predictor of a maladaptive behavior identified as sloth ignores, for example, the role played in unemployment in racism. That the advocate of herd immunity counts on it that there exist social and economic conditions which make for reliable disease exposure ignores the fact that the majority of low-wage workers at grocery stores, service stations, restaurants, hospitals, and nursing homes are disproportionately female and/or black or brown. Although the eugenicists specifically identify negative behavioral traits with race, advocates of herd immunity know who will bear the brunt of widespread infection. Although eugenics sterilization programs executed profoundly invasive human rights violations, a program seeking to achieve herd immunity in the midst of a deadly pandemic is effectively genocidal. While compulsory sterilization was codified in some states such as Virginia and Connecticut as statute, it's clear that herd immunity has been adopted in some states, for example, South Dakota, as public health policy. *Both traffic in varieties of racism masquerading as public health.* Both tacitly assume as morally defensible an order of nature and society that systemically disvalues and exploits the many to protect a privileged few. Both discount science in favor of a pseudo-science that conveniently supports a status quo whose long history tells the story of how human chauvinism, or more truthfully, heteropatriarchal and racist human chauvinism has wrought twin catastrophes: pandemic and the climate crisis, each the potential end of human history.

6.6   Human-Centeredness, the Aesthetic *in* Experience, and the Desirable Future

6.6.1   The Aesthetic Value of Natural Objects as a Vital Element of an Ecofeminist Ethic

While ecofeminism spans the full range of approaches to environmental ethics, and while every ethic, as John Dewey shows, includes some element of appreciation for what he called the aesthetic *in* ordinary experience, it may be that this variety of *axiology*—theories of value—has more to offer the life worth living than any of these approaches have fully theorized. Aesthetic value, in other words, may have something to offer to the morally defensible life not captured by analyses of moral principle or by accounts of social and economic injustice. As David Wood argues, incorporating the value of aesthetic experience into moral judgment is unlikely ever to be intended as a replacement of moral value, but rather as an avenue for deepening our capacity for why science and history matter to articulating the future. Appealing once more to Dewey, for example, Wendy Lynne Lee argues that the aesthetic elements of our ordinary experience of nonhuman nature is more vital to sound moral judgment than we often recognize. Wedding aspects of an eco-phenomenological approach to the utilitarian's emphasis on consequences, she argues that "where the motivation supplied by moral obligation, assessment of possible consequences, or even empathy for nonhuman subjects fails to move us to action, we may yet be able to be moved by the awe we experience in the beauty of natural objects and phenomena" (Lee, "On Ecology and Aesthetic Experience," p. 23). "Where the autonomic compulsion of duty fails to deliver sufficient moral impetus," argues Lee, "aesthetic response may stand a better chance" (pp. 23–4).

Lee makes clear that what she's proposing isn't intended to replace other systems of moral value, but rather supplement them with an understanding of experienced value that can prod us to "deeper questions about why our relationship with nonhuman nature has netted so much damage—despite our claim to value its aesthetic worth." She goes on to argue that

> If we took the aesthetic value of natural objects more seriously than we do now as a value worth cultivating, we might find ourselves nearer to an ethos whose vision of moral action…is justified at least in part by the *possibility of experience whose loss we cannot endure* and whose objects we cannot but know to be vulnerable to our present state of environmental abuse. ("On Ecology and Aesthetic Experience," p. 24, my emphasis)

If aesthetic experience has value for environmental ethics, in other words, it's because "it can encourage actions that condition the ecological stability requisite to aesthetic experience in the future" moving us "to a greater recognition of the extent to which our conceptions of beauty are relative to culture and historical moment" (p. 24). The danger, in other words, that we could squander future opportunities to appreciate the diversity, multiplicity, and fragility of nonhuman nature through recklessness, consumption, and waste has a moral *and* an aesthetic dimension, and it takes seriously a responsibility to our successors not merely to leave them a sustainable, but denuded, planet, but rather a verdant planet that can support opportunities for aesthetic experience. To value that future is to value what makes aesthetic experience possible, and that in turn requires not only a planetary ecology capable of recuperating and restoring itself, but also social and economic conditions capable of genuine moral progress—even revolutionary change.

Consider once more arguments for herd immunity where the goal is to allow a viral outbreak to spread in the hopes of infecting a high enough quotient of citizens that their putative immunity will protect the more vulnerable from contracting the disease. We know that black and brown people will be disproportionately represented among the millions who would likely die given social and economic condition that make them more vulnerable to infection.[82] We know that because the herd immunity strategy gives license to ignore the causes and origins of the disease as largely irrelevant in favor of letting it run its course, we're less likely to come to a mature understanding of environmental issues relevant to future pandemics.[83] We know the history of herd immunity is littered with bad science,[84] and we know that there are intimate, but inadequately understood, links between the emergence of novel viruses and the climate crisis.[85] Each of these presents us with critical questions about the morality of pursuing herd immunity as a strategy for combatting a pandemic, and each demonstrate a decisive ethical failure. But, each also provide a site to consider important questions concerning whether the prospect of a future bereft of opportunity for the aesthetic *in* experience *matters*. Adopting a herd immunity strategy is, for example, an effective denunciation of the value of the ethnic and cultural diversity that lends an aspect of aesthetic richness and depth to our lives. Perhaps even worse, herd immunity forfeits the value of at least some human lives, and with it the value of our potential experience *of those people*, their stories, their ideas, their uniqueness. Herd immunity also evokes the long shadow cast by Eugenicism and with it images of devastating loss not only for human communities, but for the aesthetic value those communities could otherwise have created.

The adoption of this effectively eugenicist strategy is an abandonment of science, the appreciation of its complex history, and its future potential to improve the life of the planet's ecosystems and their inhabitants. But it's also a dismissal of the value of wonder, of exploration, and of adventure—vital aesthetic components of scientific work. Indeed, even as we must combat Covid-19, few would dispute the beauty and complexity of its chemical and biological character or its capacity to reproduce itself. Perhaps most telling, however, is that a negligent disposition to one science, in this case epidemiology and virology, too often reflects neglect of (or the willingness to distort) other vital scientific enterprises—for example, climate science. As a recent Harvard study suggests, the possible nodes of connection between a changing climate, habitat erosion, species migration, virus evolution, and consequent interaction with human populations are legion:

> As the planet heats up, animals big and small, on land and in the sea, are headed to the poles to get out of the heat. That means animals are coming into contact with other animals they normally wouldn't, and that creates an opportunity for pathogens to get into new hosts. Many of the root causes of climate change also increase the risk of pandemics. Deforestation, which occurs mostly for agricultural purposes, is the largest cause of habitat loss worldwide. Loss of habitat forces animals to migrate and potentially contact other animals or people and share germs. Large livestock farms can also serve as a source for spillover of infections from animals to people. Less demand for animal meat and more sustainable animal husbandry could decrease emerging infectious disease risk and lower greenhouse gas emissions. We have many reasons to take climate action to improve our health and reducing risks for infectious disease emergence is one of them.[86]

Given these many factors and intersections, all of which have impact on what the future can sustain, it's not hard to see what are the moral issues with respect to adopting a herd immunity strategy. While it might offer temporary respite from the most devastating effects of pandemic outbreak for a fortunate few, its willful ignorance of the relevant sciences sets the stage for a future characterized by inescapable suffering and loss. But the moral perversity of taking such a course is the way loss may come to be magnified such that what makes striving for the future worth the struggle, namely, the aesthetic *in* experience, is diminished. As Dewey argues, while the moral may command us to do the good even when it's difficult, even when it demands risk, self-sacrifice, and hardship, it's the hope of the aesthetic *in* experience that makes the good worth doing. That is, it's the hope of a future experience of beauty and diversity, of shared values like compassion, patience, and joyfulness, that we cannot afford to jettison—at least if we want to avoid the ultimate nihilism inherent in the worldview that makes herd immunity, like climate change denial, seem plausible.

Lee argues that "if aesthetic experience has moral value for feminist theorizing, it is because in cultivating it we simultaneously cultivate those relationships upon which it depends, relationships whose value, given this experience, are by definition more than merely instrumental" ("On Ecology and Aesthetic Experience," p. 25). We're more than commodities, and the value of our relationships with human and nonhuman others is more than can be exhausted by their usefulness. We could settle for a world where moral authority is premised on maintaining the hierarchical relationship of, say, Peterson's masculine order versus feminine chaos, superiority versus inferiority, exchange value versus intrinsic value. Or, argues Lee, we could reimagine a *human-centeredness* grounded not in the logic of domination, but rather in the *epistemic* (what we can know), *moral* (what we should do), and *aesthetic* (what future experience we hope to be possible) value that accrues to taking responsibility for conserving and, where necessary, restoring the conditions that make a desirable future possible. We could reimagine our always changing and evolving relationships as forms of interdependency, as opposed to fixed forms of competition. We can listen objectively to the sciences, a disposition that requires a moral commitment to act on what science tells us is in the best interest of *all* of the planet's constituencies, not just those that occupy the "worlds" we prefer. We can take aesthetic experience seriously as something the loss of which transforms living into mere surviving and the future into desolation. No better future is possible, of course, without mammoth struggle, one that must be taken up not only by those who stand to lose the most, but by those who can come to see the cost of their privilege. The struggle, moreover, is not against the Jordan Petersons or Scott Atlases of the world who'll become more and more irrelevant as our attention becomes taken up by the crises we must face. The real struggle is against the sheer nihilism of what they represent, a worldview that presupposes its own annihilation in virtue of the fact that the planet cannot sustain it, but that arrogantly assumes its patriarchs and profiteers will be the last to go.

To try to build optimism about our uncertain future into the environmental ethic that must confront it is a tall order. But there may be more ways than we realize to articulate how the aesthetic *in* experience can potentially disrupt the routinized waste, thoughtless decision-making, or the quiet despair that too easily permeates our thinking about the future. Consider, for example, just one example: satire, specifically that of the anonymous artist Banksy. In his performance of *Sirens of the Lambs*,[87] Banksy puts the lie to the notion that non-human animals are incapable of any form of sentience, reciprocity, fear, or anxiety, and in so doing undermines the claim that they're beyond the scope of moral considerability. Banksy solicits our thinking and feeling without an argument, without premises or a conclusion. *Sirens of the Lambs* is a theatrical work. As Lee argues in *Eco-Nihilism: The Philosophical Geopolitics of the Climate Change Apocalypse*, Banksy, like Ludwig Wittgenstein, tells us not merely to see, but to *look*:

> In this piece, a "farm fresh meat" truck chugs up and down city streets. It's filled with cuddly stuffed animatronic lambs, pigs, chickens, and cows—baaing, mooing, and cheeping from between jagged cargo slats. The truck pauses in front of a butcher shop. Adorable pink and yellow, spotted and snuggly critters peer out at us—seeming to call to us for help, creating *an* experience at once jarring and perplexing. Onlookers look confused; children cry. The meat-shop workers gaze out a window hung with leg-of-lamb. "Sirens" repudiates wholesale the idea that some animals are worth saving while others exist to be food, that polar bears can be our spirit animals, but pigs are just bacon ... Banksy's incarnation of the aesthetic *in* experience is neither comfortable nor cheery; it's not pretty. It's *an* experience pierced with anxiety and embarrassment... We know instantly and viscerally what Banksy is saying. (*Eco-Nihilism*, p. 379)

What Banksy's performance embodies is the possibility that sometimes art can show us that with which reason struggles, in this case that, however we may deny it, however we may deflect using euphemisms like "meat" or "pork," we're made to see we're hypocrites about what we eat. The aesthetic experience of *Sirens of the Lambs* can drive moral insight. Our experience of *Sirens* is aesthetic because it's creative, but it also disrupts the banality of our assumptions about what counts as food. It makes us think and reflect what we are if we continue to ignore these others. The discomfort and anxiety Banksy's performance solicits derives from the fact that our relationship, however momentary or fleeting, with the *idea* of an animal on its way to slaughter bleating for us to save it *is* a relationship, a *reciprocity*; we don't merely see the truck pass, we're commanded to *look* at it. We recognize it as such in the visceral nature of our response to the prospect of suffering and our complicity in it. We know we don't want to be on the "Fresh Meat" truck; and we know that while cows and pigs and chickens may not know where they're going in such a circumstance, their terror is as real as ours would be, for example, on the way to an emergency room because we cannot breathe, or deciding not to go because we have no health insurance, or as we sit in a fast food restaurant eating a hamburger as we await the call from a nurse who tells us our mother or father or child has died.

Banksy appeals to both our anxiety at participating in cruelty and our optimism that we can end it. This is the point of *Sirens*. We're amused that these are fluffy stuffed animals calling to us, that this gives us an "out"; but not really, especially if we're standing outside the meat shop holding a bloody package for our "all-meat" diet. If the aesthetic element of experience in performance-pieces like Banksy's *Sirens* has the power to elicit anxiety in us about what counts as food, it's because we know there exist sentient entities besides us, and that just because they can't voice the right not to be made to suffer unnecessarily does not mean their terror counts for less; after all, did the capacity for reciprocity, or empathy, or compassion, require a language we could just as well imagine babies propped up in the window of the meat-truck, or senile grandpa. Perhaps fluffy stuffed babies or straw-man grandpa wouldn't elicit the same sense of dread; but perhaps it would solicit even more. And that may well be what Banksy's opportunity for aesthetic experience offers to moral judgment, but it is no small thing.

6.6.2   The Standpoint of the Subjugated

Satire offers one example of the aesthetic *in* experience that can often, if not always, raise our attention to significant issues worthy of moral reflection. Yet insofar as the aesthetic aspect of experience ranges over virtually every part of human life, we needn't look far to discover other examples whose relevance to environmental ethics is, if very different, nonetheless an opportunity for insight into the importance of aesthetic value to moral judgment. Consider, for example, what Lee calls the *standpoint of the subjugated*: imagine a subsistence farmer, perhaps in a region of the world straining under the weight of drought. Contrary to Peterson's view that the experience of our relationship to our own existential conditions is determined by our effort to find our place in a dominance hierarchy, the farmer has no time for sterile abstractions. Her world is deeply enmeshed in the contingencies of her daily struggle for life (*Eco-Nihilism*, p. 396). Her every waking moment is colored by the survival of herself and her children. Perhaps she has a husband who works miles away at the factory whose emissions sometimes putrefy the air she breaths and compel her to walk ever further out to fetch water that doesn't smell acrid.

The farmer's existential conditions, her *life*, cannot be captured in the simple binary terms of masculine versus feminine or, as Peterson puts it, hardness versus softness. She has work to do. "It is to women's clear advantage," writes Peterson, "that men do not happily put up with dependency among themselves … A woman should look after her children—although that is not all she should do. And a man should look after a woman and children—although that is not all he should do. But a woman should not look after a man, because she should look after children, and a man should not be a child" (*12 Rules*, p. 329). The farmer doesn't have time for this nonsense; her family needs to eat. She may or may not know that it's the actions of privileged men like Peterson, captains of industry collectively culpable for the absence of her own husband, the dirty smudge that is her sunset or the foul smell that taints her water. Peterson's proscription of male/female relationships offers her no help at all when it's all hands on deck to get in what meager harvest she can manage on the land left to her village by the multinational who leased it from her government without consulting her.

The only scenario Peterson's "to women's clear advantage" fits is the stay-at-home affluent white domesticity of a 1950s for which he appears nostalgic; a house-wifedom repudiated as a suffocating instance of structural inequality in the trailblazing work of feminist theorists like Betty Friedan whose *The Feminine Mystique* gave birth to a new wave of the Women's Liberation Movement,[88] and later in the work of developing world ecofeminists like Vandana Shiva who expand the critique of inequality to nonhuman animals and nonhuman nature.[89] The farmer does look after her children, but her world bears little more than faint resemblance to the *Father Knows Best* imagery of Peterson's heteropatriarchal fantasy. The farmer, the movements of her body, her children, and everything in her world is permeated by the vicissitudes of a nonhuman nature that doesn't readily submit to assignments of hard or soft, strong or weak, appropriate or renegade. Carrying water, tilling soil, harvesting crops, washing children's faces, gathering firewood: activities that cannot be corralled without distortion to the tidy "although that is not all she should do" of Peterson's trite prescription. Her relationships are themselves irreducible to use, even though they're firmly rooted in interdependence, because in her world of *subsistence* little is disposable. References to "the farmer and her environment" thus seem an inadequate description since, in her experience of her own visceral life of lifting and leaning, hoisting and turning, the only border that exists between herself and "the environment" is her skin and her resolve.

In short, the life of the farmer offers a realistic image of the components necessary to an environmental ethic. But a key aspect of what makes this image realistic is that it takes into consideration the aesthetic *in* the farmer's experience of a real material world that yields as little to abstraction as it does to need. The farmer doesn't have time for the myth of endless resources, the simplistic assignment of social place, or solicitations of make protection. Yet she *feels* the heft of wood gathered in her arms, the smell of it burning mixed with the smell of fish and vegetables over a cook stove, the sound of children jostling to wash their hands before eating at the end of the day, the weight in her chest as she breaths out finally able to sit and smoke. The farmer's experience is what makes a mockery of rigid proscriptions or sets of "rules." Perhaps a more nuanced and complex account of the relationship of the farmer to her land, her family, her duties, one that includes the aesthetic *in* her experience can provide a place to begin thinking about an environmental ethic that, while moral principle needn't be abandoned, also needn't be a singular point of departure for a life worth living:

> [P]art of what deepens the satisfaction of reaping a harvest under *subsistence* conditions...is that for the subsistence farmer resources are not only *not* endless, they're tenuous, potentially scarce, precious; they're reminders of vulnerability. Insofar, moreover, as the farmer plants and harvests for her family's *survival*... her disposition to land, water, space and time, necessity, living and dying—*farming*—reflect not exchange value, but that array of values accruing to life. The farmer personifies vulnerability not just as responsibility to herself, but to others in an interdependent web of relationships. She can't afford denial because she can't afford recklessness. Her family's life depends on the epistemic responsibility she assumes in understanding whatever's necessary to insuring that harvest. Her family depends not merely on her work ethic, but her aesthetic appreciation of what counts as good seed, clean water, healthy soil. The very pleasure she takes in eating derives not merely from the provision of sustenance, but in avoiding the miseries of going hungry, or worse, watching her children go hungry. While the farmer's responsibility is a heavy one, it's for just that reason that the satisfaction she's surely entitled to take in it is that much deeper, more vibrant, and more enduring. But most important of all is this: the intimacy of the relationship between the farmer and the land creates interdependency, *but not subjugation*. (*Eco-Nihilism*, p. 396)

The farmer's culture may be male-dominated, but it cannot exhaust her experience as a subsistence farmer; it cannot capture her knowledge, her intimate connection to the land, her relationships, human and nonhuman, to a spouse or child, parent or sibling, village or far-away city. What is to the farmer's advantage has, in fact, little to do with whether the men in her orbit "put up with dependency among themselves," but much to do with whether every able body adds to the life of the farm, its access to clean water, and its relationships with its neighbors. Care-taking, moreover, is not likely to divide along the static lines of gender alone, but along the more complex fissures that define who can afford to stay at home, who leaves for the factory miles away, and who's needed in the fields in any given season.

In short, what this approach to environmental ethics—one that seeks to theorize important insights from ecofeminism and eco-phenomenology along with the appeal to principle—asks us to undertake is a paradigm shift from thinking in terms of fixed convention to thinking in terms of organic "interdependencies." On this construal, nonhuman nature acts neither merely as inert background awaiting human design nor as a malevolent "Mother" looking to inflict chaos and misery; human relationships are less dictated by domination than by the necessities of food and water security. Nature does not dominate us; it *is* us, as the farmer knows as clearly and intimately as she knows the life growing inside her, the miles she'll walk tomorrow for kindling, or the sunset she can feel on her back as she walks home at dusk. In experiencing the sheer variety of such things, we come to know ourselves. In appreciating the aesthetic *in* experience as both a source of sublimity and suffering, we come to comprehend the strong and the tenuous. In it, we can perhaps come to comprehend the magnitude of loss we will surely suffer—even if we survive into the future we are now creating.

6.6.3   We Must Do Better

The logic of domination is a human fiction crafted for specific purposes, few of which serve either the present need for greater attention to matters of social justice or the future of environmental sustainability. While considerable cynicism may be warranted, and fear of ecological apocalypse seems plainly insufficient to incentivize real change in human behavior, it's not too late to create an environmental ethic capable of replacing the logic with a moral compass designed to help us work toward ecological *and* social justice. After all, what's the point of an ecologically sustainable world that remains mired in the social injustices of the present? We must do better. The only question is whether it's too late. We have to hope not, for books like this aren't meant to be assigned merely as history; they're meant to be roadmaps for the desirable future. They're meant to provide secure anchor in the broad bend of the *precautionary principle*: Will this action contribute to suffering? Will it contribute to the erosion of future experience worth wanting? Who and what does this action value, and why? What kind of life do my actions embody? Settling for the well-worn path of a logic that informs us of our place, our worth, and our prospects is the easy thing. Charting a course disabused of myths and unearned privileges is by far the harder course. But, given the crises we face, it's also likely the only course.

6.7   Summary and Questions

In this final part, we return to the distinction between "worlds" and the planet and to the central idea that connects all the questions, issues, arguments, and ideas we've explored throughout: the life worth living. But we've also reserved some of the most important of these for last. Truth be told, the vital intersection of environmental, social, and economic justice has been with us since the beginning in examples and illustrations, but also in the effort to explore the implications of a range of principles and insights. In this last section, however, we turn our attention squarely to the intersections themselves, introducing the work of a handful of ecofeminist thinkers whose work in one of the most vibrant growing domains of environmental philosophy seeks to theorize not merely the connections, but the importance of the relationship between thought and action in the pursuit of the moral life.

Among the key insights offered to the project of drafting an environmental ethic by the ecofeminists is that we won't be able to effectively deal with any of the issues that confront us without working to address them all. Environmental justice *is* social justice *is* economic justice. All are global in nature and scale. They must be dealt with all at once, and often enough against the backlash of a reactionary and intransigent heteropatriarchy that clings to the unearned authority supported by the myth of endless resources and the fictions of dominance hierarchies. What ecofeminists like Karen Warren show us is that a planetary future whose ecosystems are sustainable but whose structural inequalities remain intact is not merely anathema to the life worth living, but as unlikely as is the worldview it depends on is false. Ecofeminists seek to identify the origins of practices and belief systems that become not only oppressive institutions but precursors to ecological deterioration. It's thus not surprising that what signifies this approach most distinctly is the critique of the capitalist idea that *everything* is a potential *commodity*, a marketable good or service whose value lay not in its ecosystemic contribution, but in its capacity to be dominated and exchanged.

What Warren's logic of domination shows is that we can draw parallels between the oppression of women, and that of nonhuman animals and nonhuman nature. The reasoning is the same in all three cases, and as an exploration of the work of Jordan Peterson shows, the logic remains entrenched if embattled throughout much of at least the Global North. Carol Adams argues that if we substitute "animal" for women in the logic we can see that the subordination of nonhuman animals is "justified" in the same way as is heteropatriarchy. In one significant way, however, Adams goes beyond Warren arguing that it's not enough to insist that women are human beings and not animals because insofar as such claims actually reinforce speciesism, they reinforce the logic itself. It's thus not really surprising that Peterson claims to eat nothing but red meat, water, and salt as the cure for a varied array of illness, or that questions like whether the obligation to avoid being party to unnecessary suffering includes nonhuman animals receives only poorly reasoned arguments such as "animals don't have rights" because "[r]ights are by definition reciprocal." The difficulty such arguments is that unless we're going to exclude human beings who are incapable of the reciprocity Peterson demands, the claim that rights-bearing requires reciprocity is false. Unless he can show that there's something about just *being* a human being that makes all human beings rights-bearers and all nonhuman beings not (or at least makes special provision for human beings who are not so capable), the argument for retaining what amounts to unearned entitlement fails. In a signal that responding to this obvious line of criticism would itself be difficult, Peterson opts instead for loaded references to the "bloody intellectual Leftists," or to the "anti-theist environmentalists." But straw fallacy isn't an argument; Peterson simply sets up an opponent he can easily knock down, avoiding the necessity of giving reasons for his position, a dishonest strategy Socrates attributed to the Sophists, "teachers" whose aim was to equip their young (male) pupils to win debates not because their arguments stood up under scrutiny, but because winning helped to sustain their privileged social status.

A climate change "skeptic," Peterson also claims that scientists focused on global warming can't "separate science from politics." But climate scientists have no more trouble separating science from politics than do epidemiologists, virologists, and public health experts aiming to combat the coronavirus pandemic. Nonetheless, figures like Scott Atlas whose argument for herd immunity disrupts the public health discourse over the best way to address Covid-19, save lives, and prevent suffering is, like Peterson's climate skepticism, seemingly driven more by the politics of preserving entitlement and authority than it is by science. The appeal in either case to pseudo-science epitomizes the rejection of almost *any* environmental ethic. Yet, while we might be tempted to reject the proponents of denial, falsehood, and prejudice as cranks, we can learn from them important lessons about why the logic of domination persists. To see this, we thus turned our attention to Friedrich Engels who argues that the beneficiaries of heteropatriarchal institutions are men for whom the control of women's bodies forms a crucial component in the accumulation of wealth. Engels condemns this "world historical defeat of women." Peterson embraces it. Engels understands that these primitive forms of commodification foreshadow the Industrial Revolution; Peterson argues that capitalism mirrors the order of nature. Both recognize capitalist commodification as correlated with social inequity, yet while Engels decries it as dehumanizing, Peterson insists that dominance hierarchies are so engrained a feature of our heritage that any effort to significantly alter them destroys the "freedom" of women to surrender to men. Evolutionary psychology has soundly refuted this view, but this doesn't deter Peterson from entertaining the idea that compulsory monogamy offers a solution to men "victimized" by women who reject their sexual advances.

While compulsory monogamy may seem a far cry from environmental ethics, it's precisely the point of an ecofeminist approach to show that current human institutions typify a worldview in which environmental deterioration is part and parcel of the logic that supports it. Nothing, however, requires us to concede to this logic; nothing compels rational creatures capable of producing science, art, and ethics to forfeit our quest for a way of life worth living to this cynical determinism. To this end, ecofeminists like Wendy Lynne Lee returns us to John Dewey's argument for the appreciation of the aesthetic *in* our experience of human and nonhuman nature with respect to its relevance for sound moral judgment. If aesthetic experience has moral value for environmental ethics, Lee argues, it's because "it can encourage actions that condition the ecological stability requisite to aesthetic experience in the future." The danger that we could squander future opportunities to appreciate nonhuman nature has, she contends, a moral and an aesthetic dimension, one that takes seriously a moral duty to the future. To value the future is to value what makes aesthetic experience possible, and that in turn requires a planetary ecology capable of recuperating and restoring itself fully. Lee offers several examples to this end, including performance artist Banksy's *Sirens of the Lambs* and, in direct contrast to what Engels might have characterized as Peterson's "bourgeois" depiction of women, the standpoint of the subjugated. In this account, nonhuman nature acts neither merely as inert background nor as a malevolent "Mother" looking to inflict chaos and misery; human relationships are less dictated by domination than by the necessities of food and water security. Nature does not dominate us; it *is* us. Echoing Dewey's notion of the aesthetic *in* experience, she argues that it's in our experience of the nonhuman nature both within and outside of ourselves that we come to know ourselves as morally capable entities. Echoing the work of her ecofeminist sisters and brothers, Lee concludes that we can, and must, do better because the alternative is not merely more of the same social and economic injustice, but rather the environmental catastrophe that is its intimate bedfellow.

1. How does the commitment to address structural inequality, including social and economic injustice across line or sex, gender, race, and species, play a key role in ecofeminist approaches to environmental ethics?
2. What is the logic of domination, and how does ecofeminist theorist Karen Warren utilize it to spell out the intersection of heteropatriarchy and environmental domination?
3. How does the work of Carol Adams concerning the exploitation of nonhuman animals supplement and illustrate the logic of domination?
4. How does Jordan Peterson's argument for "dominance hierarchies" illustrate the logic of domination, including its ungrounded premises, especially with respect to his defense of heteropatriarchal institutions, climate change "skepticism," and meat-eating?
5. How do arguments for herd immunity offered by figures like Scott Atlas as a strategy for addressing the Covid-19 pandemic illustrate the racism implicit in the logic of domination, particularly insofar as the argument embodies elements of American Eugenicism?
6. What is Wendy Lynne Lee's argument for taking the aesthetic *in* experience as an important feature of an ecofeminist environmental ethic? Why does she offer the performance artist Banksy as an example?

7. What is the standpoint of the subjugated, and how might we incorporate it into an environmental ethic that aims not only to confront injustice but offer a vision of a future both sustainable and desirable, especially to those most harmed by our current social, economic, and environmental crises?

Annotated Bibliography

Adams, Carol (2015). *The Sexual Politics of Meat: A Feminist Vegetarian Critical Theory* (London: Bloomsbury).
Adams shows how cultural misogyny is intimately connected to masculinity and meat-eating in patriarchal cultures.
Adams, Carol (2015). *Neither Man nor Beast: Feminism and the Defense of Animals* (Brooklyn, NY: Lantern Books).
Essentially a manifesto, Adams traces the complex and multiple relationships between the ways in which nonhuman animals and women have been conceived as commodities by a patriarchal and human-centered Western culture.
Engels, Friedrich (2010). *The Origin of the Family, Private Property, and the State* (New York: Penguin Classics). https://www.marxists.org/archive/marx/works/1884/origin-family.
In this classic work, Engels lays out the essentially Marxist argument concerning the origin of property in the commodification of women and nonhuman animals.
Gaard, Greta (2017). *Critical Ecofeminism* (Lexington Books, Rowman and Littlefield).
Distilling from an expansive body of work, Gaard argues for a maturing ecofeminism able to make sense of the intersections of ecological destruction, masculinism, racism, speciesism, and economic oppression. She also offers a very concise analysis of much of the terminology that's come to identify the modern environmental movement—such as "sustainability" and "nature's services."
Gaard, Greta. "Ecofeminism and Climate Change." *Women's Studies International Forum* 49, (2015).
Gaard argues that "issues that women traditionally organize around—environmental health, habitats, livelihoods—have been marginalized in debates that treat climate change as a scientific problem requiring technological and scientific solutions without substantially transforming ideologies and economies of domination, exploitation and colonialism. Issues that GLBTQ people organize around— bullying in the schools, hate crimes, marriage equality, fair housing and health care—aren't even noted

in climate change discussions. Feminist analyses are well positioned to address these and other structural inequalities in climate crises..."

Gaard, Greta. "Ecofeminism Revisited: Rejecting Essentialism and Replacing Species in a Material Feminist Environmentalism." *Feminist Formations* 23 (2), (Summer), pp. 26–53.

Gaard surveys the roots of the backlash against early ecofeminist essentialism, arguing for a reclamation of the ecofeminist project.

Hultman, Martin and Paul Pulé (2018). *Ecological Masculinities: Theoretical Foundations and Practical Guidance* (New York: Routledge).

In this critique of contemporary capitalist industrialization, Hultman and Pulé argue that the wealthy mostly white men of the Global North are primarily responsible for environmental disaster including mass extinctions and climate change. They argue that even "ecomodern" masculinities have failed, and that we must look far more closely into ecofeminist and deep ecological approaches.

Lee, Wendy Lynne (2010). *Eco-Nihilism: The Philosophical Geopolitics of the Climate Change Apocalypse* (Lexington: Rowman and Littlefield). ch. 2, p. 102–15.

Lee argues for an ecofeminist approach to the climate crisis as a way to address issues of environmental, social, and economic justice as aspects of the same forms of structural inequality.

Lee, Wendy Lynne. "On Ecology and Aesthetic Experience: A Feminist Theory of Value and Praxis." *Ethics and the Environment* 11 (1), pp. 21–41.

Lee develops a feminist theory of value—an axiology—which unites two notions that seem to have little in common for a theorizing whose ultimate goal is justice–driven emancipatory action, namely, the ecological and the aesthetic. In this union lies the potential for a critical feminist political praxis capable of appreciating not only the value of human life, but those relationships upon which human and nonhuman life depend.

Lee, Wendy Lynne. "The Aesthetic Appreciation of Nature, Scientific Objectivity, and the Standpoint of the Subjugated: Anthropocentrism Reimagined." *Ethics, Place, and Environment* 8 (2), (2005), pp. 235–50.

Lee argues for an alternative anthropocentrism that, eschewing failed appeals to traditional moral principle, takes as its point of departure the cognitive, perceptual, emotive, somatic, and epistemic conditions of our existence as members of Homo sapiens, and one feature of our experience of/under these conditions particularly seriously as an avenue toward articulating this alternative—the capacity for aesthetic appreciation

Lee, Wendy Lynne. "Anthropomorphism Without Anthropocentrism: A Wittgensteinian Ecofeminist Alternative to Deep Ecology." *Ethics and the Environment* 1 (2), (1996), pp. 92–102.

Lee argues that Carol Bigwood's feminized deep ecology reproduces important elements of the deep ecologist's essentializing discourse that ecofeminists rightly argue is responsible for the identification with and oppression of women and nonhuman nature. She proposes an alternative model for conceiving and describing human and nonhuman nature modeled on Ludwig Wittgenstein's remarks concerning anthropomorphizing.

Lee, Wendy Lynne. "Women, Animals, Machines: A Grammar for a Wittgensteinian Ecofeminism." *The Journal of Value Inquiry* 29, (1995), p. 89–101.

Lee argues for an ecofeminist standpoint that avoids "eliminativist" objections and is modeled after a later Wittgensteinian variety of naturalism. Her alternative avoids both Cartesian dualism and that variety of eliminativism that antiquates the use of psychological terms often deployed to justify psychological and epistemic oppression.

Mallory, Chaone. "Who Knows? Ethics and the Epistemology of Climate Change and Environmental Justice," *Conference Presentation, Villanova*, November 11, 2010, https://www.academia.edu/32045105/Who_Knows_Ethics_and_Epistemologies_of_Climate_Change_and_Environmental.

Mallory explores the relationship between non-expert knowers and their response to climate change in light of our evolving understanding of climate and environmental justice.

Marx, Karl. (2012). *The Communist Manifesto: Norton Critical Edition*, 2nd edn, ed., Fredric Bender. (New York: W.W. Norton and Company).

In this edition of *The Communist Manifesto*, editor Fredric Bender provides a selection of critical analyses of Marx' work, including several that advance the critique of capitalism in relation to its environmental consequences.

Mies, Maria, and Vandana Shiva (2014). *Ecofeminism: (Critique, Influence, Change)* (London: Zed Books).

Mies and Shiva offer and analysis of environmental issues relevant to the relationship between the so-called Global North versus Global South from an ecofeminist perspective.

Miller, Peter and Laura Westra (2002). *Just Ecological Integrity: The Ethics of Maintaining Planetary Life* (Lanham, MD: Rowman and Littlefield).

This is a collection of essays originating from a conference and the *Global Ecological Integrity Project*. Among its aims are devising indices of ecology health and measurement toward ecological objectives, including a varied selection of case studies.

Peterson, Jordan (2016). *12 Rules for Life: An Antidote to Chaos* (New York: Penguin).

A mix of popular psychology, psycho/social determinism, and self-help, Peterson lays out his argument and advice for avoiding the chaos he identifies as "feminine" and the order he identifies as "masculine." Although his view is not intended as an environmental ethic per se, following Peterson's twelve rules could have a profound implication for the future of the planet's ecological integrity, the survival of nonhuman life, human destiny.

Plumwood, Val (1993). *Feminism and the Mastery of Nature* (New York: Routledge).

Plumwood lays out a key eco-phenomenological and ecofeminist argument that, following Warren, demonstrates a number of linkages between patriarchal domination and the human exploitation of nonhuman nature.

Rose, Deborah Bird. "Val Plumwood's Philosophical Animism: Attentive Interactions in the Sentient World." *Environmental Humanities* 3, (2013), pp. 93–109.

Rose argues that Plumwood makes "connections with animism as a worldview, but rather than mimic or appropriate indigenous animisms she was developing a foundation that could be argued from within western philosophy. Her beautiful definition of philosophical animism is that it 'opens the door to a world in which we can begin to negotiate life membership of an ecological community of kindred beings' provides a groundwork to ecofeminist work relevant to indigenous peoples.

Sallah, Ariel, and Vandana Shiva (2017). *Ecofeminism as Politics: Nature, Marx, and the Postmodern* (London: Zed Books).

The authors argue that ecofeminism "reaches beyond contemporary social movements" and can offer the bridge that connects the feminist movement to postcolonial struggles.

Shiva, Vandana (2016). *Staying Alive: Women, Ecology, and Development* (Berkeley, CA: North Atlantic Books).

Expanding on her argument that what Westerners call "development" is really "maldevelopment" from the point of view of the developing world and ecological integrity, Shiva shows how "ecological destruction and the marginalization of women are not inevitable," but they are deeply interconnected.

Shiva, Vandana. (2015). *Earth Democracy: Justice, Sustainability, and Peace* (Berkeley, CA: North Atlantic Books).

In her most biting critique of capitalism yet, Shiva explores a number of issues in an effort to bring international attention to environmental issues ranging from cultural theft and seed piracy to the implications of Genetically Modified Food (GMOs).

Terry, Geraldine, ed. (2009). *Climate Change and Gender Justice* (Oxford: Oxfam Publications).

Terry offers a wide selection of case studies from the developing world that highlight both the obstacles and the strategies employed to combat climate change—with a specific emphasis on its impacts for women.

Warren, Karen. "The Power and the Promise of Ecological Feminism." *Environmental Ethics* 1 (2), (1990), pp. 125–46. (Summer).

In this landmark essay, Warren lays out her argument demonstrating how a logic of domination is at work in patriarchal as well as anthropocentric (human chauvinist) relationships.

Warren, Karen and Jim Cheney. "Ecological Feminism and Ecosystem Ecology." *Hypatia* 6 (1), (1991), pp. 179–97. (Spring).

In this essay Warren and Cheney show how the objectives of ecofeminism and those of the science of ecology are "engaged in complimentary, mutually supportive projects."

Warren, Karen, ed. (1997). *Ecofeminism: Women, Culture, Nature* (Bloomington, IN: Indiana University press).

In this edited anthology is included a wide selection of early ecofeminist approaches to environmental philosophy and to feminist issues. It counts as one of the touchstone works for anyone interested in the intersection of environmental philosophy and ethics and feminist theory.

Warren, Karen (2000). *Ecofeminist Philosophy: A Western Perspective on What It Is and Why It Matters* (Lanham, MD: Rowman and Littlefield).

Warren surveys a number of positions in the emergent field of ecofeminism, seeking to connect it to issues in social justice. Deploying her work on the logic of domination Warren further develops the relationship between the patriarchal domination of women and the human domination of nonhuman nature.

Online Resources

1. Caitlin Brown and Martin Ravallion, "Poverty, Inequality, and Covid-198 in the U.S.," *VOX-EU*, August 10, 2020, https://voxeu.org/article/poverty-inequality-and-covid-19-us.
2. "Coronavirus and Inequality," *United Nations*. https://feature.undp.org/coronavirus-vs-inequality.
3. Ibid. "Coronavirus and Inequality," *United Nations*.
4. "Jamal Khashoggi: All You Need to Know About Saudi Journalist's Death," *BBC News*, July 2, 2020, https://www.bbc.com/news/world-europe-45812399.
5. Scott Simon, "Parents of 545 Children Separated at U.S.-Mexico Border Cannot Be Found," *NPR*, October 24, 2020, https://www.npr.org/2020/10/24/927384388/parents-of-545-children-separated-at-u-s-mexico-border-have-not-been-located.
6. Orion Rummler, "Infectious Disease Expert: Scott Atlas' Herd Immunity claims are 'Pseudoscience,'" *Axios*, October 18, 2020, https://www.axios.

com/scott-atlas-herd-immunity-coronavirus-c8511115-0f39-4d0a-a1a8-44dd7560c7f1.html.

7. Christian Parenti, "Tropic of Chaos: Climate Change and the New Geography of Violence," *YouTube*, https://www.youtube.com/watch?v=Rl0K4-IBIFY.

8. See *Save the Rhino International*. https://www.savetherhino.org/rhino-info/threats/poaching-rhino-horn.

9. See *Polar Bears International: Climate Change*, https://polarbearsinternational.org/climate-change.

10. Taylor Telford, et. al., "Trump Orders Meat Plants to Stay Open in Pandemic," The Washington Post, April 20, 2020, https://www.washingtonpost.com/business/2020/04/28/trump-meat-plants-dpa.

11. "What is Ecofeminism?" *One Million Women*, February 13, 2017, https://www.1millionwomen.com.au/blog/what-ecofeminism.

12. "Gender Equality," *United Nations: Sustainable Development Goals*, https://www.un.org/sustainabledevelopment/gender-equality.

13. Audre Lorde, "The master's Tools Will Never Dismantle the Master's House," *Middlebury College*, http://s18.middlebury.edu/AMST0325A/Lorde_The_Masters_Tools.pdf.

14. Javier David, "'Beyond Petroleum' No More? BP Goes Back to Basics," *CNBC*, April 23, 2013, https://www.cnbc.com/id/100647034.

15. "Smithfield Foods Announces Landmark Investment to Reduce Greenhouse Gas Emissions," *Smithfield*, October 25, 2018, https://globenewswire.com/news-release/2018/10/25/1627553/0/en/Smithfield-Foods-Announces-Landmark-Investment-to-Reduce-Greenhouse-Gas-Emissions.html.

16. Kip Anderson and Keegan Kuhn, *Facts and Sources: Cowspiracy*, http://www.cowspiracy.com/facts.

17. Marx, Karl, "The Commodity," 1867, *The Karl Marx Archive*, https://www.marxists.org/archive/marx/works/1867-c1/commodity.htm.

18. John Gibbons, "Climate Deniers Want to Protect the Status Quo that Made Them Rich," *The Guardian*, September 22, 2017, https://www.theguardian.com/environment/2017/sep/22/climate-deniers-protect-status-quo-that-made-them-rich.

19. *Clean Choice (Ethical Electric)*, https://cleanchoiceenergy.com.

20. "Why Capitalism Can't Be Sustainable," *The Green Economist*, http://www.greeneconomist.org/page.php?pageid=capitalism.

21. Juliann Emmons Allison, "Ecofeminism and Global Environmental Politics," *International Studies Association*, March 2010, http://oxfordre.com/internationalstudies/view/10.1093/acrefore/9780190846626.001.0001/acrefore-9780190846626-e-158.

22. Kimberly Amadea, "Structural Inequality in America," *The Balance*, September 25, 2018, https://www.thebalance.com/structural-inequality-facts-types-causes-solution-4174727.

23. K Norlock, "Feminist Ethics," *The Stanford Encyclopedia of Philosophy*, August 27, 2019, https://plato.stanford.edu/entries/feminism-ethics.

24. "Proud Boys," *Southern Poverty Law Center*, https://www.splcenter.org/fighting-hate/extremist-files/group/proud-boys.

25. Ben Sales, "Not NAZI Enough: Proud Boys Leaders Want Group to Fully Embrace White Supremacy," *The Times of Israel*, November 12, 2020, https://www.timesofisrael.com/not-nazi-enough-proud-boys-leader-wants-group-to-fully-embrace-white-supremacy.

26. Jason Wilson, "Proud Boys are a Dangerous White Supremacist Group, Says U.S., Agencies," *The Guardian*, October 1, 2020, https://www.theguardian.com/world/2020/oct/01/proud-boys-white-supremacist-group-law-enforcement-agencies.

27. Emily Atkin, "Proud Boys and Petro-Masculinity," *Heated*, October 1, 2020, https://heated.world/p/proud-boys-and-petro-masculinity.

28. John L. Smith, "Proud Boys and Pandemic Politics as Trump's Deadly Mask-Free masquerade Ends," *The Nevada Independent*, October 4, 2020, https://thenevadaindependent.com/article/proud-boys-and-pandemic-politics-as-trumps-deadly-mask-free-masquerade-ends.

29. Martin Gelin, "The Misogyny of Climate Deniers," *The New Republic*, August 28, 2019, https://newrepublic.com/article/154879/misogyny-climate-deniers.

30. Ibid. Martin Gelin, "The Misogyny of Climate Deniers." *The New Republic* August 28, 2019.

31. Ewan Palmer, "BLM Accuse Police of Emboldening 'White Supremacists" After Linking Them to Proud Boys Attack," *Newsweek*, November 5, 2020, https://www.newsweek.com/proud-boys-attack-washington-blm-election-1545049.

32. Rachael Levy, "Who are the Proud Boys? The Group that Trump Told to 'Stand back and Stand By'," *The Wall Street Journal*, November 6, 2020, https://www.wsj.com/articles/who-are-proud-boys-11601485755.

33. Julia Jones, and Sara Sidner, "MAGA March Brings Together Trump Voters, Far Right leaders, and Counterprotesters, Ending in Some Clashes," *CNN*, November 15, 2020, https://www.cnn.com/2020/11/14/us/trump-washington-voters-rally-far-right/index.html.

34. Rebecca White, "Group Takes Responsibility for Taking Down Covid-19 Crosses at City Hall," *The Spokesman Review*, May 18, 2020, https://www.spokesman.com/stories/2020/may/18/proud-boys-claim-responsibility-for-taking-down-co.

35. Jonathan Oosting, "Militias, Far Right Groups Recast Themselves as Mainstream at Lansing Gun Rally," *Bridge, Michigan*, September 17, 2020, https://www.bridgemi.com/michigan-government/militias-far-right-groups-recast-selves-mainstream-lansing-gun-rally.

36. Colleen Clemons, "What We Mean When We Say 'Toxic Masculinity," *Teaching Tolerance*, December 11, 2017, https://www.tolerance.org/magazine/what-we-mean-when-we-say-toxic-masculinity.

37. Richard Twine, "Masculinity, Nature, Ecofeminism," *Richard Twine Blog*, http://richardtwine.com/ecofem/masc.pdf.

38. "Lawsuit Claims Tyson Food Managers Bet Money on Employees Getting Covid-19," CBS News, November 19, 2020, https://www.cbsnews.com/news/tyson-foods-lawsuit-managers-john-casey-tom-hart-bet-money-covid-19-employees.

39. Timmons Roberts, "One Year Since Trump's Withdrawal from the Paris Climate Agreement," *Brookings*, June 1, 2018, https://www.brookings.edu/blog/planetpolicy/2018/06/01/one-year-since-trumps-withdrawal-from-the-paris-climate-agreement.

40. Laura Zuckerman, "Scientists Voice Opposition to Weakening of U.S. Endangered Species Act," *Reuters*, September 24, 2018, https://www.reuters.com/article/us-usa-wildlife-endangered/scientists-voice-opposition-to-weakening-of-u-s-endangered-species-act-idUSKCN1M42PG.

41. "Developing Countries Are Responsible for 63 Percent of Current Carbon Emissions," *Center for Global Development*, https://www.cgdev.org/media/developing-countries-are-responsible-63-percent-current-carbon-emissions.

42. John Cushman, "Harvard Study Finds EXXON Misled Public about Climate Change," *Inside Climate News*, August 22, 2017, https://insideclimatenews.org/news/22082017/study-confirms-exxon-misled-public-about-climate-change-authors-say.

43. Martin Hultman, "Climate Change Denial," *En(Gender)ed*, April 30, 2020, https://engendered.us/episode-99-martin-hultman-on-misogyny-and-masculinities-on-climate-change-denial.

44. Avi Selk, "Trump Suggests Rakes Could Prevent California Fires, but the Reality is Far More Complicated," *Chicago Tribune*, November 18, 2018, https://www.chicagotribune.com/nation-world/ct-trump-california-fire-comments-20181118-story.html.

45. Emily Holden, "Climate Change Skeptics Run the Trump Administration," *Politico*, March 7, 2018, https://www.politico.com/story/2018/03/07/trump-climate-change-deniers-443533.

46. Sara Chodosh, "Please Do Not Try to Survive on an All-Meat Diet," *Popular Science*, August 2, 2018, https://www.popsci.com/carnivore-all-meat-diet.

47. James Hamblin, "The Jordan Peterson All-Meat Diet," *The Atlantic*, August 28, 2018, https://www.theatlantic.com/health/archive/2018/08/the-peterson-family-meat-cleanse/567613/.

48. Jordan Peterson, "Jordan Peterson Denies Animal Rights," *YouTube*, https://www.youtube.com/watch?v=1GUy-uCiWSM.

49. Jordan Peterson, "Jordan Peterson: The Fatal flaw in Leftist American Politics," *Big Think, YouTube*, April 1, 2018, https://www.youtube.com/watch?v=8UVUnUnWfHI&list=PLaYTNyxIsdw995OJM79N7oe1foL5Fihaw&index=14.

50. Michael Favata, "A Christian Case for Veganism," *The Reasoned Vegan*, June 4, 2018, https://thereasonedvegan.com/2018/06/04/a-christian-case-for-veganism.

51. Zack Beauchamp, "Jordan Peterson, The Obscure Canadian Psychologist Turned Right-Wing Celebrity, Explained," *VOX*, May 21, 2018, https://www.vox.com/world/2018/3/26/17144166/jordan-peterson-12-rules-for-life.

52. Stephen Anderson, "Animal Communication and Human Language." *Cambridge Encyclopedia of the Linguistic Sciences*, https://cowgill.ling.yale.edu/sra/animals_cell.htm.

53. "Jordan Peterson—Humans are a Cancer on the Planet? What a Hell of a Thing to Say!" *Bite-Sized Philosophy, YouTube*, https://www.youtube.com/watch?v=Dr5z_hFzQhw.

54. Jordan Peterson, "Environmentalists and the Garden of Eden," *YouTube*, https://www.youtube.com/watch?v = xIN-KyrU7aA.

55. Gyrus, "Jordan Peterson and Environmentalism," *Dreamflesh*, October 2018, https://dreamflesh.com/essay/jordan-peterson-environmentalism.

56. "Sophists." *Internet Encyclopedia of Philosophy*. https://www.iep.utm.edu/sophists.

57. Michael Bastasch, "Jordan Peterson Says Global Warming Hype is 'Low Resolution Thinking," *The Daily Caller*, November 8, 2018, https://dailycaller.com/2018/11/08/jordan-peterson-global-warming-hype.

58. DYSOT, "Jordan Peterson Attacks the Degenerate Feminism and Reminds You That Cucks Do Not Deserve Respect," *YouTube*, https://www.youtube.com/watch?v=f_J3HAncB9w.

59. "Jordan Peterson Attacks Postmodern Leftist Thinkers," *Conservative Debates, YouTube*, https://www.youtube.com/watch?v=S-X1UY92nL4.

60. "Jordan Peterson on the Plight of Young Men," *Independent Man*, January 28, 2018, YouTube, https://www.youtube.com/watch?v=BZiceARmNvc.

61. "Proud Boys Rally," *Reddit*, https://www.reddit.com/r/JordanPeterson/comments/j4nbtd/proud_boys_rally.

62. Matt Sheedy, "3 Things I Learned from Attending a Jordan Peterson Rally, Part Two," *Culture on the Edge*, October 3, 2018, https://edge.ua.edu/tag/the-proud-boys.

63. Matt Languedoc, "How I Escaped the Proud Boys Ideology," Amherst Wire, October 29, 2020, https://amherstwire.com/35329/opinion/how-i-escaped-the-proud-boys-ideology.

64. Scott Oliver, "The Fundamental Errors of Jordan Peterson," *Vice*, June 4, 2018, https://www.vice.com/en/article/evqekn/the-fundamental-errors-of-jordan-peterson.

65. Jordan Peterson, "Mother Nature; Mother Earth; Natural Environment; Unchecked, Killers All," Mare Pacificum Publishing Blog, September 24, 2019, https://marepacificumpublishing.com/2019/09/24/mother-nature-mother-earth-natural-environment-unchecked-enemies-all.

66. Ben Burgis and matt McManus, "Why Jordan Peterson is Always Wrong," *Jacobin*, April, 2020, https://jacobinmag.com/2020/4/jordan-peterson-capitalism-postmodernism-ideology.

67. "Richard Lindzen," *DeSmogBlog*, https://www.desmogblog.com/richard-lindzen.

68. Joseph Romm, "Climate Scientist Mann Gets Final Exoneration from Penn State," *Grist*, July 2, 2010, https://grist.org/article/2010-07-01-climate-scientist-michael-mann-gets-exoneration-penn-state.

69. Katie Herzog, "Jordan Peterson Pushes Dangerous Myths About Climate Change," *The Stranger*, August 3, 2018, https://www.thestranger.com/slog/2018/08/03/30143461/jordan-peterson-pushes-dangerous-myths-about-climate-change.

70. Friedrich Engels, "*The Origin of the Family, Private Property, and the State*," *Marxist Archives*, https://www.marxists.org/archive/marx/works/download/pdf/origin_family.pdf.

71. Jordan Peterson, "Why Capitalism is Highly Effective in the West," *Exclusive Conservative, YouTube*, https://www.youtube.com/watch?v=KO_JXeluzSw.

72. Jordan Peterson, "Capitalism is NOT Responsible for Inequality," *Conservatively Right, YouTube*, https://www.youtube.com/watch?v=wpcHDNdCC8c.

73. Jordan Peterson, "Oppression of Women by Men or Nature?" *Essential Truth, YouTube*, May 29, 2018, https://www.youtube.com/watch?v=4hf1XvpiUYo.

74. Nellie Bowles, "Jordan Peterson: Custodian of the Patriarchy," *New York Times*, May 18, 2018 https://www.nytimes.com/2018/05/18/style/jordan-peterson-12-rules-for-life.html.

75. John Horgan, "Do Women Want to be Oppressed?" *Scientific American*, December 29, 2017, https://blogs.scientificamerican.com/cross-check/do-women-want-to-be-oppressed.

76. Tabitha Southy, "The Context of Jordan Peterson's Thoughts on 'Enforced Monogamy'," Macleans, May 25, 2018, https://www.macleans.ca/opinion/the-context-of-jordan-petersons-thoughts-on-enforced-monogamy.

77. *The Great Barrington Declaration*, https://gbdeclaration.org.

78. Bruce Y. Lee, "White House Considering the Great Barrington Declaration Herd Immunity Strategy for Covid-19 Coronavirus," Forbes, October

14, 2020, https://www.forbes.com/sites/brucelee/2020/10/14/the-great-barrington-declaration-herd-immunity-strategies-for-coronavirus-overlook-8-problems/?sh=7e8a5081bf70.

79. Aneri Pattani, "Corralling the Facts on Herd Immunity," *KHN*, (*Kaiser Family Foundation*), September 29, 2020, https://khn.org/news/corralling-the-facts-on-herd-immunity.

80. "U.S. Blacks 3 Tomes More Likely than Whites to Get Covid-19," *CIDRAP* (*Center for Infectious Disease Research and Policy*), August 14, 2020 https://www.cidrap.umn.edu/news-perspective/2020/08/us-blacks-3-times-more-likely-whites-get-covid-19.

81. Steven A. Farber, "U.S. Scientist's Role in the Eugenics Movement (1907-1939): A Contemporary Biologist's Perspective," National Library of Medicine: National Institutes of Health, December 5, 2008, https://www.ncbi.nlm.nih.gov/pmc/articles/PMC2757926.

82. "Health Equity Considerations and Racial and Ethnic Minority Groups," CDC (Centers for Disease Control), July 24, 2020, https://www.cdc.gov/coronavirus/2019-ncov/community/health-equity/race-ethnicity.html.

83. Canelle Poirier, et al., "The Role of Environmental Factors on Transmission Rates of the Covid-19 Outbreak: An Initial Assessment in Two Spatial Scales," *Nature*, (Scientific Reports), October 12, 2020, https://www.nature.com/articles/s41598-020-74089-7.

84. David Jones and Stefan Helmreich. "A History of Herd Immunity." *The Lancet: The Art of Medicine* 396 (10254), pp. 810–11. (September 19, 2020). https://www.thelancet.com/journals/lancet/article/PIIS0140-6736(20)31924-3/fulltext.

85. "Coronavirus, Climate Change, and the Environment: A Conversation on Covid-19 with Dr. Aaron Bernstein, Director of Harvard Chan C-Change," *Harvard T.H. Chan School of Public Health*. https://www.hsph.harvard.edu/c-change/subtopics/coronavirus-and-climate-change.

86. Ibid. "Coronavirus, Climate Change, and the Environment: A Conversation on Covid-19 with Dr. Aaron Bernstein, Director of Harvard Chan C-Change." *Harvard T.H. Chan School of Public Health*.

87. Banksy, *Sirens of the Lambs*, *YouTube*, https://www.youtube.com/watch?v=WDIz7mEJOeA.

88. "Betty Friedan," *Biography*, April 7, 2020, https://www.biography.com/activist/betty-friedan.

89. *Navdanya*. https://www.navdanya.org/site.

INDEX

This is Environmental Ethics: An Introduction, First Edition. Wendy Lynne Lee.
© 2022 John Wiley & Sons, Inc. Published 2022 by John Wiley & Sons, Inc.
Companion Website: https://thisisphilosoph.wordpress.com